Villa I Tatti Series
34

Cover

Giovanna Garzoni, *Still Life with Bowl of Citrons*, late 1640's, tempera on vellum.
Los Angeles, The J. Paul Getty Museum.

I TATTI
THE HARVARD UNIVERSITY CENTER
FOR ITALIAN RENAISSANCE STUDIES

Villa I Tatti – The Harvard University Center
for Italian Renaissance Studies
Via di Vincigliata, 26
50135 Florence, Italy
www.itatti.harvard.edu

Villa I Tatti Series; 34

Published and distributed in Italy and France by

OFFICINA
LIBRARIA

Officina Libraria
Via Carlo Romussi, 4
20125 Milan, Italy
www.officinalibraria.net

Art direction and Cover Paola Gallerani
Graphic Design and Layout Chiara Bosio
Color separation Giorgio Canesin
Printed and bound by Monotipia Cremonese, Cremona

Worldwide distribution by Harvard University Press
Italian and French distribution by Officina Libraria

ISBN 978-0-674-24408-5 (Harvard University Press)
ISBN 978-88-3367-039-3 (Officina Libraria)

Allen J. Grieco

FOOD, SOCIAL POLITICS AND THE ORDER OF NATURE IN RENAISSANCE ITALY

Contents

Acknowledgements

While many cooks are said to spoil the broth, this multi-course work owes whatever success it might encounter to the many people who have contributed to its final form. Not only were there innumerable helping hands when these articles first came out, but also, more recently, hands were not lacking in pulling together this quasi-monographic book. Yet, no matter how long this list of friends and colleagues might be, there is always the risk of forgetting someone, especially since, in some cases, the articles re-published in this volume date back several decades. But first and foremost I would like to thank three people in particular who first cooked up the idea for this book, unbeknownst to me, and have been constantly reminding me of the deadline, or should I say the deadlines, which have provided a challenge to this admittedly slow writer. Since order matters, and an historian sensitive to classification systems knows this all too well, it is not easy to come up with one that would do justice to this trio. For once let it be clear that whatever the order they appear in, they can be considered to be fully *di pari merito*. Richard Goldthwaite showed much patience and humor in discussing many of the decisions that had to be made regarding this volume. Dick would be disappointed if I did not mention the fact that he kept tabs on me (overt and covert) while we were working on our own archival project to bring together food history and economic history. Nicholas Terpstra, despite the very heavy workload he carries with apparently so little effort, also closely followed the developments of this manuscript, and kindly arranged for Sara Patterson to undertake the normalization of notes that had appeared in widely different publications and in different languages, each with their own formatting conventions. Nick also periodically turned up the heat in repeated attempts to keep this project within an unreasonable amount of overtime. The third person who has put up with me in all stages of this project is Sara Matthews-Grieco. Sara has been, now and for many years, an exigent and patient "copy editor," whose close reading of my work has been, to say the least, invaluable. She will forgive me if I have not taken into account every editorial suggestion. Each one of this trio has contributed in their own very distinctive way to get the project going and then keep it on track. There is no need to say more since they know full well that this book would never have come into being without them... and many a virtual *bastonata* offset with a shot of Fernet.

I also would like to thank Lino Pertile who, as the director of Villa I Tatti, took this project on board when it was first hatched in late Winter 2015, and who has been instrumental in getting this book published in what are certainly the best possible conditions. Villa I Tatti funding for the translations and a number of the illustrations has contributed enormously to a volume that aspires to demonstrate, once again, the extent to which images can constitute a primary source for historical research. Thanks are also due to Alina Payne, the present director of the Harvard University Center for Italian Renaissance Studies, who has patiently seen this through the protracted final stages of completion. I would also like to acknowledge the assistance received from Jonathan Nelson and Thomas Gruber. Jonathan dealt with securing some tricky copyrights for the articles and for the images, and Thomas saw this through to publication, with all that entails. The VIT team—past and present—has made an invaluable contribution to this volume.

Amongst the other personalities who have made a significant difference to this book, I would like to especially thank Jim Hankins, who was primarily responsible for my sojourn in Cambridge as a De Bosis fellow in Spring 2009. That semester (teaching what I have been told was the first course in Medieval and Renaissance Food History at Harvard) crucially allowed me to keep the scholarly fires going at a time when they risked being smothered by other concerns.

I also have a deep debt to the many U.S., French, Belgian, English, Swiss, and Italian colleagues with whom I have carried on a scholarly dialogue since the days of Jean-Louis Flandrin's seminar at the *Ecole des Hautes Etudes en Sciences Sociales* (EHESS) in 1980, when food history was more of an idea than anything else. Since that formative period, my circle of colleagues and friends has been increased by numerous historians and social scientists sharing similar interests. This expanding group has participated with me in the ongoing development of the IEHCA—*Institut Européen d'Histoire et Cultures de l'Alimentation* (founded in 2001)—led under the expert guidance of Francis Chevrier. The numerous conferences organized over the years at the headquarters in Tours, as well as the yearly meetings of the Scientific Committee, have quite literally provided a global forum for exchange; the most recent Congress (June 2019) brought together speakers from no less than twenty-six different countries.

Many of the people who contributed to this volume over past decades are thanked in specific notes for their references, suggestions and help. While acknowledging every person who has somehow contributed to this book is an impossible task, in conclusion I would like to mention some of my oldest friends and colleagues. Their advice and critical input regarding my research has proved invaluable over many years. Warm thanks are due to Christiane Klapisch-Zuber, Bruno Laurioux, Marilyn Nicoud, Françoise Sabban, Phil and Mary Hyman, Peter Scholliers, Alberto Capatti, Claude Fischler, Pierre Lieutaghi, Gregorio Saldarriaga, Irma Naso, Antonella Campanini, Steve Maganon, Martin Bruegel, Andrea Rizzi and Andrea Barlucchi. Friendship and esteem also requires mention of two departed friends, Jean-Louis Flandrin and Odile Redon.

Each one of the people listed here, as well as the many others cited in notes, and those whom I have unforgivably omitted, have contributed to this volume in one way or another from their own very diverse fields of expertise, not only enriching my research but also remaining through the years valued friends. My heartfelt thanks to you all.

Foreword

Christiane Klapisch-Zuber

"All things ... must have another that is opposite ...
and this is the reason we find ... plants that are quite different
and opposed to one another..."[1]

This remarkable principle of opposites, here formulated by Restoro d'Arezzo (1282), permeates all medieval thought on food and dietetics. While this notion continued to hold sway for several centuries, it was not until the closing decades of the twentieth century that its wider implications were brought into focus.

In the early 1980s in France, a new disciplinary area (the history of food) was producing new perspectives on the past while, at the same time, the notion of the "mental universe" (as defined by Lucien Febvre) provided an opportunity for exploring the social and symbolic meaning of foodstuffs. Pioneers, such as Jean-Louis Flandrin and Philippe Ariès, expanded the history of food to include a cultural history of eating habits. These innovators extended the analysis of diet and the dining table (as originally launched by Fernand Braudel) beyond the study of material life and biological behavior.[2] Other scholars, such as Louis Henry and Pierre Goubert, brought attention to the history of subsistence and supply, of climate and population, and of historical demography. Out of the collective heritage of all these fields of research arose original questions that led to a new field: the history of taste.[3]

Jean-Louis Flandrin insisted on "distinction through taste," thereby linking Pierre Bourdieu's notion of social distinction with a more anthropological interest in the diner himself: the individual seated at the table. What Flandrin moved into the foreground were the social distinctions of taste. Not only did his research focus on the "man of taste," who knew "how to eat," but he also made connections between the theoretical knowledge shared by doctors and dietitians (influenced by Aristotelian philosophy) and by culinary practice itself. Henceforth cookbooks, collections of recipes (*ricettari*), and conduct literature became as vital an historical source as the learned treatises that had long constituted the standard fare of cultural and intellectual scholars. In this new approach to the history of food, quantitative and economic approaches dwindled in importance with respect to qualitative studies of the preparation of dishes and table manners (two aspects of food history whose potential was first explored by Norbert Elias). Issues such as the relations between those eating at table, diners sharing the same trencher, the appreciation of the dishes served and the associations triggered by combinations of tastes or colors in various dishes became topics that whetted the appetites of historians, struck by the evolution of recipes between the late Middle Ages and the nineteenth century.

In France—as well as in Italy, Spain, and (to a lesser degree) Germany and Britain—a social and cultural history of food that explored the symbolism of taste and tastes gained momentum in the later 20th century. The historical horizon was broadened by an interest in sources that had previously been relegated to anecdotal histories of manners and material life. Cookbooks, as a genre, were now seen as a fully-fledged source for the study of Western medieval history.[4] New research materials on the preparation of food, contextualized by the theoretical knowledge of food and dietetics circulating in the past, led to the renewal of historical thinking about eating habits.

This was the path that Allen Grieco took right from the outset. His doctoral thesis, defended in 1987, explored a hitherto unknown corpus of material: the archives of the "Mensa dei Priori," the table of the Priors of the Florentine Signoria between 1344 and 1428.[5] Confined for a two-month term of office within the Palazzo della Signoria (now the Palazzo Vecchio, Florence), the nine citizens who had been appointed through a complex selection process could look forward to a substantial daily diet, and honor occasional visitors with even more sophisticated fare. While ostentation was required when those governing the city welcomed elite guests at their table, the ordinary provisioning of the Priors was similar to the quotidian habits and tastes of those they governed; the content of their meals and how they were distributed throughout the day corresponds with the practice of the general population.

Grieco's research has since taken a special interest in the dining habits of different social classes. For example, his analysis of princely repasts highlights aspects that are peculiar to the tables of the nobility and banquets (ch. 3). The ritualization of dining not only dictates the place assigned to each diner according to rank, but also table manners, the ritual of hand washing, and the material setting of the meal. The display of tableware, precious glass and centerpieces heaped with every sort of viand and fruit, along with the musical accompaniment provided by official *canterini* (ch. 8), provide both visual and aural components of a highly structured, stylized event in which the master of ceremonies surpassed the cook (ch. 3).

This brings us to one of the greatest problems faced by food historians: the question of how to interpret sources, since most surviving documents relate to the more privileged social classes. Should historians resign themselves to a study of the elites, without endeavoring to discover anything about the food of the poor other than what archaeology reveals about the scraps from their tables? Allen Grieco has nonetheless managed to explore the eating habits of social groups other than princes and patricians: chapter 4 of this book, for example, analyses the procurement of food and everyday meals in the Florentine foundling hospital, the *Ospedale degli Innocenti*. While it is impossible, in this and in other studies on institutional fare, to calculate the precise calorie intake of the food eaten by the staff and children living in the Ospedale, it is nonetheless possible to see how the diet of each group was differentiated and adapted according to individual factors of age, health and position within the institution. Florentines would have normally eaten two main meals a day, but the children and wet nurses lodged in the hospital were given four repasts. Eggs, which were regarded as being readily digestible by everyone, were given in particular to children and those confined to bed, while a special menu was reserved for the Prior of the *Ospedale* and those who were ill.

Food historians have long remarked that the composition of meals differed according to who was eating, and contemporary accounts testify to the fact that diet reflected social inequalities. Thus, whether they were employed by ecclesiastics, princes or private households, cooks rigorously respected food hierarchies, which in turn reflected social hierarchies. The rich ate fruit and certain meats rather than others, and drank humorally "hot" wines. The poor, on the other hand, ate vegetables, tubers and bread, for food prices condemned the lower classes to a modest (and socially degrading) vegetarian diet. The guidelines set out by doctors and dietitians reinforced this *status quo,* but at the same time asserted that certain foods could constitute an exception, correcting humoral imbalances in individual temperaments and preserving both health and social station.

Undoubtedly one of Allen Grieco's most original contributions is to have found, in the *Great Chain of Being,* the common denominator that would lead to an overall understanding of dietary regimes. Evoked in more than one chapter in this book, the *Chain of Being* links the various hermeneutic systems through which nature was understood. The relative hierarchies of elements, humors, temperaments, seasons, flavors and colors are ranked between their own extremes of hot/cold, high/low, bitter/acid, etc. These classificatory principles provide the basis for a "unified dietary system," while the corresponding pairs of opposites acquire full value when linked to social hierarchies. One of the greatest merits of the essays in this volume is their insistence that alimentary regimes must be understood in terms of social status. As Allen puts it, "society had a 'natural' order, and nature had a 'social' order, both clearly intended by God" (ch. 5). This notion is further developed in chapter 10, which provides a wonderful explanation of the classifications and combinations of foods that differentiated the menus of rich and poor.

By identifying this common denominator, Allen Grieco challenged the primarily economic view of diets and tastes promoted by earlier studies based on quantitative (albeit still useful) methods. While economic analysis saw diets as being specific to different sectors of society, reacting primarily to vagaries of climate and market trends, Allen's approach interprets them in another light. Readers of the essays in this volume will note that the author, far from disavowing the conclusions of the founding fathers of food history, remains sensitive to their material foundations while incorporating them into a larger interpretative system of social and cultural values.

This volume repeatedly demonstrates the extent to which the concepts underlying the *Chain of Being* expanded well beyond the educated elites. While these notions were intrinsic to cookbooks addressed to the rich, thereby influencing what was put in their cooking pots, dietetics also became a subject for poetry, where rhymers detailed the qualities of fruit, wines and fish (ch. 6 and 7), even singing their verses before the *Signoria* (ch. 8). The influence of the *Chain of Being* theory was thus far from being limited to a particular social group, although it was the elites—cushioned from market oscillations by their social position, and never deprived of spices, meat, or fruit (even out of season)—who most resorted to the written page as a means of expressing their culinary preferences ... along with their social prejudices. Cookbooks and recipe collections served to disseminate the culinary practices of the wealthy while sumptuary laws effectively banned these same eating habits among the lower classes. A detailed examination of recipe books is thus far from superfluous as a means of gauging the part played by class prejudice in the formation of taste. To a certain extent, the alimentary regimes of the poor can be seen as the negative of the recipes for the rich, who scorned humble foods as being unworthy of their status.

By relegating the poor to the lowest level of the *Chain of Being*, to earthy, "cold" and unrefined foods, the cuisine of the late Middle Ages and Renaissance brings food systems and social values into sharp focus. The essays contained in this volume demonstrate how theoretical knowledge ranging far beyond simple dietetics was used to justify class prejudices, thereby adding an ideological dimension to the historic construction of taste.

Notes

Translated by Lucinda Byatt with revisions by Sara Matthews-Grieco.

1. "E ogne cosa ... dea avere lo suo oposito ... e per questa cascione trovamo .... plante tutte opposite e variate e contrarie l'una a l'altra," Restoro d'Arezzo, *La Composizione del mondo colle sue cascioni,* edited by A. Morino, (Florence: Accademia della Crusca, 1976), 146.

2. Cf. the fundamental article by F. Braudel, "Alimentation et catégories de l'histoire," *Annales. Economies, Sociétés, Civilisations,* 16, 1961, 723–728. J.-J. Hémardinquer, "Pour une histoire de l'alimentation," *Cahier des Annales,* 28, 1970, relaunched the work initiated by F. Braudel on the history of consumption. See also the pages dedicated to "Anthropologie historique" by André Burguière in *Nouvelle histoire,* edited by J. Le Goff, R. Chartier and J. Revel, (Paris: CEPL, 1978), 37–64, especially 45–48.

3. For a rapid overview of food history, see the excellent summary by Odile Redon, "Histoire de l'alimentation, entre Moyen Âge et Temps Modernes," which introduces *Le désir et le goût. Une autre histoire (XIII-XVIII siècles),* edited by O. Redon, L. Sallmann, S. Steinberg, (Saint-Denis: Presses Universitaires de Vincennes, 2005), 53–84, accompanied by an extensive bibliography put together by Bruno Laurioux, 85–96. On the way in which food systems have evolved since Antiquity and on the link between economy and food, see the summary by Massimo Montanari, "Alimentation," in *Dictionnaire raisonné de l'Occident médiéval,* edited by J. Le Goff and J.-C. Schmitt (Paris: Fayard, 1999), 20–31.

4. Bruno Laurioux, *Les Livres de cuisine médiévaux,* (Turnhout: Brepols, 1997).

5. Allen J. Grieco, *Classes sociales, nourritures et imaginaire alimentaire en Italie (XIVe-XVe siècles),* 3e cycle [Ph.D] thesis, supervised by C. Klapisch-Zuber, Paris, EHESS, 1987.

Introduction

"Niuno luogo dimostra e' buoni costumi d'un bene allevato quanto la mensa."
"Nowhere are the good manners of a well brought-up person more apparent than at table."
Leon Battista Alberti, *De Iciarchia*, Libro II, 16–18[1]

As banal as it might seem, the act of eating, and the repetitious nature of this basic human need, can hide all too easily the fact that choices made regarding food and its consumption rank among the most quotidian and deeply-rooted cultural acts of all societies. It is often forgotten that eating is not simply about food choices but also about what is produced locally, what is brought in from afar, how it is prepared, and the rituals accompanying its consumption. The intense familiarity bred by constant repetition results in perceiving the act of eating as something "ordinary" or even "natural," and this bears much of the responsibility for keeping food—as an object of study—distinctly below what might be called the "historicizing threshold." As a consequence, much of what is actually a complex social and cultural construct, characteristic of different historical periods and geographic locations, has been frequently confused with "biological" needs shared by all human beings. The misleading confusion of these two distinct aspects of food consumption—the biological and the cultural—was understood and dealt with by anthropologists much before historians, who had to wait for the cultural turn of the early 1980s, when these distinctions were integrated into food history. Thanks to this "turn," food history has enlarged upon and integrated prior economic and dietetic approaches to food, as it has grown into a full-fledged disciplinary field.

The social and cultural dimensions of food are perhaps most easily perceived when we are exposed to cultures other than those most familiar to us. For example, eating the food of another country focuses the diner's attention on the ingredients used, the way in which the meal was prepared, the rituals of service and the order in which the food is served (the "grammar" of the meal), especially when these differ vastly from the diner's habitual food culture. The same distancing effect can come about in a variety of situations even within a single country; for example, when we are exposed to the eating habits of different social, religious or even regional groups, to mention only some of the more easily recognized variables. Another variable is the historical one; an eating culture of the past presents more challenges for understanding its workings since we cannot rely on any direct experience. While some kind of simulacrum of historical meals can be produced, at best it remains a very distant approximation of the original that cannot recreate the most important aspect of these events for food historians: the social and cultural context in which food was consumed. Every context for food consumption is chronologically and geographically specific, and while we can rely on a variety of available sources—whether textual, visual or archaeological—even these have limits in terms of the information they convey.

Even just a few decades ago, the idea that food might have a history comprising more than an "anecdotal approach"[2] struggled to surface in the field of historical writing. While economic history had for a long time paid close attention to certain aspects of food—including the means of production, the functioning of markets (above all grain), the history of prices, etc.—it was not readily apparent that other approaches were either possible or necessary. Yet there had been a few exploratory forays into a more culturally nuanced approach to the history of food, even preceding the historiography Christiane Klapisch has sketched out in the foreword to this volume. Roland Barthes' trail-blazing work in semiology suggested the wealth of possibilities that a decidedly cultural approach to food could unlock, even though this early lesson fell on deaf ears. His book *Mythologies* (first published in 1957),[3] dealt with a variety of cultural objects and foods in the chapters devoted to "Le vin et le lait" and "Le bifteck et les frites." Less playful and more analytical, his brief article "Pour une psycho-sociologie de l'alimentation contemporaine"[4] (1961) highlighted the importance of studying food in its specific cultural context. This latter essay appeared in one of a series of dossiers on *"Vie matérielle et comportements biologiques,"* published by the journal *Annales. E.S.C.* that were largely devoted to food and diets.[5] Barthes' brief article represented a distinct and dissenting social/cultural perspective, in contrast to the economic/dietetic determinism that underpinned the series. It is therefore hardly surprising that the lesson was not picked up by historians, who at the time were pursuing radically different goals: Barthes' particular approach placed foodstuffs in an essentially a-historical and synchronic, semiotic framework that was far from the diachronic approach pursued by historians. While his work was not immediately taken into account, it was nonetheless a reminder to all disciplines that food was *also* part of a cultural network of meaning, which aspect became the principle focus of interest of food history some two decades later.

As of the early 1980s, the "cultural turn" began to make itself felt in a variety of fields in addition to the nascent discipline of food history. As it broke down closely guarded disciplinary confines,[6] it threw open the door to sociological and anthropological theories and methods, focusing attention on sources that had, for the most part, been excluded from the historian's repertoire. Scholars exploited the serial use of literary texts and visual documents as sources, employed in combination with other, more traditional and "erudite" approaches practiced in more canonical fields, such as medical history or the history of ideas. This new, interdisciplinary approach, with its specific interest in social and cultural history, revealed itself to be remarkably productive for food historians. Situated at the intersection of a variety of major disciplines, food was studied from almost endless points of view, ranging from economic history to the history of technology, from the history of agriculture to the history of taste. If there was any one way to hold these diverse approaches together it was under the umbrella concept of cultural history, which is ultimately implicated in all fields and disciplines. This is also why understanding food and food-related practices, in any given historical period, depends on situating them (as much as is possible) in the cultural framework they belong to.

The present volume has been long in the making and is the result of research that spans over two decades. Although many of the following chapters were originally published as separate articles and self-contained case studies, they were always meant to take their place in a larger project. Here they have come together to explore a variety of sources for food history while demonstrating a consistent analytical method that brings food, in all of its diversity, firmly into the arena of late medieval and Renaissance history. The task of pulling together a volume of complementary essays, published over a long period of time, was somewhat complicated by the fact that they originally appeared in three different languages (English, French and Italian) and dealt with fields that, at first glance, might seem relatively disparate, such as medieval dietetics, fresco painting and botanical classification systems.[7] Yet these different perspectives, grouped into the three sections of this volume, deliberately draw upon a variety of sources and analytic approaches that together reveal how food and meals functioned in late medieval and Renaissance Italy.

The first of the sections, "The Renaissance Table in Theory and Practice," comprises four relatively descriptive chapters that constitute an introduction to the kinds of food consumed at different types of "tables" in the Renaissance, and provide a first encounter with some of the analytical tools developed more fully in the rest of the volume. The chapters in this first section thus concentrate on food/recipes and on the variety of meals served to different social groups in different contexts. In chapter 1, "Meals and Mealtimes in Late Medieval and Renaissance Italy," the subject is approached over a broad social spectrum. This social focus becomes more specific when looking at the food consumed in one of Florence's most important charitable institutions, the *Ospedale degli Innocenti,* examined in chapter 4, "Diets at the *Ospedale degli Innocenti*: Practice, Social Differences and Medical Theories in the Mid-Quattrocento." The other two chapters in this first section deal with elite social groups, concentrating on the higher social strata for which more abundant documentation survives. The intersection between recipes in cookbooks and the actual food served at the table of the Florentine *Mensa della Signoria* in the mid-fourteenth century is analyzed in chapter 2, "From the Cookbook to the Table: The *Mensa della Signoria* and Italian Recipes of the Fourteenth and Fifteenth Centuries," while the organization of food supplies at the court of Urbino in the last years of the Quattrocento comes under scrutiny in chapter 3: "Conviviality in a Renaissance Court: the *Ordini et Officij* and the Court of Urbino."

The first section of this volume draws attention not only to the variety of food practices that coexisted in this period, but also points out the importance of observing differences in diets according to different social classes. Far from constituting a theoretical abstraction, the social parameter carried an inordinate amount of weight in pre-modern societies. The later Middle Ages and the Renaissance witnessed a rapidly developing stratification of society, especially in urban centers, accompanied by a diversification of consumption patterns in food and wine. The extent to which these dietary changes were consciously perceived by contemporaries manifests itself in the significant amount of sumptuary laws that dealt with food (and clothing), issued as of the end of the thirteenth century to curtail what was deemed extravagant and unacceptable behavior. Moralists of the fourteenth and fifteenth centuries reminded their readers that the public consumption of excessively luxurious food not only contravened communal laws, but also constituted socially inappropriate behavior.[8]

The second part of this volume brings together six essays that pursue the theme of social distinction, beginning with chapter 5 on "Food and Social Classes in Late Medieval and Renaissance Italy." These investigative studies explore yet other sources to evaluate how social categories were reinforced and even legitimized in subtly pervasive ways, via dietetic theories and classificatory systems. Dietetic information was often dispensed by medical doctors, who composed widely-read treatises on the subject that usually gave considered attention to socially distinct groups.[9] Dietary treatises become very numerous after the middle of the fourteenth century, presumably instigated by the devastation wrought during the Black plague. These treatises first circulated in manuscripts and, by the end of the fifteenth century, in the form of conveniently small, printed volumes. Some publications reached as many as 30 re-editions by the early seventeenth century, testifying to both the popularity of this genre and its considerable readership.[10] Advice on dietetics can be found most easily in the work of doctors, but it was not exclusively circulated by them. It also surfaces in a great variety of other sources, such as encyclopedias, *ricordanze*, letters, *novelle*, poetry and even sermons, suggesting that dietetic theory was part of a pervasive, commonplace knowledge as of the middle of the fourteenth century. Dietary knowledge circulated by popular medical treatises, and relayed via so many other channels, would have had a significant impact on the way in which food was consumed.[11]

While dietetic lore bolstered notions of social status, the classification of food and foodstuffs in a hierarchical system, understood and practiced by the consumer of pre-modern Italy, also played an important role in making dietary and social distinctions appear "logically" grounded. This hierarchically constructed system—known as the *Great Chain of Being*—continued to play an important role well into the 17th century, and was, for the most part, derived from Aristotelian cosmological theory. It seems to have both informed and reinforced the widely held notion that a kind of symmetry existed between an ordered nature and an equally ordered society. This parallelism, pursued above all in chapter 9, "The Social order of Nature and the Natural Order of Society in Late Thirteenth and Early Fourteenth-Century Italy" and again in chapter 10, "The Social Politics of Pre-Linnean Botanical Classification," created a bridge between specific social groups on the one hand, and their hierarchically "appropriate" food consumption on the other. Yet another example is the classification of fish, discussed in chapter 7 : "Fiordiano Malatesta da Rimini and the Ichthyological Treatises of the Mid-Sixteenth Century." Ideas about socially appropriate fare were, however, hardly limited to the natural world, since they also surface in other dietary contexts, such as the classification of wines, examined in chapter 6 on Medieval and Renaissance wines: "Taste, Dietary Theory and How to Choose the 'Right' Wine (Fourteenth-Sixteenth centuries)." All of these apparently quite different essays share a common, hierarchically ordered principle that gave a concrete and "objective" explanation to the presumed needs of different social groups.

The third and final part of this volume moves onto a more theoretical and abstract plane where food is observed above all through literary and visual sources. The reason for choosing these sources is based, above all, on the fact that food and "foodways"[12] are embedded in social and cultural practices that are difficult to access. Furthermore, this type of information is not available in most written sources relating directly to food; it can only be perceived via a contextualized, descriptive evocation of the circumstances in which food plays its specific (and never negligible) role. From this point of view, literary and visual sources, no matter how slippery and difficult they can be to analyze, provide the best kind of "virtual" description of the context we are trying to observe.

The caveats for such an enterprise are many, but first and foremost is the fact that single occurrences, or even a small number of examples, do not provide enough documentary evidence, whereas a serial approach to both literary and visual sources, cumulating and comparing numerous examples, can effectively minimize the risk of mis-reading limited or eccentric documentation.

Both literary texts and images are "informants" of a sort, precisely because they were made to communicate and were meant to be understood. Those who read (or listened to) literary texts, or viewed images that featured food in either a literal or a metaphorical guise, necessarily participated in a shared cultural background. Today, however, this common culture has been lost, which means that "reading" these sources effectively requires decoding them. References that were once transparent are no longer such. However, while a complete reconstruction of the meanings conveyed by references to food is beyond the purview of a single volume, the four chapters constituting the last section of the book aim to contextualize a group of particularly eloquent cases in which food culture—*au sens large*—plays a central and revelatory role. These essays range from actual and documented food consumption, as in chapter 11: "What's in a Detail: More Chickens in Renaissance Birth Scenes." to more discourse-based practices that shed light on the imaginary dimension of food. Chapter 13, "The Eaten Heart: Social Order, Sexuality and the Wilderness," and chapter 14, "Vegetable Diets, Hermits and Melancholy in Italy in Late Medieval and Renaissance Italy," reveal the rich symbolism evoked by imaginary or exotic diets. This last section brings to light some of the more hypothetical contexts in which food discourse could operate and, in the process, demonstrates the wealth of meaning that can be extracted from literary and figurative sources.

As a whole, this book aspires to provide a cultural history of food in late medieval and Renaissance Italy, seen through a variegated prism of sources, analytical methods and theoretical approaches that confirm the importance and complexity of food... if ever this was necessary. While no single volume could ever hope to adequately cover such a vast subject, the essays in this volume provide a selection of diverse sources and tools that should prove useful in continuing to make inroads on this topic.

Notes

1. In *Opere Volgari*, edited by Cecil Grayson, (Bari: Laterza, 1966), vol. II, 231. Thanks go to Gian Mario Cao who spotted this citation and drew my attention to it.

2. A term often used by Jean-Louis Flandrin.

3. Paris: *Les Lettres Nouvelles*, 1957.

4. Published in *Annales. Économies, Sociétés, Civilisations*, vol. 16, n. 5, (1961), 977–986.

5. The journal published a series of 18 distinct *Bulletins* as of vol. 16, n. 3 (1961), comprising some 48 articles until the series ended with vol. 24, n. 2 (1969), which was followed up by a final "Dossier Histoire de l'alimentation," in *Annales ESC*, vol. 30, n. 2–3 (1975) containing a further 17 articles.

6. For a recent historiographical look at this phenomenon, see Peter Scholliers, "Twenty-five years of studying *un phénomène social total*. Food history writing on Europe in the 19th and 20th centuries," *Food, Culture and Society*, vol. 10, n. 3 (2007), 450–471, and his follow-up article on "The Many Rooms in the House: Research on Past Foodways in Modern Europe," in *Writing Food History. A Global Perspective*, edited by Kyri Claflin and Peter Scholliers, (London/New York: Berg, 2012), 59–71. A full account of the historiographical development for the pre-modern period, keeping in mind both the French and English language contributions to the field, still needs to be written. As they first developed in an age where internet did not exist, these two major strands of the cultural history of food developed in a more or less discrete way and, as a consequence, have never ended up merging.

7. In reprinting articles that first came out over a long period of time, the temptation to update them was very strong indeed. This temptation was all the greater given that three of them were translated from Italian and three from French, all by Lucinda Byatt. After much deliberation, it was decided that bringing the texts (or even just the notes) up to date would have required rewriting the articles. As a consequence the articles and the notes are substantially the same, although I have not resisted making slight changes in the newly translated articles to improve the clarity of certain passages and to mention important contributions to the field that have appeared since the original publication date. Two exceptions to this rule are chapters 4 and 5. The first of these, "Diets at the *Ospedale degli Innocenti*: Practice, Social Differences and Medical Theories in the Mid-Quattrocento." had been updated for a prospective publication that never took place. The second one "Food and Social Classes in Late Medieval and Renaissance Italy," first appeared without any notes at all, as per the publisher's request; for the sake of consistency with the rest of this volume a few notes have now been integrated.

8. The pithiest statement of the ideals regulating the diet of the urban upper classes was formulated by Leon Battista Alberti in his *Libri della famiglia*, edited by Ruggiero Romano and Alberto Tenenti (Turin: Einaudi, 1969), Book 3, 234: what he called a "mensa cittadinesca" (see chapter 1, page 27).

9. The standard work on this literature is, of course, Marilyn Nicoud, *Les régimes de santé au Moyen Âge: naissance et diffusion d'une écriture médicale, XIIIᵉ-XVᵉ siècle*, (Rome: École Française de Rome, 2007), 2 vols.

10. For information on this literary genre in the age of the printing press see Ken Albala, *Eating Right in the Renaissance*, (Berkeley: University of California Press, 2002).

11. The exact relationship between medical discourse and social practice remains an

open question, as does the debate regarding which drives the other or, indeed, whether they reciprocally influenced each other. These questions have given rise to a lively scholarly discussion since the 1980s, when the importance of dietetic literature began to be widely recognized by historians of food, producing a considerable amount of publications over the past decades.

12. This useful term, commonly used in the social sciences, refers to the complex of cultural, social and economic practices regarding both the production and the consumption of food.

I. The Renaissance Table in Theory and Practice

Chapter 1
Meals and Mealtimes in Late Medieval and Renaissance Italy

Most people eat every day of their lives, and every time they eat they renew the most basic of cultural acts; yet this most basic cultural act remains elusive for a variety of reasons. In part this is due to an historical paradox whereby quotidian or commonplace practices (such as meals and meal times) have left less surviving documentation than more sporadic or special events. The dearth of sources regarding meals is inversely proportional to the frequency of such ephemeral occasions: most meals, and especially those eaten every day, did not give rise to any archival records worth speaking of and, for that matter, practically no iconographic ones either.

The lack of surviving documents is especially true for the lower social orders, although, in the upper echelons, "special occasion" meals and notably banquets have left a more abundant documentation. Usually the reason for this was linked to the expenses incurred for extra-ordinary meals, and the need to keep track of such expenditures: both because an accounting had to be rendered to the master of the house and because extravagant spending on food conveyed the importance of a specific event. Unfortunately, this means that there is a very real risk of generalizing about meals on the basis of those hosted by the wealthy and/or followed on festive occasions. One of the ways to avoid this bias is to have recourse to literary sources—with all due caution in terms of interpretation—since these contain information on what simple meals might have looked like for the laboring and artisan classes, for whom much less documentation survives.

Festive and Ordinary Meals of the Wealthy

The surviving evidence on "exceptional" meals is—true to the historical para-dox—both varied and plentiful. Information on special or festive meals appears in the accounts of many a memorable occasion (such as from state marriages, visits of potentates, meals celebrating a newly acquired knighthood), in sumptuary laws bent on curbing excessive luxury in the Italian city states, in cookbooks (mostly designed for an upper class clientele),[1] and even in a variety of medical texts on di-etetics. Equally informative are surviving account books for both families and in-stitutions that help us understand what foods were acquired, and to a lesser degree, the organization of meals. Yet it would be entirely illusory to attempt to define what the "standard" or "typical" medieval and Renaissance Italian meal was like.

Even a cursory glance at the sources confirms that there were, then as now, many different types of meals depending on a number of variables. The most obvious of these was, of course, the social class of the people who sat at the table. In a society where social distinctions were made manifest in a variety of ways, food constituted a particularly important distinguishing element, not only between different social classes but also between rural and urban cultures. From this point of view, literary texts again provide a valuable source as they often describe the cultural context of meals, and thus provide insights into the social codes that held sway over such events on both mundane and special occasions.

In his *Libri della Famiglia* composed between 1432 and 1434, Leon Battista Alberti makes a point to remind his readers that the family should be served meals that are both abundant and composed of what he describes as "good" but not "elect" food (in Italian he uses the term *elettissimi*). He specifies that the food to be eaten by the family should not include "...peacocks, capons and partridges nor other such refined foods that are usually served to those who are sick but rather make sure that you serve a meal for city dwellers."[2] Excessive luxury is thus condemned and the guidelines to be followed are ex-plicitly associated with urbane city living. At the same time, it was also pos-sible to err through parsimony and serve food that was excessively poor. As we shall see, it was a fine line that divided what was considered to be "good enough" (but not lavish) fare, and food that was considered to be too miserly.

The idea that one had to serve food that was appropriate for a given occasion was a deeply rooted cultural convention, as is conveyed by the so-called *"Lettera a Raimondo"* (incorrectly attributed to St. Bernard) that circulated in manuscripts throughout the Italian peninsula from the thirteenth to the fifteenth centuries. According to this letter "Marriages or meals of great cost do damage without bringing you any honor. Expenses incurred in obtaining a knighthood are honorable, those incurred in helping friends are reasonable, those incurred to help gluttons and prodigal people are lost forever."[3] It is significant that meals are described, at least in part, in terms of honor, a public virtue that came to the fore precisely in festive celebrations that confirmed social status and/or sealed social contracts such as marriages (although marriages were considered less important than consecration ceremonies for a knighthood). When the anonymous author of this letter addresses the problem of how to feed one's own family (a term that was more far-reaching than today since it included all those who lived under the same roof, including servants and possibly animals), he suggests that they be fed with "coarse foods, not delicate ones" and stresses that such food was also appropriate for holiday meals, although in this case it should be copious. As he puts it: "During the solemn festivities feed your family abundantly but not with delicate foods."[4] The conclusion this author finally comes to in order to solve the problem (of how grand or how simple food should be) was, quite simply, that there should be a "struggle" between the desire for good food and the reasons dictated by the purse.[5]

Although there are endless condemnations of how food occasioned lavish spending and excessive luxury, it is also possible to find counsel against being too parsimonious. Overly simple fare is implied in the "Lettera a Raimondo" (especially in regard to inadequate menus for the festivities celebrating a knighthood), but it is an idea that recurs in literary sources, at least until the end of the sixteenth century. In Stefano Guazzo's *La civil conversazione*, begun in 1567–68, a concern with just measure in the choice of foodstuffs surfaces quite explicitly at the end of a long and detailed passage dealing with gluttony and excessive expenditure. In conclusion to this passage, Guazzo observes:

> just as we feel that condemnation must be heaped on those whose gluttony causes them to never be satisfied with the food they eat and who spend excessively to

satisfy their appetite, so do I feel that one can hardly hold up as an example those whose avarice keeps them from living properly according to their rank in society.[6]

This very upper-class view of the dilemma of excess versus parsimony at the table was seen somewhat differently by the merchant classes. A mid-fifteenth-century manuscript by Benedetto Cotrugli on the "perfect" merchant (first published in Venice in 1573) devoted part of a chapter on temperance to the issue of how merchants should behave when it came to consuming food. According to Cotrugli, great restraint should be demonstrated regarding both food and drink, for it was seemly to "eat only in order to sustain your body." The reasons given were many, including damage to the public reputation of a merchant (he should not absent himself from his shop due to having indulged in food and drink) and his financial interest (notably the risk of making a mistake when adding up what he owed or was owed). Too much food was seen as being dangerous because it provoked slothfulness, sleepiness, slow wits and many other defects. The author then quotes Thomas Aquinas when listing the five different habits that contribute to the sin of gluttony:

> ...first of all, when you eat earlier than is wont; second, when after one kind of food you desire another; third, when you desire precious foods; fourth, when you want great quantities of food; fifth, when you are not careful to be clean but rather eat avidly and without any order.[7]

The opposition between "public" or ritual meals, in which the food had to measure up to certain standards in order to uphold the honor of those who were offering it, and meals consumed in "private," where it was possible to eat in a very modest if not downright parsimonious way, seems to have been a fundamental divide that runs through Italian food history for this period. The excesses public meals could entail—due to the wish (or need) to display the wealth and power of a family—were above all associated with the patrician (magnate) classes, but not entirely restricted to these social circles. Ritual displays of wealth and power were an important part of life for the merchant classes as well, especially since the late medieval and Renaissance ruling classes, in central and northern Italy, were often recruited from the ranks of the wealthier merchants. Town authorities undertook to resolve the political unease incurred by conspicuous consumption, and the accompanying risk of blurring social boundaries, with the promulgation of sumptuary laws. From the late thirteenth century to the end of the sixteenth century, practically every Italian city-state had passed sumptuary legislation that was regularly updated.[8] Although most of such legislation dealt with the even more sensitive issue of clothing, it often included a set of laws devoted to curbing excessive alimentary luxury displayed in public. These laws were ultimately quite ineffective in containing the ostentation of opulence, especially as they often could be circumvented by paying a fine. They do, however, tell us something about how lavish meals were structured and, incidentally, reveal details about what was considered the maximum amount of luxury that could be allowed.

The amount and variability of the norms imposed by Italian sumptuary laws can be quite bewildering, but upon careful comparison, it becomes obvious that strikingly similar criteria were applied in a number of cities. To begin with, sumptuary laws dealt almost exclusively with meat dishes (sometimes, but more rarely, with fish and with sweetmeats), thus clearly indicating that vegetables and fruit were not considered special items. Legislation also tried to curb the amount of people that could be invited to an event with a clear public dimension: such as marriages, wakes, and celebrations in honor of a knighthood. It also set limits on the amount of "dishes" that could be served during banquets, a standard that was complicated by the fact that each "dish" (each course) could be made up of several meats. Thus, for example, a sumptuary law promulgated by Siena in 1343 forbade serving more than three dishes at marriage banquets: a first course in which there could be only one kind of boiled meat (six pounds for two people being the maximum allowed), a second course in which there could be two different kinds of roasted meat—*excepting* capon, goose and duck (in which case only one bird could be served per trencher)—and, finally, a third course of sweets in which, if marzipan was served, no other sweet could be featured. The law also stated that *"confectiones sive confectos"* (candied fruit and seed) could only be served at the beginning and at the end of the meal, but that there were no restrictions as to the type or amount of fruit offered.[9]

A roughly contemporary Florentine law (1356) also specified that a maximum of three courses could be served at wedding banquets and that there could not be more than twenty-five trenchers per banquet, which meant no more than fifty people could attend since trenchers were shared by two diners.[10] This particular law included any kind of pasta (*raviuolos*) as comprising one of the three courses allowed. This provision, of course, makes it hard not to think that the typical Italian meal today still respects this structure, even though to jump to such a conclusion is not advisable before knowing more about Italian meals and their evolution in the intervening centuries. The law also specified that banquets in honor of a knighthood could be open to an unlimited amount of people, and furthermore, that one supplementary course could be served, thus tacitly admitting that the honor of a knight required a greater display of food (thus wealth) than a wedding (an opinion already encountered in the *"Lettera a Raimondo"*).

In Florence, over a century later, the laws had not changed much. The banquet regulations of 1473 seem to be more restrictive, since they allowed only two courses (one of boiled meats and one of roasted meats), but in actual fact they were probably more lenient since a greater variety of meats was allowed in each one of these courses.[11] Thus, for example, a course of boiled viands could include three different kinds of meat, while courses of roasted meats could include up to four. Interestingly, this law also mentions that anything made with eggs, cheese or milk, was not considered an "extra" course, nor was blancmange, pies of different kinds, soups, *maccheroni*, pork, salted meats or fish, aspic nor many other items considered separate courses, and therefore could be freely served. The phrasing of the law is significant because it provides a loophole that confirms and explains the impression that festive meals became increasingly complex affairs in the course of the fifteenth century, reaching unprecedented heights in the sixteenth century. In fact, the phrasing of the law allowed for any number of side dishes to be served alongside the main courses and, presumably, this was fully taken advantage of without incurring the wrath of the civil authorities.

Abundant accounts survive for festive banquets, and testify to the fact that, in most cases, such repasts tended to respect current sumptuary laws, although these laws could occasionally be bent. If, for some reason, it was decided that a banquet menu needed to transgress the restrictive terms of the law, usually all that was necessary was to pay a fine. However, as the payment of this same penalty would have added to the display of wealth and power sought by any given family, the penalty system ultimately turned the purpose of the law against itself. It must not be forgotten that sumptuary laws were aimed, above all, at conspicuous display, as was made pointedly clear by the same Florentine law of 1473, which stated that a private meal at home with only family members need not observe any of the rules and regulations decreed for public events.[12]

The information that survives about festive banquets also confirms that the structure of the meal, and the order in which dishes were served, largely respected the norms imposed by the sumptuary laws. Thus, for example, the festive meals served in Pistoia and Florence in honor of Giovanni Panciatichi's knighthood in 1388 were quite similar to the banquet served more than sixty years earlier in honor of Francesco di Messer Sozzo Bandinelli's knighting in Siena.[13] In both cases it is clear from the list of food acquisitions that the structure of the meals resembled each other closely, and conformed to the type of meal that the sumptuary laws described as being appropriate for such occasions. All three of these banquets began with a first course of sweetmeats, continued with a dish of boiled meats followed by a course of roasted meats, and finally ended with a course of yet more sweetmeats. Alongside the meat dishes there were also some pies, blancmange and other dishes, the exact number of which is hard to determine. These relatively simple festive meals of the fourteenth century nonetheless tend to become more elaborate in the course of time, with the number of courses increasing exponentially. The festive meals mentioned in a 1557 cookbook by Messisbugo, for example, shows that the two, three or four course meals of the past had become a distant memory by the mid-sixteenth century. Not only had the number of courses (which he referred to as *vivande*, i.e. different dishes served together) increased to as many as seventeen, but the number of dishes composing each course had also grown to anything between seven and nine.[14] Much the same can be said about the (only slightly more restrained) festive meals noted by Bartolomeo Scappi, the cook of Pope Pius V, who published his well-known cookbook a little more than two decades after Messisbugo. The meals he describes were made up of anywhere from three to eight courses, which he refers to as *servizi di cucina* or *servizi di credenza*, depending on whether they were hot dishes that came from the kitchen or cold dishes prepared by the *servizio di credenza*. Each of these multiple courses was then composed of as many as thirty dishes, although significantly less (between eight and sixteen) were more usual.[15]

Of course it would be an error to think that such festive / special meals resembled in any way the daily fare of the urban upper classes. An example of the difference between daily and festive fare for this social group can be found in the meals of the *Mensa della Signoria* (the table of the highest executive body in the city of Florence after 1282), which did not even come close to the luxury fare served at banquets in the fourteenth and early fifteenth centuries. While the detailed day-by-day food acquisitions of the Florentine governing body does not allow us to determine the exact menu served at their table, the much more modest amount of items bought for their meals suggests that they were nowhere as grand and varied as were the festive occasions mentioned by Messisbugo and Scappi. In most cases the *Signoria* ate no more than two or three different meats every day (usually veal, mutton and fowl of various kinds), with side dishes like blancmange but also salad, vegetables and fruit. The shopping list does, however, become more varied when an important visitor had to be honored (such as an ambassador or a prince) or for special occasions (Christmas, last day of Carnival, etc.).

The extent to which festive meals were altogether exceptional, and far removed from a more quotidian way of eating, is also borne out by a little-studied treatise by Domenico Romoli on the princely table and its management in the early sixteenth century. Book four of his treatise is devoted to the menus he prepared and served from 10 March 1546 to 9 March 1547. These meals, which he carefully annotates from the outset as being "Of ordinary meals, day by day"[16] show a relative restraint despite the fact that they were meant to be fare for a prince. While exhibiting a certain amount of variety, these "ordinary" meals show, once again, that the basic structure of the repast was not very different from the one described by sumptuary laws. The main meal of the day was at midday, usually made up of three courses on normal days and four courses on lean days. Each one of these courses included some four or five different dishes.

Thus, on lean days, the meal began with an *antipasto*, followed by a second course referred to as an *allesso* (boiled), a third course referred to as *fritto* (fried) and finally ended with a last course which Romoli refers to as *frutte* but which included something more than just fruit since he also mentions vegetables and sometimes even candied fruit. On normal (fat) days the *fritto* course was simply dropped and not replaced by anything else. Supper, on the other hand, was almost invariably made up of four or five different dishes but was not subdivided into courses. Once a month there was a day in which Romoli served two special meals, both of which he calls *convito,* although one of these seems to have been a regular banquet. Interestingly enough, this practice of having at least one day a month in which to have special meal recalls a 1343 sumptuary law of Siena, which specified that citizens were allowed only one banquet a month.[17] On these more elaborate occasions, Romoli served luncheons that were much smaller than the evening dinner, typically made up of a series of seven to ten dishes that, in most cases, were not subdivided into courses. The dinners, however, featured more courses than "normal" meals, as well as a greater amount of dishes. In most cases, dinners comprised six or seven courses, each of which included as many as six to ten different dishes, and were thus comparable to the festive banquets mentioned in the works of Messisbugo and Scappi.

The tendency towards increasingly varied meals (at least on festive occasions) in the period under examination did not, of course, mean that individuals would actually eat all the different foods. In fact, there is ample evidence to suggest that individuals chose from what was served according to their "constitution," and avoided many of the other dishes available. And, as might be expected, the abundance and luxury displayed at banquets was not always seen to be necessary or even fitting by everyone at the time. The advocates of moderation were, presumably, among the many who bought and read Alvise Cornaro's treatise on sober life. First published in 1558, Cornaro's treatise became something of a best seller, whose popularity (some twenty-five editions published well into the nineteenth century) never seemed to falter. Cornaro lamented the fact that in Italy "excessive eating is seen as a virtue and an honorable thing to do while a sober way of living is seen not only as a dishonorable custom but also one followed only by the avaricious."[18]

The criticism that Cornaro leveled at those who ate and drank excessively was doubtless aimed more at people who made it a practice to eat a lot at public banquets insofar as private meals were, on the whole, much more restrained affairs. While the princely "everyday" meals mentioned by Romoli would have been excessive for a merchant but modest in the case of a Prince, many other examples of private meals reinforce the (relative) restraint of the domestic table. Stefano Guazzo, for example, writing at much the same time as Cornaro, opposes the noise and confusion of public affairs with the more restrained, simple and satisfying meals in which family and friends dined together.[19]

The clear distinction that existed between public and private meals can also be deduced from Sir Robert Dallington's comments based on a trip he made to Tuscany in 1596. In fact, although accounts of festive meals clearly underline the conspicuous consumption of meat, he soon came to the conclusion that less public occasions were dealt with in a very different way. Dallington noticed that "...for every horse-load of flesh eaten, there is ten cart loades of herbes and rootes, which also their open Markets and private tables do witness." For an Englishman presumably used to eating large amounts of meat, the surprising consumption of vegetables (a relatively recent phenomenon in the upper classes) was explained in the following way:

> Concerning Herbage, I shall not need to speake, but that it is the most generall
> food of the Tuscan, at whose table a Sallet is as ordinary, as Salt at ours; for being
> eaten of all sorts of persons, & at all times of the yeare: of the riche because they
> have to spare; of the poor, because they cannot choose; of many Religious, because
> of their vow, of most others because of their want...[20]

Food, Table Manners and the Lower Classes

While the food that was consumed during festive meals can be documented with some accuracy—at least for the better-documented tables of the wealthy and the powerful—poorer meals are better perceived through literary texts. Literature is, of course, a source that is often hard to decode as authors use *topoi* that contain a certain amount of veracity, but the exact degree of realism is difficult to gauge with any reliability. And even in literary sources, the meals of the poor are seldom described with much detail, as authors tend to limit themselves to mentioning what was consumed. Nonetheless, the most recurrent description in novelle is of meals in which onion (or garlic) and bread are eaten, a fare that seems to have constituted the simplest and most basic type of repast in medieval and Renaissance Italy.

As might be expected, mentions of such humble fare occasionally appear in sources other than literature. This was the food given, two or three days a week, to the North African slaves building the Florentine fortifications in the sixteenth century. Much the same meal was also consumed, albeit in a pinch, by none other than Pope Pius II who, in the mid-fifteenth century, found himself one evening in the little town of "…Formello where he did not find anything to have been prepared: no food, no drink and no beds. It became necessary to look in the houses of the farmers for something to eat; but all that was available were bread and onions. As the wine had just been made it was better to drink water."[21] Such poor meals are never elaborated upon, and therefore it is quite impossible to know what kind of meaning might be attributed to these simple foodstuffs other than it was fare more frequently consumed by farmers, laborers and slaves.

Both the food that a person chose to eat (or, in some cases, was obliged to eat) and their table manners were considered fundamental elements in determining the social class to which they belonged. A telling example of this is illustrated, with an abundance of details, by one of the stories in a collection of early fifteenth-century *Novelle* by the Sienese author Gentile Sermini.[22] The story is actually an elaborately constructed mockery (a *"beffa"*) at the expense of Mattano, a rather wealthy young man from the Sienese *"contado"* (outlying districts) who thinks that he should be eligible for a high political position in the city just because he has money.[23] During a plague year he takes refuge in the nearby town of Abbadia a Isola, where he imitates a group of young men belonging to the urban upper classes who have also taken refuge there. He ostentatiously spends money in much the same way they do, but it is obvious to them that his type of spending is not germane to his social rank (while theirs is). This group of young men, who were all born within the city walls (a *sine qua non* condition for holding high political office), decide to play a trick on Mattano and, in doing so, make him understand that his lowly rural birth and his un-couth manners will always preclude him from holding office. Interestingly enough, one of the judges chosen to decide on the outcome of this trick to determine Mattano's (in)eligibility for a public position is none other than a cook from the kitchens of the Bishop of Abbadia, able to determine the social extraction of diners simply by observing what and how they ate.

According to the cook, Mattano will never hold office in Siena for three rea-sons: because he was not born in the city, because he has no table manners, and because he eats what are considered to be revolting dishes fit only for country dwellers. The list of his transgressions is telling because, although the intent is clearly satirical, it does give us an idea of the code that allowed people to distinguish sophisticated city dwellers from rustic country folk. First of all (and probably most important of all, since more text is dedicated to this than to any other aspect) is the fact that Mattano does not follow urban rules of etiquette. Intriguingly, some of the rules mentioned in the story are identical to those mentioned in Bonvesin da la Riva's handbook of etiquette *De Quinquaginta curialitatibus ad mensam,* composed almost a century earlier.[24] Thus, for example, both handbook and novella make a point of mentioning that it was bad-man-ners to slice bread by resting the loaf on one's chest, since this was seen as being typical of peasants (handbook rule twenty-two). Both texts also agree on the impropriety of licking fingers when eating (rule thirty-five in Bonvesin) and the faux-pas of putting too much bread into the soup bowl or trencher containing meat[25] (rule forty-six), both of which practices are decried as rural bad manners. Sermini's story also isolates other distinguishing transgressions. It is pointed out that Mattano is guilty of repeatedly dipping his bread into the bowl or trencher before putting it in his mouth, and when his hands are greasy he does not know what to do and wipes them off on his clothing in order not to dirty the white tablecloth.[26] Finally, he is also guilty of eating all of his soup before beginning on the meat dish, which suggests that these typical dishes served in fourteenth- and fifteenth-century meals were not meant to be eaten successively, but rather contemporaneously in the urban context.

Equally noteworthy is the fact that the Bishop's cook judges Mattano as be-ing a plebeian because he eats unrefined foods such as geese,[27] warmed-up cabbage and soup with vast amounts of garlic. A love for garlic was thought to be an almost innate quality found among the poor and the rural populations (to the extent that it is often referred to as the "spice" of the poor), and thus it confirmed his lowly status when he ate garlic with everything, even with delicate meats: "...he would eat that powerful garlic even with capons, pheasants and partridge just as he had done with the rancid lard he fed on when he lived in the *contado*."[28] Eating garlic with refined bird dishes meant that he was guilty of mixing unrefined foods with refined ones, thus further demonstrating that he did not have the discerning taste of his social betters.

Finally, the Sermini story underscores the fact that even the schedule followed by Mattano's meals betrays his social origins: "...he is not a city dweller but rather born and brought up in the *contado,* he is want to take *panebberare* breaks to eat and drink something no less than two or three times a day not counting the break he takes to eat his snack (*merenda*) and then having his dinner..."[29] This observation, which launches a long condemnation of Mattano's typically rural habits, cannot just be seen as a literary conceit. It actually introduces revelatory details such as the two terms, *panberare* and *merenda*, which had typically lower-class associations. *Panberare*, a conflation of *pane* = bread and *bere* = drink, was closely associated to the mid-morning break of the workingman and, in some cases, was even part of their daily pay. *Merenda*, instead, conjured up the mid-afternoon or evening meal that rural people ate in the fields. Thus, the text in question should be seen as only a slight exaggeration of what seems to have been a habit practiced by the lower classes in general, and yet more "proof" of Mattano's socially inappropriate behavior and failure as a social climber.

Meals and Mealtimes in Late Medieval and Renaissance Italy

The idea that Mattano could only be a lower class person since he ate so often in the course of the day was a relatively common prejudice that also appears in the writings of doctors and dietitians. Michele Savonarola, for example, whose treatise on diets was completed sometime between 1450 and 1452, explained that "peasants, masons, cart drivers, carpenters and other such people … eat three or four times per day and yet manage to digest everything."[30] As he points out a little further on, the question of how often to eat is also a moral issue: insofar as "man is a reasonable animal, he must give himself up to intellectual activity. In this he distinguishes himself from animals that are always looking for food."[31] Yet Savonarola does not propose any particular rule to be followed but rather suggests different timetables according to the constitution of individuals. Thus he advocates one meal a day for those who are fat but two meals for young people, individuals who are thin and for adolescents who are fourteen or more years old. Children under the age of thirteen and people who work physically, on the other hand, are advised to eat "two, three or more times." Old people, "who are decrepit," should also eat often but must eat little at a time, whereas those who are not decrepit are thought to be best off if they eat three meals in the course of two days (a suggestion already mentioned in Arabic medical treatises).[32]

The variability of meals and mealtimes suggested by reading Savonarola's treatise should probably not be taken too literally since the guidelines proposed by doctors were respected only in part. In fact, the doctors themselves pointed out that an individual's habits were a decisive factor to be taken into consideration, and could easily modify the theoretical rules they proposed. Domenico Romoli, while not a doctor himself, repeated medical advice in his influential treatise on food and diets (Venice, 1560): "…if a man is used to eating twice a day, and it does not harm him, then he must continue as long as it does not disturb him, because if he stopped this habit he would be weakened." Romoli also uses much the same reasoning to determine at what time of the day a particular meal had to be eaten: "…everybody should eat at the time of day they are used to eat and above all if this has become an old habit."[33] This flexibility in terms of appropriate mealtimes is echoed by Stefano Guazzo, who adds another, socially determined criteria when one of the characters in his *La civil conversazione* (1574) state that the hour for dinner is relative since "The hour for the wealthy is when they want to and that of the poor is when they can."[34] On the whole, however, counsel on mealtimes seems to have been largely for the benefit of the rich and privileged upper classes, who had less constraints as to when they ate.

In the Middle Ages and Renaissance, most large-scale construction sites had rules regulating when food was to be consumed. These rules seem to have varied from one city to another and may have been determined by the work to be done. They also varied according to the seasons. For example, the workers co-opted into building the Bucintoro for the ritual marriage of the city of Venice to the sea were allowed two meals a day in winter and three in summer. Similarly, the Venetian statutes of the glass blowers (a guild that featured prominently in the export economy of the city) stated that the guild would not allow more than three meals a day, possibly to curb the workers' tendency to increase the number of meal pauses.[35] According to the 1421 statutes of the Orvieto *Opera del Duomo*, the workers involved in the construction of the cathedral had a lunch break that lasted one hour and were then allowed another pause of a half an hour in the afternoon to eat their *merenda*. In summer, from the beginning of May to the end of August, when both daylight and working hours increased, the statutes deemed two breaks not to be enough and thus added a third one, lasting half an hour, *"pro mistu sumendo"* (for eating "the mixed"—presumably bread and wine).[36]

The amount of time allowed for meals does not seem to have been the same all over the Italian peninsula and in all walks of life. Breaks were measured with inexpensive yet precise hourglasses that became common on building sites as of the end of the fourteenth century. The workers engaged in caulking in the shipyards of Genoa, unlike those working on the cathedral of Orvieto, were accorded shorter breaks that depended on the kind of work they did. Those involved in *"opera veteri"* ("old work" i.e. maintenance?) had half an hour for lunch and a quarter of an hour for the other breaks, which were referred to as *"panberandi vel xorvendi aut merendandi"*[37] (these are three different terms for brief snack breaks). Those who were employed in the *"opera nova"* ("new work" i.e. building new ships?) had double the amount of time both for lunch (one hour) and for the other breaks (half an hour).[38]

The meals of breakfast and supper do not appear in the sources examined above. This omission can be explained, at least in the case of the statutory literature, by the fact that statutes were only concerned with what happened during working hours, and not before or after. However, in the case of breakfast (consumed shortly after getting up or, in any case, before beginning work), it does not seem to have been a customary meal, even though it was not entirely unknown. References to an early morning repast are quite rare and indicate that, if anything, it would involve a minimal amount of food: usually some toasted bread, or just a small glass of sweet wine in winter to "comfort" the body before going outside.[39] In fact, breakfast seems to have been a meal prescribed by doctors rather than something that was commonly practiced. In one of the stories of the Decameron (X,2), breakfast is served to an abbot who has been taken prisoner by the famous bandit Ghino di Tacco. The person serving this breakfast—consisting in two big pieces of toasted bread and a big glass of *"vernaccia da Corniglia"* (the well known vernaccia of Corniglia, Cinque Terre)—remarks ironically that Ghino was providing this refreshment because, as a young man he had studied to become a doctor. Even the dietary suggestions of Giovanni di Pagolo Morelli, whose *Ricordi* were composed in the 1380s for the benefit of his sons, presume a medical approach to this meal since he suggests a series of possible breakfasts to avoid the dangers of the plague. Morelli points out that they should eat

> ...a little something according to what you feel like: either a little bread and a half a glass of good wine or malmsey ... and if you have a weak or cold stomach eat some candied ginger root and a half a glass of malmsey ... or then chew on a clove or on some cinnamon, eat a spoon of jam or four *derrate* (literally four pence worth) of saffron, two or three cooked walnuts, two or three figs without any bread, or a little something that you have been recommended.[40]

It is quite possible that the idea for a breakfast meal might have originated with the medical profession, even though the term usually used in medieval Italian, *asciolvere* or sometimes *sciolvere*, came from abbreviating the Latin *absolvere jejuna* (end fast), a term that came from the ecclesiastical milieu.[41] The literal meaning therefore refers to ending the night's fast, as in the English word "breakfast." A seventeenth-century commentary of the *Malmantile*,[42] for example, points out that this is a meal that can be eaten any time between dawn and noon, and makes it clear that the term refers to a food break that was quite separate from the first main meal of the day. Significantly, the word *asciolvere*

was also used in Italian to mean "something that is not very important, something that lasts for a short time, or an instant," and thus an appropriate term
for breakfast. Yet another word used for this meal (though much less frequently) was *colazione,* a term that emerges in the course of the Cinquecento as a
descriptor for a variety of meals.[43]

Whatever the term adopted, it is clear that, as of the middle of the Trecento,
it was not uncommon for a certain amount of people to eat a little something
in the morning for reasons that were not strictly medical. Donato Velluti
(1313–1370), for example, mentions in his *Ricordanze* that one of his ancestors
ate only two rolls of bread at breakfast but then ate quite heartily at lunch.
Domenico di Cambio, one of Datini's correspondents, boasted in a letter that
his wife gave him some chestnuts to eat before he left the house every day
because she wanted to pamper him.[44] At times this very first meal of the day
was even an occasion for inviting a guest. This can be seen in a letter that
Francesco Datini wrote to his wife Margherita on 7 April 1410 in which he
asked her to invite Messer Giovanni Genovardi "either for breakfast or for
lunch and do for him what you can."[45]

The next meal of the day was the *desinare,* sometimes referred to as *pranzo,*
which was considered the most important meal of the day.[46] Not much can
be said about the time at which this meal was eaten because the evidence is
somewhat contradictory. Although more than one author makes a point of saying that this meal, like any other, should be eaten at the "right" moment, it is
worth noting that they never commit to a time of day. Thus, Giovanni di Pagolo
Morelli tells his sons to "*Desina* at the right time" and a fourteenth-century vul-
garization of St. John Chrysostom criticizes "Those who have always lived an
easy life, and ... are used to extend their *desinare* to the hour of vespers and their
dinners until midnight."[47] Neither specify when it would be appropriate to eat
this particular meal, and to further confuse things, a passage from a sermon of
Fra Giordano da Pisa (1260–1311) points out that *desinare* "can also be called *cena*
because in ancient times it was like this and, inversely, *cena* was called *desinare.*
This was the case because in the past people used to eat meals that lasted until
after the hour of *nona.*" We therefore have to surmise that at the beginning of
the fourteenth-century lunch was consumed before noon, although this does

not help much since it is a well-known fact that the hour of *nona* was not fixed, and slowly moved from what at present would be about 2:00 pm to 12:00 noon, as has been pointed out by historians such as Jacques Le Goff.[48]

What is more certain is that *desinare* was considered the most important meal in the day, to the extent that the prescriptive literature of the period stressed the fact that it should be the only meal for which one was to cook. The fourteenth-century Tuscan moralist, Paolo da Certaldo, thought that it was best to "Cook only once a day in the morning and keep part of this food for the night…"[49] Michele Savonarola, a doctor at the court of the Este at Ferrara in the mid-fifteenth century, did not provide such a a simple formula. He suggested that a bigger luncheon and a smaller supper was best for sick people, but also for "healthy people doing civil service, merchants and other such professions," as well as for those who did heavy physical work. The only cases for which Savonarola prescribed a different distribution of meals was for athletes and those who did a lot of exercise, such as riding or walking. In these cases, proba-bly due to the subjects' constant movement (but not as much physical effort as the laboring classes), it was felt that a light lunch and more substantial supper were more appropriate. The exceptions were thus relatively few within the gen-eral consensus that most people were meant to have a more copious luncheon.[50]

There is some reason to believe that the moral and medical rules associated with mealtimes were observed by the population at large, even though there are indications that a slow evolution between the late thirteenth and sixteenth centuries was turning the evening meal into a more copious repast, something that was closer to the larger luncheon. Evidence for the thirteenth and four-teenth centuries indicates the prevalence of two different daily meals, of which the first was more abundant and the second quite plain. Even a bon vivant, such as the Sienese poet Cecco Angiolieri (before 1260-1311/1313), refers to them in a line of his poetry implying their different status when he observes: "Do you know what I have too much of? Bad lunches and even worse suppers."[51] Ser Lapo Mazzei, one of Datini's most assiduous correspondents, apparently observed the rule voiced by Paolo da Certaldo regarding the simplicity of an evening meal which did not require cooking when he wrote, "…often at night I sup frugally, and nothing is better than a handful of olives: so the doctors will tell you."[52] Yet, by the end of the fifteenth century, evidence on the quantity of food appropriate to each meal becomes somewhat more contradictory. On the one hand, the custom of a more copious lunch and more frugal dinner seems to have survived, since Bartolomeo Scappi mentions (more than once) in his well-known cookbook, that the food prepared for lunch should also be served for dinner.[53] On the other hand, Bartolomeo Sacchi (Platina) stated in his *De Honesta voluptate* (written sometime after 1467 and first published without a date but probably 1473/75) that he felt the main meal of the day should be supper, affirming explicitly that this was in contradiction with what his ancestors had always done.[54] A little after the middle of the sixteenth century, one of the great experts on all of the aspects of dining and meals, Domenico Romoli, affirmed that a healthy person should eat a bigger dinner and smaller lunch, but cautiously tempered this affirmation by saying that if a person is used to the opposite it is not a good idea to change this habit.[55] Curiously enough, Romoli's sample menus in book four of *La singolare dottrina* (1560) seemingly contradict his own advice in that they invariably call for a large lunch and a decidedly smaller dinner. Despite this apparent contradiction, it seems that the sixteenth century was moving, generally speaking, toward the practice of a more substantial dinner. An opinion reinforcing this impression is voiced by the sixteenth-century naturalist Costanzo Felici, who wrote in his long treatise on salads (probably sent to Aldrovandi in 1569) that the "rule is that a healthy person should eat a dinner that is more copious than lunch."[56] Worth mentioning is also the fact that the Florentine painter Jacopo da Pontormo, whose eating habits are well known due to a diary he meticulously kept for a year from 1555 to 1556, ate only one meal a day, a dinner, except on Sundays when he also treated himself to lunch.[57]

The next meal in order of time after lunch, usually referred to as a *merenda*, was consumed in the afternoon sometime before dinner, and appears to have been more commonly eaten in the summer months, as Costanzo Felici also suggests in his treatise.[58] Various proverbs mention *merenda*, generally when they point out that this meal should be dropped after the day of St. Luke (18 October).[59] This light afternoon refreshment possessed some interesting connotations that are worth examining in more detail because they constitute clues to understanding the social context of this food break. The literary uses of the term show that it was often associated with the peasantry, or at least with the outdoors world since these meals are usually brought by women to their husbands in the fields or are consumed in a rural setting. Considering the violent diatribes against the peasantry that are part of medieval and even later Italian culture, it hardly comes as a surprise that a word like *merendone*, quite obviously related to this repast, was used as of the mid-fifteenth century to speak of a slow-witted and obtuse person, as if the practice of eating a *merenda* ended up making everybody as dull as the peasants who ate this meal.

It would, however, be quite wrong to conclude that the *merenda* was an exclusively lower class meal since it can also appear in a very different social context. This very same term described meals that were eaten by groups of young, upper class people in the open air, sometimes in the countryside after a walk and sometimes in an enclosed garden in the city.[60] Such exceptions can be documented quite easily as they appear in many *novelle*, but this practice did not alter the fact that *merenda* was ultimately seen as a meal more fit for lowly field workers than for the higher classes. In the beginning of the seventeenth century, this social conceit is expressed quite clearly by Secondo Lancellotti (1583-1643), when he asserted that this meal was "named this way in ancient times by Noia and Festo, [and] was the food eaten after lunch and was more suitable, as in our own time, for farmers who because they work in the fields would seem to deserve that small meal, more than any civilized and good mannered person."[61] Lancellotti seems thus to have known (or at least intuited) that the etymology of this word that effectively comes from the Latin word *merere* = to deserve.

The next meal punctuating the day was *cena,* which was eaten at the end of the working day, when it got dark. A variety of literary sources from Boccaccio onwards[62] mention that the signal for this meal was, in fact, the coming of darkness, with the exception of the months in which the days were particularly long. Machiavelli pointed out this nuance when he wrote: "It was in the month of May, when most Italians eat their supper at a time of day when there still is daylight." The very formal banquets celebrated at the Este court in Ferrara between 1524 and 1543 show that, on these occasions, the time for a *cena* could be quite variable, since some dinners began two hours before dark

(20 May 1529), while others began as much as three and a half hours after dark (14 February 1543).[63] Part of this variability was due, of course, to the fact that the meals were held at different times of the year, but this is not enough to account for a difference of five and a half hours.

In sixteenth-century Italy, a dinner that took place at nine or ten o'clock at night was considered nothing less than an extravaganza. Francesco Priscianese, author of an important treatise on food-related topics published in Rome in 1543, tells a highly significant story concerning a Neapolitan count who poured over his books until nine or ten o'clock at night, and thus prevented his family from having dinner at the "right" time. After suffering his extravagant ways, they decided to punish him by having dinner at the correct time, and told the house personnel to tell him, when he finally appeared, that they thought he had already had his dinner some four hours earlier and that there was no more food for him.[64]

At times the last meal of the day, as distinct from dinner, was a relatively light one that could be served any time after dark, either quite early on or much later, and was usually referred to as a *colazione* (sometimes spelled *collatione*). Although the term was often used for the refreshments served during an evening affair, there are also some examples of the same term being used for a light meal served in the morning. Examples of this second use of the term appear in Domenico Romoli, who speaks of this custom as being a French import[65] that was beginning to be fashionable in Rome at the time when he was writing his treatise (before 1560).

An early use of the word *colazione*, referring to a light evening repast, can already be found in the fifteenth century,[66] but more copious examples come from sixteenth-century sources. According to Messisbugo, such a meal was eaten quite a few hours after dinner but never replaced it, despite a certain variability in the hour at which it was served. The examples he provides are in Winter (24 January and 14 February), but both of these *colazioni* took place several hours after dark (once at nine o'clock and the other at eleven o'clock).[67] Bartolomeo Scappi uses the same word to speak of a rather different custom, since the examples found in his cookbook describe a meal taken in a garden (or in a vineyard) during the warm season, while in winter it was served in an enclosed space. The summer versions, which sound like they might have been nothing more than a renaming of the *merenda* (since this term had too many negative connotations?), were invariably served just after vespers and thus in the early evening. In winter, *colazione* took place at approximately the same hour, but as a consequence ended up being served increasingly longer after dark. Scappi is particularly clear as to timing: in the summer months *colazione* was served "after vespers"; at the end of October and in the month of November, one hour after nightfall; at the end of December, two hours after nightfall; and at the end of February it was again only one hour after darkness set in.[68] Despite the fact that the term could be used for a meal that varied enormously as to when and where it was served, what characterized the *colazione* was the fact that it was always a cold meal that did not come from the kitchen but was rather a *servizio di credenza*, a kind of buffet. In terms of the menu, there was a certain amount of variability when seen from the point of view of a modern sensibility: these meals could consist of sweet things (candied fruit, sugar water, jams, etc.) and fruit of all kinds, but could also feature cold meats and even fish, depending on the day of the week they were served.

Meals: Rituals and Food

To return to the abundantly documented, lavish meals in the Middle Ages and Renaissance, sources indicate that they all began the same way, with the observation of an elaborate hand-washing ritual. This custom is not only mentioned in literary texts but also depicted in paintings and frescos. Thus Italian paintings of the fourteenth century representing the *Last Supper*, the *Wedding at Cana* and other meal scenes often include a significant detail: the towel that was used for drying the hands of the diners, usually hanging from a wooden railing in the back of the room (See Plates 1, 2 and 14). The hand-washing ritual was considered an important part of table etiquette, to the point that Bonvesin da la Riva mentions it twice in his list of fifty "courtesies" to be observed when dining. In his late thirteenth-century treatise on good manners, Bonvesin reminds his reader that pouring the water for guests should be "a refined gesture" and that it is important not to do it "in a villainous way." The instructions are quite specific and even mention that, in summer, one should make sure to pour enough water, but not too much, whereas in winter, since it is cold, it is best to pour only a small amount on the hands of the guests.[69]

The hand-washing ritual before beginning a meal was observed throughout the period under examination and, in the case of the *Mensa della Signoria* in the fourteenth century, even called for special tin-lined silver bowls, used exclusively for this purpose.[70] In some situations the degree of sophistication was pushed even further, since in the sixteenth century (and maybe even earlier) this ritual was performed using perfumed water, in order to make it even more pleasant and refined.[71] This ablution remained current until at least the end of the Renaissance, even though the actual moment in which the hands of the guests received this treatment in the course of a meal might have changed in the course of time. In the late thirteenth century, according to Bonvesin da la Riva, the diners first washed their hands and then the meal could begin; a second hand washing then took place at the end of the meal, before a last drink of quality wine. In the sixteenth century, it would seem that this custom had not changed much since Messisbugo mentions that all banquets began with a washing of the hands, after which the diners sat down and began to eat a first course (more precisely, a cold course from the *credenza*) that was already on the table when the diners came into the room. Both Messisbugo and Scappi mention the fact that hand washing also occurred towards the end of the meal, when a second round of ablutions took place, before a very last course of candied fruit, fruit in syrup and candied seeds. It might well be that, in the sixteenth century, this last course had developed into a more ambitious affair than it had been at the time of Bonvesin da la Riva, when a drink of good wine was all that was needed in order to conclude a meal in a fitting way. The *purpose* of the last course—a series of sweet dishes meant to cap the meal—is discussed by a variety of authors in terms of an aid to digestion (as we will see further on). In the meantime, it is worth remembering that, by the early sixteenth century, a final small meal composed of fruit, candied seeds, and sugar water (referred to by Messisbugo as a *"collatione per la notte"*) had become customary and was served several hours after dinner. In this case, of course, the sweets did not end a meal but rather concluded the food intake of the day.

Tableware, Cutlery and Serving Dishes

In medieval Italy, as in the rest of Europe, people did not have their own individual tableware. Knives and spoons were shared by diners, while bowls and trenchers contained food for two or more people. In the thirteenth and fourteenth centuries, trenchers were made with maple or beech since these light-colored woods allowed for fashioning much prized "white" ware[72] (possibly a forerunner of the white plates still much in use today). This taste for white surfaces to eat on continued despite the craze for a new kind of tableware—fashionable and colorful majolica—which soon replaced the old-fashioned wooden bowls and trenchers in comfortable households. Majolica (and glass) are often portrayed in Italian paintings, where their pictorial effect is fully exploited,[73] but they were relatively rare on contemporary tables until the end of the fourteenth century, and probably still relatively scarce in the beginning of the fifteenth century, when a kind of mass production began in a number of Italian centers, and "an extraordinary elaboration of forms and decoration" began to develop.[74] Nonetheless, a taste for white surfaces not only seems to have remained (despite the newly available colors), and seems to have become fashionable once again in the early seventeenth century, when the author of a well-known treatise on the management of a noble house observed that "many gentlemen, princes and cardinals want their food served up on dishes of white majolica…"[75]

The sharing of a trencher and other tableware determined a particular dynamic, as it caused a diner to have more intimate contact with his or her partner than with the rest of the people sitting at the table. Bonvesin da la Riva makes a long list of rules regulating the "cohabitation" of these couples of diners. He reminds his readers that it is polite to swallow the food in one's mouth before drinking from the common cup, since a full mouth might disgust the other diner (rule ten); one should wipe one's mouth before drinking (rule twelve); one should not play with the food on the trencher since this too is indelicate (rule twenty); and one must refrain from

putting bread in the wine since, as he points out with a good dose of ironic un-
derstatement, this would disgust at least brother Bonvesin (rule twenty-three), and
so on. Curiously enough, although this dynamic of delicacy is quite explicitly discussed by Bonvesin da la Riva, it hardly ever appears in iconographic sources from
the period in which it was most common. Nevertheless, in some frescos (see, for
example, a *Last Supper* of Ugolino di Nerio in the Metropolitan Museum in New
York, and that of an unknown artist in the church of Bessans, Savoie) it is possible
to see how the diners turned more towards their partner, forming couples that partially turned their backs to their other neighbors (Plates 1 and 2).[76]

The sharing of trenchers and silverware gradually disappeared, although
we do not know much about the chronology of this change. The available
data suggests that the process might have begun earlier in the upper classes
and then slowly made its way down into the lower classes. As of the mid-fourteenth-century there are clear signs in the Florentine *Mensa della Signoria* of a
move towards an individualization of silverware. The list of such tableware,
recorded in the 1360s by a friar acting as a notary to the *Signoria*, shows that
the Priors of Florence not only possessed individual knives but also, more surprisingly, their own forks (to my knowledge the earliest mention of individual
forks in Italy), as well as personal salt cellars and containers for the sauces that
were commonly served at meals.[77] The earliest mention of individual plates
for each diner (but further research might very well push this date back considerably) is at a banquet served in Ferrara in 1530, where the chronicler specifically mentions that each diner had his own *tondo* (quite literally "roundel")
and therefore an individual plate to eat from.[78]

Although the details of this significant transformation in table manners are
not yet known, what is certain is that the process began in Italy earlier than
in most European countries, and that these "new" table manners were subsequently adopted by northern European countries. The use of forks seems
to have been more generalized in Italy by the end of the fourteenth century,
above all as an instrument for eating pasta, since it is mentioned for this purpose in one of Sacchetti's *novelle*.[79] The use of forks most probably became fairly widespread by the fifteenth century, as can be surmised by their appearance
not only in Florentine *ricordanze*[80] but also in frescos such as Pietro Perugino's

Last Supper in the refectory of Sant' Onofrio di Fuligno in Florence (1493). In Perugino's fresco appear several rudimentary kinds of forks—a finely shaped wooden instrument with two prongs—used to spear food and bring it to the mouth, as well as to hold food in place while cutting it.[81] This precursor of the fork might have at first been used for only these two tasks, and not in the various ways that later developed for this implement.

Although it is not easy to follow the development of individualized tableware, it is more than likely that by the end of the sixteenth century (or at the very latest at the beginning of the seventeenth century), individual cutlery had become widely accepted, even in modest social milieus. Paintings from this period often portray this new custom, and even the English traveler Fynes Moryson, who embarked from Venice in 1595 on a trip to the Levant, was struck by a fashion that was—at least for him—quite a novelty. In his account, he wrote that everyone on the boat ate "with his knife and spoone, and his forke to hold the meat whiles he cuts it, for they hold it ill manners that one should touch the meat with his hand and with a glasse or cup to drinke in peculiar to himselfe."[82]

The Order of the Meal

Meals for which reliable documentation has survived reveal not just conventions regarding the succession of viands and the gradual introduction of individualized eating utensils, but also the extent to which they followed the dietary precepts of the time. Dietary prescriptions remained much the same from the late thirteenth century until the mid sixteenth century and beyond, and were repeated in a widely disseminated genre of popular literature that specifically treats the properties of foodstuffs. This kind of literature, it is important to emphasize, was consumed not only by the wealthy and the powerful but also by urban artisans, and circulated orally amongst all social classes thanks to a considerable number of well-known proverbs.[83]

According to this prescriptive literature (and as confirmed by the menus of banquets), an ideal multi-course meal during the period under consideration was meant to begin with a first course in which fruit, salads and other foods were served because they were considered to be "cold" according to humoral theory. The humanist Bartolomeo Sacchi—better known as Platina—pointed out in his cookbook (composed in 1467) that meals should begin with apples, pears, lettuce and more generally, "all raw and cooked foods that are served with oil and vinegar." However, he points out that it was considered unhealthy and dangerous to eat fruit and vegetables together: their excessively cold nature and humidity could upset the digestive process, thus endangering healthy people. According to Platina it was better to eat fruit before a meal, but if there was none to be had he suggested it be replaced with salads.[84] This opinion was also mentioned by contemporary doctors and literary texts and, above all, was practiced in the more complicated meals where several courses were served.[85]

The custom of starting with a salad was certainly known as of the fourteenth century since it is frequently mentioned in literary sources although, oddly enough, the various festive meals for which we have accounts do not seem to mention this feature. It was probably not until the fifteenth century (but certainly by the sixteenth) that this "first" course became an important part of the meal. Once such first courses were adopted they comprised varying amounts of cold dishes (depending on the grandness of the meal served) and were characterized by their not being brought directly from the kitchen but rather prepared at the *credenza* in full view of the diners. The fact that the *antipasto, insalata* or *primo servizio di credenza*, as it had come to be called, was a rapidly evolving and fashionable custom can also be seen from the various treatises that were devoted to this subject in the second half of the Cinquecento. Thanks to these it is possible to define, in a more precise way, what dishes the diners expected when they were served a first course, although under the term "salad" were often dishes that, in most countries today, would not be defined as such.

Costanzo Felici, whose second and longer treatise on salads was completed in March 1572, defines the term for his readers in a very concise and even analytical way:

> ...salad is a term that is only used by the Italians and is a term derived from one of the elements used in the dressing: salt. The term is used for a kind of green leaf or several kinds of green leaves mixed together, or any other thing (sic) that is usually

mixed with oil, salt and vinegar, but some people also add *sapa* [a sauce made with boiled grape juice], honey, sugar, and such things…

He also points out that salads could be made with "…either cooked or raw things that are all mixed together…"[86] This definition underscores the fact that it is not the basic foodstuff used to make this dish that determined its being a "salad" but rather the dressing that made it such. This definition is also borne out by the banquets of the sixteenth century in which salads made with green leaves (cooked or raw) represent a minority of the dishes.[87] A great variety of first course *antipasti* included items such as boiled tongue, fried raw ham, sage on slices of bread, sausages boiled in wine, capon served cold with capers, "salad" made with kid feet, aspic made with meat broth, "salads" made with different kinds of salted fish, etc. These essentially acidic-tasting dishes might remind one of the traditional French *hors d'oeuvres* or *crudités* more than the present-day Italian *antipasto*.

There were two other groups of dishes that were normally served as part of the first "salad" course. The first of these was basically sweet-tasting and consisted in fruit of various kinds as well as sweet dishes: strawberries with sugar, plum savory, lemons with sugar and rosewater, grapes, marzipan, cookies of various kinds, different kinds of pies made with apples, quince and marzipan, etc. The second group of "salads" that could be served included various types of fresh cheeses, milk and butter,[88] which at times were served by themselves and sometimes were used to make prepared dishes, such as fresh butter with sugar and rosewater or *ricotta* (a kind of cottage cheese) mixed with sugar and rosewater, etc.

One of the functions of the first course was to sharpen the appetite of the diners and therefore, as Costanzo Felici points out, such dishes could also reappear towards the middle of the meal. "Salads" could be served in order to help those whose hunger was already satiated to continue eating. However, Felici hastens to say that "…this habit does not please me very much since it ends up stretching the skin of the diners from too much eating." In fact, according to him, salads should be consumed above all before the evening meal,[89] which is also what Domenico Romoli indicates as being the correct thing to do,[90] although this was not always respected in contemporary practice.

Following the "appetizer" or salad course, the meal proper could begin with a first part that consisted of a variable number of courses composed of an equally variable number of dishes. The exact number of courses and dishes depended not only on the occasion but also on the period in question. The evidence at our disposal suggests, unsurprisingly, that the higher the social class and the more festive the occasion, the more courses and more varied dishes were served. This profusion increased over time, since the rich banquets of the sixteenth century certainly outdid those of earlier centuries, but in these increasingly complex affairs it is hard to find an exact rule (or set of rules) that structured the various courses.[91] To a certain extent, the great quantity of dishes might be ascribed to the triumph of medical and dietary concerns, which had always stressed the fact that every guest needed a different diet reflecting their age, sex, social extraction, professional occupation, constitution and a series of other parameters particular to an individual. As this is not the place to enter into much detail about such dietary rules, let it suffice to say that the profusion of dishes allowed each person to eat what suited them best. The abundance of dishes was thus not meant to provide the individual with a vast amount of varied foods but with a "healthy" choice. Indeed, both doctors and cooks made a point of saying that "…dishes made with many different ingredients will become corrupt more easily than those made with few ingredients" and thus by extension it became obvious that "…nothing is more pernicious than mixing many different foods in your stomach…"[92]

Despite the variables governing an individual's dietary needs, there was also a general rule to be observed by all diners, based on what was thought to be the physiological basis of digestion. According to this rule it was important to follow up the first course, which prepared the digestive process, with "coarser" foods (such as the meat of four legged animals and their internal organs), considered "cold" food requiring a long digestion. Since the stomach was thought to be hottest at the beginning of the digestive process, it was believed that this was the moment when it could cope best with "cold" food. Next came the dishes made with more refined foods (especially birds of all kinds) which were thought to be digested more easily.[93] The meal finally ended with a last course comprised of one or more dishes (cooked apples and pears, candied coriander and aniseed, chestnuts, fennel, etc.), which were meant to help complete the digestion and, above all, "seal the mouth of the stomach and stop the digestive fumes from going to the brain."[94]

These were some of the basic rules structuring the meals of the period, according to both dietary theory and actual practice, although specific menus can appear to be very different at first glance. Thus in some cases the first "salad" course might be missing, in others there might be a far greater variety of dishes served as the main courses, but basically the same overall structure is respected over a long period of time. Some concrete examples of how these rules were observed will demonstrate the prevalence of the late medieval and Renaissance order of the meal.

The dinner offered in honor of the knighting of Giovanni Panciatichi in April 1388 began with salted veal, chicken giblets and kid feet. The next course called for capon, chicken, pigeon and a pie. At the end of the meal came cheese, fruit (presumably cooked even though it is not mentioned explicitly) and, finally, candied seeds.[95] On a more lavish scale, the banquet celebrated on the 24th of January 1416 for the marriage of Antonio di Niccolò Castellani began with a gilded cake made with pine nuts, followed by veal and ravioli, after which the guests were served capon, partridge, and meat pie. The meal then ended, predictably enough, with cooked pears and candied seeds.[96] Moving into the sixteenth century, the first impression is that this linear progression is lost except for the fact that the meal begins with sweet things (but also with salads) and ends in the same way. What seems to have happened in the evolution of increasingly complex and long banquets is that, in any given course, appear what seem to be contradictory dishes from the point of view of the earlier, standard progression. This apparent contradiction can be explained by the fact that each diner not only ate according to their constitution, but also that they progressed through the meal at different rhythms. On the whole, however, the principle of progression according to digestive theory appears to have been respected since there tend to be more dishes of "coarse" foods at the beginning than towards the end of the meals,[97] and that the catering to individual tastes and needs ended at the last course, when everybody shared the same sweet items that concluded the repast.

Conclusion

At the end of this brief and summary look at Italian medieval and Renaissance meals, it is essential to reiterate, once again, that the closer we look at these meals, the more difficult it becomes to formulate generalizations that are valid in all cases. Such generalizations all too often end up simplifying and obscuring the variety that existed in reality. For example, what has not been discussed, for want of space are all kinds of unusual and yet regularly recurring meals. In this category would be those served to the sick (both in homes and in hospitals), that still need to be studied more closely.[98] The little we know about the food served to the ailing indicates that they followed a rather different logic than meals served to the healthy.[99] To the list of important, though infrequent, meals that have not been specifically examined in the previous pages might be added marriage banquets. These deserve a study unto themselves since they were the central event of a complex social occasion celebrating a fundamental institution in this period.

Two more examples, that certainly do not exhaust the list of types of meals that have been excluded, are funeral meals commemorating the dead and the numerous festive meals linked to a specific date (All Souls' Day, Christmas, Easter, Carnival "Fat Thursday" called *Berlingaccio*, etc.). All of these occasions were celebrated by menus, customs and rituals that were specific to that given occasion, and had a religious or lay meaning shared by all those who sat down to eat together. In medieval Florence, for example, a goose was consumed (at least by those who could afford it) only on one occasion during the entire year: All Souls' Day. The association of the goose with this particular day of the year commemorating the dead was so strong and pervasive that it ended up creating a macabre association used with great dexterity by Franco Sacchetti in one of the stories of his *Trecentonovelle*.[100]

Even if the cyclical recurrence of "special" occasions and holidays are excluded from an examination of the late medieval and Renaissance meal in Italy, a bewildering variety of appropriate viands, courses and dietary concerns remained. Eustachio Celebrino, in his concise but analytical treatise on how to serve food to guests (first published in 1526), points out that meals can be divided into no less than eight different types.[101] After detailing the ways of setting the table—more or

less the same for all of the meals—he goes on to define the first of these categories: "lunches served to important guests in winter," a category, it turns out, that
included only lunches served outside of Lent. The second category is the companion to the first since it concerns dinners served to the same kind of important
guests at the same time of year. The third category concerns lunches served to
important guests in winter, but this time during Lent. Oddly enough Celebrino
does not have a category for dinners served to important guests during Lent, a
configuration that might have been deemed unacceptable due to the continent
spirit of this time of the year. He then cites a fourth category made up of lunches
served during the "the season of fruit." In this category he considers roasted and
boiled meats (which meant that it had to take place outside of the Lenten period
and lean days) and carefully specifies what fruit is to be served at what point in the
course of the meal. The last four categories mentioned by Celebrino all concern
meals that share the fact that they are offered to a guest who is also a "family
friend" (*amico domestico*, as he puts it). Categories five and six are devoted to domestic lunches and dinners outside of Lent, whereas categories seven and eight
are those devoted to lunches and dinners during Lent.

The different types of meals listed by Celebrino are nothing more than a
permutation of three fundamental oppositions: lunch/dinner, Lent/not Lent,
and important guests/intimate friends. The only meal that does not fit into
this permutation are the lunches in fruit season. It is, however, highly significant (and this is also a cautionary note with respect to the attempts to system-
atize a biological necessity shaped by social and cultural norms) that Eustachio
Celebrino concludes his list of different types of meals by adding a last brief
chapter dedicated to what he calls the *parlamento universale*, i.e. "universal way
of speaking about" meals. Rather than claiming to have described the quintes-
sential structure of meals, he reminds his reader that,

> Although I have described to you the types of meals observed in Venice, this does
> not mean that you can practice and know the universal way of speaking of meals.
> It is said that every region has its own way of doing things and every house has its
> own customs. Therefore, you will eat according to the way in which it is done in
> your lands or then according to how you like to do things in your house.[102]

Notes

First published as "Le repas en Italie à la fin du Moyen Age et à la Renaissance," in *Tables d'hier, tables d'ailleurs*, edited by J.-L. Flandrin and J. Cobi, (Paris: Odile Jacob, 1999), 115–149.

1. On cookbooks and social classes see chapter 2.

2. "...paoni, capponi e starne, ne simili altri cibi elettissimi, quali s'apparecchiano agl'infermi, ma pongasi mensa cittadinesca..." Leon Battista Alberti, *Libri della famiglia*, edited by R. Romano and A. Tenenti (Turin: Einaudi, 1969), book 3, 234 (all translations, unless otherwise specified, are my own).

3. "Le noze, overo conviti di grande spesa, fanno danno senza onore. La spesa fatta per cavallaria è onorevole, la spesa che si fa per aitare gli amici è ragionevole, la spesa che si fa per aitare e goditori e' prodighi è perduta." "Dottrina del vivere o Lettera a Raimondo," in *Scrittori di religione del Trecento*, edited by Don G. De Luca, (Turin: Einaudi, 1977), vol. 3, 461–462.

4. "Ne' dì solenni e pasquarecci pasce la tua famiglia con abundanzia, ma non dilicatamente." Ibid.

5. As he puts it: "Fa che la gola litighi co' la borsa." Ibid.

6. "...sì come vogliamo che meritino gran biasimo quei che per crapula non finiscono mai di saziarsi de' cibi e di spendere soverchiamente nel diletto della gola, così istimo che meritino poca lode quei che per avarizia restano di vivere convenevolmente secondo il loro grado." Stefano Guazzo, *La Civil conversazione*, edited by A. Quondam (Modena: Panini, 1993), 277.

7. "...prima, quando mangi innanzi tempo; secondo, quando di poi uno cibo vuoi l'altro; terzo; quando vuole cibi pretiosi; quarto; quando ne vuole in quantità; quinto, quando non serva politia nel mangiare, ma mangia avidamente et senza hordine." Benedetto Cotrugli

Raguseo, *Il libro dell'arte di mercatura*, edited by U. Tucci (Venice: Arsenale, 1990), 226.

8. On sumptuary laws and banquets see Odile Redon, "La réglementation des banquets par les lois somptuaires dans les villes d'Italie (XIIIe-XVe siècles)," in *Du manuscrit à la table*, edited by C. Lambert (Montréal/Paris: Champion-Slatkine/Les Presses de l'Université de Montréal, 1992). Concerning Florentine sumptuary laws and marriage banquets see Christiane Klapisch-Zuber, "Les noces florentines et leurs cuisiniers," in *La sociabilité à table. Commensalité et convivialité à travers les âges*, edited by M. Aurell, O. Dumoulin and F. Thelamon, (Rouen: University of Rouen, 1992).

9. The text of this law is now published in Maria A. Ceppari and Patrizia Turrini, *Il Mulino delle vanità. Lusso e cerimonie nella Siena medievale* (Siena: Il Leccio, 1993), 188–90.

10. For an edition of this particular sumptuary law see Paolo Emiliani-Giudici, *Storia politica dei municipi italiani* (Florence, 1851), 431–432 or Ronald E. Rainey, *Sumptuary Legislation in Renaissance Florence*, PhD thesis, Columbia, 1985 (University Microfilms International, 1987), 677.

11. Rainey 1985, 783–88.

12. Rainey 1985, 784.

13. The festivities celebrating Giovanni Panciatichi are published in Luigi Passerini, *Genealogia e storia della famiglia Panciatichi* (Florence, 1858), 245–267. Those celebrating Francesco di Messer Sozzino Bandinelli are published in *Cronache Senesi* in *Rerum Italicarum Scriptores* (Bologna, 1934), t. XV, part 6, 450.

14. Christoforo di Messisbugo, *Libro novo nel qual s'insegna a far d'ogni sorte di vivanda* first published in Ferrara but I am citing from the anastatic reprint of the edition printed in Venice in 1557 (Bologna: Forni, 1982). See

above all the first part of the volume in which various meals are described in detail.

15. Bartolomeo Scappi, *Opera*, (Venice: 1570; Bologna: Forni, 1981), book 4, 169–327.

16. "Del mangiare ordinario di dì in dì," Domenico Romoli, *La singolare dottrina* (Venice: 1560), 32 v°.

17. Ceppari and Turrini 1993, 194–195.

18. "…nientedimeno è sentita la crapula per cosa virtuosa e onorevole, e la vita sobria disonorevole e da uomo avaro…" Alvise Cornaro, *La vita sobria*, edited by A. Di Benedetto (Milan: Tea, 1993), 29.

19. Guazzo 1993, vol. 1, 175.

20. Sir Robert Dallington, *A Survey of the Great Dukes State of Tuscany, in the Year of Our Lord 1596* (London: Edward Blount, 1605; facsimile reprint, Amsterdam: Walter J. Johnson/ Theatrum Orbis Terrarum, 1974), 34.

21. "Ipse Formellum petiit, ubi nihil omnino parati repperit: non cibus, non potus, non lecti reperiebantur. Quaesita sunt a rusticis quae famem auferrent panis cepae. Vinum, tum primum ex uvis expressum, aquae cessit eaque sitim extinxit." Enea Silvio Piccolomini, *I Commentarii*, edited by L. Totaro, (Milan: Adelphi, 2004), book 4, ch. 41, vol. 1, 818.

22. The name of this author has now been shown to be an 18th century invention and is now often referred to as Pseudo-Sermini.

23. Gentile Sermini (Pseudo), *Novelle*, critical edition and comment by Monica Marchi, (Pisa: ETS, 2012), novella XXV, 451–465.

24. Bonvesin da la Riva, *De quinquaginta curialitatibus ad mensam*, in *Poeti del Duecento*, edited by G. Contini, (Milan/Naples: Ricciardi, 1960), vol. 2, tome 1, 703–712.

25. This rule is, of course, partially due to the fact that bowls and trenchers were usually shared by two or more people until the late sixteenth-century.

26. This particular passage is not easy to interpret but might suggest that tablecloths were probably used more or less the way we use napkins today. In any case, it is noteworthy that in Central Italy rural families were in the habit of cleaning their hands on the tablecloth until the 1950s.

27. Concerning the lowly status of geese and aquatic birds, as well as the question of what was considered to be rich or simple fare, see Allen J. Grieco, "Food and Social Classes in Late Medieval and Renaissance Italy," in *Food: A Culinary History*, edited by J.-L. Flandrin and M. Montanari, (New York: Columbia University Press, 1999). (Chapter 6 in the present volume).

28. "…et così vorrebbe il forte aglione con capponi o fagiani o starne, come col vieto lardo che usava in contado." Sermini, 2012, 458.

29. "…lui non è cittadino ma nato et allevato in contado, uso panebberare la mattina duo o tre volte, et merendare, et poi cenare la sera…" Sermini, 2012, 458.

30. "…i villani, muratori, carari, marangoni e somegianti … questi tali per la usanza manzano tre e quattro volte al zorno e pur bene padiscono." Michele Savonarola, *Libreto de tutte le cosse che se magnano*, edited J. Nystedt, (Stockholm: Alquist & Wiksell, 1988), 183–184.

31. Ibid., 185.

32. Ibid., 186 where he cites al-Rhazi (Rhazes) but see also Romoli 1560, 257v°–258r°.

33. Romoli 1560, 258r°. Concerning the importance of individual habits see also, Savonarola 1988, 184.

34. "L'ora de' ricchi è quando vogliono, e quella de' poveri è quando possono," Guazzo 1993, vol. 1, 271.

35. Sante Polica, "Il tempo del lavoro in due realtà cittadine italiane: Venezia e Firenze (secc. XIII-XIV)," in *Lavorare nel Medio Evo. Rappresentazioni ed esempi dall'Italia dei secc.*

X-XVI, Atti del Convegno del Centro di Studi della Spiritualità medievale (12–15 ottobre 1980), (Todi: 1983), XXI, 45.

36. Lucio Riccetti, "Il cantiere edile negli anni della Peste Nera," in *Il Duomo di Orvieto*, edited by L. Riccetti (Bari: Laterza, 1988), 190.

37. The term is most probably a corruption of the Latin *sorbendi* and therefore "sipping." I would like to thank Giulia Torello Hill for helping me sort this out.

38. Laura Balletto, "I lavoratori dei cantieri navali (Liguria secc. XII-XIV)," in *Artigiani e salariati. Il mondo del lavoro nell'Italia dei secoli XI-XV* (Pistoia: 1984), 147.

39. This is mentioned both by doctors and by the authors of *novelle*. See, for example: Tommaso del Garbo, *Ordine e reggimento, che si debbe osservare nel tempo di pistolenza...*, edited by P. Ferrato (Bologna: G. Romagnoli, 1866), 33; Giovanni Boccaccio, *Decameron*, edited by V. Branca (Torino: Einaudi, 1980), X,2, 1122–1123.

40. Giovanni di Pagolo Morelli, *Ricordi*, edited by V. Branca (Florence: Le Monnier, 1957), 295–296. Although this is proposed as a protective measure to be employed during the winter, when premonitory signs suggested the arrival of the plague, it must be pointed out that plague tractates usually reconfirm the importance of not deviating from usual and healthy behavior.

41. For the following discussion I have used Salvatore Battaglia, *Grande Dizionario della Lingua Italiana*, from now on GDLI (Torino: UTET, 1961), s.v. asciolvere.

42. Ibid.

43. A more complete discussion of the use of this word will be dealt with later on in this chapter.

44. Letter quoted in Iris Origo, *The Merchant of Prato*, (Harmondsworth: Penguin, 1979), 285.

45. "...che ll'abiate a 'sciolvere o desinare e fategli ciò che voi potete." Francesco Datini, *Le Lettere di Francesco Datini alla moglie Margherita*

(1385–1410), edited by E. Cecchi, (Prato: Società Pratese di Storia Patria, 1990), 297.

46. The etymology of *desina*, from the Latin *de-ieiunare*, suggests that the term *sciolvere* or *asciolvere* used for breakfast might have been a more recent one. What is certain is that the Latin *de ieiunare* gave rise to Europe-wide terminology (in French both *déjeuner* and *diner*, English dinner, Spanish *desayunar*, Catalan *dinar...*)

47. This and the following citation are taken from GDLI, s.v.

48. Jacques Le Goff, "Au moyen âge. Temps de l'église et temps du marchand," in *Pour un autre Moyen âge* (Paris: Gallimard, 1977), 46–65.

49. Quoted in Origo 1979, 286. It is worth mentioning, as evidence of the "longue durée" of some of these practices, that until the mid-20th century, the rural populations of central Italy cooked at lunch for the whole day and warmed up the leftovers for dinner in a designated alcove, recessed below the (raised) hearth.

50. Savonarola 1988, 183–184.

51. "Ma sapete di che i' ho abbondanza?/ Di ma' desnar con le cene peggiori." Cecco Angiolieri, *Rime*, edited by G. Cavalli (Milan: Rizzoli, 1959), 83.

52. Quoted in Origo 1979, 286.

53. Scappi 1570, 234 v° and 263 r°.

54. Platina, *On Right Pleasure and Good Health, A critical edition and translation of* "De Honesta Voluptate et Valetudine," by Mary Ella Milham, (Tempe Arizona: Medieval and Renaissance Texts and Studies, 1998), 109.

55. Romoli 1560, 376 r°.

56. "...regola per l'homo sano che la cena debba esser più copiosa del desinare..." Costanzo Felici, *Dell'insalata e piante che in qualunque modo vengono per cibo del'homo*, edited by G. Arbizzoni (Urbino: Quattroventi, 1986), 29.

57. Jacopo Pontormo, *Il libro mio*, edited by S. Nigro (Genoa: Costa e Nolan, 1984), 49.

58. Felici 1986, 30.

59. For the following discussion see GDLI, s.v. *merenda* and *merendone*.

60. An example of this is to be found in the *Decameron*, IV, 7.

61. "La merenda, nominata antichissimamente da Noio e Festo, ch'era il cibo doppo mezzo giorno, conveniva più, come ancora nei nostri tempi, a contadini, i quali lavorando colà nel campo, pare che meritino quel poco rinfrescamento, che a persona civile e costumata" quoted in GDLI, s.v. *merenda*.

62. For the following examples, unless mentioned otherwise, see GDLI, s.v. *cena*.

63. Messisbugo 1557, 9r° and 36r°.

64. I would like to thank Andrea Manciulli for this reference. Francesco Priscianese, *Del Governo della corte d'un Signore in Roma*, edited by L. Bartolucci (Città di Castello, 1883; 1st ed., Rome, 1543), 34.

65. Romoli 1560, 57r°, 64r°, 65r°, 72r°, 80r° etc.

66. See GDLI, s.v.

67. Messisbugo 1557, 19v° and 38r°.

68. Scappi 1570, 192r°, 204v°, 214r°, 226r°, 250r°, 264v°, 276v° and 104r° (but paginated incorrectly and really between 303 and 303 bis).

69. Gianfranco Contini, 1937, numbers two and fifty.

70. Concerning these silver bowls see Curzio Mazzi, "La mensa dei Priori di Firenze nel secolo XIV," *Archivio Storico Italiano* 5, 20, 1897, 337.

71. See, for example, Messisbugo 1557, 29 v°, 31 r°, 32 r°, etc.

72. Concerning the kinds of wood used for bowls and trenchers, as well as for references to the whiteness of trenchers, see Giovanna Frosini, *Il Cibo e i signori. La mensa dei Priori di Firenze nel quinto decennio del sec. XIV*, (Florence: Accademia della Crusca, 1993), 206.

73. On pictorial effects and how representative this tableware might have been see chapter 14.

74. As it has been put by Goldthwaite 1989, 2.

75. Antonio Adami *Il Novitiato del Maestro di casa*, (Rome, 1657), 165, quoted in the useful article by Richard Goldthwaite, "The Economic and Social World of Italian Renaissance Maiolica," *Renaissance Quarterly* 42, 1, 1989, 21.

76. See Allen J. Grieco, "Cibi e buone maniere nei sacri conviti," in *La Tradizione fiorentina dei cenacoli*, edited by C. Acidini Luchinat and R. C. Proto Pisani eds., (Florence: Scala, 1997), 76–77. (Chapter 12, page 213 in the present volume).

77. Mazzi 1897, 338.

78. Messisbugo 1557, 27 r°.

79. Franco Sacchetti, *Il Trecentonovelle*, (Florence: Sansoni, 1984), n. CXXIV, 251.

80. See, for example, Francesco di Matteo Castellani, *Ricordanze I. Ricordanze A (1436–1459)* and *Ricordanze II. Ricordanze e Giornale B (1459–1485)*, edited by G. Ciappelli (Florence: Olschki, 1992 and 1995), vol. 1, 107 and 158; vol. 2, 60, 115–116 and 152. Castellani mentions forks more than once between 1436 and 1485. In 1447 he gives "twelve little silver forks" to a friend as a marriage present, while in 1452 he pawns a set of forks. In 1460 he lends forks to a friend.

81. I would like to thank Stefanie Ohlig, who was doing her doctoral dissertation on Florentine refectories when this article was first published. Her thesis has now come out as *Florentiner Refektorien. Form, Funktion und die Programme ihrer Fresken*, (Engelsbach/Frankfurt/Munich/New York: Hänsel-Hohenhausen, 2000).

82. Quoted in Ugo Tucci, "L'alimentazione a bordo delle navi veneziane," *Studi Veneziani*, n.s. XIII (1987), 107.

83. For an overview of this problem see Allen J. Grieco, "Medieval and Renaissance Wines: taste, dietary theory and how to choose the "right" wine (14th-16th centuries)," *Mediaevalia*, 30, (2009), 17–21. (Chapter 6, page 118 in the present volume).

84. Concerning Platina's opinions on how to begin a meal see pages 122–23 and 212–13.

85. Insofar as doctors are concerned see, for example, Savonarola 1988, 178, also under individual entries on fruits like cherries,

apples etc. Concerning the actual meals and the fact that they began with fruit, salads, etc. see the meals mentioned by Messisbugo, Scappi and Romoli.

86. "...l'insalata è nome de' Italiani solamente, havendo la denominatione da una parte del suo condimento, cioè dal sale, perhò che si chiama così un'herba o più miste insieme a questo nostro proposito, o altra cosa con condimento d'olio, sale et aceto generalmente (che altra cosa ancora da alcuni in questa si suole aggiongere, como sapa, mele o zuccaro, o simile cose ... o cotte o crude che siano, misticando il tutto in un corpo." Felici 1986, 25. See also what he says about salads made without any green leaves, 30–31.

87. For the following examples I have relied on the banquets mentioned by Scappi in his *Opera*, but much the same habits can also be observed in the banquets described by Messisbugo and by Romoli.

88. Already in the middle of the fifteenth century Platina wrote that milk and freshly made cheeses (a few days old) was served at the beginning of a meal, while aged cheeses were to be eaten at the end. Platina 1998, 158–159.

89. Felici 1986, 28.

90. Romoli 1560, 206 v°.

91. Since this piece was written, much more work has been done on this subject—but not on Italy—See above all the last and unfortunately incomplete book by Jean-Louis Flandrin, *L'ordre des mets*, Paris: Odile Jacob, 2002. See also by the same author, "Structure des menus français et anglais aux XIVe et XVe siècles," in *Du manuscrit à la table. Essai sur la cuisine au Moyen Age*, (Paris/Montréal: Champion/Slatkine and Les Presses de l'Université de Montréal, 1992), 173–192 and Gilly Lehmann, "The Late Medieval Menu

in England. A Reappraisal," *Food & History*, vol. 1, n. 1 (2003), 49–83.

92. Romoli 1560, 258 v°.

93. Ibid., 362 r°.

94. Platina 1998, 462–463 but see also Girolamo Manfredi, *Libro intitolato il perché* (Bologna: 1629; first ed. Bologna: 1474), 53 and Savonarola 1988, 178.

95. The accounts for this meal are in Passerini 1858, 250.

96. Archivio di Stato di Firenze, *Acquisti e Doni*, 302, 1. I would like to thank Christiane Klapisch-Zuber for this reference.

97. This conclusion has been reached on the basis of the large number of banquets described by Messisbugo and Scappi, as well as the meals recounted by Romoli.

98. Some useful new material has come out since this article was first published. For a brief bibliographical update see chapter 4, notes 1 and 3.

99. For an example of this see Leon Battista Alberti's comment about meals for the sick, note 1 *supra*.

100. Sacchetti 1984, novella CLXXXV, 413 but see also novella CLXXXVI, 417 for another story regarding the custom of eating a goose on this day.

101. For the following discussion see Eustachio Celebrino, *Refettorio, Opera Nova che insegna apparechiar una mensa* (Venice, 1526; reprint edition, Campoformido (Udine): Ribis, 1993), 25 passim.

102. Ibid., 36–37, "Ben ch'io te habbia scritto questo ordene al modo proprio de Venetia, el non è che tu possi far et saper l'ordene universale; perché si dice: ogni terra la sua usanza et ogni casa ha il suo costume. Pertanto tu tenirai gli ordeni secondo gli tuoi paesi o secondo che ti piacerà di fare in casa tua."

Chapter 2
From the Cookbook to the Table:
The *Mensa della Signoria*
and Italian Recipes of the Fourteenth
and Fifteenth Centuries

Over the past few decades, food historians have increasingly turned to cookbooks and to recipes as a source for writing the history of food.[1] Although a variety of publications have already demonstrated the usefulness of cookbooks as an historical source, the problems posed by this kind of document should not be forgotten. Just because a recipe appears in a cookbook does not mean that it was ever actually prepared, served or eaten. This is, of course, a rather extreme example of how such a source could be unreliable, and there is a wealth of indirect evidence that suggests that certain dishes were made on certain occasions. Nonetheless, cookbooks and their recipes, when examined serially, show developments in taste and in culinary choices that can be confirmed by other sources.[2]

In order to work with this type of source in an effective way, at least four separate questions should be asked of each cookbook:

- The first and probably most important question has to do with the relationship between cookbooks and culinary practice. To what extent do the cookbooks of the past actually reflect a culinary practice or not? What sources best provide evidence as to recipes actually prepared and consumed?

- The second question depends partially on the answer to the first. If the recipes in question were actually prepared, what do we know about the target group of these cookbooks? Who were they meant for? What social class used them?

- The third question has to do with the context in which recipes were prepared and eaten. In other words, it should be determined whether a given recipe was meant for banquets, for everyday meals, for the sick, etc.

- The fourth question concerns the frequency with which recipes were used. Were they all equally well known and prepared equally often, or were some of them practically never eaten, reserved for special occasions or requiring ingredients that were expensive or difficult to obtain?

An exhaustive answer to all of these questions is, of course, impossible, even when limiting the scope to the Tuscan cases and examples being focused on in this essay.[3] In the following pages, I will examine the eating habits of a specific group of people (the Priors of Florence) and the recipes served to them, comparing this data to contemporary cookbooks in order to give some summary and provisional answers to the four questions mentioned above.

Florence and the *Mensa della Signoria*

The sources used for this essay are the accounts of all the foodstuffs bought for the Florentine *Mensa della Signoria* ("Table of the Lords").[4] This archival source allows for an extremely precise analysis of what a small group of Florentines ate between 1344 and 1428. The *Signoria*, created in 1282, was the highest executive body in the city of Florence until the Medici take-over in the 1430s. A total of nine Priors were elected to hold office for two months at a time and, in order to curb corruption and protect them from various pressure groups, they were obliged to work, sleep and eat in the town hall.

Unlike hospital accounts, which are a frequently used but frustratingly incomplete source for late-medieval food history,[5] the records kept for the *Signoria* cover *all* of the food bought, cooked and served at table. Hospitals often had vegetable gardens or farms to supply food, which would therefore not appear in the institution's accounts since there was no monetary transaction; the result is that fruit, vegetables and even meat are distinctly under-represented in most surviving records. In the case of the *Signoria*, however, all foodstuffs had to be acquired through monetary transactions, and accounts were kept on a day-by-day basis, documenting with great precision what was eaten. The fidelity of the daily accounts with regard to the Priors' menu is demonstrated by the fact that when an acquisition was forgotten, it could be added even several weeks later with a note specifying on what day it was actually served. Similarly, food could also be bought several days before use, but in such cases the accounts always specified the day on which it was supposed to be consumed.

The accounts relating to the Prior's table comprise long lists of bread, wine, meat, fowl, eggs, cheese, spices, fruit, vegetables, etc. Each line in the account books mentions the type of food bought, the quantity or weight, the name of the person who sold it, his or her trade (such as butcher, poulterer), and the total cost. At times items are grouped, especially when they do not cost much (this is often the case with vegetables), but often these long and rather dry lists contain somewhat more information. For example, if special food is bought for only one of the members of the *Signoria* the reason for this is mentioned (usually it is food for someone who has been taken ill). Unless there was a good reason for such special treatment, all of the Priors seem to have been fed the same food. In exceptional cases, the accounts end a list of ingredients with a lapidary statement specifying that the items mentioned were bought to make a named dish, although such information remains frustratingly scarce. In fact, among the accounts that have survived (circa 550 days), there are only eighty-seven references (to some twenty different recipes or dishes) that can be identified in contemporary cookbooks.

Although the accounts of the *Signoria* are very detailed and precise by medieval standards, they do not permit any calculation of the exact food intake of those who sat at the table (amounts of proteins, calories, etc.), since the exact number of people sitting at the table seems to have varied from day to day. The Priors of Florence often entertained diplomatic representatives and other guests. Furthermore, some of the food bought for the *Signoria* was given to their attendants and to the poor, not to speak of leftovers, which were most probably distributed in different ways.

Fortunately, it is easy to tell whether a banquet was served on a given day since the most important guests are usually mentioned in the accounts, as if to justify the additional expenses incurred. Such information distinguishes banquet fare from everyday meals and, in turn, provides essential information about the context in which certain recipes were prepared.

It should also be pointed out that the account books of the *mensa* do present a very specific limitation for medieval food history: this source describes the consumption patterns of an elite and is thus far from being representative of the entire Florentine population. As I have shown elsewhere,[6] the *Mensa della Signoria* served very formal and refined foods that were considered by contemporaries as unfit, and even morally dangerous, for men who were not called to exercise such a responsibility. The banquets held to honor visiting potentates and ambassadors, as well as military leaders like the English mercenary John Hawkwood (known as Giovanni Aguto in the Italian peninsula), can be compared to the meals served in the most official state banquets of the time. What was eaten by the Priors of Florence was far from what the average Florentine ate, and even quite different from what wealthy patricians usually consumed. Nonetheless, this very specific documentation will allow us to draw some conclusions as to the target public of Italian cookbooks in the fourteenth and fifteenth centuries.

The accounts of the *Mensa* name some twenty different dishes which, in most cases, can also be found in any Italian cookbook from the period. Interestingly enough, the dishes mentioned by the accounts of the *Mensa* are usually designated by a generic name that refers to a category of recipes. In other words, one encounters standard names of dishes—*torta, erbolato, fritellette, migliacci, pevero, ravioli,* etc.—for which the cookbooks usually give variant recipes.[7] Let us take the example of the *torta*, a kind of pie (usually savory but sometimes sweet), which seems to have been one of the signature dishes of Italian medieval cookery.

While the accounts of the *Mensa* mention only the word *torta*, contemporary cookbooks are more specific, since out of a total of 131 recipes for making pies that appear in the database of fourteenth and fifteenth century Italian cookbooks (see notes 1 and 7), only two recipes do not identify the exact type of pie. The rest either specify the dominant ingredient (*torta de herbe, de gamberi...*), the occasion on which it is eaten (*torta di quaresima, nera di carnovale, per feste in venerdie...*), a supposed place of origin (*torta parmesana, inglese, d'ormania...*) and, less frequently, the colours it is meant to have (*torta verde, di tre colori, di quattro colori...*). While the notary responsible for the *Mensa* bookkeeping often used rather laconic terms (such as *torta*), this shorthand should not lead us to think that the *Mensa* always ate the same type of pie. In fact, the shopping list shows that the ingredients used for a *torta* were not always the same, and in some cases the pies had to be made with elements compatible with a special occasion or with Lent. The ingredients listed thus seem to suggest that behind the rather generic term for a category of dishes there is a somewhat less generic recipe. The mushrooms, pumpkin and milk occasionally mentioned in the accounts of the *mensa* as being intended to make pies would have presumably been the main ingredient used to make the *torta di funghi, torta de zucche* and the *torta de latte* that are found in contemporary cookbooks.[8] Yet, in only two cases, the accounts of the *mensa* come up with ingredients and terms which can be equated, without any shade of doubt, to cookbook recipes. The two dishes are: 1) a *savore* (basically a kind of sauce to be eaten with meat or fish) which was made with *rughetta* (rocket) and 2) *salsiccetti* (sausages made with fish meat). The first of these recipes can be found in the *Libro di cucina del secolo XIV* which is usually considered to be a Venetian cookbook,[9] while the second recipe can be found in the fifteenth century south Italian cookbook known as *Anonimo meridionale, libro A.*[10]

It is worth reflecting on the reason(s) why the accounts of the *Mensa* mention generic recipe names and never bother with more specific ones. A possible explanation is that banquets and meals of a certain importance (for which more sources survive) were composed of a set of dishes that followed a fairly rigid convention. This hypothesis seems to be confirmed by what sumptuary laws tell us about the more luxurious meals and their structure. Banquets and festive meals were usually constructed around one or, at most, two meat dishes, which were the center-piece of the meal. During Lent or on lean days, these dishes were quite simply replaced by fish, thus leaving the structure of the meal unchanged. For example, a law adopted in Florence in 1356 specified that no meal could include more than three *vivande* (a term which is difficult to translate since it can refer to just one dish or to a course with several items). The main *vivanda* mentioned in this law (as in all of its successive variants), was a meat course with specified combinations of roasted meats and a pie (*torta*), which together constituted one of the three *vivande*. The law also pointed out that *ravioli, tortelletti,* or *biancomangiare* (blancmange) should each be considered a separate *vivanda*,[11] but the main or central meat dish (the most expensive item in the meal) was the one most carefully controlled by sumptuary laws. However, the use of accompanying sauces and *gelatine* (aspics made with meat or fish and often colored in order to achieve a pleasurable visual effect) remained quite unrestricted.[12]

Sumptuary laws used much the same kind of generic terminology as found in the accounts of the *Mensa dei Signori*, which implies that certain dishes were required for entertaining special guests, and constituted the core structure of a banquet. Yet the rather repetitious and rigid structure of banquets and elite meals should not mask the fact that an endless amount of variations could exist within this mold. For example, although the documents often speak in a generic way of *torte* or of *biancomangiare*, the cookbooks and the habits of the *Mensa* show us that there are an almost infinite variety of recipes which were loosely grouped under the generic term. As a consequence, it must have made perfect sense to both the lawmakers and the bookkeepers to refer generically to an element of the meal rather than to a specific variant.

Blancmange: A Cookbook and its Uses

I would now like to take a closer look at one recipe or, more precisely, at a group of recipes, since it would be too long to examine all of the twenty named dishes found in the accounts of the *Mensa dei Signori*. This dish, blancmange, seems to have been of great importance in Italian and European cookery as of the late thirteenth century. Although this recipe has not survived in European cuisine, other than in Sicily, England and Canada (and even then only in name),[13] it seems to have been essential since it appears in many banquet descriptions of the fourteenth and fifteenth centuries as well as in literary sources.[14] Blancmange, according to the etymology of the word, was an original contribution of French cuisine, exported all over Europe as of a date that is impossible to determine since even the earliest medieval cookbooks mention it. In Italy it was known under a variety of names which were all corruptions of the French *blanc manger*, such as *bramangere*, *bragiere*, *blamangere*, and *biancomangiare*, to give just a few examples.

Jean-Louis Flandrin has shown that this dish varies from one country to another and from one cookbook to another, and thus should be considered a rather loose term for a whole series of recipes.[15] As he pointed out, there is no common characteristic in the thirty-seven English, French, Catalan, and Italian recipes he analyzed. No ingredients in common, no spices in common, and even the color does not seem to be an essential characteristic. European cookbooks mention tinted blancmange, using saffron to make it yellow, herbs to make it green, or sandal wood to make it red. In Italian cookbooks, however, the latitude for variations was not quite as great. In Italy, it would seem that the recipes for blancmange were very similar to each other. Essentially there are two, or at most three, basic versions of this dish. The most common was made with a base of ground capon (or hen) breast, almond milk (or animal milk), rice and lard, all of which, after cooking, was meant to produce a rather thick cream. The spices used in this dish were usually sugar, cloves and rose water, although at times variants on this basically sweet dish were made using acid ingredients such as verjuice or orange juice. Another approach, very similar to the basic Italian recipe, replaced the poultry with different kinds of fish and eliminated the lard so that it could be served during Lent and on days when a lean diet was required. The mentions of blancmange that appear in the accounts of the *Mensa della Signoria* list much the same ingredients as those required by contemporary cookbook recipes. Moreover, the *Mensa* records also contain information about the context in which this dish was served.

In the Priors' accounts, blancmange is mentioned eleven times, which makes it the second most often named dish (*gelatina*—aspic—is mentioned twelve times). However, the frequency with which *biancomangiare* appears must not be taken as proof that it was a banal or everyday dish. Most of the dishes identified in the accounts of the *Mensa* are found on the days in which this institution served banquets to honor foreign dignitaries or other official visitors. This concentration of named dishes in coincidence with such days is a tacit confirmation of their exceptional status. Furthermore, even the days of the week on which blancmange was served confirm the rather exceptional nature of this dish. The *Mensa della Signoria* modulated the wealth and refinement of the foods served according to a weekly cycle.[16] Sundays and Thursdays (a survival from classical antiquity or the day before lean Friday?) were the days devoted to the richest and most lavish meals. Tuesdays were somewhat less important days, while Mondays and Wednesdays were usually devoted to simple and unassuming meals (dried meat, pork, etc.). This rule was followed unless an unavoidable banquet (with the usual special foods) had to be held on a Monday or Wednesday. Fridays and Saturdays were, of course, lean days. Blancmange made with a base of poultry was served by the *Mensa* ten out of the eleven times this dish is mentioned in the accounts. In the eleventh case, the dish was made with fish in order to conform with the regulations for a lean day (the fish used by the *Mensa* was tench, the same fish as is usually specified by cookbook recipes for this purpose). Out of the ten fat days in which blancmange was served, we find it four times on a Sunday, three times on a Thursday, and once each on a Monday, Tuesday, and Wednesday.

Generally speaking, the *Mensa* accounts only specify how much poultry or fish was used to make this dish. This is a significant detail since it confirms that these two ingredients were considered the most important ones, despite all the other elements needed to make this recipe. In one case, however, practically all of the components are mentioned. On Sunday 22 August 1344, blancmange was made using six capons, six pounds of lard, two pounds of sugar, three ounces of cloves, seven pounds of almonds, as well as one and a half pounds of pine nuts. The proportions of these ingredients are practically identical to those mentioned by contemporary cookbooks.[17] The only item missing is rice, an element that is almost always mentioned in cookbooks, but appears only in one case in the accounts of the *Mensa*.[18]

While the records of the *Mensa dei Signori* detail the ingredients acquired for making specific dishes—thus permitting a comparison with Italian recipes of the fourteenth and fifteenth centuries—these same account books also convey information about the social and cultural context of meals that is lacking in contemporary cookbooks. For example, the Priors' daily market expenditures can give an idea of what was eaten with certain dishes. In the case of standard blancmange, it was invariably eaten with capons, chicken and other fowl, while the lean version of blancmange was eaten with tench. Thus, in both cases, there is an interesting duplication, since the Priors ate at least two dishes made with the same ingredients, capon and capon cream, tench and tench cream. What we do not know is whether they were served simultaneously or successively.

The blancmange dish served at the *Mensa* was often accompanied by other named dishes such as *savore*, (a kind of sauce), *gelatina* (aspic), and *peverata* (a pepper based, strong tasting sauce). This should not come as a surprise, since recipes for *savore* and *peverata* are to be found in literally *all* cookbooks of this period, although the terminology used by the *Signoria* bookkeepers is generic while the cookbooks almost always are much more specific. These two sauces were served with the main dish whether it was meat, fowl or fish. *Gelatina* usually contained some meat but mostly jelly and spices, and according to the cookbooks, there were many different recipes for preparing it, including a lean version with fish. The accounts of the *Mensa* do not give details on how the cooks prepared aspic because they mention only the basic ingredients, while the jelly, which took a long time to cook, was sometimes bought from a tradesman. However, they do confirm the fact that both fat and lean versions of this dish were served to the Priors. Thus a banquet held on Friday the thirteenth of December 1398 featured a dish of *gelatina* made with twenty-six pounds of tench, along with a *"bramangiere"* made with seventeen pounds of tench. Aspic could also be given different colors: the accounts of the *Mensa* often refer specifically to *gelatina vermiglia* (red aspic), which predictably also appears in an anonymous fifteenth-century cookbook that has a recipe for a bright red aspic: *vole essere colorito* (!) *e ben vermeglia.*[19]

Some Conclusions and Working Hypotheses

Such a brief comparison of the actual dishes served to the *Signori* of Florence with cookbook recipes does not permit many general conclusions, although it does answer some of the questions asked at the outset of this chapter. It is quite certain that the recipes found in fourteenth- and fifteenth-century cookbooks were not simply a literary exercise but reflect a cuisine which was actually cooked and served. Furthermore, the apparently very close link between contemporary cookbooks and the food prepared for the *Mensa* is contextualized by the well-defined social milieu in which this cuisine was served, and thus helps to clarify the circumstances that entailed this type of cookery.

Until recently, it was thought that most medieval Italian cookbooks were intended for a middling and maybe even patrician public. However, such an hypothesis does not appear to be tenable after looking at the accounts of the *Mensa*. The eating habits of the *Signori*, seem to have been determined by their elite institutional role. But these refined culinary habits were not strictly limited to the Priors since they were also practiced in Florentine society on special and solemn occasions such as marriages and other types of celebrations. Furthermore, the fact that many of the generic recipe names also appear in sumptuary laws can be seen as a confirmation that such food was reserved for state banquets or marriage festivities, where the degree of luxury foods extended to the limit of what was legally acceptable. In any other context, however, such refined food was considered immoral or even dangerous. A good example of this distinction was formulated by Ser Lapo Mazzei in a reproachful letter to his wealthy friend, Francesco di Marco Datini:

> Please stop sending me your partridges and other such things which, God knows, I do not like … If I were serving my town, as has been the case in the past [in fact, Lapo Mazzei served a term in the *Signoria*] then [the partridges] would have been my food in order to do my job.[20]

With regard to the geographical and temporal dimensions of the cookery practiced by the *Mensa*, it is difficult to draw any firm conclusions. All of the twenty named dishes served to the Priors of Florence can be found in cookbooks as early as 1300 and as late as the end of the fifteenth century. This apparently "timeless" quality of the recipes is not their only distinguishing feature, since they are also characterized by the fact that they are not specific to any particular Italian region. In fact, some of the dishes served to the Priors (*salsiccetti*, *savore* and various types of *torte*) are to be found in what is called the "Tuscan cookbook" (the *Libro della cucina* edited by Zambrini in 1863), which is geographically consistent, but they also appear in the so-called "Venetian cookbook" (the *Libro di cucina* edited by Frati in 1899), and the two southern Italian texts published by Bostrom in 1985.[21] These dishes are therefore not exceptional: all of the named dishes mentioned in the *Mensa* accounts can be traced to cookbooks and have an equally cosmopolitan identity. How should these facts be interpreted? Were South Italian and Venetian recipes used in Tuscan cookery? Or might Tuscan cookery have influenced the rest of Italy? This latter hypothesis would certainly please all those who still believe in that hard-to-die myth that Catherine de Medici and her cooks brought the refinement of Tuscan cuisine to France.

Nevertheless, this apparent culinary consistency in time and space might be taken as an indication that there was a strong peninsular character in late-medieval and Early Renaissance Italian cooking, if it is not an illusion created by a paucity of available documents. There certainly appears to be a kind of "inter-peninsular" cuisine for special occasions and state affairs that had little to do with everyday eating habits, but then that raises the question if Italian cookbooks have survived only because they catered to just such a diplomatic and geographically specific cuisine? Given the present knowledge of cookbooks and cookery in Italy, it is quite impossible to give a satisfactory answer to any of these questions, although further research will certainly continue to make headway in our understanding of the social and cultural context in which such cookbooks were used.

Notes

A first version of this essay was published as "From the Cookbook to the Table: a Florentine Table and Italian Recipes of the 14th and 15th centuries," in *Du Manuscrit à la table: essai sur la cuisine au moyen âge*, edited by Carole Lambert, (Montréal/Paris: Presses de l'Université de Montréal/Champion/Slatkine, 1992), 29–38. Since the publication of this article too much has been done on cookbooks for me to provide an even summary bibliography.

1. One of the more ambitious undertakings in this direction was the "Enquête sur les traités culinaires anciens," a group research project created under the direction of Jean-Louis Flandrin at the Centre de recherches historiques de l'École des Hautes Etudes en Sciences Sociales in Paris. Unfortunately this project was never completed.

2. See, for example, Jean-Louis Flandrin, "Les légumes dans les livres de cuisine français du XIVe au XVIIIe siècle," in *Le Monde végétal (XIIe-XVIIe siècles): savoirs et usages sociaux*, edited by A. J. Grieco, O. Redon and L. Tongiorgi Tomasi, (Saint-Denis: Presses Universitaires de Vincennes, 1993).

3. This essay was meant to be a first and summary report of my findings in preparation for a more thorough treatment in the unfortunately never published "Enquête sur les traités culinaires anciens" (see note 1).

4. Archivio di Stato di Firenze (ASF), *Camera del comune, mensa dei Signori* above all no. 13, no. 15, no. 17, no. 26 and no. 68; Biblioteca Medicea Laurenziana di Firenze, *Ashburnham*, no. 1216.

5. On this problem see the discussion in chapter 4, 86–87.

6. See Allen J. Grieco, *Classes sociales, nourriture et imaginaire alimentaire en Italie (XIVe-XVe siècles)*, PhD thesis, École des Hautes Études en Sciences Sociales, (Paris, 1987).

7. I would like to thank Bruno Laurioux for having helped me with a search in the database of the "Enquête sur les traités culinaires anciens." In March 1991 the Italian section of the data base contained all of the recipes to be found in thirteen cookbooks from various Italian regions. The cookbooks entered by that date were:

I. *Liber de coquina*, edited by Mulon, Marianne, "Deux traités inédits d'art culinaire medieval," in *Bulletin philologique et historique (jusqu'a 1610) du comité des travaux historiques et scientifiques (1968)* (Paris: Bibliothèque Nationale, 1971), I, 396–420; early fourteenth century.

II. *LVII ricette d'un libro di cucina del buon secolo della lingua*, edited by Salomone Morpurgo, (Bologna, 1890), 1338–1339, Tuscany.

III. *Frammento di un libro di cucina del secolo XIV edito nel di delle nozze Carducci-Gnaccarini*, edited by Olindo Guerrini, (Bologna, 1887); fourteenth century, Tuscany.

IV. *Il libro della cucina* edited by Francesco Zambrini, (Bologna, 1863; reprint Bologna: Forni, 1968); fourteenth century, Tuscany.

V. *Anonimo meridionale. Due libri di cucina (libro A)*, edited by Ingemar Boström (Stockholm: Almqvist & Wiksell, 1985); end of fourteenth or beginning of fifteenth century, southern Italy (hereafter *Anonimo meridionale A*).

VI. Ibid., *libro B*, (hereafter *Anonimo meridionale B*).

VII. *Liber coquine*, MS Nice, musée Masséna, Bibliothèque de Cessole, 226; fifteenth century, Umbria (hereafter Nice).

VIII. *Di buone et dilicate vivande*, MS London, British Library, Additional 18165; fifteenth century.

IX. "Manuscrit napolitain," MS New York, Pierpont Morgan Library, Bühler 19; fifteenth century, Naples?

x. Maestro Martino, *Libro de arte coquinaria*, edited by Emilio Faccioli, in *Arte della cucina. Libri di ricette, testi sopra lo scalco, il trinciante e i vini dal XIV al XIX secolo* (Milan, 1966), 115–204; ca. 1450 (hereafter Martino).

xi. *Liber bonarum coquinarum*, MS Chalon-sur-Marne, Bibliothèque municipale, 319; 1481, Bergamo.

xii. *Libro di cucina del secolo XIV*, edited by Ludovico Frati, (Livorno, 1899; reprint Bologna, 1970); end of fifteenth-century, Venice-Romagna.

xiii. *In questo loco servirro tutte le vivande*, MS London, Library of the Wellcome Institute of the History of Medicine, 211; end of fifteenth century.

8. A *torta de funghi* can be found in *Anonimo meridionale B* (no. 46, p. 44) and Frati (no. 98, p. 52), a *torta de zucche* in Martino (160) and Frati (no. 102, p. 56), and in the table of *Anonimo meridionale B* (no. 44, p. 33), while the *torta de latte* is found in Morpurgo (no. 6, p. 22), Guerrini (40), Nice (no. 5) and Frati (no. 106, p. 55).

9. Frati, no. 83, 45.

10. *Anonimo meridionale. Due libri di cucina (libro A)*, edited by I. Boström (Stockholm: Almqvist & Wiksell, 1985), no. II, 7.

11. See, for example, the "Ordinamenta circa sponsalitias" of 1356 published by Paolo Emiliani-Giudici, 1851, 431; and Antonio Bonardi, *Il Lusso di altri tempi in Padova: studio storico con documenti inediti*, (Venice, 1909), 164.

12. See the banquet regulations voted 27 April 1473 and published as an appendix in Ronald Rainey, *Sumptuary Legislation in Renaissance Florence*, PhD dissertation, Columbia University, 1985, 785.

13. For the survival of blancmange in Canada, see Carole Lambert, "Survivance d'usages culinaires anciens dans la cuisine québécoise." In *Actes du colloque "Manger: de France à la Nouvelle-France,"* Textes colligés et présentés par Yves Bergeron et Gérald Parisé, *Ethnologie* XII, no. 3 (1990): 61–64.

14. See, for example, Giovanni Boccaccio, *Il Corbaccio*, edited by P. G. Ricci (Milan/Naples: Ricciardi/Einaudi, 1977) 49, where he accuses the woman he criticizes throughout this text of eating fowl of all kinds, blancmange, etc., and thus showing her lack of self-control.

15. Jean-Louis Flandrin, "Internationalisme, nationalisme et régionalisme dans la cuisine des XIVe et XVe siècles: le témoignage des livres de cuisine," in *Manger et boire au Moyen Âge*, (Paris: Belles Lettres, 1984), II, 75–76.

16. Grieco 1987, 122.

17. Guerrini, no. 1, 19.

18. Since rice was used as a kind of thickener in blancmange, it might well be that the dish served to the Florentine Signori was a particularly rich version in which rice was not used.

19. Frati, *"gelatina de zascuna carne,"* no. 31, 16–17.

20. Ser Lapo Mazzei, *Lettere a Francesco Datini*, edited by C. Guasti (Florence, 1880), 25. For other examples, see Grieco 1987, above all chapter three.

21. See notes 7, 8 and 9.

Chapter 3
Conviviality in a Renaissance Court:
The *Ordine et Officij*
of the Court of Urbino

The importance of meals, banqueting and food in the context of the Italian Renaissance court is clamorously apparent in the *Ordine et officij* of the Court of Urbino, an extraordinary document rich in details about court life and special events in the mid-fifteenth century.[1] However, as often happens with documents relating to material culture, the importance accorded to food and dining has not always led to the type of in-depth research that would help to better understand this key aspect of courtly living.[2] This lacuna is all the more surprising as historians have become increasingly interested in practically all other aspects of court life,[3] yet tend to neglect the fact that banquets—and meals in general—were an important part of this world. Meals were not only a pretext for ceremonial conviviality, they were also meant to impress all those who visited a court, as well as those who never actually visited it but read or heard about feasts in which conspicuous consumption played an important role.

The grandeur of court banquets was intended to have an afterlife, insofar as the details of splendid repasts were broadcast to a vaster public in descriptions of feasts that circulated as early as the fourteenth century in a variety of forms: in "official" manuscripts/chronicles, in letters sent by attending ambassadors, and in private epistolary correspondence. In the course of the fifteenth and sixteenth centuries, these accounts became nothing less than a literary genre, whose circulation increased widely following the invention of the printing press.[4] The descriptions of court banquets and festive occasions broadcast the magnificence of these events, not only affirming the power of the courts that organized such affairs, but also serving as an instrument of political propaganda for those who could decipher the list of the guests, the seating arrangements, the program of the decoration and *intermezzi,* as well as a series of other clues that are mostly lost to all but historians versed in the context of these events.

The significance accorded to meals and related aspects of courtly life is elegantly expressed by the Neapolitan humanist Giovanni Pontano, who dedicated one of his five treatises on "social virtues" to the virtue of conviviality. His *De Conviventia* (first published in 1498, but originally composed about a decade after the *Ordine et officij*)[5] examines a banquet culture that is both a style of life and a way of ruling through the distribution of regal largesse. The first sentence of Pontano's treatise highlights the attention paid to sharing meals, thus linking the somewhat more general concept of conviviality to the more specific one of commensality. He begins with the observation that: "Though it is nature itself, dear Ioannes Pardo [the Aragonese nobleman to whom the treatise is dedicated], that reconciles man with man, nevertheless it seems to me that the two most important factors contributing to this natural togetherness are sharing common interests and the custom of eating together."[6] Although he admits to the possible dangers of spending a life going from one banquet to another—because of the costs that would be incurred and the sin of gluttony engendered by such a practice—he nevertheless underlines the importance of conviviality by inventing the term *inconviventia* to denote "the defect consisting in not being convivial." The newly-coined term is then explained by saying that it is formed in much the same way as the purely negative concepts of "inconstancy and incontinence"[7] are formed.

The somewhat general principle of "natural togetherness" with which Pontano begins his disquisition is far from being the only reason for which he deemed convivial occasions to be important. In the second chapter of his treatise, he draws up a brief list of the other motives for which the practice of conviviality at the table is an essential virtue. This list mentions above all meals that are bent on obtaining "the gratitude of many people all at once, as when offering banquets to the population" but adds to these occasions "yet others [that] respect the customs of civility as when friends, parents and acquaintances are invited to a marriage."[8] Pontano's implication that meals can demonstrate the power of a host—an objective that is also implicitly recognized by the *Ordine et officij*—is deemed important enough to deserve being developed and illustrated in another chapter dedicated specifically to this topic.

The fourth chapter of Pontano's treatise (entitled *De conviviis splendoris gratia susceptis)* recapitulates the reasons for which rulers and even less august families put so much emphasis on the meals and banquets they served. While in most cases meals should be neither too sumptuous nor too poor (a frequent topos in literature on food),[9] Pontano explains that this principle should be disregarded in the case of banquets, in order to demonstrate the magnificence of a prince or a ruler. As he puts it:

> When meals are served, aiming to be as splendid as possible, then not only should you not leave anything behind or forget anything, you should actually loosen the bridle somewhat and not proceed dragging your feet, as the expression would have it, but rather run. In such occasions you should bring out all of the objects of the house, load the abacus and the marble sills with gold and silver, cover the floors and place objects in the house in such a way that the house smiles, as Horace once said.[10]

Pontano further develops the concept of an ostentatious conviviality by pointing out that it is not enough to serve food that is produced locally or even in the same country, but also appropriate to select foods that come from abroad, so as to provide the guests of the court with a greater variety, an exquisite meal and a display of greater refinement.[11] Pontano's ideas reflected a way of thinking that went well beyond the Neapolitan court he was primarily writing for, as demonstrated by much the same conceit expressed in the Urbino *Ordini et officij*. Writing on banquets to be held at the Montefeltro court, the anonymous author declared that "The comfits coming from Damascus will be more praiseworthy than those from Sicily or ours," and pointed out that the exotic provenance of the candied fruit gave it an extra cachet that was fitting "not only for your excellency but also for the entire family."[12]

The *Ordine et officij* consecrates a significant amount of pages to the way in which food was sourced, paid for, prepared and served to ensure a grand and dignified commensality in one of the most important courts of central Italy.

Out of a total of sixty-four chapters, touching on practically all aspects of life in the Urbino court, no less than twenty-three are exclusively dedicated to the many tasks connected to supplying food for the duke, for those who sat at his table, for those who visited him and, finally for those who served him in various capacities. This last category—that of service—included a great number of people who sat at a series of different tables that were regularly laid in the ducal palace.

The complexity of a system that ministered to the needs of the court is also born out by the number and variety of places where people were fed. To begin with, there were the members of the ducal *famiglia*: the personnel that took care of the Duke's many and varied needs.[13] While the staff serving this table were less in number than those who attended the Duke's table, the ceremony observed there was almost as complex. Meals dispensed to the *famiglia* took place in specifically designated places referred to as *tinelli*. The term *tinello* can be translated somewhat approximately—according to John Florio's late 16th-century dictionary, *A World of Wordes*—as a "common dyning room where servants used to dyne in a gentleman's house."[14] Served in the *tinelli*, the *famiglia*, was put under the vigilant eye of the family seneschal (*scalco della famiglia*) who, while taking orders from the duke's personal seneschal, had under him "one or two cooks … one or two people to set the table … and one or two people to serve the wine."[15]

The various *tinelli* in the Urbino court respected a strict hierarchical principle, where the seating of staff and servants was reminiscent of the social order that reigned at the ducal table. According to the author of the *Ordini,* there were at least two *tinelli*, one of which was reserved for "the more prominent" members of the *famiglia*, while the lower ranking members were relegated to a second *tinello* that had to be "closed off by a door." The justification for this division was that the "stable boys and the lowly people" were supposed to eat together, quite separate from the more exalted staff, because "in the end of it all there would be more order in things and [the] stable hands and their likes would be more satisfied."[16]

The hierarchical separation of different members of the staff seems to have run quite deeply. For example, while the hand-washing ceremony practiced at the Duke's table was also practiced by the *famiglia*, it does not seem to have been extended to all tables. The *Ordine et officij* thus specify that "In the *tinello* one should 'give water' [i.e. wash hands] both before and after, at least in the main *tinello*."[17] This somewhat cryptic message implies that the hand washing ceremony took place both before and after the meal, but only in the *tinello* reserved to the higher-ranking staff. Apparently, the stable hands and the lower sort in the second *tinello* did not necessarily participate in this refined ritual.

The leitmotif of "order" often appears in the course of the Urbino treatise, and is particularly apparent in the pages dedicated to meals taken by the *famiglia* in the *tinelli*, where it serves as a reminder of the extent to which meals could both reflect and reinforce social hierarchies. For the anonymous author of the *Ordine et officij*, order is maintained by enforcing a strict seating plan based on the rank of each person, which plan also determined the sequence in which each person was served. The significance accorded to orderly seating becomes all the more apparent when the author suggests that the *scalco della famiglia* (the seneschal of the *famiglia,* who was quite distinct from the higher-ranking seneschal attached to the Duke) should ensure that each table had a "public list" of the seating arrangement. This list had to be drawn up for each of the three distinct sittings at each meal, a number of sittings that was required to feed everybody in this numerous household.

Seating order was a serious matter, given that the seneschal in charge of the family was required "not [to] let any person disregard the order," and, when needed, "make the culprit aware that he is breaking the rules."[18] These measures were meant to ensure that everybody had their designated place but also, as the author of these rules puts it, that "nobody ends up standing." This somewhat curious detail is oddly reminiscent of an anecdote related by Baldassarre Castiglione in *The Book of the Courtier*, set in Urbino in roughly these same years, involving two gentlemen who found themselves without a seat but were saved by the gallantry of one of the guests.[19]

In addition to the numerous chapters that deal exclusively with food and the rules of dining, other food-related chapters, such as the *Officio del spetiale et spetiaria* on the spices used in the kitchen and supplied for medicinal purposes, bring the total number up to thirty-three: no less than fifty percent of all the chapters comprising the *Ordini et officij.* This alone is a vivid measure of how much attention was paid to acquiring foodstuffs, cooking and serving them to all the different personages and personnel that lived and worked in the court, thereby ensuring the conviviality and commensality of a particularly large Renaissance household.

The priority given to the *servizio di bocca* (all those positions connected to preparing and serving food and drink at the table) is also made apparent by the order in which these are dealt with by the author. After opening with a brief introductory chapter on general principles, lauding the virtues of an orderly approach to managing the household, the *Ordini et Officij* proceeds in a series of chapters to examine the group of offices that comprise the *servizio di bocca*, each in turn, following their order of importance. The first office (chapter 2) is that of the *maestro di casa,* a term that is not easy to translate (translation is difficult for all of the titles encountered in the *Ordini*). John Florio, in his Italian-English dictionary, chose to translate it as "steward of the house."

The *maestro di casa* was undoubtedly the most important officer in the management structure of the household.[20] His tasks were, among others, to supervise and control the work done by all of the personnel in the palace, with the exception of a few members of the administrative staff (such as those employed by the Chancery). The *maestro di casa* was responsible, among other things, for supervising and countersigning all of the accounting that went into a complex bookkeeping system that recorded the food, drink and other supplies that entered the court. He also supervised a parallel set of volumes that kept track of the silverware as it was used or kept in the *credenza,*[21] in a meticulous and almost obsessive network of accounts that were intended to reduce the likelihood of anything being lost or stolen.

Immediately after a long chapter dedicated to the qualities demanded of the *maestro di casa* and the tasks required of him, there follows a group of seven chapters devoted to all of those offices belonging more specifically to the *servizio di bocca*. The position they occupy at the beginning of the treatise (chapters 3–9) underscores the importance accorded to them, coming as they do right after the chapter dedicated to the "steward of the house." Those who serve at table are dealt with in a descending hierarchical order, beginning with the most important office and then working down to the lesser ones. This order manifests itself via an explicitly stated chain of command and the salaries that these individuals were paid.[22] The seven chapters dedicated to the *servizio di bocca* begin with the *scalco del signore* (a term that is particularly difficult to translate),[23] followed by the *coppieri* (the cupbearers), the *dapiferi* (dapifer, whose task it was to bring the food from the kitchen to the table), by *"chi ha a servire da cortello"* (i.e. the carver) and by *"chi ha a dare acqua"* (those who ensured the hand washing ceremony performed at the beginning and end of each meal).[24] The eighth chapter describes the various tasks assigned to the *credenzieri*, who were meant to prepare and serve the cold courses (the so-called *servizio di credenza*), but who were also in charge of the silverware and "other things" that the *maestro di casa* and the *scalco* had put in their care. Finally, the last (ninth) of this group of chapters on dining-related topics deals with some of the finer points of the Duke's meal, such the complex procedure to be followed in serving different dishes, decorating the room with tapestries and flowers, and arranging the lighting.

The group of seven chapters that deals with most of the offices that were necessary to ensure that the duke's meals were served in a manner deemed appropriate and fitting for his status do not include the various *soprachochi* and *cochi principali* whose responsibility it was to cook *all* of the food that was served at the court. The cooking staff surface only much later in the text (chapters thirty-five, thirty-six and thirty-nine), as befits their rather lowly status in comparison with those responsible for orchestrating the magnificence of the court: the much more exalted *servizio di bocca*.

Specific table arrangements were made for the frequent visitors to Urbino, both when the Duke was in residence and when he was away. Guests merited a deployment of expert help, albeit somewhat simplified with respect to the Duke's table. The visitors entertained in Urbino were subdivided into those who got the most honorable treatment and those who were simply put up at an inn, where they were fed and taken care of at a price that had been previously agreed upon. The higher-ranking visitors clearly rated a very different treatment since they were put up in houses that belonged to the court and were taken under the wing of an especially designated staff member led by another seneschal, the *scalco di foristhieri*. The measure of how delicate the task of taking care of visitors could be is conveyed by the fact that the *scalco di foristhieri* reported directly to the two highest-ranking officials, the *maestro di casa* and the *scalco del signore*, for whatever the guest might require (chapter fifty-seven). The well-being of prestigious guests was essential, and the explicit order was to err on the side of excess rather than be too parsimonious (*peccare più tosto nel superchio che altramente*).

The seneschal assigned to visitors had under his command a *credenziere* in charge of the silver lent out by the *guardarobba*, a helper for menial tasks (chapter fifty-eight) as well as a special cook (chapter fifty-nine). This small group of assistants was meant to be always on duty, although some visitors came with their own staff, who made sure they were served *"a loro modo"* (in their own way), a practice that was quite common throughout the Middle Ages and during the Renaissance.[25] The fact that some guests of the court of Urbino would travel with their own servants (who were expected to work with the staff *in loco* to assure a guest's comfort) might seem an anecdotal detail, but it brings home the extent to which the *ufficiali di bocca* were considered essential in ensuring that the convivial machinery required by a court could function at all times, in all circumstances, and with all types of visitors.

Notes

An earlier and somewhat shorter version of this text was published as "Conviviality in a Renaissance Court: the *Ordine et Officij* and the Court of Urbino," in *Ordine et Officij de Casa de lo Illustrissimo Signor Duca de Urbino*, edited by Sabine Eiche, (Urbino: Accademia Raffaello, 1999), 37–44.

1. For a transcription of this document, see: *Ordine et Officij de Casa de lo Illustrissimo Signor Duca de Urbino*, edited by S. Eiche, (Urbino: Accademia Raffaello, 1999), 89–141.

2. Pierre Hurtubise is one of the first to have remarked on the importance of banquets in court culture, see: "La table d'un cardinal de la Renaissance. Aspects de la cuisine et de l'hospitalité à Rome au milieu du XVIe siècle," *Mélanges d'archéologie et d'histoire de l'École française de Rome* 92, 1 (1982), 249–282.

3. For example, this aspect is not examined by Piergiorgio Peruzzi, "Lavorare a Corte: 'ordine et officij.' Domestici, familiari, cortigiani e funzionari al servizio del Duca d'Urbino," in *Federico di Montefeltro: lo Stato*, edited by G. Chittolini, *et al.* (Rome: Bulzoni, 1986), 225–96, The dearth of publications pointed out in the earlier version of this essay (almost twenty years ago) has been since somewhat remedied thanks above all to the book by Giancarlo Malacarne, *Sulla mensa del Principe. Alimentazione e banchetti alla corte dei Gonzaga*, (Modena: Il Bulino, 2000).

4. For examples limited to marriage festivities see Olga Pinto, *Nuptialia. Saggio di bibliografia di scritti italiani pubblicati per nozze dal 1484 al 1799* (Florence: Olschki, 1971).

5. On the dating of this document to the late 1480s see John E. Law, "The *Ordini et officij*: aspects of context and content," in *Ordine et officij de casa de lo illustrissimo Signor Duca de Urbino*, edited by Sabine Eiche, (Urbino: Accademia Raffaello, 1999), above all 17–18.

6. "Tametsi, Ioannes Parde, hominem homini natura conciliat, ad hanc tamen naturae conciliationem duae cum primis res mihi vedentur plurimum conferre, eorundem scilicet studiorum societas consuetudoque convivendi..." Giovanni Pontano, *I Trattati delle virtù sociali*, edited by Francesco Tateo (Rome: Edizioni dell'Ateneo, 1965), 141.

7. "Defectum igitur ipsum nunquam convivendi appellabimus inconviventiam, ut incostantiam uncontinentiamque, quod a convictu ipsoprorsus abhorreat." Pontano 1965, 143.

8. Ibid., 145–46.

9. For more on this see chapter 1, pages 27–29, in the present volume.

10. "Aut cum solius splendoris gratia convivia parantur, tunc non modo remittendum aut omittendum nihil est, verum etiam habenae ipsae liberius laxandae sunt, neque passibus, ut dici solet, plenioribus accedendum, sed currendum potius. Explicandus tunc est domesticus apparatus, onerandi auro atque argento abaci et plutei, coenationes exornandae, sternenda pavimenta et ita quidem omnia disponenda, ut, quod air Horatius." Pontano 1965, 150.

11. Ibid., 150.

12. "Seriano anchora più laudate le confectione de Damascho che quelle de Sicilia o le nostre ... non solo per la sua Excellentia ma per tutta la famigli," *Ordine et Officij*, 1999, chapter 14, 102.

13. For more considerations on what the term *famiglia* comprised see Law 1999, 20–21.

14. *A World of words or the most copious, and exact Dictionarie in Italian and English* (London, 1598), 421.

15. *Ordine et officij*, 1999, chapter twenty-two, 106–107.

16. "...li famigli da stalla et vile persone mangiasseno uniti per sé ché in fine seria ordine et loro più satisfacti." *Ordini et officij,* 1999, 107.

17. "Nel tinello se vole dare l'acqua et denante et deretro almeno al tinello principale." Chapter twenty-three, 107–108.

18. "Et non lassare prevarichare l'ordine a persona cum farlo acorgere de lo erore suo." Ibid, 107.

19. The anecdote involves the Spanish Gran Capitano Diego de Chignones, who was already seated but had everybody stand up from the dinner table in order to seat "due gentilomini italiani." Baldassarre Castiglione, *Il libro del Cortegiano,* edited by G. Preti, (Turin: Einaudi, 1965), II, lxv, 174.

20. It should be pointed out that not enough has been written to date on this key figure who worked in lay and ecclesiastical courts as well as other, major households in Renaissance Italy. A few exceptions are David S. Chambers, "Bartolomeo Marasca, master of cardinal Gonzaga's household (1462–1469)," in *Renaissance Cardinals and their Worldly Problems* (Aldershot/Brookfield: Variorum, 1997) and Gigliola Fragnito, "La trattatistica cinque e seicentesca sulla corte cardinalizia," in *Annali dell'Istituto Italo-germanico di Trento,* 1991.

21. A kind of storeroom that was kept locked by a *credenziere.*

22. See, for example, the scalco of the family and the scalco assigned to the "foristhieri" i.e. visitors who both were meant to report to the Duke's personal scalco (chapter three), the carver who also reports to the scalco (chapter six), etc. Concerning the hierarchy of these officials see Andrea Manciulli, "Le arti della tavola," in *Et coquatur ponendo. Cultura della cucina e della tavola in Europa tra medioevo ed età moderna,* (Prato: Istituto Datini, 1996), above all 340–41.

23. Etymologically speaking, a better translation might be "the Duke's personal Seneschal." However, in English usage, a Seneschal was "An official in the household of a sovereign or great noble, to whom the administration of justice and entire control of domestic arrangements were entrusted" (according to the Oxford English Dictionary), an office far exceeding the tasks of the Italian *Scalco.*

24. This ceremony was considered of some importance since it is often mentioned in treatises on good manners. For an early example of this see Bonvesin da la Riva, *De quinquaginta curialitatibus ad mensam,* in *Poeti del Duecento,* edited by Gianfranco Contini, Milan/Naples: Ricciardi, 1960, vol. 2, tome 1.

25. *Ordine et officij,* 1999, chapter sixty, 136.

Chapter 4
Food at the *Ospedale degli Innocenti*: Medical Theory and Social Groups in Mid-Quattrocento Florence

Sources and Historiography: an Overview

Hospitals in the late Middle Ages have been the focus of a renewed historical interest over the past couple of decades, resulting in a series of monographs dedicated to individual institutions.[1] These monographs have revitalized a field that had been largely stagnant since the erudite contributions of the nineteenth and early twentieth centuries. However, in almost all cases, these studies have continued to neglect the question of food that was served in hospitals. Indeed, with the exception of some mentions of the provisions purchased by these institutions,[2] or the occasional short appendix containing details on diets catering to specific individuals or groups (such as the sick, or wet nurses), there is an historiographical vacuum for this aspect of hospital life in the period prior to the mid-sixteenth century.[3] This vacuum cannot, however, be attributed to a simple oversight, but should be understood as a result of the objective difficulties facing any historian who attempts a study of food consumption in late-medieval and Renaissance hospitals.

The difficulties encountered in studying food issues in the context of charitable institutions are particularly critical for any quantitative approach to provisioning. To begin with, the relatively basic accounting system used by large fifteenth-century hospitals does not make it possible to determine, with any accuracy, the actual recipients of the different foodstuffs that were purchased. Such information would be, of course, particularly important in a society where social stratification was matched by an equally diversified consumption of food and drink. Even more difficult to resolve is the problem posed by the fact that almost all hospitals—and in this respect, the Florentine *Ospedale degli Innocenti* was no different—owned country estates that provided a range of different foodstuffs. These supplies were not included in lists of food acquisitions insofar as they were produced by the institutions themselves. An example of how some provisions were grown in the kitchen garden or even in the other properties owned by the *Ospedale,* (but not accounted for as cash outlay), appears on Friday 24 October 1483.[4] A concise entry refers to "oil used for cooking and to dress the salad and the supper" *"olio per condire la cucina et insalate e lla ciena,"* an item for which there is no documented expenditure in the account books.

Even the most meticulous reconstruction of what a hospital received in the way of its own produce—possible in theory, but difficult in practice—could never guarantee a reliable picture of its food consumption. This is because we will never know precisely how many persons were present at any given time in a particular institution, and because produce had to be transformed before being consumed. A good example is the case of wheat, which could be used to make very different quantities of both white and brown bread. Add to these variables the fact that, in many institutions (as in the *Ospedale degli Innocenti*), food was also produced inside the complex itself (vegetable gardens, chicken coops), and while the end products might be known or guessed, they elude all attempts of quantification.

With regard to the *Ospedale degli Innocenti*, Philip Gavitt has published some interesting data, collected and analyzed for the months of October and November 1483. This was a period when Messer Francesco di Martino della Torre, the newly appointed *spedalingo* or prior, embarked on what the American historian calls "a major administrative reorganization." As a result, the *spedalingo* started to keep a register filled with much more detailed information than is usually found in such account books. Not only was the food consumption for the Ospedale recorded but also annotated as pertaining to individuals or groups of consumers. In other words, distinctions were made between various categories of those fed (the *commensali*), and in some cases even their number was recorded.[5] It appears that around 200 individuals (it is not possible to be more exact) ate at the various tables on a regular basis. In addition to the "shared" table (*tavola comune*), there was a table for clergy and one reserved for the infirmary. On average, these persons shared 369 pounds of bread a day, which represented approximately 625 grams per head (the Florentine *libbra* being equal to 339 grams). Bread could be of different qualities: at breakfast on certain days (such as Sunday, 26 October 1483), the accounts record that an *"inferigno"* bread, one made with flour containing bran, was served "at breakfast to the entire group."[6]

What today might seem to be a relatively large amount of bread per capita can be explained by the well-known fact that bread was the staple food, above all in poor diets where it was proportionately more important. The quantities recorded in Florence are very similar to those estimated by Archbishop Giovanni Visconti in 1453, for the planned *Ospedale Maggiore* in Milan. According to the Archbishop, it was to be hoped that "each poor man would receive a daily ration of thirty-two ounces of well-made bread made from mixed flours ... [and the]... sick ... would be given a daily ration of twenty-four ounces of well-made wheat bread."[7] Bearing in mind that the Milanese ounce was a different measure, it can be calculated that the poor would receive 870 grams of mixed bread, while the sick had to make do with 650 grams, although in their case the bread would be made from finer white flour.

The records kept by the Florentine *spedalingo* reveal that bread rations in the *Innocenti* were also apportioned according to different groups. These groups were identified as follows: "boys and girls of the house" (*fanciulli e fanciulle di casa*), "little children" (*fanciulli piccini*), "boys and girls who work in a *bottega*" (*fanciulli e fanciulle che vanno a bottega*), "the sick" (*infermi*), "wet nurses" (*balie*), and lastly "priests" (*preti*). The distinction is interesting, although in some cases there was undoubtedly some overlap between the various categories. The different groups were certainly not given the same quantities of bread, but if we try to calculate their consumption, it becomes clear that the accounts contain insufficient detail to differentiate between meals provided by the *Ospedale* for its different categories of residents.[8]

The accounts of the *Innocenti* are unfortunately even less precise when it comes to other important foodstuffs, such as wine, oil, meat and cheese. Judging by the records, a minimal quantity of meat was available, but it certainly could not have been shared among all those being fed in this institution. This was doubtless the case with the two pounds of dried meat (ca. 680 grams) purchased on Sunday, 26 October 1483, presumably reserved for a special guest or a restricted number of people. A similar situation can be observed in relation to cheese, which is also recorded in limited amounts: for example, 8 pounds (equivalent to approximately 2.7 kilograms) of cheese were served on Friday, 24 October. This amount is still too little to have provided cheese to all those in the *Ospedale,* since it would have meant serving just 13 grams per person.

While the information contained in the Ospedale account books certainly does not permit the calculation of precise food rations, it is nonetheless useful for other purposes. The children living at the *Innocenti* were in all likelihood given four meals a day, starting with an *"asciolvere"* (breakfast), and then lunch and supper. There was also a *"merenda"* (snack)[9] given to them, although it is unclear whether this meal was served in the morning or afternoon. Interestingly, this number of meals confirms the precepts of contemporary medical literature, which stressed that certain groups of the population (including children) required more meals than a healthy adult. Variations in the number of meals were also noted by Michele Savonarola, cited often in this chapter because of his alignment to medieval dietetic theories and his chronological/geographical proximity to the source here discussed. A physician at the Este court, Savonarola, composed his well-known dietary treatise between 1450 and 1452 wherein he observes that an adult only had to eat once or only twice, except for "those who labor and earn their bread with their hands," noting that "from experience we see that these persons are accustomed to eat three or four times a day."[10] According to this same author, youths and adolescents aged over fourteen should eat twice, but "children" (*putti* as he calls them) who were not yet fourteen should eat not only often, but plentifully. This custom was probably not always taken for granted since Savonarola asserted that "some teachers err by keeping their pupils on such short rations and so do pious mothers who make them fast too much, too often, or even continuously."[11]

The main meals in this period, also eaten by everyone in the Hospital, were lunch and supper. To these was added *"asciolvere"* (breakfast), a meal that often consisted of very little indeed. Just how little Giovanni di Pagolo Morelli noted in his *Ricordi* (memoirs) written for his sons in the 1380s.[12] However, the breakfast meal was not much practiced in normal circumstances, being limited to specific groups, such as growing children or laborers. Yet, at the *Innocenti*, it would seem that as many as four meals a day were served to the wet nurses. One of the entries (dated 24 October 1483) mentions: "to the wet nurses for breakfast and lunch, afternoon snack and supper, namely to 13 wet nurses and 4 weaned children, 15 pairs of loaves, 34 pounds."[13] This was certainly an indirect but eloquent way of including wet nurses amongst those who earned their living through heavy physical labor.

The details contained in the 1483 registers do not allow much further progress in analyzing the food provisioning of this Florentine institution. Nonetheless, by a stroke of serendipitous luck, an isolated notebook of expenses has survived that throws more light on provisions and diet at the *Ospedale degli Innocenti* in the mid fifteenth century.[14] Unfortunately, it is the only example of such a notebook to have survived.

The Accounting System Used at the *Ospedale*

In April 1451, new statutes and regulations were drawn up and approved by the Consuls of the *Arte di Por' Santa Maria* for the *Ospedale degli Innocenti*. From the outset, these provisions stipulated how the treasurer [*camerlingo*] should keep the accounts. The treasurer was "obliged and beholden to keep a book titled income and expenditure [*entrata ed uscita*] relating to produce from the land."[15] Moreover, the treasurer then in office also had to keep "a long notebook in which he recorded day by day all the minor expenses [*spese minute*] for the residents [*boche*, literally "mouths"] at the charge of the said hospital now and in the future." The sole surviving notebook here examined is indeed long and narrow (42 × 16 cm), above all if compared to credit and debit books, which are almost square (29 × 23 cm). Even the *incipit* to this notebook, "Minor expenses to be made for the house and for the children commencing on the first day of December 1451 in which a daily record will be kept,"[16] confirms that this is precisely one of the *spese minute* notebooks required by the statutes.

The notebook in question (referred to as a *Libro giornale*) was not used to keep the definitive and final accounts recording the expenditures of the *Ospedale*, but rather kept track of daily outlays, which were then transcribed into the credit and debit accounts. Unlike the *libri giornali*, the *entrate e uscite* account books have all survived and form a complete series. The schedule whereby the details were to be transferred from one account book to another is specified by the statutes: "all the said minor expenses [*spese minute*] recorded in the above notebook must be entered as debits on a monthly basis by the said treasurer."[17] There was also another series of accounts referred to in the statutes as belonging in the *Libro grande* (large register), and this type of register has also survived. Indeed, at 42 × 32 cm, these registers are even larger than the credit and debit books. The statutes further stated that the scribe had to record "all of the general expenditure of the hospital so that it can be seen in the *Libro grande*, year by year, what is consumed and what the individual costs are, item by item."[18] Unfortunately for food historians, these latter registers record financial outlay only in terms of the supplier, not in terms of types of food.

Nearly all the detailed descriptions of the operations related to food were lost when the records of acquisitions were transferred from the notebook of *Spese minute* to the register of *Entrata ed Uscita* and then to the *Libro grande*. Moreover, the successive transferal of accounts regarding expenditure was not always undertaken on a monthly basis, nor even annually, despite the stipulations of the 1451 statutes. Thus the annotations in the notebook dedicated to daily expenses has an entry on one of the butchers who supplied the *Ospedale*, where it is possible to identify not only the quantity but also the type of meats, and even the days when it was bought and eaten. Instead, in the *Entrata ed Uscita* register, these same expenditures are recorded in a single line mentioning the total weight of the meat purchased (without even specifying what the different kinds were) and its overall cost. This latter kind of information is not very useful, not only because the types of meat are unspecified, but also because it does not link the consumption of meats to a specific moment in time: the *Entrata and Uscita* registers list payments that were often made many months after the original acquisition.

The details of the *Spese minute* notebook and its function as a daily memorandum help us to understand why nearly all the other notebooks in this series have been lost: records of minor expenditures were grouped and sub-sumed into the more general bookkeeping effort that aimed at monitoring and controlling the *Ospedale* accounts. Logically, at the top of the pyramid of account books were the series of *Libri grandi*, which gave a more general over-view and followed the long-term patterns of expenditure, and have survived almost entirely.[19] Yet the administrators of the *Arte di Por' Santa Maria* knew that the long, narrow notebooks of daily expenses were extremely important as a means of tracking costs during the period between the initial acquisition and the final annotation in at least one of the two series of surviving account books. The statutes stated quite clearly

> that all the records kept by the scribe must be kept on the desk of the chancellery of the said hospital and must not be locked up, so that the prior or others on his behalf may see them, whether by night or by day, and the same [should be the case for]... the long notebook of the minor expenses incurred day by day, so that the scribe may read them at any time of day.[20]

Uninterrupted access to these accounts was a guarantee, albeit a partial one, against misuse of the hospital's resources because these notebooks—even if they have now vanished without trace—served as the foundation on which the entire accounting system of the organization was built.

Food and Minor Expenses

Before taking a closer look at the contents of the sole surviving notebook of *spese minute*, it is important to remember that this source, although exception-al in many ways, does not provide sufficient data for a quantitative history of food provisioning in this institution, not the least because, in all likelihood, the notebook was not the only means of recording expenditure. This hypoth-esis is suggested by the fact that the accounts, grouped under different head-ings (minor expenses, extraordinary expenses, meat expenses, etc.), contain chronological gaps. In other words, while it is true that we have a large part of the minor expenditures from 1 December 1451 to 14 May 1454, it is also true that there are inexplicable gaps from 29 September 1452 to 15 October of the same year, and from 26 November 1452 to 1 November 1453. Moreover, if we attempt to cross-reference minor expenses with the so-called "extraordinary expenses," we find that the latter stretch over an unbroken period between 1 December 1451 and 14 October 1452, but only overlap with some of the days covered by the "minor expenses." Such gaps may be due, in part, to the influx of other food resources that required no cash outlay.

The foods recorded as *spese minute* were those that the *Ospedale* purchased, either because its properties and estates did not produce enough (as in the case of meat, which was often bought), or because certain items were not produced at all (as in the case of fish and the limited quantities of spices mentioned in the accounts). Despite the problems related to the *quantification* of food consumption created by the *Innocenti*'s un-recorded farm produce, this little account book contains important details regarding the hospital's food provisioning, and provides *qualitative* information that is particularly useful when compared with other sources regarding diets in Florence in the mid-Quattrocento.

The *spese minute* notebook offers, first and foremost, unprecedented insights into daily life at the *Ospedale*, and a window onto a reality that the other sources usually conceal. For example, there is information on the productive capacity inside the walls of the *Innocenti*. Although often considerable, such production normally eludes the records kept by such institutions. In this case, perhaps the most important element was the kitchen garden, which was topped up by the already significant quantities of leaf and root vegetables purchased at the city market. In addition to the kitchen garden, there was also a henhouse, mentioned more than once in the *spese minute*: on 3 November 1453, for example, there was a purchase of "5 pairs of chickens to rear as hens [*chaline* (sic.)]," i.e. meant to produce eggs.[21] Eggs seem to have been deemed particularly important in the diet of the *Ospedale* residents, judging from the fact that they were also bought quite consistently.

The size of the kitchen garden is emphasized by the fact that expenses are recorded for keeping tools in good repair (an example is the entry for '*asotigliare maretti*', sharpening the cutting edge of hoes).[22] There were also large numbers of seedling sets purchased on various occasions, to be grown on in the plot of land behind the *Ospedale* where the kitchen garden was located. As is clearly visible in the late sixteenth-century *Buonsignori* map of Florence,[23] the Innocenti garden was an important area within the building complex, and was to remain active until the nineteenth century. On Friday, 21 April 1452, "350 onions were bought to plant out," but on 5 April of that year 1,200 "onions" had already been purchased, which says a lot about the significant dietary role of this root vegetable.[24] On Saturday 4 March, another note records a total of "500 lettuces to plant," while on 20 May appear "8 bunches of basil to plant" (an unusual acquisition in this period).[25] On 30 May the *Ospedale* acquires "1000 young leeks,"[26] which would have been consumed during the following winter. Yet it must be remembered that the considerable number of seedlings purchased for the kitchen garden almost certainly only ensured a limited amount of produce that was augmented by more substantial production from the *Innocenti*'s agricultural holdings and eventually acquisitions at the market.

All the food provisions for the *Ospedale*, including the hens in the henhouse, were kept under lock and key, as is documented, for example, by an entry on 28 November 1453 that records the purchase of "2 keys, one for the kitchen garden and one for the henhouse" which cost 7 *soldi* and 8 *denari*.[27] High importance was given to protecting all stocks, stored both outside and inside. On 20 February 1454 a further 4 *soldi* and 8 *denari* were spent on "the key to the bread room,"[28] while the distilling room used by the pharmacy also had to be locked: a note dated 5 July 1452 records 13 *soldi* spent on "a lock and 1 key for the still room door opposite the bath house where the dried meat is kept in summer."[29]

The *spese minute* accounts are even more useful as a source to study details of diet. Records listing grain and flour, purchases of meat, fish, cheese and many other foodstuffs, are often accompanied by short annotations. A double entry bookkeeping system was used, with credit and debit columns to keep track of the quantities of grain that the foundling home sent to be ground by various millers. When it returned from the miller (with deliveries that varied but often took place every two or three days and at most every two weeks), the flour, weighed exactly the same as the grain sent, always around 660 *libbre* (circa 224 kilograms), from which it can be deduced that it contained all of the bran. Yet, while the *Innocenti* might have usually served dark bread, white bread was not unknown. This inconsistency is made evident by the purchase, on 7 December 1451, of "two cheese-cloth bags for bolting (sifting),"[30] indicating that the process of separating the flour from the bran could well have been undertaken in the *Ospedale* itself. Whatever the case, we also know that the bread baked with this flour was not top quality, as is suggested by the white bread regularly bought for the prior, Lapo di Pacino, for whom a number of special purchases were made.

The account book also provides interesting details regarding the meat that was purchased and consumed. On the whole, the quantities bought were always very small, but there is no way of knowing whether these were supplementing the meat produced on the *Ospedale*'s own estates. On average, the quantity purchased never exceeded 16 or 17 *libbre* a day (5.5–6 kg), and usually included two or even three different types of meat. It is worth noting that the seasonal variations that appear in other accounts of the period also occur here. Kid meat was thus bought in Spring, even though in small quantities, presumably since it was the most expensive meat available. Lamb appears in larger quantities, as it was less prized and cost less than kid. In the Autumn and Winter what stands out is the typical predominance of pork.

Pork acquisitions started in September, even though it would have been deemed an injudicious choice by all the dietary treatises of the time, whose authors condemned it not only as a vulgar meat but also as being responsible for a large number of illnesses. Michele Savonarola's treatise emphasizes that pork "is certainly more suitable food for the winter," but also points out some more positive aspects of a meat that might have applied to the foundling home, even though it was widely scorned by medieval culture: "It is a meal for strong stomachs and for children, because they have a strong digestion and need much nourishment."[31] A similar opinion regarding pork (minus the explicit reference to children) can be found in many texts dealing with dietary matters in the fifteenth century. An example is the *Trattato utilissimo circa la conservazione della sanitate*, first published in Milan in 1481 and often incorrectly attributed to the Sienese philosopher and physician Ugo Benzi (1376–1439).[32] Benzi's treatise restated information that had been in circulation for a long time and in turn was nothing more than a translation of Benedetto Reguardati's earlier *Libellus de conservatione sanitatis* (composed between 1427 and 1430).[33]

The only meat that shows no seasonal variation was *castrone* (mutton), that usually came from animals that were one or two years old. This was purchased all year round and in large quantities (usually two thirds of expenditures on any given day). To the *Innocenti's* acquisition of meats was added, on very rare occasions, veal. This would not be the milk-fed veal regarded as the best quality, but rather a type of veal described as *"grossa"* (best translated as "coarse"). Equally rare in the accounts, but for quite another reason, was ox meat, a type of meat that was held in very little regard because it came from animals at the end of their working lives.

More important in the *Innocenti* diet, certainly in quantitative terms, was salted meat. The accounts often record the purchase of meat destined to be salted, an operation that was always carried out by the "porters" [*portatori*] who carried the meat to the *Ospedale* and were supervised on site (presumably to make sure that the right amount of salt was used).[34] The modest payments for this operation also suggests that the salt, which was required in significant quantities, was provided by the *Innocenti* itself from a special room set aside for salt stocks. An entry on 2 December 1451 mentions having to buy 3 *libbre* of salt "because the key to the room containing the rock salt and the sea salt broke." Two days later, another entry appears for the cost of "opening the door to the rock salt and sea salt [room] which was broken."[35] Regardless, meat to be salted was purchased quite frequently (at least once a month), with purchases ranging from a minimum of 35 kilos to a maximum in excess of 150 kilos. Once dried, this meat was stored in a special room that seems to have changed according to the season; in summer, as mentioned earlier, it was located "opposite the bath house where distilling is carried out."

Spices also make a timid appearance in these accounts, and their relatively high cost indicated a certain degree of luxury in food preparation for select individuals. On Saturday 11 December, 1451, a lean day, an entry records the purchase of "1 ounce of sweet spices."[36] A fifteenth-century cookbook from the Veneto mentions these same sweet spices and describes them as a mixture of ginger, cinnamon, cloves and a mysterious, unidentified "leaf." The cookbook in question specifies that the blend was especially suited to "lamprey in pastry and for other good freshwater fish baked in pastry…"[37] Food historians have noted repeatedly that these spices, considered hot and dry according to humoral medicine, were often used to correct the overly wet and cold nature of fish. It was no coincidence, therefore, that the purchase of "1 pound of whole pepper" (another hot and therefore "corrective" spice) on 11 March 1452 occurred in the middle of Lent, when at least the most important people at the *Ospedale* would have eaten fish practically every day. [38]

Occasionally, the entries in these accounts offer specific details about how certain foodstuffs were used. In one case, "20 pounds of pig's heads and trotters" were purchased "to make *aspic*."[39] At first, this might seem strange, as aspic was a festive dish, often purchased from those specializing in making it. Aspic was sold to top-ranking institutions (such as the *Mensa della Signoria*, the high table of the ruling Priors of Florence), and was often made using more than one food color to make it more attractive (the cookbook mentioned earlier contains at least three different recipes for making aspic).[40] However, it seems unlikely that this specialty would have been served to all those residing at the *Ospedale*, both because it was considered a refined and rich dish, and because there certainly would not have been enough for all of the staff and inmates.

Some purchases were intended for just one privileged individual, or at most for a handful of people. There are countless examples of this, starting with the *lasagne* purchased for festive meals, such as Christmas, but in quantities that usually did not exceed 3 *libbre* (approximately one kilo). Another special entry dates from Carnival 1454, when on 28 February the purchase mentions "12 thrushes and sausage for Fat Thursday."[41] This prized meat would have been sufficient for the Prior's table alone; indeed, the accounts demonstrate the extent to which his diet was exceptional. The Prior of the time, Lapo di Piero di Pacino Pacini, had donated all his possessions to the *Innocenti* in a solemn deed dated 11 January 1444, and had taken up "the rule and clothing of the *Spedale*," but this did not mean that he would have set aside the dietary privileges that distinguished him from other individuals in the institution. Luxury purchases for the Prior were recorded on other occasions as well, such as the "six warblers for Lapo" that cost 4 *soldi*, or "two pairs of capons... for Lapo,"[42] not to mention the numerous times that white loaves and fresh eggs were bought (fresh eggs cost almost twice the price of normal eggs: 6 *denari* each compared to just over 3 *denari* for eggs destined for the *famiglia* on the same days).

In some cases, purchases of special or expensive foods were justified by the fact that Lapo was unwell, and it is no coincidence that in these instances the items purchased were those that were believed (by both doctors and patients) to have therapeutic properties. The most striking example of a specific type of food for the ill appears on 8 July 1452, when a capon was purchased "to be ground for Lapo as medicine for his stomach disorder."[43] This rather odd note is difficult for modern readers to interpret, but can be explained by the contemporary belief whereby the flesh of capons and chickens was thought to be particularly healthy for the sick. It was minced to form a paste and then diluted with almond milk and various spices to create a dish that was widely known in late-medieval Europe. Regarded as a tonic, this dish was geographically very widespread (it appears in Catalan, French, English and German cookbooks), and numerous variants existed, even if it was always known as "*biancomangiare*" (i.e. blancmange, from the French *blancmanger*).[44]

The institution's concern for the sick and their diet was not restricted solely to the Prior because a series of specific purchases were made for other people, starting with the frequent mention of fresh eggs "for the sick" and "white loaves for sick children"[45] (apparently of a better quality than the normal bread served by the *Ospedale*). The importance of giving fresh eggs to the sick is explained by dietary treatises. Michele Savonarola, for example, stated that "...eggs are regarded by [medical] authors as the food of foods. Very nutritious ... they have almost no 'superfluous' [elements] but are entirely converted into nourishment. They are easy to digest, and appropriate food for the weak, the infirm, and when the feverish patient is weak, that is when they are most suitable..."[46] More costly, medicinal foods for the sick were bought and accounted for, as in an entry that reads, "1 chicken for two children who are sick," or "a chicken bought by Pucio for Piero ... sick at home."[47] When a certain Dianora (perhaps the Prior's wife) fell sick, the various foods bought for her were also recorded. In her case, there are not only the customary "fresh eggs" praised by doctors, but also on the same day "5 pills for the aforesaid," and again a few days later some white loaves, other fresh eggs, "4 ounces of Manus Christi [*manoscristo*]" and "distilled waters and electuaries"[48] which appear to indicate a deterioration in her condition necessitating not only a special diet but recourse to actual medicaments.

This brief look at some aspects of food provisioning and diets at the *Ospedale degli Innocenti* underscores the fact that we continue to know very little about the normal everyday practice of a large institution that must have relied considerably on produce from its properties in addition to occasional purchases. Although the isolated account book on *spese minute* shines a bit more light on the little-studied subject of hospital food and provisions, it also offers a skewed picture precisely because it records events that could be extra-ordinary rather than normal practice. A small detail, like the "basket of cherries I bought for the children and the household on 24 May," (an entry that is also repeated a few weeks later), would count for very little in a quantitative study.[49] Yet this human touch offers us a richer qualitative view in addition to what was undoubtedly a very serious, quantitative problem for the period in question: food for survival.

Notes

This is a slightly revised version (notes and bibliography) of an article that was first published as "Il vitto di un ospedale: pratica, distinzioni sociali e teorie mediche alla metà del Quattrocento" in *Gli Innocenti e Firenze nei secoli: un ospedale, un archivio, una città*, edited by Lucia Sandri, (Florence: Spes, 1996), 85–92. Translated by Lucinda Byatt with revisions by the author.

1. See, for example, Lucia Sandri, *L'Ospedale di S. Maria della Scala di S. Gimignano nel Quattrocento* (Castelfiorentino: Biblioteca della Miscellanea Storica della Valdelsa, 1982); Philip Gavitt, *Charity and Children in Renaissance Florence: The Ospedale degli Innocenti*, (Ann Arbor: University of Michigan Press, 1990); Giuliana Albini, *Città e ospedali nella Lombardia Medievale*, (Bologna: CLUEB, 1993). For a useful bibliography on Medieval and Renaissance hospitals see the excellent online compilation put together by Marina Gazzini, http://www.rm.unina.it/rmebook/index.php?mod=none_Gazzini. (Last accessed 22/08/2018). See also John Henderson, *The Renaissance Hospital. Healing the Body and Healing the Soul*, (New Haven and London: Yale University Press, 2006) and Allen J. Grieco and Lucia Sandri, eds. *Ospedali e città: Italia del Centro-Nord, XIII–XVI secolo*, (Florence: Le Lettere, 1997).

2. Used above all for establishing prices, not to study diets. For Florence the most complete

study is Charles de La Roncière, *Prix et salaires à Florence au XIVe siècle, 1280–1380*, (Rome: École française de Rome, 1982).

3. At the time this article was first published in 1996, an exception to this rule were two articles: Lucia Sandri, "I regimi alimentari negli ospedali fiorentini alla fine del Medio Evo e in Età Moderna" in *Aspetti di vita e di cultura fiorentina*, (Florence: Accademia della Fiorentina, 1995); Alfio Cortonesi, "Le spese 'In victualibus' della Domus Helemonsine Sancti Petri di Roma," In *Archeologia Medievale*, vol. 8 (1981), 193–225. Since this article came out, some excellent work on this topic has appeared. See above all Christine Jéhanno, "L'alimentation hospitalière à la fin du Moyen Âge. L'exemple de l'hôtel Dieu de Paris", in *Hospitäler in Mittelalter und Früher Neuzeit. Frankreich, Deutschland und Italien. Eine vergleichende Geschichte, Hôpitaux en France, Allemagne et Italie: une étude comparée (Moyen Âge et Temps modernes)*, (Munich: Oldenbourg, 2007), 107–162, and Maddalena Belli, Francesca Grassi and Beatrice Sordini, *La Cucina di un ospedale del Trecento. Gli spazi, gli oggetti, il cibo nel Santa Maria della Scala di Siena*, (Ospedaletto (Pisa): Pacini, 2004), which contains long lists of food but very little analysis. Much more consistent are the following three contributions: Barbara Krug-Richter, *Zwischen Fasten und Festmahl. Hospitalverpflegung in Münster 1540 bis 1650*, (Stuttgart: Steiner, 1994); Giuliana Albini, "Ospedali e cibo in età medievale" in *Carità e governo delle povertà (secoli XII-XV)*, (Milan: Unicopli, 2002), 211–225 and Lucia Sandri, "Alimentazione e salute negli ospedali fiorentini tra Medioevo e Età Moderna," in *I Gusti della salute. Alimentazione, salute e sanità ieri e oggi*, (Silea, Centro Italiano Storia Sanitaria Ospitaliera, 2000), 199–211. See also Henderson (2006) 63–65 and 206–209, and the special issue dedicated to "Food and Hospitals" *Food & History*, vol. 14, 1 (2016).

4. On such properties owned by the *Innocenti* see Simona Gelli and Giuliano Pinto, "La

presenza dell'Ospedale nel contado (sec. XV)," in *Gli Innocenti e Firenze nei secoli: un ospedale, un archivio, una città*, edited by L. Sandri, (Florence: Spes, 1996), 95–108.

5. Concerning this assessment, see Gavitt 1990, 170–73; for a partial transcription of the daily expenditure on food made by the *Ospedale*, see his Appendix, 307–309.

6. "...allo sciolvere di tutta la brighata...," Archivio dell' Ospedale degli Innocenti Firenze (AOIF from now on), s. XII, no. 2, c. 51.

7. "...quotidiana a ciascun povero si diano trentadue once di pane di mistura ben fatto ... [e a] ... gl'infermi ... si diano ogni giorno ventiquattro once di pane di frumento ben fatto," cited in Giacomo C. Bascapè, "L'assistenza e la beneficenza a Milano dall'alto medioevo alla fine della dinastia Sforzesca," in *Storia di Milano*, vol. VIII, Milan, 1957, 404–405.

8. Only part of the staff seems to have been present for all of the meals. From this point of view, the rations calculated by Gavitt (1990) 170 are not wholly convincing.

9. For a more thorough discussion of meals, when they were consumed and contemporary nomenclature, see chapter 1.

10. "...a chi se fatica e guadagna il pane cum le mani ... nui videamo per experientia che questi tali per la usanza manzano tre e quattro volte al zorno," *Michele Savonarola, Libreto de tutte le cosse che se magnano, un'opera di dietetica del sec. XV*, edited by J. Nystedt, (Stockholm: Almqvist & Wiksell International, 1988), 184.

11. "...errano alcuni pedagogi che voleno tenere i suoi discipuli a tale abstinentia e anco le madre che troppo sono divote a farli dezunare troppo o spesso o continuo." Ibid., 186.

12. For a more complete discussion of this point, see chapter 1.

13. "...alle balie per sciolvere e desinare et merenda e ciena che ssono 13 balie e 4 fanciulli svezzi coppie 15 di pane libre 34," cited in Gavitt 1990, 308.

14. The document in question is in the AOIF, *Spese minute et straordinarie dello Spedale delli Innocenti* B (1451–1463), 5342. I thank Lucia Sandri for having brought this interesting notebook to my attention.

15. "...tenuto e debbi tenere j libro si chiama entrata ed uscita delle richolte delle possessioni..." I quote here and further on from the transcription published by Ugo Cherici, *L'Assistenza all'infanzia ed il R. Spedale degli Innocenti di Firenze*, (Florence: Vallechi, 1932), 60–67.

16. "Ispese minute si faranno per la chasa e per i fanciugli chominciata adì primo di dicembre 1451 dove si scriverà partitamente di dì in dì...," AOIF, 5342, c. 2.

17. "...tutte dette spese minute, scritte in su detto quaderno, il detto chamarlingo le debba mettere a uscita mese per mese..." Cherici 1932, 60.

18. "...spese generali dello spedale per maniera che anno per anno si possa vedere in sul libro grande quello s'è logoro anno per anno a chosa a chosa ognuna per sé..." Ibid., 64.

19. "...acciò sia manifesto e veghasi le variazioni che seguiranno anno per anno," ibid., 64.

20. "...che tutte le scritture che si tengono per lo scrivano, tutte le debba tenere sul descho della cancielleria del detto spedale sanza serrarle, acciò che lo spedalingo o altri per lui le possa vedere di dì e di notte chome ... il quaderno lungo delle spese minute che di dì si faranno, acciò che lo scrivano a ogn'ora le possa leggere." Ibid., 62–63.

21. "...5 paia di pollastre per fare chaline..." Ibid., c. 20.

22. AOIF, 5342, c. 21.

23. Behind the main cloister of the *Ospedale* and indicated by regularly spaced hatching. See http://cds.library.brown.edu/projects/florentine_gazetteer/map_page.php?p=11 (last accessed 22/08/2018) for a closeup view.

24. "...350 cipolline per porre..." AOIF, 5342, c. 4v. and c. 133v. On the importance of bread and onions in lower class diets see chapter 1.

25. "...8 mazuoli di basilico per porre..." Ibid., c. 4v.

26. "...1000 porrine..." Ibid., c. 134v.

27. "...2 chiave, una all'orto e una al pollaio..." Ibid., c. 20.

28. "...la chiave all'uscio del pane..." Ibid., c. 20v.

29. "...una toppa e 1 chiave per l'uscio do' si stilla dirimpetto alla stufa dove istà la carne secca d'estate..." Ibid., c. 135v.

30. "...due barategli di stamigna per aburattare..." Ibid., c. 2.

31. "E' pasto da stomeghi forti e da putti, il perché hanno forte digestiva e bissogno de molto nutrimento..." Savonarola 1988, 134.

32. Ugo Benzi, *Tractato utilissimo circa la Conservazione della Sanitade*, Milan, Petri de Corneno, 1481, 23v–24v.

33. Concerning the real author of the *Tractato utilissimo* see Juliana Hill Cotton, "Benedetto Reguardati: Author of Ugo Benzi's *Tractato de la Conservatione de la Sanitade*," Medical History, vol. 12 n. 1 (1968), 76–83. However, even Reguardati's *Libellus de conservatione sanitatis* was not an entirely original piece of work since it too was based on a yet older text, the *Compendium de naturis et proprietatibus alimentorum* composed by the mid-fourteenth-century doctor, Barnabas Riatini da Reggio (ca. 1300–ca. 1365).

34. Stories about under-salted meats that end up going bad appear in *novelle* as metaphors of shortsighted stinginess. One example is in Franco Sacchetti, *Il Trecentonovelle*, edited by A. Lanza (Florence: Sansoni, 1984), novella CCXIV, 504–507.

35. "...perché la chiave dove està el sale e la salina si guastò." AOIF, 5342, c. 2.

36. "...1 oncia di spezie dolci..." Ibid., c. 2.

37. "...per lampreda in crosta e per altri boni pessi d'acque dolze che se faga un crosto..." Anonymous, *Libro di cucina del secolo XIV*, edited by Ludovico Frati, (Leghorn, 1899; anastatic reprint, Bologna: Forni, 1979), 40. This

cookbook is, linguistically speaking, from the Veneto and was incorrectly dated by Frati, who believed it to be a fourteenth-century text. As is well known, however, elite cookery during this period was very similar across the entire Italian peninsula. On the intricate question of Italian cookbooks see Bruno Laurioux, "I libri di cucina italiani alla fine del Medioevo: un nuovo bilancio," *Archivio Storico Italiano*, vol. 154, n. 1 (1996), 33–58. Concerning this particular type of spice mixture see Enrico Carnevale Schianca, *La Cucina medievale: lessico, storia, preparazione*, Florence, Leo Olschki, 2011, 627–28. See also chapter 2 in the present volume.

38. "...1 libra di pepe sodo..." AOIF, 5342, c. 4.

39. "...libre 20 di capi e pie' di porco... per fare gelatina" Ibid., c. 3v. For more on aspic see chapter 2, 68 and 71.

40. Anonymous, *Libro di cucina*, op. cit., 16–19.

41. "...adì 28 per berlinghaccio per 12 tordini e salsiccia" AOIF, 5342, c. 20.

42. "...due paia di capponi ... per Lapo" Ibid., c. 6.

43. "...è per pestare per Lapo, e medicina per lo suo male dello stomaco" Ibid., c. 5.

44. Much has been written on this popular dish, known in English as blancmange, and whose etymology suggests that it had to be white even though many surviving recipes do not bear this out. For an introduction to the history of this interesting dish and its context

see the landmark article by Jean-Louis Flandrin, "Internationalisme, nationalisme et régionalisme dans la cuisine des XIVe et XVe siècles: le témoignage des livres de cuisine," *Manger et boire au Moyen âge*, vol. 2 *Cuisine, manières de table, régimes alimentaires*, edited by D. Menjot, (Paris : Belles lettres, 1984), vol. 2, 75–91.

45. "...pani bianchi per fanciulli infermi..." AOIF, 5342, c. 2v., c.3, etc.

46. "L'ovo è posto dali autori cibo fra i cibi. Molto nutritivi è ... non hano quasi alcuna superfluità ma tutti se convertono in nutrimento. Sono facili da padire, e cibo conveniente a debili e anco a infirmi, dove quando il febriente è debele alora ben ge conveneno..." Savonarola 1988, 145.

47. "1 pollastra per due fanciulli ànno male," "...una pollastra comprò Puccio per Piero ... malato in casa." AOIF, 5342, c. 2v. On chickens and birds more generally and their supposed effect on the human body, both as medicine and as an aphrodisiac, see my essay, "From Roosters to Cocks: Renaissance Dietary Theory and Sexuality," in *Erotic Cultures of Renaissance Italy*, edited by S. F. Matthews-Grieco, (Aldershot: Ashgate, 2010), 89–140.

48. "4 once di manoscristo" and "aque istilate e latovari," Manus Christi being the name given to a type of cordial, ibid. c.2v.

49. "...ciestarella di ciriege comprai pe' fanciulli e per la brigata di casa adì 24 maggio..." Ibid., c. 4v.

II. Social Distinctions, Dietary Theory and Classificatory Systems

Chapter 5
Food and Social Classes in Late Medieval and Renaissance Italy

According to a medieval convention, human beings were believed to survive by drinking wine (or ale and beer in northern Europe), eating bread, and eating "all those other things" that could be eaten with bread. This third category of food-stuffs was usually referred to by a highly significant Latin term: *companagium* (*companatico* in Italian, *companage* in French).[1] When dealing with medieval food history, this ubiquitous trio of categories turns out to be both a useful and a fundamental way to subdivide human fare, especially when examining the diets of the poor. Economic considerations, but also economic imperatives, limited both the choice of what people ate and how much they ate. This was particularly true in a society where the surplus produced tended to be very limited indeed. Furthermore, even slight price differences seem to have put certain food items beyond the reach of the lower social classes, thus relegating many products to the realm of the desired rather than to what was actually eaten. The reduced margins within which the poor could make food choices are encountered by economic historians whenever they compare the incomes of the working classes to the cost of wheat, which imposed a very different price structure in the realm of foodstuffs than the one we are familiar with at present.

By present day standards, it might come as a surprise to know that in late-medieval and Renaissance Italy the cost of wheat flour—from which bread, the real staff of life, was made—seems to have been abnormally high, especially if we compare its cost to that of meat products. In late fourteenth-century Florence, for example, one pound of the cheapest meat (pork) cost only twice as much as the best quality flour, whereas the most expensive meat (veal) cost only two and a half times as much as wheat flour.[2] Today, of course, we are used to a much greater price differential since meat is usually ten to fifteen times more expensive than flour, depending on the kind of meat and the cut. However, what might seem to have been only a slight price difference between meat and wheat must not be underrated since, as I have suggested, it constituted a major discriminating barrier in the eating habits of a large segment of the population, especially in those areas of Europe where wheat and other grains were used either to bake bread or boiled to make gruel.

It is now a historiographic commonplace to point out the clear link between bread consumption and social rank. The lower a person's social rank, the greater the percentage of income spent on bread.[3] For example, historians have found that the percentage of the dietary budget devoted to bread on one of the properties of King René of Anjou in 1457 varied from a minimum of 32 percent for the overseers to a distinctly higher figure (47 percent) for the cow herders and mule drivers; it reached a maximum of 52 percent among the shepherds, who were considered the lowest-grade workers. The percentage devoted to wine, on the other hand, was less variable, ranging from a minimum of 28 percent for the overseers to a maximum of 34 percent for the shepherds. The most radical discriminant was the percentage devoted to the *companagium*, the various kinds of food that brought a bit of variety to what was otherwise a diet consisting of vast amounts of bread or gruel and wine. Only 14 percent of the lowly shepherds' dietary budget was devoted to this item, whereas the overseers, responsible for managing the property, were able to devote as much as 40 percent of their budget to something other than bread and wine. In short, bread occupied an increasingly conspicuous percentile share of the diets of the lower social classes; inversely, this proportion shrank as one rose through the social hierarchy.

This state of affairs does not seem to have been limited to Mediterranean Europe. Christopher Dyer, in *Standards of Living in the Later Middle Ages*,[4] has shown that the importance of grains (wheat, barley, and oats) was just as fundamental in English peasant diets, even though these were integrated, as in most other European countries, with large quantities of inexpensive or home-grown vegetables (onions, garlic, leeks, and cabbage being the most often mentioned) and small quantities of more costly meat and cheese.

In a society where social distinctions were made manifest in a variety of ways, food was an important distinguishing element, not only between the different social classes but also between rural and urban culture. Literary texts are particularly sensitive indicators of the cultural value attributed to different foods and therefore allow us to penetrate the social codes with which foodstuffs and meals were invested. For example, any number of texts can be found that underscore the fact that the daily consumption of white bread distinguished city dwellers from rural populations, who were more likely to eat bread made with a mixture of grains (wheat or millet, for example) or who, more simply, boiled their grain and ate it in this less refined form. That this distinction was not a just a literary topos can be seen from the fact that social and dietary differences were also recognized in the confined spaces of fifteenth-century ships, where at least two different tables existed. According to Benedetto Dei's report to the *Consuls and Masters of the Sea* of Pisa in 1471, there was a strict scale of salaries respecting the hierarchy of the men on board ship and similarly rigid distinctions made in the food served.[5] The owner of the ship and the "officers" were served white bread, whereas the rank and file had to be satisfied with rations of dry biscuit.

Literary texts also draw attention to the importance given to a "proper" choice of foods, especially on public occasions when banquets and meals commemorated an important event linking a given family to the community at large (birth of a child, marriage, knighthood, death). There was, in fact, a fine line between what was considered to be good enough and yet not excessively lavish fare, and that which would be considered too poor and therefore not becoming the status of the family and the occasion on which it was being served. An excessive display of wealth was controlled and sanctioned by sumptuary laws promulgated not only by the Italian city-states, but also elsewhere in Europe. These laws (a rich source for food historians) stipulated with great precision what foods could be served, how much at a time, and to how many guests. The opposite extreme—too frugal a meal—seems to have been a rare occurrence, condemned by the community (only morally speaking, of course), as being just as reprehensible as was excessive luxury.

The diets of the wealthiest members of the community present a rather complex but interesting problem as they require a more sophisticated approach than simply calculating the percentile incidence of bread in their general intake. In fact, for the classes other than the laboring ones, it would seem that social distinctions on the basis of diets became apparent primarily in their choice of food stuffs other than bread. In this case, it is not advisable to rely entirely on literary texts as a source, since there are many other sources—such as letters, travel accounts, and private memoirs—that allow us to penetrate into an everyday world, where the relationship between food quality and social status moves from a more abstract plane to a perfectly explicit one.

An excellent example of the connection between food and social status can be found in a letter written in 1404 by Ser Lapo Mazzei, a Florentine notary known to us for his voluminous correspondence with his friend, Francesco di Marco Datini, a rich merchant who lived in the city of Prato. In one of these letters, he thanked Datini for what was meant to be a handsome gift of partridges, but reminded him that those birds were not appropriate food for his sort of person. In fact, Lapo complained to his friend, saying, "You will not leave me in peace with your partridges and God knows I do not like to destroy so many all at once, considering their price, and I would not give them to the gluttons, and it would grieve my soul were I to sell them."[6] He then proceeded to explain that, had he still been a servant of his people (a euphemism by which he reminded Datini that he had formerly served in the governing body of the city of Florence), it would then have been his duty to eat such fowl.[7] This statement might seem curious but his comment should be taken quite literally. The Signori of Florence were, in fact, required to eat great quantities of partridges and fowl in general, since this was seen as an outward sign of the civic and political power they wielded. Such food, however, was not considered fit for normal people, both in a medical and a moral sense.

Not only was it thought dangerous to eat foods (such as partridges) that would produce excessive "overheating" in the human body, but those who were imprudent enough to eat such fare risked being led directly from the sin of gluttony (*gula*) to the closely associated and even more dangerous sin of lust (*lussuria*). This was something that Lapo must have believed to be true, as did most of his contemporaries, since in another letter to Francesco Datini, Lapo made a reference to the partridges Datini had eaten in Avignon in his younger years, as a clear allusion to his mistress in that city. Even a great theologian and preacher like Bernardino of Siena believed that eating fowl could be dangerous; he made a point of telling the assembled crowd in Siena on the Piazza del Campo in 1427 that widows (the subject of this sermon) had to be especially careful in choosing their food. He reminded his audience to avoid foods that "heat you up since the danger is great when you have hot blood and eat food that will make you even hotter," and therefore : "Let me tell you, widow, that you cannot eat this or that.... Do not try to do as you did when you had a husband and ate the flesh of fowl."[8]

In any case, Lapo made it clear that such presents were not welcome, but if his wealthy friend wanted to give him coarser foods, fit for working people, these he would accept with pleasure. Lapo, it must be said, did not change much over the years; in a letter he wrote some fourteen years earlier, when he first met Francesco, he told his new friend, "I like coarse foods, those that make me strong enough to sustain the work I must do to maintain my family. This year I would like to have, as I once had, a little barrel of salted anchovies."[9]

The austere nutritional guidelines followed by Lapo were not followed by everyone, and his friend Francesco was quick to break dietary rules for he continued to consume (even after his Avignon interlude) the diet of a man who was anything but temperate. Iris Origo's study of Francesco di Marco Datini, *The Merchant of Prato*, points out that food was an important matter: the food Datini bought was closely linked to his social status, as it was for many of his contemporaries. Thus, meat that was not considered worthy of his standing could unleash a rather indignant reaction. On one occasion he was sent some veal that was not up to par (probably from an animal that was too old). His reaction was to write to the agent who provided it : "You should feel shame to send such meat to as great a merchant as I am! I will not forgive you, save you make amends, and I will come and eat it in your house (sic), and only then shall we be friends again!"[10]

The notion that "good" quality meat was suitable for the higher social strata and lower-quality meats were fit for less elevated members of society was considered to be a "scientific" fact even by doctors writing about diets, as is borne out by another of Datini's letters. In this letter he asks a man by the name of Bellozzo to go to the market "where there are most people and say, 'give me some fine veal for that gentleman from Prato,' and they will give you some that is good.”[11] For a man that was so conscious of his status and the food that went with it, it became a matter of some importance if he managed (or, for that matter, did not manage) to buy the same food that was allotted to the Priors of Florence whose high table (the *Mensa dei Signori*) saw the best food to be had in Florence. On various occasions he either complained that the *Signori* of Florence had bought up the best fish available, or he boasted to his wife that he had bought the same veal as was reserved for the Priors.

Literary texts also suggest that it was considered quite normal that exceptional items (such as those of an unusually large size)—as long as they belonged to what was considered a "noble" food group, such as fish or fowl— would be reserved for exceptional people, usually the local ruler. A novella that has survived in a fifteenth-century manuscript contains an anecdote that is probably more than just a literary topos: a pair of exceptionally large capons appeared on the market in Milan where they were immediately bought up by a gentleman who, far from having them cooked for his own table, thought it fitting to send them as a present to Bernabò Visconti, the ruler of Milan.[12]

At times hierarchical distinctions were observed in an even more extreme way—to the point of seeming an over-determined mechanical exercise. A particularly good example of this appears in the meals served to two Bavarian princes who visited Florence with their retinue in 1592.[13] This group of visiting dignitaries and their hangers-on were offered a highly varied meal that was meant to respect the social hierarchies at play. Thus, the two princes were served a dish with five different fowl (fowl being the noblest food possible). The "second table" (the one for the nobility accompanying the princes) was served dishes with only four different fowl. The cupbearer and the other top-ranking "servants" were also given dishes with four different fowl, but they were to eat their food in a private room separate from the banquet hall. Then came the lower-ranking servants (thirty in all) who had to share five dishes, each made with one fowl. These servants ate in the *tinello*, a kind of antechamber used for this purpose.[14] This document then specifies that the horses and mules of the visitors were to be stabled and fed. Ending the list, even after the animals, were the very lowest-ranking servants (a total of 140), who were put up in two different hostels in the city. Hierarchies were thus expressed not only in terms of the diversity of food served, but also in terms of the location where it was consumed (the distance from the master being inversely proportional to importance).

Food and Worldview

Distinctions through food, whereby the upper classes ate more "refined" fare and the lower classes coarser foodstuffs, were omnipresent in late-medieval culture. Sixteenth-century treatises on nobility explicitly dealt with this issue, reminding their readers (in something of a tautological statement) that the "superiority" of the social elites was due, at least in part, to the superior way in which they ate. Thus, Florentin Le Thierriat de Lochepierre, in his *Trois Traictez*, asserted that "we eat more partridges and other delicate meats than they do [i.e. those who are not of the nobility], and this gives us a more supple intelligence and sensibility than those who eat beef and pork."[15]

All of the examples cited above suggest that there was something like a code that made a meal either noble or poor, and that this code was not based on personal preference but rather on ideas about food shared by most people. The idea that the rich and poor were meant to eat in very different ways may seem more or less senseless to us today. Yet in the late Middle Ages and the Renaissance, this notion was grounded in the prevailing worldview, according to which there existed a series of analogies between the natural world created by God and the world of human beings. It was deemed self-evident that God had created the world as well as the laws that governed human society, both of which were structured by a vertical and hierarchical principle.

Human society was therefore seen as being subdivided in a hierarchical way, like nature, in a ladder-like structure usually referred to as the *Great Chain of Being* (see figure 5.1). This great chain was thought to give a particular order to nature since it not only connected the world of inanimate objects to God but also linked all of creation together in a grand design.

Between the two extremes of the chain were all the plants and animals created by God (including even mythological animals such as the phoenix),

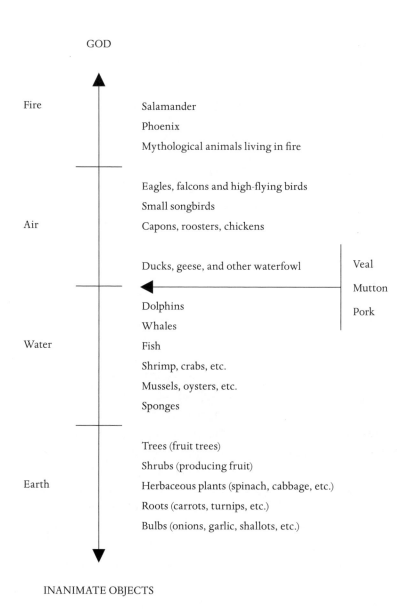

Fig. 1 The *Great Chain of Being*

arranged in a perfectly hierarchical sequence in which everything respected an ascending or descending order. Each plant (or animal) was thought to be nobler than the one below it and less noble than the one above it, so each had a different position according to their degree of nobility.

The *Chain of Being* subdivided all of creation into four distinct segments that represented the four elements (earth, water, air, and fire), in which all plants and animals (both real and mythological) were to be found.[16] Earth, the lowest and least noble of the elements, was the element in which all plants grew, but even within this segment there was a perfectly hierarchical system at work. According to the botanical ideas of the time, the least noble of edible plants were those that produced a bulb underground (such as onions, garlic, and shallots). After these came slightly less "lowly" plants with edible roots (turnips, carrots, and many root crops no longer in use). The next tier belonged to all plants whose leaves were eaten (spinach and cabbage, for example), and at the top came fruit, the most noble product of the plant world.[17] Fruit was considered to be entirely superior to all other produce, and therefore more fit for the upper classes. The supposed nobility of fruit was due to the fact that most of it grew on bushes and trees, and thus grew higher off the ground than all the previously-mentioned plants.

Moreover, plants were thought to actually digest the terrestrial food they absorbed with their roots and turn it into sap, which continued to improve as it rose up through the plant and produced leaves, flowers and, best of all, fruit. It was even thought that the taller a plant grew, the more the rising sap "digested" and transformed the cold and raw humors of the earth into something increasingly better. Even on the same tree, the fruit that was higher off the ground was thought to be better than the rest. This rather mechanical application of a theory led people to think of strawberries and melons as very poor fruit, a consensus that was further confirmed by medical doctors and dietary theory.[18]

The second segment of the *Chain of Being* (associated with water) produced, at the very bottom, lowly sponges that seemed more plants than anything else; nevertheless, they were considered somewhat sentient since they responded to touch. One step up from sponges, but still at the low end of this category, were mussels and other shellfish that cannot move about on their own and that were considered to be partially inanimate because of their hard shells. Higher up on the Chain, and therefore more "noble" than the previous group, were the various kinds of crustaceans (such as shrimp and lobsters) that crawled on the floor of the sea. Yet more elevated were various kinds of fish, although they were distinctly overshadowed by another group of aquatic animals at the top of the category: all those animals that, like dolphins and whales, tend to swim on the surface of the water and, at times, even emerge from this element into the next segment of creation (air) as if they were striving upward, to greater perfection. It is perhaps no coincidence that, given such ideas about the nobility of dolphins and whales, their superior "nature" contributed to their being hunted and eaten in this period of European history.

Much like the two segments below it, the third segment of the *Chain of Being*—the element air—, has its own hierarchy of values. It begins, at the bottom, with the "lowest" kinds of birds, those that live in water: ducks, geese, and wild birds living in or near water (such as the cormorant) were all thought to reveal their lowly status by being associated with that lower element. Other fowl, such as chickens and partridges, were considered to be much better fare since they were more obviously aerial animals; in fact, any respectable banquet had to include such birds. The next step up was occupied by songbirds, a late-medieval and Renaissance culinary passion, and at the top of the category were the highest-flying birds, such as the eagle and falcon. The latter were not really considered to be food but rather were kept as pets and were trained by the upper classes for hunting. A story in Boccaccio's *Decameron* (V,9) concerning the unrequited love of Federigo degli Alberighi reveals an intriguing use of these ideas. Federigo, who has been reduced to poverty in his efforts to win over his beloved monna Giovanna, ends up living in a little farm outside Florence with his last earthly possession: a falcon whose hunting talents manage to keep him fed. Many years later Giovanna comes to see him because her son is convinced that the only thing that will cure him from a sickness is to own Federigo's falcon. Unfortunately, the noble Federigo has no food on the day that he receives Giovanna and, although it causes him great anguish, he decides that the falcon is a *"degna vivanda di cotal donna"* (a worthy dish for such a woman). The pathos of the story is developed around the idea that the falcon is both a companion and a noble food, and that Federigo has no other choice than to transform his faithful pet into a dish for his beloved.

Like most general theories, the *Great Chain of Being* did not manage to account for everything. One of its problems was in the classification of quadrupeds, since they were difficult to assign to any one element. One the one hand, while they were obviously earthbound, they could hardly be considered in the same way as plants. On the other hand, quadrupeds could not be associated with the element air, and thus not be grouped with birds. In practice, they were somewhat awkwardly inserted in the middle of the Chain, insofar as they were considered nobler fare than what the plant world produced, and yet less prized than birds.[19] Predictably, the meat of quadrupeds, like everything else on the *Chain of Being*, was ordered according to a strict hierarchy. At the very top was veal, which was also the most expensive meat on the market and second only to fowl. At banquets, such as the one that was held in honor of the marriage of Nannina de' Medici to Bernardo Rucellai in 1466, veal was given to the more important people who came from the country properties of these two families, whereas the most notable guests were served capons, chickens, and other fowl.[20] In the hierarchy of meats, mutton (the everyday fare of the merchant classes) was placed below veal, while pork occupied the lowest rank. The latter was looked down upon, especially when salted, probably because it was the meat most available for the lower classes.

The hierarchical structure of both society and nature suggested that these two worlds mirrored or paralleled each other. As a consequence, it was believed that society had a "natural" order whereas nature had a kind of "social" order. One of the outcomes of this parallelism between the natural and the social worlds was the general view that the upper strata of society were destined to eat the foods belonging to the upper reaches of the realm of nature. In fact, the idea that the produce of nature was not all the same (since it was hierarchically ordered), and that specific foodstuffs were associated with specific sectors of society, became increasingly plausible. It seemed to make perfect sense that fowl be considered the food, par excellence, for the rich and mighty of the earth. The tautological reasoning of dietetic theory would have it that the social elites needed to eat birds precisely to keep their intelligence and sensibility more acute. Doctors like the Bolognese Baldassare Pisanelli, whose treatise on diet was first published in 1583, could say without a hint of irony: *"Le pernici non nuocono se non a gente rustica"*[21] (Partridges are only unhealthy for country people). While the meat of birds was thought most appropriate for the upper classes, the meat of quadrupeds, considered heavier and more substantial, was deemed more suitable for the merchant classes insofar as their lifestyle called for somewhat more sustenance. Pork and old animals in general (such as sheep, goats, and oxen that were no longer useful) otherwise provided the meat for the lower classes, who were understood to be in need of yet more coarse but hearty nourishment.

The working classes might have been destined some meat, but they were considered best off eating vast amounts of vegetables. There is no doubt, of course, that vegetables had a prominent part in the poor man's diet in Western Europe from the fourteenth through the sixteenth century, primarily for economic reasons. In fact, vegetable gardens all over Europe produced relatively cheap and abundant quantities of edibles. However, this kind of diet was also invested with a strong class bias that surfaces in all kinds of documents. The link between vegetables and the lower social orders is always very evident, to the extent that it sometimes constituted a quasi-symbiotic relationship. Doctors, dietitians, and the authors of *novelle* often reveal a contemporary cultural bias when they affirm that the great quantities of vegetables eaten by the poor are the result of a physiological necessity rather than a diet imposed on them for economic reasons. A well-known example of this is to be found in the late sixteenth-century tale of Bertoldo by the Bolognese author Giulio Cesare Croce. In this story, a peasant from the mountains, accustomed to eating turnips and other lowly food, is adopted by a king and lives at his court. As time passes, the peasant Bertoldo becomes increasingly ill, and as the doctors do not know his social origins, they give him the wrong remedies. Bertoldo, who knows what is really wrong and the remedy required, asks for nothing more than some turnips cooked in the ashes of the fire and some fava beans (also associated with the diet of the peasantry). Unfortunately, nobody sees fit to provide him with this simple fare and he finally dies a miserable death. The ironic epitaph on his tomb reminds everyone that, "He who is used to turnips must not eat meat pies."[22]

The *Great Chain of Being* can thus be said to have had a double function. On the one hand, it ordered and classified the natural world; on the other hand, it provided a social value for all the foodstuffs used by man. This double function of classifying and evaluating created a code that could be used to communicate social differences in a subtle way. Every foodstuff had a specific connotation, and even curative diets prescribed by doctors took social status into account as an important variable. As a consequence, all foodstuffs were invested with an outward and apparent value (very much like clothing) and communicated social differences. Little wonder that sumptuary laws paid so much attention to what was served on everybody's plate. In Florence, for example (but one could look elsewhere and find the same phenomenon), a city statute passed in 1415 specified that the course of roasted meats served at wedding banquets could consist of only one capon and a meat pie on each trencher. However, it was also possible to serve a duck and a pie, or two partridges and a pie, or two chickens and a pigeon, or two pigeons and a chicken, or a duck and two pigeons, or even just two chickens. These laws and their obsessive attention to details tried to anticipate all the possible combinations and permutations of an alimentary system that was highly codified. Nevertheless, just as the lawmakers did not manage to foresee new accessories that allowed people to circumvent the rules in the realm of clothing (such as studs instead of buttons), so too did banquet menus find endless loopholes in the laws. Sumptuary laws might have aspired to set limits on constantly evolving concepts of luxury, but in a society where food (and dress) were inextricably associated with social distinctions, legislation did not succeed in disciplining behavior, and ultimately failed.

Notes

First published in English as "Food and Social Classes in Late Medieval and Renaissance Italy" in *Food: a Culinary History*, (New York: Columbia University Press, 1999), 302–312. This essay has been copy-edited for this volume. Notes (which the publisher did not allow in the original version) have been added for the sake of consistency.

1. The English equivalent is companage, a word that the Oxford English Dictionary specifies as being "Now historical and rare."

2. Grieco, Allen J. *Classes sociales, nourriture et imaginaire alimentaire en Italie (XIVe-XVe siècles)*, unpublished PhD thesis, École des Hautes Études en Sciences Sociales, (Paris, 1987), 147.

3. Already pointed out by Louis Stouff, *Ravitaillement et alimentation en Provence aux XIVe et XVe siècles*, (Paris/The Hague: Mouton, 1970), 222 *passim*.

4. Christopher Dyer, *Standards of Living in the Later Middle Ages: social change in England, c. 1200–1520*, (Cambridge/New York: Cambridge University Press, 1989).

5. Benedetto Dei, *La Cronica*, edited by Roberto Barducci, (Florence: Papafava, 1984), 181.

6. "Voi non mi lasciate stare con vostre starne, e cose che Dio sa io non veggio volentieri, e per lo costo; che non mi diletto tanto struggere a uno tratto, e a' goditori non mi contento mandarle, e vendelle non me lo patisce l'animo." Ser Lapo Mazzei, *Lettere di un notaro a un mercante del sec. XIV*, edited by Cesare Guasti, (Florence, 1880), vol. 2, 25.

7. Another excerpt from this extraordinary letter is dealt with in chapter 2, 72.

8. "Così voglio dire a te, vedova, che non puoi mangiare né questo né quell'altro … non voler fare come quando avevi marito, che stavi a polpe d'uccellini." Bernardino da Siena, *Le prediche volgari dette nella Piazza del Campo l'anno 1427*, 3 vols., edited by Luciano Banchi, (Siena: 1880–1888), vol. 2, n. 22, 84.

9. "Io mi diletto di grossi cibi, e quegli più mi fanno forte alle fatiche che porto per regger la famiglia. Avrei vaghezza in questo anno, com'altra volta ho auto in casa, d'uno bariletto picolo di acciughe salate…" Mazzei 1880, vol. 1, 7.

10. Cited without an exact reference in Iris Origo, *The Merchant of Prato*, (Harmondsworth: Penguin, 1979; first English edition, 1963), 288.

11. Ibid.

12. For an example see *Novelle inedite intorno a Bernabò Visconti*, published by Piero Ginori Conti, (Florence: Fondazione Ginori Conti, 1940), VI, 53.

13. Archivio di Stato di Firenze, *Diari di Etichetta*, 1: 43–44 cited by Marcello Fantoni, "Feticci di prestigio: il dono alla corte medicea," in *Rituale, Cerimoniale, Etichetta*, edited by Sergio Bertelli and Giuliano Crifò, (Milan: Bompiani, 1985), 159.

14. For a more complete discussion of *tinelli* see chapter 3, 79–80.

15. "…nous mangeons plus de perdrix & autres chairs delicates qu'eux, ce qui nous rend un sens & une intelligence plus desliée qu'à ceux qui se nourissent de beuf & de pourceau." Florentin de Thierriat, *Trois Traictez scavoir, 1. De la Noblesse de Race, 2. De la Noblesse Civille. 3. Des Immunitez des Ignobles*, (Paris: Lucas Bruneau, 1606), 47–48.

16. The following description of the *Great Chain of Being* is repeated and developed later in this volume, but in both cases it is essential to the development of the argument.

17. On the importance accorded to fruit see chapter 8 in the present volume.

18. For more on plant classifications see chapter 10, 187 *passim*.

19. This is not the exact conclusion I have come to since writing this article. A closer examination of the evidence suggests that quadrupeds were, in fact, considered to be located at the top of the element earth. On this see chapter 14, Figure 14.3, 250 and discussion of the same.

20. Giovanni di Pagolo Rucellai, *Zibaldone*, edited by Gabriella Battista, (Florence: Sismel, 2013), above all 111–112.

21. Baldassare Pisanelli, *Trattato della natura de' cibi et del bere*, (Bologna: Forni, 1980 anastatic edition of the Venice, 1611, ed.), 98.

22. "Chi è uso alle rape non vada ai pasticci." Giulio Cesare Croce, *Le Sottilissime astuzie di Bertoldo; Le Piacevoli e ridicolose simplicità di Bertoldino*, edited by Piero Camporesi, (Turin: Einaudi, 1978), 75.

Chapter 6
Medieval and Renaissance Wines: Taste, Dietary Theory and How to Choose the "Right" Wine (Fourteenth–Sixteenth Centuries)

Reconstructing the taste of the wine made at the end of the Middle Ages and in the Renaissance is a practically impossible task. Although we cannot satisfy this curiosity, it is possible, nevertheless, to analyze what consumers of this period said and thought about the tastes they perceived in the wines they drank. Then, as now, taste, color and provenance were some of the most important criteria in the process of choosing a wine. However, it would be entirely erroneous to think that the tastes, colors or provenance that were sought after, the way of talking about them, the way of classifying them, or, for that matter, their imaginary dimension, have remained the same. The changes that wine has undergone over time have ended up making the evaluations of the past regarding this beverage exceedingly difficult, if not impossible, to understand. Only a full-fledged reconstruction of the ideas and theories in circulation in the past can permit some conclusions about what, at first sight, might seem an inextricable jumble of somewhat recondite concepts. Yet, no matter how abstruse these concepts might seem today, it must be pointed out that they had an undeniable influence on the consumers of the past.

Before going any further, it is necessary to draw attention to how important it is for the historian working on food (and therefore also on wine) to adopt the cognitive categories of the period. In fact, a simple projecting of today's categories on former times is not of much use and often ends up hiding the real reasons influencing behavior. For example, the attempt to understand the choices made by wine drinkers in the Middle Ages and the Renaissance according to the concept of *terroir* (the place where the wine was produced)—now such an important criterion—will not help much in the period we are dealing with. Such an approach, attempted more than once by wine historians,[1] has ended up hiding the fact that most wines, until the end of the sixteenth century, were evaluated and chosen not so much in terms of their provenance (although geographic origin is often mentioned) as for the characteristics tied to the taste they had. This is because it was thought that taste was nothing less than an indicator of the humoral composition of any given wine.

While accounting documents can sometimes mention the provenance of wines, this has been misinterpreted to reflect the precocious emergence of prime production areas. However, such a reading poses more than one problem. First of all, even though the documentation may indicate a production area, it is almost immediately apparent that most areas would have been quite different from the ones we know today. An examination of the wine producing territories mentioned in the past shows that some of these have been forgotten over time or, even more significantly, are now famous for quite another kind of wine. An example of this phenomenon emerges when comparing a wine production map of today with a map derived from the taxation tariffs established in Florence in 1427 by the *Ufficiali del Catasto* [Officers of the Cadaster, the tax and census office].[2] The tariffs established for the *Catasto*, have often been understood as testimony regarding the emergence of recognizable production areas,[3] but, far from corresponding to today's viticulture/vineyards, they suggest a map of quality production that is radically different. Two examples will be enough to illustrate this point. The wine of the upper Valdarno (to be exact the present day Communes of Bucine, Montevarchi and San Giovanni) had the highest tariffs in Tuscany, which indicated a supremacy that it eventually lost, whereas the wine of the Chianti area that was considered most valuable in the past was not the usual red we know today, but rather a white wine.

After the middle of the sixteenth century, the importance of a wine production area seems to emerge in a more explicit manner, as is documented by the famous *lettera* of Sante Lancerio.[4] But here too, referring to a wine's provenance was clearly not enough to characterize it in a satisfactory way. While Sante Lancerio's *lettera* adopts a classification of wines that is based on the areas from which they were sent to Rome, this does not turn out to be a conclusive criterion since even a superficial reading of this text reveals that any given region produced a variety of different wines. In order to somewhat clarify things, the author specifies the characteristics to look for in the best wines of any given region by mentioning the color, the taste (according to a very precise terminology) and often adds some considerations on when and how a specific wine should be drunk.[5]

The behavior of the past, the preferences in terms of taste and the choices made are dictated by criteria that are often (and mistakenly) not taken seriously given that they are deemed devoid of any "scientific" basis, and thus often appear driven by no verifiable motive or, worse still, by purely nonsensical ones. Yet, if we accept to examine such behavior according to the criteria of the past, not only do the elements of choice become more understandable, but even the concepts and the terminology linked to certain choices become more transparent, as I shall demonstrate here through an examination of late medieval and Renaissance dietary lore.

Dietary and Medical Treatises

It is well known that the theory of the four elements—water, earth, air and fire—and the related theory of the four qualities—hot, cold, dry and wet—constituted the backbone of scientific thought in this period, and maybe more importantly for our purpose here, formed the basis of everyday thinking of people for over a millennium.[6] According to these theories, there were correspondences between the elements, the four qualities, the seasons, the different times of the day, and the ages of life. These correspondences meant that it was possible to understand the "order of things" which, in turn, allowed people to make "appropriate" choices in terms of food and diet in order to maintain a balanced humoral constitution necessary for good health. In summer, for example, with its warm and dry weather, humorally "cold" foods and beverages were meant to be consumed, thus allowing the human body to become as ideally "temperate" as possible. Inversely, for old people, who were considered to be naturally "cold," it was suggested that they should be consuming humorally "hot" foods and drinks so as to correct their cooler constitution.[7]

These general dietary rules were asserted and disseminated by doctors, as well as by authors of literary works and even members of the merchant class, who passed such information on to their offspring in household recipe books. Dietary rules were also spread beyond the closed ranks of medical professionals by a variety of other advice literature on diet, derived from various versions of the medieval *Regimen sanitatis salernitanum* and the *Tacuinum sanitatis*.[8] In the following centuries, these texts turned out to be "best sellers," copied in manuscript form and even printed well into the eighteenth century, thus creating and maintaining a medical lore that is still very much rooted in rural areas of Italy and France today.[9] The medieval texts, which were mostly the work of anonymous doctors, were soon joined by yet other medical writings that were no longer anonymous. As of the thirteenth century appear *Regimina sanitatis*, authored by well-known doctors and often dedicated to equally well-known patients. Examples of such works are the *Libello per conservare la sanità* composed by the Florentine physician Taddeo Alderotti for Corso Donati sometime after 1260,[10] and the treatise on healthy eating by Aldobrandino of Siena, *Le Régime du Corps,* composed sometime between 1234 and 1256.[11] The latter text was written in French, a choice that demonstrates to what extent the author, who lived in Troyes (in the Champagne area), wished to reach the broadest possible public. In fact, a large amount of manuscript versions of Aldobrandino's treatise have survived: no less than sixty-eight manuscripts can be dated to the period preceding 1500 (not all of them are complete), which certainly confirms the interest of the French speaking world for this particular work. It was also translated into Latin, Italian, and other European languages, and with four Italian versions, it had a parallel life in this language. A first reconnoitering of the surviving manuscripts has turned up at least 18 manuscripts in various Italian libraries, as well as two printed editions.[12]

In the fourteenth century, treatises on dietary matters continued to elicit a great deal of interest. A clear proof of this are the surviving *Tacuina sanitatis*, of which the more prestigious, illustrated versions[13] are better known, although many manuscripts can be found without any illustrations. Unfortunately these texts, which are often very simple in appearance and circulated in large numbers, have not been much studied at all, even though they can be found in practically any important European library with a manuscript collection. Dietary literature of this sort continued to be popular in the fifteenth and sixteenth centuries, and actually underwent a major transformation that ended up modifying the somewhat standardized presentation of the *Tacuina*, even though the content was not changed. For example, even a superficial examination of the well-known treatise of Michele Savonarola composed between 1450 and 1452 and presented to Borso d'Este,[14] reveals how close this text is to the *Tacuina*. Much the same could be said about the work of Baldassarre Pisanelli, first published in 1583.[15] Pisanelli adopts the typical *Tacuina* layout, which tended to follow a kind of standardized form in which would be listed, amongst other things, the humoral composition of any given food or drink, who would benefit from consuming it, what season it should be consumed in, and so forth. Pisanelli's innovation on this time-tried genre lies in an additional paragraph of what he calls *"Historie naturali"* for each one of the foodstuffs examined. Here he presents curious details and at times even classical anecdotes on the foods and drink he is examining, with quotes from Latin and Greek authors.

Above and beyond this already abundant literature, ideas concerning dietary notions could also be derived from the great number of plague treatises that began to proliferate immediately after 1348, and continued to be written as late as the end of the fifteenth century.[16] These treatises contained almost always one or two chapters on dietary matters, since certain precautions were considered important in order not to fall prey to the plague. Tommaso del Garbo's *Consiglio contro a pistolenza*,[17] for example, composed shortly after 1348, dedicates no less than ten chapters (out of thirty-two) to what should be eaten in order to avoid the plague, while four deal with what should be drunk.[18]

The dietary notions contained in these different types of texts were repeated and circulated so often that they finally constituted a body of knowledge adopted well beyond the medical profession. The spread of this information came about, however, not so much via the high-end treatises composed for famous and important patrons, but rather via the diffusion of letters and recommendations composed by more humble doctors, writing for patients who belonged to the merchant middle classes. A letter written by Lorenzo Sassoli in May 1404 to Francesco di Marco Datini, the wealthy merchant of Prato who was both his patient and benefactor, is an excellent example of how a great deal of dietary notions could be circulated in quite informal ways. Sassoli informed Datini as to what he could eat and what he should eliminate from his diet. These recommendations, however, were not delivered in the usual, rather rigid, framework of a treatise, but rather in a much more personal letter to his patient. That this advice was actually taken seriously can be surmised by the fact that Datini wrote on the back of this letter that the prescriptions sent to him by this doctor were meant for his own "person."[19]

Similar medical/dietary advice was proffered by another doctor, Ugolino da Montecatini, writing for Averardo de' Medici just a few years later than Sassoli.[20] In this text, as in all others from this period, are repeated guidelines that were, by then, generally known. Merchants and literary figures knew these rules and replicated them in their own writings. In his *Ricordi*, Giovanni di Pagolo Morelli explained to his sons (for whom he was writing) the way to behave when a new wave of the plague seemed to be approaching. His practical advice begins with how the plague spread, where best to take refuge, and how much money to take with you when fleeing the city. All of these aspects are more or less rapidly dealt with. However, much more attention is devoted to the problem of how to eat and drink (both before and after the plague) so as not to be predisposed to this terrifying illness.[21] The recommendations written up by Morelli closely follow the advice found in all treatises dedicated to the plague, and were thus not offered as the recommendations of a specialist but only as general rules that any doctor would confirm and elaborate on. As Morelli himself pointed out: "at present I will not write any more about this matter because, to tell the truth, trusted doctors who know your nature would be the best people to instruct you as to these measures. Therefore, as I have told you, you should take counsel with them..."[22]

The massive and capillary circulation of medical knowledge deeply influenced the way in which consumers behaved, even though this knowledge could not be considered to be foolproof. Medical recommendations regarding food and health that had originally developed in the medical milieu were considered valuable in everyday life, but especially appropriate in periods when plague was known to be arriving. This, at least, is what Giovanni di Pagolo Morelli suggested when he wrote in his memories that "…it is quite clear that in mortal combat those who are well armed have a greater advantage and less of them die than those who are disarmed; so, I would like to say that remedies are a good thing."[23]

The dissemination of information on plague and on appropriate diets to be followed in such circumstances was so widespread that by the fifteenth century it was hardly necessary to be a doctor to write on dietary advice. An example of this general medical knowledge appears in Marsilio Ficino's *Consilio*, published in Florence in 1481, a treatise that went through a good number of editions in both Italian and in Latin.[24] Yet another example of dietary information having expanded beyond the exclusive preserve of doctors comes from a very successful book published by the Bolognese humanist Geronimo Manfredi: *Libro intitolato il perché*. In this volume Manfredi not only answers a variety of questions linked to human diets but also discusses different foods in rime, a mnemonic device reminiscent of the canonical Salernitan model. Manfredi's book was first published in Italian in 1474 and only later translated and published in a Latin version, but was to be reprinted in both languages up until the middle of the seventeenth century.[25]

In fact, doctors and the conceptual framework that structured their medical knowledge not only ended up determining a way of thinking about food and drink but, predictably, they exerted an influence on the way in which people ate. An indication of how successful these ideas really were comes from the fact that these concepts were not limited to the upper strata of the patrician and merchant classes, but percolated down to the lower levels of society, where they ended up being lodged in an oral tradition that has survived more or less to the present. Proverbs and folk sayings are notoriously difficult to date, but some of those recorded in the mid nineteenth century clearly demonstrate continuity with medieval dietary concepts.[26]

The Axes of Taste

Medieval and Renaissance dietary theory applied to all foodstuffs including wine, a product that was as ubiquitous as bread on the tables of this period.

Understanding the humoral characteristics of wine entailed, however, a greater attention to the taste and color of this drink than for foodstuffs in general. In order to understand the criteria used by the *consumers* of the fourteenth to the sixteenth centuries for choosing their wines, it is necessary to turn to the cognitive categories of the past. In an earlier article on medieval wines, the premises of medical and literary sources, corroborated by the account books of the Florentine *Signoria,* revealed the longue durée of terminology used for the taste and color of wine from the Trecento to the Cinquecento.[27] Out of this analysis emerged what seems to have been a widespread binary system, an opposition between strong sweet wines at one end, and sharp or bitter (hence weak wines) on the other. This opposition, a kind of taste "axis," permitted an unlimited series of intermediate tastes between the extremes. The late medieval "taste axis" is worth exploring, not so much from the point of view of antiquarian erudition, but above all because the opposition between sweet wines and acid ones had an impact on the ways the wines were used, and structured the imaginary associations that accompanied them.

Both doctors and moralists recommended that sweet and powerful wines (*malvasia* and *vino greco* being the best known examples) be consumed only in very small quantities and, in any case, on particular occasions (such as festivities or marriage banquets) or then, alternatively, for strict medical reasons. That these recommendations were not purely theoretical but also respected in practice can be inferred by looking at the account books of the Florentine *Signoria,* as well as at evidence from literary texts.[28] If a limited consumption of sweet wines was not respected, it was believed that a rich and varied series of consequences would follow. It was commonly thought that a person risked both physical and "moral" problems, because such wines produced a dangerous over-heating of the body.[29] Inversely, the acid and weak wines were considered to be "healthier," both from a purely physiological point of view as from a "moral" one.

Wine, or more correctly wines in the plural, were considered by both doctors and authors of dietary texts as having humorally variable characteristics. Such variability was entirely atypical insofar as concerns food and drink derived from other plants and animals, since all other foodstuffs were assigned a univocal humoral characteristic.[30] Yet the illustrated *Tacuina* of the late fourteenth century dedicated at least three or four separate chapters (and illustrations) to wine, in order to document the humoral differences that they were believed to have. Normally the *Tacuina* speak of *vinum citrinum, vinum album, vinum rubeum grossum, vinum vetus odoriferum*. This classification of wines into four categories was to be picked up and recirculated by the dietary treatises of the fifteenth and sixteenth centuries. More than reflecting actual market denominations, the various categories of wine seem to have furnished a useful "scientific" description that also allowed consumers to extrapolate the humoral characteristics of any given wine, even though these same categories, which can be found in all of the *tacuina*, never seem to appear in accounting documents.

The differences between wines and their supposed humoral characteristics can best be understood by moving beyond the somewhat laconic treatment of the *tacuina* and delving into the more prolix explanations provided by medical and dietary treatises. Such treatises not only permit a reconstruction of the ways in which wines and their characteristics were understood, but define the criteria that were adopted when it became necessary to choose, according to these same criteria, the "right" wine for a specific person.

The first problem raised by medical and dietary texts is how to understand the "nature" of a given wine. Michele Savonarola, for example, dedicates a whole chapter of his treatise to identifying the various types of wine and concisely summarizes the basic humoral definition of his time: all wines can be considered to be "hot." One century later, Cesare Crivellati, a doctor from Viterbo and the author of the *Trattato dell'uso et modo di dare il vino nelle malattie acute*, (published in Rome in 1550), confirms the "hotness" of all wines in the third chapter of his treatise dedicated to "What Wine Is." While he acknowledges that it is difficult to generalize about the nature of wine, he nonetheless asserts: "...most doctors have said that wine is hot and wet, an opinion which to my mind has more reason behind it than other opinions..."[31] Yet such a generalization could not cover all possible variants: Crivellati himself points out the complexity of wines by observing that "there are different types of wines, since some of them are new wines, some old ones, some white, some red, some sweet, some "austere," some raw, some cooked, some navigated,[32] others not navigated, some odorous, others lacking odors, some from the mountains, others from the valleys, some powerful, others weak, some fine, others gross, some tasty, others insipid…"[33]

Michele Savonarola is much less detailed in his description of wine, but equally careful not to generalize. He specifies that all wines can be considered to be "hot," but possess this quality in differing degrees. In fact, they distinguish themselves from each other according to four different degrees of heat, in the same way as all the other qualities (dry, wet and cold), which also have four different degrees. According to Savonarola: "…the smallest wine is in the first degree, the next is more powerful but still small is in the second degree, and then come the others such as 'vernaccia' wines, malmsey, 'maroa' and similar wines which are in the third degree. However, *eau de vie* or 'spirit of vine', or fire water, although made with wine, is in the fourth degree…"[34] It would seem, therefore, that at least one of the criteria that contributed to make a wine more (or less) "hot" is what we today call its alcoholic content.

"Heat" was only one of the many criteria that determined the nature of a wine. Another was smell, which conveyed yet other information regarding its nature. In writing about the taste and odor of wine, Savonarola describes a way of tasting wine that might seem to be a very modern practice but was actually dictated by very different reasons. First of all, he reminds his reader that "…the one [wine] that has a good odor, a strong one, and a pleasant one, this one is hotter and more powerful … the middling one does not have a strong odor…"[35] He then goes on to say that "…the inhabitants of Padua, who know this better, always shake[36] the wine first in the glass and then put their nose to it in order to judge it. If they do not perceive an odor they make fun of the wine saying that it is a very 'weak' one."[37]

The criterion of smell relative to the analysis of wines was, however, insufficient to determine with absolute certainty the nature of a wine. The humoral composition was influenced by a series of factors, amongst which might be remembered the growing of grapes in different sites such as those mentioned by Crivellati (hillsides, valleys, swampy areas, etc.).[38] Furthermore, it is important to point out that both the ageing of wine and the color it presented were thought to influence its humoral nature. Savonarola reminds his readers that "...the more it ages, the more it gets hot and dry..." and that "white wine, all things being equal, is less powerful, because it has less 'matter' and the more it is white the more this is so. Dark wines [literally:*"black"* wines] are more powerful, such as *cropelli*.[39] The wines between these two [extremes] are midway in strength."[40] The oppositions described by Savonarola were, however, hardly original. As Crivellati points out in a more philological vein, they were already put forth by Galen: "...the strength of wine, as Gal.(en) points out in more than one passage, can be deduced from many different things such as the color, the taste & and the age..."[41] Even agricultural treatises, while constituting a more practical approach to the cultivation of vines and to the making of wine, mention the link between the color of a wine and its humoral configuration. A treatise composed by Corniolo della Cornia between the end of the fourteenth and early fifteenth century draws attention to the evolution in the color of wine over time, and points out how the two factors of color and age could reveal the nature of a wine:

> White and black are simple colors while red and gold are composed with them. Glaucous or greenish and pinkish are between red and white. Pallid and 'sub-pallid' are between golden and citrine colored. All of these are generated in the following manner. Clearly wine made from white grapes is, at first, white due to its watery nature and its rawness but also to its lack of natural heat. However, once it will have aged more than a year, heat begins to develop and the humidity decreases. It then changes color and becomes off-white. But if it is aged for more than two years it becomes increasingly hot and less humid while becoming '*palmeo*'[42] in color. If it is aged more than four years ... it will have a citrine color...[43]

This analysis of wine color and characteristics by Corniolo della Cornia does not end with the various kinds of white wines since he also examines red ones and the so called "black" wines (what today are considered the darkest reds). These passages in his treatise, too long to cite here, reconfirm the theories that circulated at the time concerning the idea that the more a wine was strongly colored, sweet or aged, the more it was humorally "hot."

Inversely, wines that tended to be white in color (transparent and not "ful-vous or tawny" as Crivellati also specifies), along with those that had a taste tending towards the acidic, and those that were young, were all humorally "colder" ones.[44]

One of the best ways for analyzing a wine and, more generally, any kind of food, was to judge it on the basis of the taste it had. Even the authors of sixteenth-century treatises mention what Avicenna had already pointed out, namely that it was easier to judge the nature of a medicine or of a foodstuff by its taste than by its appearance, its smell or by touching it. This predominance of taste over the other senses seems to have been determined by the fact that it was informed by the tongue, which combines both a tactile sense as well as that of taste.[45] Medieval theory distinguished a greater number of tastes than the four that we recognize today as being fundamental (salty, sweet, acidic and bitter);[46] depending on the treatise, there were anywhere from a minimum of seven to a maximum of thirteen distinct tastes attributed to food (and medicines). All of these tastes had quite different qualities associated with them that determined whether the food in question was closer to the "cold" side of things, or veered towards the "hot" (see Fig. 2).[47] In this way it was also possible to judge, on the basis of the tastes perceived, the humoral composition of a wine.

The Right Wine for the Right Person

Once the nature of a given wine was determined—according to its degree of "heat," provenance, color and taste—there were at least four other conditions that had to be taken into consideration in order to choose the most appropriate wine. First of all, it was essential to know the humoral constitution of the person who was going to drink it. Secondly, it was important to determine what food was going to be eaten with it. Thirdly, it was necessary to take into account the time of the year in which the wine was to be drunk and, finally, it was important to consider the geographic location the wine came from.

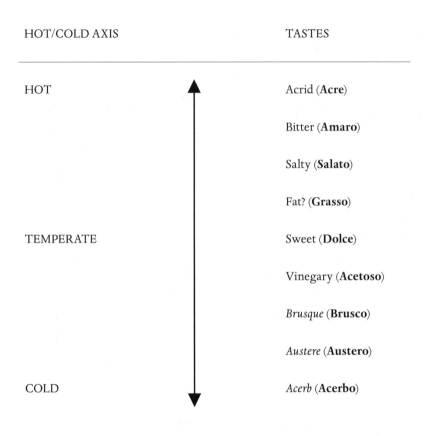

HOT/COLD AXIS	TASTES
HOT	Acrid (**Acre**)
	Bitter (**Amaro**)
	Salty (**Salato**)
	Fat? (**Grasso**)
TEMPERATE	Sweet (**Dolce**)
	Vinegary (**Acetoso**)
	Brusque (**Brusco**)
	Austere (**Austero**)
COLD	*Acerb* (**Acerbo**)

Fig. 2 The Medieval ladder of tastes.*

* This table constitutes a partial reconstruction of the terms used to describe tastes in the later Middle Ages and Renaissance. More terminology is mentioned in Rashmi Patni's thesis (see note 46). The Italian terms in brackets are not easily translatable into English, even though most of them have antiquated English equivalents (here in italics), cited in the *Oxford English Dictionary*.

Insofar as the humoral constitution of the consumer was concerned, there were some general rules that defined the specific constitution of each age group without having to go into the type of more refined diagnosis proper to doctors. The younger a person, the hotter they were supposed to be; consequently wine, a "hot" substance, was not appropriate for consumption by the young and thus not recommended. Baldassarre Pisanelli uses a telling metaphor in his *Trattato della natura de' cibi et del bere* when he says that wine should not be served to children "because it adds fire to fire on top of weak wood." Even young people that are still growing, according to him, should not drink wine "because since they have a hot and fervent nature they risk their soul and their body catching on fire and becoming furiously agitated." Inversely, for old people who become increasingly "cold" because of their age, wine was considered almost a medicine. In fact, wine: "is given to the elderly as a suitable thing for their nature and because its heat reduces the coldness of that age to the point of reaching a good and proper temperament."[48] Typical in medieval and Renaissance medical theory, these ideas continued to enjoy great success throughout the early modern period, penetrating social and cultural strata quite distant from those addressed by authors of dietary advice literature. Even proverbs declared, for example, that "Old age does not want games but rather wine, heat and fire,"[49] a notion clearly based on the idea that "We are born hot and die cold."[50]

It was also important to choose the right wine in function of what was eaten. Such a choice was not meant to combine tastes in a pleasurable way, but rather to oppose hot and cold elements in an ideal equilibrium that would bring about the best constitution possible, a temperate constitution. If, for example, fish were eaten (considered cold and humid) or various kinds of fruit (also considered mostly cold), it was thought best to drink a humorally "hot" wine that would correct the "coldness" of the food eaten.[51] The practice of such "compensatory drinking" ended up having a long success, as can be seen again in proverbs that reiterated such notions. Unfortunately, some of the variants that illustrate this mechanism are practically impossible to translate, and lose their original catchy rhythm or rhyme: "With fish, serve wine,"[52] "Cow's ribs and wine without water,"[53] or "Peaches, pears and apples require good [strong] wines."[54]

The two final variables that had to be taken into account—the time of year and the provenance of wine—were somehow connected to each other. The season in which a type of food or a kind of drink was consumed would be conditioned by its geographic origin, insofar as the degree of heat or cold that reigned in its place of production would become one of its characteristics. According to the "compensatory" theory regarding food/drink, it was necessary to consume (humorally) cold things in summer so as to compensate for seasonal heat and, inversely, to eat and drink (humorally) hot things in winter. Similarly, places that were prone to warm weather called for the same kind of precautions regarding food and drink. Pisanelli, like most authors of dietetic treatises at the time, wrote that: "…if the heat of the air, of the season, and of the region is moderate, it will be suitable for the cooling to be moderate, but if (the heat) is a lot it will be necessary for a lot of cooling since cooling is nothing else than the tempering of heat." This generalization then leads Pisanelli to a consideration that demonstrates the practical consequences of this theory: "…in the island of Sicily, where the heat is excessive, and the water is not very cold, before they introduced the use of snow,[55] every year, in the course of the Summer, a great many people died of fevers and pestilence…"[56] More than a century earlier, Michele Savonarola advised his ward Borso d'Este with regard to the same "compensatory" rule. During the cold months of the year, he imposed food that was particularly nourishing and humorally "hot," to compensate the loss of the "natural heat" of the body at this time of the year. According to Savonarola "…in winter one must not eat light things that are not nourishing, nor should one eat vegetables, but rather eat solid things that provide good and abundant nourishment. The reason for this is that the [body's] natural heat will thus be greater in this time of the year while in summer it should be the opposite."[57]

If a wine drinker wanted to respect current dietary theory, they were faced with a series of problems that were not easy to solve. The first task was to determine the humoral qualities of the wine to be drunk, according to a number of variables such as color, taste and provenance, all of which could be mutually reinforcing or even cancel each other out. Once the qualities of a wine had been established, there was still the problem of matching a given wine with the age and constitution of the drinker, the season in which it was consumed, and the food it was to accompany. This complexity might suggest that consumers would not have worried too much about all of these theories, and would have ended up simply drinking the wines most easily available on the market. Yet a variety of documents—such as the *lettera* composed by Sante Lancerio concerning the qualities of the different wines[58] drunk (but also declined) by Pope Paul III—amply support the premise that current dietary guidelines were respected whenever possible. A reading of the Lancerio text, and a careful comparison of the fifty-seven entries it contains, make it clear that the Pope closely followed the prescriptions of doctors and dietary experts. In fact, in summer he drank "small" wines with low alcohol content as they were considered "cold" wines. In winter he chose sweet and more alcoholic wines, which were thought to be "hotter."[59] He also drank some "hot" wines because of his advanced age.[60] In consonance with the dietary code is the fact that the Pope chose to drink "smaller" wines whenever he could, and that he never allowed himself to drink the most powerful and sweet wines, even when the weather was very cold. This was, of course, because the latter would not have been considered appropriate for a Pope, given the relationship between strong and sweet wines and the sin of lust. The wines of "Mangiaguerra," for example, were considered particularly "hot" since, according to Lancerio, "...on the whole they are wines for courtesans intended to excite lust." Appropriately, he concludes this entry with the mention that "Such wine was never drunk by his Holiness..."[61]

The rules that Pope Paul III followed in choosing his wines were widely respected by many other consumers, long before the middle of the sixteenth century. Literary texts of the fourteenth century specify that the wines served at banquets were chosen in terms of the time of the year in which they were drunk. Giovanni Gherardi da Prato, for example, in his *Paradiso degli Alberti*, mentions that in banquets there was a "great wealth of very precious wines in function of what the time of the year required..."[62] But it is above all private correspondence that reveals individuals' behavior with regard to wine. Thanks to the letters of Lapo Mazzei, that often deal with such issues, it becomes obvious that both he and his rich friend Francesco di Marco Datini bought special wines for the first hot months of the summer. These wines came from the Arno valley upstream from Florence (Bucine, Torre, Galatrona, San Leolino, etc.) and had qualities that made them particularly appropriate for a limited period of the year. In a letter dated 8 December 1400 Ser Lapo wrote to Francesco saying that "I bought two *cogna* of wine from Torre... I want to give some to the *Signori* (of Florence) and to you if you come back for the summer."[63] Some years earlier, on 20 June 1395, he had been even more explicit when he wrote that:

This morning while Sandro, Niccolò d'Andrea and I were walking towards Orto Sa' Michele, Sandro was so thirsty, because of the heat of last night, that he had a dry mouth. Not finding anybody who would invite us for anything [i.e. a drink] which we had decided to accept, I said, if Francesco were here we would have been able to have some [wine] from Bucine. Because of this and since he is a lively person, he answered: 'Ser Lapo, please tell him that I said that after the middle of July that wine tastes of leather and that, by God, he should drink it. However, before that date, it is the best wine in the world...'[64]

The wine referred to by Ser Lapo was produced in a circumscribed area in the Valdarno Superiore, where the high quality of produce was documented, as we have seen, in the 1427 Catasto.[65] But even much earlier, Giovanni di Pagolo Morelli, whose *ricordanze* were written in the course of the 1380s, suggested that his sons buy the wine from this area in order to be able to offer some to their neighbors in summer.[66] No less than two centuries later this wine was still known and much appreciated by Sante Lancerio, who referred to it as "Trebbiano," and according to whom "it comes to Rome from the Florentine state of the upper Valdarno and from many other places but the best (wines) are from San Giovanni and Figline." In the meantime, however, this slightly sweet wine was no longer recommended for the beginning of the summer but rather "in autumn, between the old and the new season."[67]

The complex and even abstruse theories that determined the choice of a wine on the part of contemporary drinkers must have been difficult to master in their entirety. In another of Ser Lapo Mazzei's letters, he accuses both his friend Francesco and his wife because, according to him, neither one of them knew how to correctly determine the humoral constitution of wines. On 27 September 1395 he wrote: "I tell you that Mona Margherita does not know anything about these things and neither do you. I would believe her about anything other than about cold and hot wines." Ser Lapo was not mentioning this issue for purely speculative reasons but for much more practical ones. As the rest of the letter shows, he was not only explaining what kind of wines were appropriate for the different seasons, but was also suggesting how to intervene and to modify the characteristics of a given vintage. In fact, he suggests mixing some sweet must into a wine that normally was not consumed (or sold) in winter, in order to make it more acceptable for that season, either for the Datini couple or for sale. In pursuing his point he writes to his friend that:

> Do as I tell you this time around. From tomorrow on make sure to get a barrel of good white wine that will be slightly, or not at all, fermented, that is to say crushed, and put in a barrel.[68] That barrel will be necessary whether you drink the wine or sell it because now that it is cold, you would not get much money for it. Once you have added that barrel [of good wine] you will see what it will do [to it] and you will see that were you to sell it, you would get two florins a barrel, if you decide not to drink it yourself.[69]

This technique was thought to be necessary to make the wine more acceptable, both for home consumption and for commercial purposes. Reminding his friend that the resulting wine could serve in either way suggests that his ideas concerning the nature of wines and the rules that were followed by the wine market were, ultimately, one and the same. Lapo also lists the wines that Datini would consume in winter and in summer, reminding him that "...make sure you have a barrel of white, sweet wine, for this winter, for monna Margherita and yourself. For summer you will get some from Vieri, I mean Trebbiano wine."[70] He then concludes the letter pointing out that the same "corrective" procedure should be carried out to improve some red wine which he perceives has a *"brusco"* (brusque)[71] taste. This taste placed it closer to the cold end of the scale (see Fig. 2), which would not have been recommended for the oncoming cold season. In fact, he explains: "And in the same way, from tomorrow on, make sure that you send two *some* [unit of measure, literally a mule load] of red wine that has not fermented very much, so it can be added to the *brusco* wine. This is the way to "fortify" it, whether you intend to sell it or to drink it yourself."[72]

Medical theories influenced not only the tastes of the consumers but also ended up influencing the way in which wines were actually made. The impact of such theories on production is much more conspicuous (even explicit) in agronomic texts dealing with wine and the growing of grapes. Two of these treatises—the *Divina Villa* by Corniolo della Cornia, dating from the end of the fourteenth or early fifteenth century, and the much later *Della eccellenza e diversità de i vini che nella montagna di Torino si fanno e del modo di farli* by Giovanni Battista Croce (published in 1606)—demonstrate the extent to which medical theories influenced authors writing on agricultural matters. Often these theories remained more or less implicit in the work of agronomists, when they recommend adding a substance to alter the characteristics of a wine. An example among many regards the so-called *"vino salviato"* (sage wine) in which sage leaves—thought to be hot and dry—were added to wine during the fermentation process.[73] The result of this addition was, of course, a wine that "Suits the winter months and cold stomachs as well as chests closed by a cold and coarse humours..."[74] Upon occasion, a more explicit statement is made regarding medical theory, such as in the description of a technique used *"A riffreddare el vino caldo"* (To cool a hot wine). This called for a phial of quick silver or a piece of lead, both "cold" metals, to be suspended in a barrel *"a mezzo il vino"* (in the middle of the wine) and then taken out to be washed every morning and evening, as if to remove the heat that they had absorbed.[75]

Writing two centuries after Corniolo Della Cornia, Giovanni Battista Croce was still concerned with much the same ideas and looked for solutions in order to satisfy the demands of a market that had practically not changed. Croce wrote, in fact, that wines are "...sought after according to the seasons. And those that are enjoyed in winter do not please in spring, nor are those of spring enjoyed in summer. This is why one needs to have wines for every season." This statement then leads him to propose his recipe for a wine he calls *"Melon"* that, as its name indicates, was meant to be drunk in summer with this fruit. Melons, like all of the family of the cucurbits, were classified as a "cold" fruit and therefore suitable for consumption in summer.[76] The nature of melons was, however, excessively cold, which was the reason why it became necessary to temper this characteristic with a "hot" wine.[77] Croce continues, specifying that

> ...during the dog days, when the natural [body] heat diminishes and the appetite decreases, when one eats a lot of fruit and above all melons, then people seek, both for taste and for health, to drink the best and the most powerful (wines) that can be found. It would be an inexcusable omission on my part were I to fail mentioning the way to make wine that is called Melon.[78]

The criteria required of a good tasting wine were, therefore, practically identical to those of a healthy wine—if, in fact, they had ever been considered different.

Notes

Translated from the Italian "I sapori del vino: gusti e criteri di scelta fra Trecento e cinquecento," in Jean-Louis Gaulin and Allen J. Grieco, *Dalla vite al vino. Fonti e problemi della vitivinicoltura italiana medievale* (Bologna: Clueb, 1994) and first published in English as "Medieval and Renaissance Wines: Taste, Dietary Theory, and How to 'Choose' the Right Wine (14th- 16th Centuries)," in *Mediaevalia*, vol. 30, (2009), 15–42. The body of the article has not been changed, compared to the original version, while some of the notes have been revised to reflect the research published in the years since this article first came out. The essay has been copy edited to better conform to the style of the present volume.

1. An excellent example of this kind of approach may be found in the work of Federigo Melis, now collected in *I Vini Italiani nel Medioevo*, edited by A. Affortunati Parrini (Florence: Le Monnier, 1984). See, above all, the four essays in the section on *"Zone di Produzione,"* 137–173.

2. Published by Elio Conti, *La Formazione della Struttura Agraria Moderna nel Contado Fiorentino* (Rome: Istituto Storico Italiano per il Medioevo, 1966), vol. 3, part 1, 46–47.

3. See Conti 1966, 46–47 but also Federigo Melis, "Il Consumo del vino a Firenze nei decenni attorno al 1400," in Melis 1984, above all 34–54.

4. *"Della qualità dei vini,"* (Of wine qualities) now also published in a more accessible form with an introduction by Emilio Faccioli, *L'Arte della cucina in Italia. Libri di ricette e trattati sulla civiltà della tavola dal XIV al XIX secolo*, (Turin: Einaudi, 1987), 329–355.

5. See, for example, what Sante Lancerio says about the *"vino corso"* (Corsican wine), *"Della qualità dei vini,"* in Faccioli 1987, 336.

6. The vast amount of publications on this topic is not always very reliable but the reader may consult the useful volume on *Les quatre éléments dans la culture médiévale* (Actes du Colloque d'Amiens, 25–27 March 1982), edited by D. Buschinger and A. Crépin (Göppingen: Kümmerle, 1983). For a more recent study see Ken Albala, *Eating Right in the Renaissance* (Berkeley: University of California Press, 2002).

7. This is not the place to examine in detail all of the variables in medieval and Renaissance dietary theories, many of which had not been investigated at the time this article was published. Since then much work has been done on the subject and it is now possible to turn to the monumental monograph by Marilyn Nicoud, *Les Régimes de Santé au Moyen Age: naissance et diffusion d'une écriture médicale. XIIIe-XVe siècle* (Rome, Ecole Française de Rome, 2007), as well as Ken Albala's book mentioned in the previous note.

8. Given the research that has been carried out since the writing of this article, it is now apparent that the world of dietary texts is far more complex than is suggested here.

9. Concerning the longue durée of this knowledge see Pierre Lieutaghi, "Commentaire historique, botanique et medical," in Platearius, *Le livre des simples médicines d'après le manuscrit français 12322 de la Bibliothèque nationale de Paris*, (Paris: Ozalid/ Bibliothèque Nationale, 1986), 284–312.

10. See the "Lettera di Taddeo Alderotti a Corso Donati e l'inizio della letteratura igienica medievale," in *Atti del XXI Congresso Internazionale di Storia della Medicina* (Siena, 1968), vol. 1, 91–99. For a brief discussion of this text see Nancy Siraisi, *Taddeo Alderotti and his Pupils* (Princeton: University Press, 1981), 292–293.

11. On problems relating to dating see Aldobrandino da Siena, *Le Régime du corps*,

edited by L. Landouzy and R. Pépin, (Paris: Champion, 1911; reprint edition Geneva: Slatkine, 1978), LIV–LV.

12. For a list of Aldobrandino manuscripts and first editions see Françoise Fery-Hue, "Le Régime du Corps de Aldebrandin de Sienne: tradition manuscrite et diffusion," in *Actes du Congrès National des Sociétés Savante, Section Histoire Médiévale* (Montpellier, 1985), vol. 1, 113–134. See also the review of this article in Odile Redon, *Bullettino Senese di Storia Patria* (Siena, 1992), vol. 99, 430–31. It is now possible to turn to the introduction and edition of the earliest known Italian translation: Rossella Baldini, "Zucchero Bencivenni, 'La Santà del Corpo'. Volgarizzamento del 'Régime du corps' di Aldobrandino da Siena (a. 1310) nella copia coeva di Lapo di Neri Corsini (Laur. Pl. LXXIII 47)," in *Studi di Lessicografia Italiana* (1998), vol. 15, 21–300.

13. Concerning these illustrated versions see Luisa Cogliati Arano, *Tacuinum sanitatis* (Milan: Electa, 1979).

14. For a critical edition and a presentation of this important text see: Michele Savonarola, *Libretto de tutte le cosse che se magnano: un'opera di dietetica del secolo XV*, critical edition by J. Nystedt, (Stockholm: Almqvist & Wiksell, 1988).

15. The edition consulted for the present article is the one published in Venice in 1611, anastatic reprint (Forni: Bologna, 1980).

16. For an overview of these treatises see Karl Sudhoff, "Pestschriften aus den ersten 150 jahren nach der epidemie des 'schwarzen Todes' 1348," in *Archiv für Geschichte der Medizin*, vol. 4 (June, 1911) and vol. 5 (January, 1913).

17. Edited by P. Ferrato (Bologna, 1866).

18. Almost all of the chapters of this treatise touch on dietary matters but the ones specifically dedicated to food are chapters nine

through eighteen while those dealing with drink are chapters nineteen, twenty, twenty-seven and twenty-nine.

19. Ser Lapo Mazzei, *Lettere di un notaro a un mercante*, edited by C. Guasti (Florence, 1880), vol. 2, 370, note 6.

20. For an edition of this and a brief comment on the text see Ugolino da Montecatini, "Consiglio medico ad Averardo de' Medici," edited by F. Baldasseroni and G. Degli Azzi, *Archivio Storico Italiano*, serie quinta, no. 38, 1906, 140–152.

21. Giovanni di Pagolo Morelli, *Ricordi*, edited by V. Branca (Florence, 1956), 287–302.

22. "...al presente non iscriverò più avanti sopra la detta materia, perché nel vero i medici fidati e che conoscono la tua natura sarebbero quelli che meglio t'ammaestrerebbono di tale provvedimento; et però, com'è ditto, il consiglio si vuole avere da loro..." Giovanni di Pagolo Morelli 1956, 301–302.

23. "...è assai chiaro che a una zuffa mortale ha gran vantaggio chi è bene armato, e meno ne muoiono che de' disarmati; e però vo' dire che' rimedi sono buoni." Giovanni di Pagolo Morelli 1956, 293.

24. For the Italian text of the 1481 edition and an introduction see Marsilio Ficino, *Consilio contro la pestilenzia*, edited by E. Musacchio (Bologna: Cappelli, 1983).

25. For information on the many editions of this curious volume see Mario Emilio Cosenza, *Biographical and Bibliographical Dictionary of the Italian Humanists and the World of Classical Scholarship in Italy 1300–1800* (Boston, 1962), vol. 3, 2117–2118.

26. Proverbs have been a relatively little-used source by Italian historians until the recent book published by Massimo Montanari, *Il formaggio con le pere: la storia in un proverbio* (Bari: Laterza, 2008). See, for example, the

work of Françoise Loux and Pierre Richard, *Sagesses du corps: la santé et la maladie dans les proverbes français*, (Paris: Maisonneuve et Larose, 1978) and Daniele Rivière, "Le thème alimentaire dans le discours proverbial de la Renaissance française," in *Pratiques et discours alimentaires à la Renaissance*, edited by J.-Cl. Margolin and R. Sauzet, (Paris: Maisonneuve et Larose, 1982). For a very complete collection of proverbs on wine that unfortunately does not follow very clear classifying rules see *Buon vino, favola lunga: vite e vino nei proverbi delle regioni italiane*, edited by M. L. Buseghin (Perugia: Electa Editori Umbri, 1992). Among the proverbs expressing medieval medical concepts see numbers 2664–2667, 2920–2922, 2952–2968, etc.

27. Allen J. Grieco, "Le goût du vin entre doux et amer: essai sur la classification des vins au Moyen Age," in *Le vin des historiens*, edited by G. Garrier, (Suze-la-Rousse: Université du vin, 1990), 89–97.

28. For a graph detailing the consumption of sweet wines by the *Signoria* see Grieco 1990, 92–93.

29. For a somewhat lengthier discussion of this phenomenon see Grieco 1990, in particular pages 94–95.

30. Products derived from animals also varied according to the age of an animal.

31. "...la maggior parte de i Medici hanno detto il vino esser caldo, & umido, la quale opinione secondo me ha molto più che le altre del ragionevole..." Cesare Crivellati, *Trattato dell'uso et modo di dare il vino nelle malattie acute* (Rome, 1550; anastatic reprint ed., Bologna: Forni, 1989), 20.

32. Crivellati is here referring to the wines transported on boats since it was thought that their trips made them better. This is a very early reference to a practice that became quite common in the eighteenth century.

33. "...diverse sono le spetie e i Vini essendo che di essi altri sieno nuovi, altri vecchi, altri bianchi, altri rossi, altri dolci, altri austeri, altri crudi, altri cotti, altri navigati, altri non navigati, altri odorosi, altri senza odore, altri di monte, altri di piano, altri potenti, altri deboli, altri sottili, altri grossi, altri saporiti, altri insipidi..." Crivellati 1989, 20–21. The many oppositions mentioned by this author might seem fanciful to the present day reader but, as we will see further on, constitute some of the variables that were thought to influence the nature of wines.

34. "...il più picolo nella prima, l'altro, ch'è più potente benchè picolo in la secunda e cussì del'altri come vernace malvasia maroa e somegianti nele mansione del terzo. Ma l'aqua de vita overo de vida, zoè ardente, fatta pur del vino nel quarto..." Savonarola 1988, 151–152.

35. "...quello che bon odore e forte è delectevole, quello tale è più caldo e più possente ...Il mezano ha odore non forte..." Savonarola 1988, 152.

36. The apparently familiar movement of the glass was therefore not meant just to liberate the aromas but rather to test the "power" of a wine.

37. "...e imperò i paduani, meio sapendo tale signo, sempre scorla prima el vino nel bichiero, dapo' lo nasa e cussì de lui iudica, che s'el non sente odore, fasse beffe de quello, dicendo dè esser molto piccolo." Savonarola 1988, 152.

38. See, for example, Crivellati 1989, same passage as the one cited in note 34.

39. Most probably the grape variety known today as *Groppello*. Known already to the classical authors (Cato the Elder and Virgil), it is also mentioned by medieval (Pietro de' Crescenzi) and Renaissance authors (Agostino Gallo, 1564 and Andrea Bacci, 1596). For more information see the *Guida ai vitigni d'Italia*, edited by F. Giavedoni and M. Gily, (Bra: Slow Food, 2005), 216–217.

40. "...più se invechia, tanto più se fa caldo e secco..." and "...il bianco, posto la parità debita, è men possente, il perché ha meno de

materia e quanto è più bianco, tanto meno; il negro è più potente come cropelli; il mezzano fra questi tengono il mezzo," Savonarola 1988, 152.

41. "...la forza del vino come vuole Gal.(eno) in più luoghi da molte cose si conosce, cioè, dal colore, dal sapore, & dal tempo..." Crivellati 1989, 39.

42. The term is not defined in the 1612 edition of the *Dizionario della Crusca* but in the *Grande Dizionario della Lingua Italiana*, edited by S. Battaglia (Turin: UTET, 1961–2008), where it is defined as "verde lucente" (shiny green), like the color of a palm leaf. The color "palmeo," here designates a darker shade of white wine. This evolution of the tonalities of white wines from colorless to increasingly tawny hues fits very well what we now know is a natural oxidation process that affects, in varying degrees, all white wines.

43. "Li colori semplici sonno el bianco et nero, el rosso et lo aureo sonno composti di questo. Sonno il glauco cio è verdigno, et el rosato, intra el rosso et el bianco; el pallido et supalido, intra lo aureo et citrino, li quali tutti se generano in questo modo. Certamente el vino dell'uve bianche prima è bianco per l'acquosità e crudità et difecto del caldo naturale, ma quando harà passato l'anno el calore si conforta, minuisce la humidità et fassi di colore sotto biancolino, ma se passa li due anni, el calore acresce, minuisce la humidità et fassi di colore palmeo, ma se passa li 4 anni ... e colore se farà citrino." Corniolo della Cornia, *La Divina Villa*, edited by L. Bonelli Conenna (Siena: Accademia dei Fisiocritici, 1982), 171.

44. Crivellati 1989, 33 points out that "...by white what is usually meant is any other color excepting red and black; but this is not a good reason for meaning a fulvous color or a tawny one such as the one in malmsey, Greek wines and the likes. What is meant is citrine or yellowish or whatever we wish to call it, colors that are not far from that of water..."

("...per bianco comunemente parlando, si può intendere ogni altro colore dal rosso, e negro in fuori; non per questo si deve intendere il colore fulvo, ò flavo, come è quello della malvasia, del greco, & simili; ma si deve intendere un cedrino, ò gialletto, che vogliamo dire, che poco sia lontano dall'acqua...").

45. Concerning tastes and the medical/alimentary theories connected to them I am much indebted to the excellent thesis, unfortunately never published, by Rashmi Patni, *L'Assaisonnement dans la cuisine française entre le XIVe et le XVIe siècle*, Doctorat de 3e cycle, Ecole des Hautes Etudes en Sciences Sociales, 1989, above all chapter 2, "Le goût et les saveurs," 135–164.

46. Umami is now considered a fifth and quite separate taste.

47. Patni 1989, 143–144.

48. These quotations are all from Pisanelli 1980, 161: "...perché gli è uno aggiugere fuoco al fuoco sopra legna deboli"; "perché havendo essi una natura calida, fervente, portano pericolo di essere infiammati gagliardamente nell'anima, e nel corpo, e di esser furiosamente agitati"; and "...si concede a' vecchi, come cosa conveniente alla natura loro, perché col suo calore riduce la fredezza di quella età ad un giusto, e convenevol temperamento"

49. "La vecchiaja nun vo' gioco ma vo' vino, callo e fuoco," in *Buon vino, favola lunga: vite e vino nei proverbi delle regioni italiane* 1992, proverbs no. 3799–3802, 242–243.

50. "Si nasce caldi e si muore freddi" in *Raccolta di proverbi toscani nuovamente ampliata da quella di Giuseppe Giusti*, edited by G. Capponi, (Florence, 1911; reprint edition Florence: Edizioni Medicee, 1971), 287.

51. This way of compensating the characteristics of a given type of food with a drink or food of the "opposite" type has been noticed by many food historians. See, for example, Jean-Louis Flandrin and Odile Redon, "Les livres de cuisine italiens des 14e et 15e siecles," in

Archeologia Medievale 8, 1981, 400 and above all the article by Jean-Louis Flandrin, "Médecine et habitudes alimentaires anciennes," in *Pratiques et discours alimentaires à la Renaissance*, edited by J.-Cl. Margolin and R. Sauzet, (Paris: Maisonneuve et Larose, 1982), 85–95.

52. "Sui pesci, mesci." See also proverbs n. 2898 and 2899 in *Buon vino, favola lunga: vite e vino nei proverbi delle regioni italiane*, 1992, 184.

53. "Costa di vacca e vino senz'acqua." Wine was usually drunk diluted with water, as this was thought to make the wine less "hot"! See also proverbs n. 2921 and 2922 in *Buon vino, favola lunga: vite e vino nei proverbi delle regioni italiane*, 1992, 185.

54. "Pesche, peri e pomi vogliono vini buoni." This proverb, as well as numerous variants, was current throughout the Italian peninsula. See proverbs n. 2953–2962 and 2964–2968 (no less than sixteen variants) in *Buon vino, favola lunga: vite e vino nei proverbi delle regioni italiane*, 1992, 187.

55. He is referring to the adding of snow and ice to wine, a practice that became very popular in the course of the sixteenth century.

56. "...se il caldo dell'aria, della stagione, e della regione sarà poco, conveniente cosa sarà, ch'ancora il rinfrescamento poco sia, ma se sarà molto, bisogna ch'ancora il rinfrescamento sia molto, poiché il rinfrescare non è altro che temperamento del caldo." and "...nell'isola di Sicilia, ove i caldi sono eccessivi, e l'Acque poco fredde, avanti che vi si introducesse l'uso della neve, ogn'anno ne' tempi dell'estate moriva gran quantità di persone, di febri pestilentiali..." both in Pisanelli 1980, 177.

57. "...d'inverno non se debbono manzar cosse leziere e de poco nutrimento, nè herbazo, ma cose solide e di nutrimento bono e assai, il perché il caldo natural, è cussì più forte ne tal tempo e in lo estate el contrario," Savonarola 1988, 177.

58. Sante Lancerio, "Della qualità dei vini" [Of wine qualities] in Emilio Faccioli, *L'Arte*

della cucina in Italia. Libri di ricette e trattati sulla civiltà della tavola dal XIV al XIX secolo (Turin: Einaudi, 1987), 329–355.

59. On cold wines to be drunk in summer see, for example, the Montepulciano wine mentioned in Sante Lancerio, 1987, 349. On hot wines for winter see the entry on "vino Sucano," 344. For an even more restrictive prescription see his comments on the wines coming from the Casentino, which he says were drunk only in the month of October, 350.

60. On wine suited for old people, see what is said about "Aglianico" wine by Sante Lancerio 1987, 346.

61. "...sono in generale vini da cortigiane per incitare la lussuria" and then "Di tale vino S.S. non beveva mai..." Sante Lancerio, 1987, 344–45.

62. "copia grande di prezziosissimi vini, secondo che l' tempo chiedeva..." Giovanni Gherardi da Prato, *Il Paradiso degli Alberti*, edited by A. Lanza (Rome: Salerno, 1975), 166.

63. "Ho comperato due cogna del vino della Torre ... vonne poter dare a' Signori e a voi, se ci tornarete alla state." Ser Lapo Mazzei, *Lettere di un notaro ad un mercante del secolo XIV*, edited by C. Guasti (Florence, 1880), vol. 1, 312.

64. "Stamane, andando Sandro, Niccolò d'Andrea e io a torno verso Orto Sa' Michele; e avendo Sandro per la sete arsa la bocca per lo caldo di stanotte passata, e non trovando chi ci invitasse a nulla, ch'avamo giurato d'accetare; io dissi: Se Francesco ci fosse, assaggeremo noi d'uno [vino] dal Bucine. Il perché di presente, come persona accesa, rispuose: Ser Lapo, sopra me digli che passato mezzo luglio, quel vino sa del guaime: che, per Dio bealo; però che, anzi il tempo, egli è il miglior vino al mondo..." Mazzei 1880, vol. 1, 101.

65. The wine of this area was considered a luxury item and was most taxed by the officials of the Catasto, as has already been mentioned at the beginning of this article.

66. Giovanni di Pagolo Morelli 1956, 260.

67. "...viene in Roma dallo stato fiorentino di Valdarno di sopra e da molti altri luoghi, ma li migliori sono quelli di San Giovanni e Figghine" and then "...nello autunno, fra la nova e vecchia stagione" Sante Lancerio 1987, 132. The slight shift in production areas that emerges in comparing fourteenth-century with sixteenth-century sources is probably due to the fact that San Giovanni Valdarno and Figline were the more important regional markets, where the produce of the surrounding hills ended up being sold.

68. What he means is that the grapes should have just been crushed recently, and thus be at the very beginning of the fermenting process (when they were sweetest).

69. "...dicovi che Mona Margherita non s'intende, nè voi, di questi fatti. Io le crederei d'ogn'altra cosa, che di vini freddi o caldi" and then further on "Fate questa volta a mio senno; che da domane in là ci venga uno barile di vino bianco buono, poco o non punto bollito; cioè pigiato, messo in barile; e o per bere quella botte, o per venderlo, e nicissità: chè ora, per che sia freddo, e' non se ne trovarebbe danaio. E messovi su questo barile, vedrete che a venderlo s'arebbe II fiorini del barile, se nol vorrete bere." Mazzei 1880, vol. 1, 112–113.

70. "...fate d'avere una botte di bianco, di vino dolce, per lo verno, per monna Margherita e voi; che per la state n'arete da Vieri; del tribbiano, dico" Mazzei 1880, vol. 1, 113.

71. The Oxford English Dictionary shows that the term was used in the seventeenth and eighteenth centuries to describe the taste of "tart" wines.

72. "E così ancora, da domane in là, fate di mandare due some di vermiglio poco bollito, per mettere in su quello brusco vermiglio; e

questo è il modo di rinfrancallo, o volete vendello o volete berlo," Mazzei 1880, vol. 1, 113.

73. See Corniolo della Cornia, who considers sage to be "calda nel primo grado, secha nel .2" [hot in the first degree, dry in the second], 1982, 230.

74. "Confassi nel verno et alli stomachi freddi et a pecti chiusi di freddo et grossi humori..." Corniolo della Cornia 1982, 175.

75. Corniolo della Cornia 1982, 163.

76. For more on the supposed coldness and danger of the cucurbit family see chapter 10, above all 196–199.

77. Some medieval guidelines have had so much success that they have survived in Italian eating habits today, such as eating (cold) melon with (hot) prosciutto (note 52). See also Allen J. Grieco, "The Social Politics of Pre-Linnaean Botanical Classification," I Tatti Studies 4 (1991), 131–149 (now chapter 10 in this volume) and Anna Bettoni, "Cibo e rimedio. I meloni di Montaigne," in Codici del Gusto, edited by M. G. Profeti (Milan: Franco Angeli, 1992), 265–274.

78. "...ricercati secondo i tempi. E quelli che gustano l'Inverno, non piacciono nella Primavera, ne quelli della Primavera la State: onde è necessario di haverne per ogni stagione..." and, further on "...ne i giorni canicolari, che scema il calor natural, diminuisce l'appetito, & si mangia quantità di frutti, massime meloni, dopo i quali ogn'uno ricerca, si per gusto, che per santà, di bever de' migliori, e più potenti (vini) che si possino ritrovare; Sarebbe inescusabile dimenticanza la mia tralasciare il modo di far vino, che si chiama Melon," Giovanni Battista Croce, Della eccellenza e diversità de i vini che nella Montagna di Torino si fanno e del modo di farli, (Turin, 1606; anastatic reprint Bologna: Forni, 1980), 35.

Chapter 7
Fiordiano Malatesta da Rimini and the Ichthyological Treatises of the Mid-Sixteenth Century

In 1576, the sole edition of a treatise composed by Fiordiano Malatesta da Rimini—*Operetta non meno utile che dilettevole della natura et qualità di tutti i pesci...* ["A brief work, as useful as it is delightful, regarding the nature and qualities of all fish..."]—was published in Rimini by Bernardino Pasino.[1] It is a minor work, both in a strictly scientific sense and as an example of typography. This unusual text in *ottava rima* can certainly not rival the outstanding treatises on fish that had emerged from the 1520s onwards, most of which are distinguished by magnificent illustrations and painstakingly researched. Both illustrations and scholarly apparatus are absent from the Malatesta treatise, but it is precisely its simplicity that makes it particularly interesting for the history of aquatic fauna in this period.

The author of the *Operetta* remains virtually unknown to historians of both literature and science. The only information that seems to have survived regarding Fiordiano Malatesta da Rimini is found in the work of Carlo Tonini, a local scholar who planned to republish the treatise in the early twentieth century. Tonini's project was never completed, but his biographical information on Malatesta was subsequently published in a volume of essays.[2] This research shows that the author of the *Operetta* had studied law and held a number of offices in the city of Rimini as of 1556, he was also interested in various aspects of natural philosophy, and had a penchant for a writing in verse. This is apparent from his treatise on fish, but also from sonnets that he published in various miscellaneous collections of poetical works, such as his *La Bellezza delle donne* (Rimini, 1562) and his *Canzone in lode alla città di Rimino* (Bologna, 1573) in praise of the city of Rimini.

The extent of Malatesta's knowledge of the natural world was acknowledged in epistolary correspondence between two contemporaries: Costanzo Felici, a physician and naturalist born in Piobbico in the Marche region who is remembered both for his treatise on edible plants,[3] and the celebrated Bolognese natural scientist Ulisse Aldrovandi (to whom Malatesta sent fish, plants and seeds of particular interest). Felici's esteem for the poet-ichthyologist from Rimini prompted him to write a letter to the great naturalist in Bologna, dated 30 March 1573, in which he introduced and recommended Fiordiano Malatesta. Felici explained:

> There is a gentleman here, a very accomplished poet, regarded and esteemed among the good poets, who has composed a short tract on fish in *ottava rima*, a delightful although very brief work, which lists all the names divided by classes and kind, together with some notable property to describe each of them more fully.[4]

Impressed perhaps more by the *ottava rima* than by the treatise's scientific content, Felici, went on to stress that, "Prompted by many friends, he [Malatesta] would like to have it printed in Bologna, and has already spoken to M. Giovanni, your bookseller and printer."[5] Unfortunately, this recommendation proved in vain, perhaps because of a problem acknowledged by Felici, namely that the *Operetta* could only be published if it were revised by the author or by another person who "was knowledgeable and had an understanding of the material" [*"fosse intelligente e capace nella materia"*]. To circumvent this publishing hurdle, Felici openly asked his illustrious correspondent to take on the task himself, and indeed went as far as to hint that he had already said as much to Malatesta:

> I put Your Excellency's name to him: I do not know if I have taken too much liberty. Pardon me, but gentlemen must always be humored. But if it would suit you and if he decides to send it to print and you were to see it and as it is printed you take a look to see if all is well, it would give me pleasure…[6]

Over and above mentioning some scientific shortcoming in Malatesta's text, Felici's letter also reveals that, in 1573, the treatise was not quite finished, or at least not to the author's satisfaction. Nonetheless it was published in 1576, the

year of Fiordiano Malatesta's death (which would have occurred after his recorded appointment to another Rimini office in August of that year). The treatise was
published in the closing months of the very year the author died, not thanks to the
prestigious intervention of Aldrovandi, but after editing by a certain Giulio Cesare
Bonadies. The two dedications at the start of the volume reveal that Bonadies was
not only a doctor in the city of Ancona, but also the author's nephew. The product
of this editorial supervision, of which few copies survive, reveals that Bonadies
was certainly not the sort of person who "was knowledgeable and had an understanding of the material," as Felici had hoped. Unfortunately, his concern that the
treatise would not be published in the best possible way proved all too true.

Fiordiano Malatesta, like many other ichthyologists of this period, had compiled information contained in other treatises, including Oppian, a classical
author from whom he seems to have taken very little, and a modern authority
to whom he owed more: Guillaume Rondelet, author of *De piscibus marinis
libri XVIII* (Lyon, 1554), and *Universae aquatilium historiae pars altera* (Lyon,
1555). However, setting aside the question of sources, the merit of Fiordiano
Malatesta's treatise is perhaps best understood in terms of some of the key
developments in fish consumption at this time.

During the Middle Ages and up until the late fifteenth/early sixteenth century,
it was believed that human food could be classified using a hierarchical scheme
dictated by the *Great Chain of Being*.[7] In the course of the Cinquecento, this medieval cosmology and the classification that depended on it were gradually abandoned, primarily on philosophical grounds. This change led to a lapse in the
strong prejudices against the animals and plants found in the two elements at
the bottom of the hierarchical scheme: earth and water. The stigma that affect-
ed both plants and fish in the early Middle Ages is confirmed by the cookbooks
of the time, which reveal the infrequency with which these ingredients were
used in the kitchens of the social elites. This diffidence was to disappear during
the sixteenth century, although the exact process of gastronomic evolution that
brought about a re-evaluation of fish and vegetables in sixteenth-century cooking is not entirely clear. Nonetheless, it is symptomatic that this re-qualification
was accompanied (even promoted) by a new and often highly prestigious scientific literature. In the field of botany, these developments were already evident in

the second half of the Quattrocento, but accelerated in the 1530s when the first major printed works appeared. In the field of zoology, interest seems to have focused above all on fish, and over the course of a few decades this led to the publication of a surprising number of lavishly illustrated, prestigious treatises.[8]

Elite food consumption had already begun to evolve in new directions as of the late Quattrocento, even if this burgeoning trend only took hold in the following century. During this period, leading humanists also became interested in gastronomy, a subject that brought together, in close symbiosis, a corpus of medical and scientific knowledge (largely inherited from the Middle Ages) with a new interest in the importance of food and all it implied. Bartolomeo Sacchi (1421–81), also known as Platina, was perhaps the first to blaze this new path with his *De Honesta voluptate* (ca. 1465). In this work he included recipes—often liberally copied from the famous Maestro Martino—as well as dietary notes, rules for table etiquette and historical information, all aimed at constructing a model for meals that was deemed modest, healthy and dignified. His treatise was enormously successful, to judge by the number of Latin editions that appeared in various European countries (no fewer than sixteen were published between 1474 and 1541), and by the large number of translations into Italian (the first dates from 1487), French and German. The work's success can also be gauged by the fact that it influenced other authors of cookbooks *cum* dietary treatises, such as Giovanni Battista Fiera, author of *Coena. De herbarum virtutibus...* printed in Rome for the first time in 1490,[9] and Helius Eobanus Hessus, author of *De tuenda bona valetudine*, first published in Erfurt in 1530.

Yet Platina, who was a spokesman for the changes that were developing in terms of the consumption of vegetables (in particular, salads which were to become fashionable in the sixteenth century), still espoused a decidedly negative view concerning the consumption of fish. Consequently, in the tenth and last chapter of the *De Honesta voluptate* (dedicated to fish) he affirmed:

All fish, however, whatever sort they are, are considered hard to digest, because of their coldness and viscous nature. Besides, they generate cold and phlegmatic blood from which various serious illnesses arise, such as weakness of nerves, a predisposition to paralysis and the feeling of intense thirst.[10]

As of the second half of the fifteenth century, a literary/scientific trend emerged (tentatively at first but intensifying in the following century) that focused on fish and on fishing, and thereby highlighted a nascent interest that appears to have been wholly lacking in medieval culture. Among the very earliest works to confirm this cultural shift was Giannantonio Campano's short text: *Trasimeni descriptio seu de felicitate trasimeni*.[11] Although this was not a work on ichthyology *per se* but rather on the art of fishing, or halieutics, it can still be regarded as one of the first Renaissance literary texts to deal with fish. The text was begun as a letter (perhaps to the author's brother)[12], composed in 1457 or the early months of 1458, and was successively re-worked before being published in 1495. Broadly speaking, it describes the various fishing techniques used on Lake Trasimeno in the mid-fifteenth century, and includes a description of the hunting methods used to trap waders and other birds normally found in the lakeside habitat. Although the documentary precision used to describe these techniques is certainly surprising for this early date, the model for this brief work is Oppian's five-book poem *On Fishing*, composed in around 180 AD, which—as mentioned earlier—was also cited in Fiordiano Malatesta's *Operetta*.

Much less literary in intent was the first true Renaissance treatise on fish, *De romanis piscibus* by Paolo Giovio (1483–1552), which was first published in 1524.[13] The author began his career as a physician, but is remembered above all as a humanist and historian. Indeed, it was these interests that made him a protagonist of sixteenth-century political and intellectual circles.[14] His well-documented presence at the most refined tables of the period suggests an interest in gastronomy that certainly went beyond the purely theoretical.[15] It was probably no coincidence that his treatise on fish was begun at the dining table, as he himself recalls in the dedication. When the fish course was served, during a meal hosted by Pope Clement VII for Jean, Cardinal of Lorraine, and Cardinal Louis of Bourbon (to whom the book is dedicated), the conversation turned to this type of food. This treatise also had an impressive number of Latin editions, first in Italy and then in northern Europe (Rome, 1524 and 1527; Antwerp, 1528; Basel, 1531, 1561, 1577, 1578, 1596; Strasbourg, 1534). The fact that the only Italian edition was published in Venice in 1560 (decades after the first Latin edition), is proof, at least indirectly, of the educated audience to whom this work was addressed.

De romanis piscibus owes much to the "humanist" gastronomic project developed by Platina in the *De honesta voluptate*,[16] even though Platina seems to have been writing for a less highbrow audience than the one addressed by Giovio. The two treatises focus on gastronomy but come to the subject through the lens of classical culture; both are sprinkled with references to classical literary texts and natural philosophy. In Giovio's case, there is also a clear philological component, as indicated by the index of *"antiqua et recentiora nomina piscium"* (old and recent names of fish), an aspect that would be expanded in the major ichthyological treatises published a few decades later. This literary-philological component should not, however, obscure the fact that *De romanis piscibus* is essentially a list of the fish sold in Rome in the first decades of the sixteenth century, and that the work should be regarded as a gastronomic program intended for high-ranking Roman ecclesiastics. This much is clear from both the dedication to Cardinal Louis de Bourbon and the contents of the work itself. The treatise proposes normative dietary guidelines as it suggests both explicitly and implicitly, a precise hierarchy of consumption to its readers, counseling them to eat the fish most suited to their status. In a telling anecdote, the author points out that humble cod was certainly not considered fitting fare for a Pope. This "particularly plebian fish" was purchased by Pope Hadrian for an excessive amount of money, to the "amusement of the entire fish market." Giovio also notes that this lack of discernment was emblematic of this particular Pope, who not only had particularly coarse taste in fish, but also demonstrated poor judgment as a ruler.[17] This passage neatly emphasizes the extent to which food consumption could be interpreted in both social and cultural terms, thereby saying more about the consumer than the product consumed.

It is important to stress the extent to which Giovio's treatise represented a turning point in gastronomy. It was indicative of a major shift in taste away from the medieval diffidence towards fish: for the first time fish is viewed as appropriate for a rich and prestigious cuisine.[18] Yet Giovio may have been ahead of his time, since the dedicatee remained unimpressed and showed little interest in this first work of the author's long and distinguished literary career. Indeed, in a letter written nearly thirty years later, Giovio admitted that,

To tell the truth, after all my work on fish, my relations with Cardinal Bourbon, to whom I dedicated the volume, went bad, since he rewarded me with a fabulous

benefice located in the island of Thule, beyond Orkney. … I made my own way after that, using my talent, and went back to the work I had started on the *Historiae*.[19]

A few decades after *De romanis piscibus* was published, interest in the study of
fish expanded rapidly all over Italy, as well as in other countries in Western
Europe. In just five years, between 1553 and 1558, five key treatises appeared
on the subject. These new works can be regarded as the first modern studies
in this field: *De piscibus marinis libri XVIII* and *Universae aquatilium historiae
pars altera* by Guillaume Rondelet (Lyons, 1554 and 1555); *De aquatilibus libri
duo* by Pierre Belon (Paris 1553); *Aquatilium animalium historiae* by Ippolito
Salviani (Rome, 1557–58); and *Historiae animalium liber IIII qui est de piscium &
aquatilium animantium natura* by Conrad Gessner (Zurich, 1558). For the first
time in natural history illustration, the images were accurate enough to permit a quasi-reliable identification of the various species.

These texts featured woodcuts based for the most part on direct observation by
the authors themselves, and in some instances on reports submitted by trusted
correspondents. One example of this practice, which was quite common at the
time, is the *Epistola de piscibus siculis* (1543),[20] sent by the Sicilian mathematician
Francesco Maurolicio to Pierre Gilles (Petrus Gyllius), a contemporary naturalist.[21] In some cases the assistance provided by correspondents was limited to reports or letters on a variety of matters, whereas in others it took the form of short
and extremely learned treatises. On rare occasions, a procedure was followed for
fish similar to the one used for plants: namely, actual specimens were sent, often
preserved rather haphazardly. A preservation accident is described in a letter sent
by Costanzo Felici to Ulisse Aldrovandi in 1557. On 19 August, Felici wrote from
Rimini to his learned Bolognese correspondent, to say that he was sending "two
fish (the cat spoiled one of them while it was [being preserved] in ash) that are
called *capo grosso* [large head] in these parts, some call it *pesce lucerna*, although I
am not sure that it is the same fish that the Ancients called *lucerna*."[22]

Despite Costanzo Felici's enthusiastic endorsement of Fiordiano Malatesta's
treatise to Aldrovandi some twenty years later, the *Operetta* published in Rimini
is certainly not in the same league as the encyclopedic works mentioned above.
This was probably due to a hybrid ambition on the part of the author, who chose

to transmit his knowledge of natural science using a poetic medium. However, it is worth remembering that, unlike Oppian (the classical model he cites in passages where literary style supersedes naturalistic content) Malatesta is careful to establish a sophisticated system of classification partially derived from Aristotle. Aristotelian influence is unquestionable in that the treatise begins by distinguishing fish with blood from those without blood, thus reflecting one of the key distinctions made in the *Historia animalium*. Furthermore, Malatesta first examines fish with blood because they are "more worthy and more powerful,"[23] a precise reference to the *scala naturae* implicit in Aristotle's work.

Malatesta's *Operetta* is divided into three different *trattati* (treatises), the first and longest of which is dedicated to classifying all the animals that live in water. The second aims, in the author's words, "to show not only how fish (which are by nature spiny) fight one another, but also how sea animals and sea monsters (cartilaginous fish and cetaceans) surpass all other animals in the world for fury and strength, as well as their disproportionate size."[24] In other words, this is a section on the wonders of the sea, in some respects similar to the *Histoire naturelle des estranges poissons marins* published by Pierre Belon in 1551 which, unlike his previously mentioned *De aquatilibus libri duo*, was dedicated exclusively to "large fish" like sturgeon, tuna, dolphins and whales. The third treatise of the *Operetta* is far shorter than the previous ones (comprising only twelve octaves) and is almost certainly incomplete. In this last part Fiordiano Malatesta set himself the task of "explaining to people the quality and nobility of *bissus* [a marine snake], coral, *purpura* [a snail producing Tyrrhenian purple?], pearls, amber and similar marine riches."[25]

The first of the three treatises is particularly interesting, perhaps because it was the only one that was actually completed before his death. Here we find the "the distinction of all the species" mentioned in the title of the *Operetta,* a subdivision of all known aquatic animals into twenty-four distinct groups which the author calls *schiere*, based in turn on at least three distinct taxonomic criteria: habitat, skeleton and morphology.[26] The different habitats frequented by fish characterize six of the twenty-four "schiere" or groups: coastal fish (i.e. what he calls *sassatili* or species that live on rocky coasts), marine species, river species and those that inhabit lakes, ponds and swamps. By adopting this criterion, he follows a classification system derived from Avicenna,[27] used by authors of dietary treatises such as Michele Savonarola,[28] and also by Giovio. The second criterion used by Malatesta is based on the skeletal characteristics of the various fish, such as the distinction, for example, between the "thorny" [spinosi] group and the "cartilaginous" [cartilaginosi] group. This approach recalls contemporary notions of comparative anatomy, which in the sixteenth century was taking its first steps through authors like Belon. Finally, the third criterion that emerges from Malatesta's classification is based on fish morphology. Thus, for example, he places all "round and reddish fish" [pesci ritondi e rosseggianti] in the fifth group, "flat thorny" [piani spinosi] fish in the seventh group, "flat cartilaginous" [piani cartilaginosi] fish in the eighth one, crustaceans in the sixteenth, and so on.

In some instances, the reasoning used to establish the groups of aquatic animals is not very intelligible, at least to the modern reader. In particular, it is worth mentioning the fourteenth group, which he dedicates to "unknown fish" [pesci incogniti], and the nineteenth group of "imperfect fish called insects" [imperfetti chiamati insetti], although it subsequently becomes clear that the latter included fish like the "sole marino" (literally "marine sun"—an unidentified species), the starfish, and the seahorse. The twenty-fourth group, is easier to understand since it included animals that are "amphibian, that is, from water and earth" [anphibi, cioé di acqua e di terra], like the crocodile, the tortoise, and the beaver, as well as ducks and geese. Indeed, according to the Great Chain of Being, this final group represents a transition between the elements water and air.

Fiordiano Malatesta's Operetta must therefore be seen as a text that developed in a scientific and cultural climate that was particularly favorable to ichthyology, even if it appeared slightly later than some of the major works published in the mid-Cinquecento. Although it is undoubtedly a minor work, the Operetta reveals the extent to which ichthyological treatises had become a scientific and literary genre in the sixteenth century. The most important works were dedicated to top-ranking ecclesiastics, like Cardinal Louis de Bourbon in the case of Giovio's De Romanis piscibus, or Pope Paul V in the case of Ippolito Salviani's beautifully illustrated Aquatilium animalium historiae; Fiordiano Malatesta somewhat more modestly followed the same path, dedicating his work to the "monsignor Vescovo di Ancona." Yet, for all the zoological interest these texts represent, it is difficult to imagine that the recent interest in ichthyology did not also have a more practical side to it, namely to inform consumers and even promote the presence of fish at elite tables.

The impact of such treatises can be measured in the number of pages dedicated to fish in sixteenth-century cookbooks, such as *La Singolare dottrina* by Domenico Romoli, published for the first time in 1560, or the even more famous *Opera* by Bartolomeo Scappi, dating from 1570. Unlike earlier texts, both these works contained numerous pages filled with descriptions of the fish used in the kitchens of the time.[29] The influence of contemporary ichthyology is confirmed not just by the number of new recipes, but also because the cooks (or at least the authors of these cookbooks) often refer to scientific knowledge. It is probably no coincidence that the third book of Scappi's *Opera*, which is dedicated to Lenten dishes, starts with a staggering twenty-six recipes for sturgeon, the one fish that Giovio had singled out as being the best of all. All the other fish listed are given up to four *accomodamenti* or recipes. In all cases, the authors of these cookbooks always mention the habitat of each, together with other characteristics such as size, the consistency of its bones, and the presence of blood or otherwise. This somewhat technical emphasis, which seems far removed from purely gastronomic concerns, was the key to understanding the alleged qualities (and demerits) of each kind of fish.[30] Such an understanding was essential for serving the "right" fish to high-ranking clergy and at the Cardinalate courts, where social distinctions were both confirmed and maintained on the basis of an informed consumption of different fish species. It was this combined scientific and gastronomic interest, from the middle of the Cinquecento onwards, that created a propitious climate for the unusual little treatise composed by Fiordiano Malatesta of Rimini.

Notes

A preliminary version of this article was presented at the conference *In principio era il mare*, San Benedetto del Tronto (5–7 December 1996).

First published as "Fiordiano Malatesta da Rimini e i trattati di ittiologia della metà del Cinquecento," in *Scrivere il medioevo: lo spazio,* *la santità, il cibo*, edited by B. Laurioux and L. Moulinier-Brogi, (Rome: Viella, 2001), 305–317. Translated by Lucinda Byatt with revisions by the author.

1. The bibliography on this virtually unknown treatise is scant. Malatesta is omitted from the otherwise exhaustive article by

Gianfranco Folena, "Per la storia della ittiono-mia volgare. Tra cucina e scienza naturale," in *Bollettino dell'Atlante Linguistico Mediterraneo*, 5–6 (1963–1964), now in *Il linguaggio del caos. Studi sul bilinguismo rinascimentale* (Turin: Bollati Boringhieri 1991), 169–199. For a few essential details, see my own contribution to *Et coquatur ponendo: Cultura della cucina e della tavola in Europa tra medioevo ed età moderna*, (Prato: Istituto Internazionale di Storia Economica "Francesco Datini" 1996), 170.

2. I would like to thank Francesco Sberlati for having kindly drawn my attention to the following publication: Carlo Tonini, "Malatesta Fiordiano. Alcuni ignoti particolari della sua vita. Poemetto dei Pesci, e altre Operette del medesimo," in *La Coltura letteraria e scientifica in Rimini dal secolo XIV ai primordi del XIX*, (Rimini: Luisè, 1988; first ed. Rimini, 1884), vol. 1, 293–314.

3. Costanzo Felici, *Del'insalata e piante che in qualunque modo vengono per cibo del'Homo*, edited by G. Arbizzoni, (Urbino: QuattroVenti, 1986).

4. "Gli è qui un galanthomo, buonissimo poeta, messo e collocato nel numero de' buoni poeti, che ha composto un trattatello de pesci in ottava rima, opera certo molto vaga, se ben piccola, dove racconta tutti li nomi suoi distinti per le sue classe e per il suo genere, retrovando per delinearlo meglio qualche sua notabile proprietà." Felici's letter is dated 30 March, not May as stated by Tonini, and is now published in Costanzo Felici, *Lettere a Ulisse Aldrovandi*, edited by G. Nonni, (Urbino: Edizioni QuattroVenti, 1982), 154–55.

5. "Istigato da molti amici, la vorria fare stampare in Bologna e già n'ha parlato con M. Giovanni, vostro libraro e stampatore."

6. "Gli ho messo inanti V. E.: non so se harò preso troppo presuntione. Mi perdoni, ché gli galanthomini se debbono sempre favorire. Perhò quando vi tornasse bene e che lui si risolva pur afatto mandarlo alla stampa e che il

vedeste e che stampandosi gli deste l'Occhio che andasse bene, a me fareste piacere..."

7. On the "Chain of Being" and its relevance for diets see Allen J. Grieco, "Food and Social Classes in Late Medieval and Renaissance Italy," in *Food: A Culinary History*, edited by J.-L. Flandrin and M. Montanari, (New York: Columbia University Press, 1999), also chapter 5 in the present volume.

8. Folena 1991, 188 traces this development of botany and ichthyology to the Latin translations of Aristotle and Theophrastus.

9. For an anastatic reprint of this work and details on editions see Giovanni Battista Fiera, *Coena. Delle virtù delle erbe e quella parte dell'Arte medica che consiste nella regola del vitto*, translation by Maria Grazia Fiorini Galassi, (Mantua: Provincia di Mantova / Casa del Mantegna, 1992).

10. "Pisces tamen omnes, qualescumque sint, durae ob eorum frigidatem et viscositatem concoctionis habentur. Sanguinem praeterea frigidum ac phlegmaticum nerant, unde variae et graves oriuntur aegritudines. Nervos molliunt et ad paralysim praeparunt, sitim excitant..." Platina (Bartolomeo Sacchi), *On Right Pleasure and Good Health: a critical edition and translation of "De Honesta voluptate et valetudine,"* Mary Ella Milham, (Tempe: Medieval & Renaissance Texts and Studies, 1998), 420–21.

11. For an edition of this text with a translation and useful comments see Bishop Giannantonio Campano, *Trasimeno felice. Trasimeni descriptio seu de felicitate Trasimeni*, edited and translated by C. Conti, introduction and notes by E. Pianta, (Foligno: Edizioni dell'Arquata, 1992).

12. Ibid., 9.

13. For an analysis of this treatise, see Franco Minonzio, "Appunti sul 'De Romanis Piscibus' di Paolo Giovio," in *Periodico della Società Storica Comense*, n. 53 (1988–1989), 87–128 with relative bibliography.

14. A more recent biography of this interesting figure is provided by T. C. Price

Zimmermann, *Paolo Giovio: the historian and the crisis of sixteenth-century Italy*, (Princeton: Princeton University Press, 1995).

15. On this aspect, see T. C. Price Zimmermann, "Renaissance Symposia," in *Essays presented to Myron P. Gilmore*, edited by S. Bertelli, G. Ramakus, (Florence: La Nuova Italia, 1978), vol. I, 363–374.

16. On this "project," see the essays by Mary Ellen Milham, "La nascita del discorso gastronomico: Platina," and Allen J. Grieco, "La Gastronomia del XVI secolo: tra scienza e cultura," both in *Et coquatur ponendo: Cultura della cucina e della tavola in Europa tra medioevo ed età moderna*, (Prato: Istituto Internazionale di Storia Economica "Francesco Datini," 1996), 125–29 and 143–53.

17. "... uti modo Merlucciae plebeio admodum pisci Hadrianus Pontifex sicuti in administranda republica hebetis ingenii, vel depravati iudicii, ita in esculentis insulsissimi gustus, supra mediocre pretium, ridente toto foro piscario, iam fecerat." Paolo Giovio, *De Romanis piscibus libellus*, Rome, 1524, ch. 1, 4.

18. For a slightly different chronology of the increasing interest accorded to fish and their consumption, see Minonzio 1988–89, 118–27.

19. "Ma, dirvi il vero, dopo che la fatica de' pesci m'andò busa col Cardinal di Borbone, al qual dedicai il libro, rimunerandomi esso con un beneficio fabuloso situato nell'isola Thile, oltre l'Orcadi... mi ritornai secondo il mio genio sopra il cominciato lavoro dell'Istoria..." Paolo Giovio, *Lettere*, edited by G. G. Ferrero, Rome: Poligrafo dello Stato, Libreria dello Stato, 1956–58, vól. 2, 205. Letter dated October 3, 1551.

20. For a brief summary of this letter, see Grieco 1996b, 169.

21. The *Epistola* form was never used by Gilles who, however, did translate Aelian's *De Natura Animalium*, which contains much information on fish.

22. "doi pesci (il gatto me ne guastò uno quando era ne la cenere) che chiamano qui

capo grosso, altri pesce lucerna, benché non so se sia la *lucerna* degl'antichi." In addition to the anecdote, the evident philological interest shown by both correspondents also emerges here. Felici 1982, 33.

23. "Più degni e di maggior potenza," Malatesta 1576, f. B(1)2.

24. "...mostrare non solo come i pesci (che propriamenti sono li spinosi) combatteno fra di loro, ma ancora come gli animali & mostri del mare che sono li (cartilaginosi e li cetacei) & di rabia & di forza e di smisurata grandezza trapassino tutti gli animali del mondo."

25. "Spiegare alle genti la qualità e nobiltà del bisso, del corallo, della purpura, delle perle, & ambra & simili ricchezze marine." Ibid., f. 2v.

26. The following discussion of the taxonomy proposed by Fiordiano Malatesta constituted a first look at such material. I have since realized that more credit is due to the importance of Aristotelian criteria.

27. Avicenna, *Canon*, Venetiis: apud heredes O. Scoti, 1520–1522, Liber II, tr. II, cap. 555, book II, 69–70 who in turn utilizes Aristotelian concepts, see note 27.

28. Michele Savonarola, *Libreto de tutte le cosse che se magnano: un'opera di dietetica del sec. XV*, edited by J. Nystedt, (Stockholm: Almqvist & Wiksell International, 1988), 139.

29. The sole exception to this "new" interest in fish is the path-breaking cookbook composed circa 1460 by Maestro Martino, employed as a cook by Ludovico Trevisan Patriarch of Aquileia.

30. See in particular Domenico Romoli, *La Singolare dottrina*, (Venice: Michele Tramezzino, 1560), especially chapters XXX–LIIII, and Bartolomeo Scappi, *Opera* (Venice: Michele Tramezzino, 1570). The latter dedicates no less than 66 chapters in Book 3 to the size and season [*statura e stagione*] of the various types of fish, and in each case notes its habitat and other characteristics.

Chapter 8
Botanical Knowledge or Poetic Understanding? Fruit in Italian Quattrocento poetry

"Trentasei fructi sum che d'albor nasse
Qual fuor, qual dentro, e qual tutti se passe."
"Thirty-six fruits grow on trees
Some are edible outside, some inside,
And some can be eaten whole."

Anonymous, late 14th cent.

The Italian poets of the late fourteenth and fifteenth centuries were particularly interested in fruit. The number of poems, sonnets and tensons (poetic debates) dedicated to fruit are a clear indication of the importance of this foodstuff, which was also a sign of wealth and power. Despite their generally "mediocre" literary value, these poems attract the attention of historians for at least two reasons: firstly, because they propose a classification of fruit, to my knowledge unknown to scholars working on botanical history, and secondly, because they highlight the dietary use of fruit.[1] In both cases, they represent a valuable source of information for food historians.

The poems that form the subject of this study are known today thanks to literary scholars of the late nineteenth century, who found them in manuscripts and published a selection with commentaries (many of which are still pertinent).[2] Their groundwork provides, above all, information on the sociocultural background of this minor literary genre in the late Middle Ages/early Renaissance. This valuable contextualization furnishes an interpretative key without which these poems would remain but simple and outmoded curiosities, whimsical texts that are more or less difficult to understand.

The Texts and the Milieu of their Production

The corpus that constitutes the focus of this essay is comprised by at least fifteen different poems on fruit deriving from a number of manuscripts composed between the late fourteenth century and the beginning of the sixteenth century.[3] All of them share a central idea that postulates—explicitly or implicitly—that there are three separate kinds of fruit: fruit whose inner part can be eaten, fruit whose outer part can be eaten, and finally fruit that can be eaten whole.

Judging from the number of manuscript poems that have survived, and the different Italian dialects they represent, it follows that the chronological range of poetic reflections on fruit was matched by an equally wide geographical provenance.[4] Leaving aside the shared characteristics unifying these texts as a whole, they can be subdivided, for the purposes of this study, into two distinct groups. The first comprises seven poems that only show slight variations, barring spelling and the choice of the names given to the fruits.[5] The poems belonging to this first group are the longest and most complete. For this reason, more of the following discussion will be based on them (an example is given in the Appendix to this chapter). The second group of poems is constituted by a much less homogeneous set of texts. While maintaining the same classification of fruit as the first set, this other group espouses a greater variety of poetic forms—notably sonnets and tensons.

The classification of fruit that was repeated in all these texts convinced the literary historians who wrote about them—all of whom had a classical nineteenth century philological training—that these poems were more or less faithful copies of a single, lost original. Yet, as we shall see, this resemblance was the result of a classification system that was commonly understood at the time when these poems were composed and recited, rather than being due to any original model. Furthermore, the number of surviving poems dedicated to fruit makes it probable that this kind of exercise was a genuine literary subgenre that enjoyed a certain vogue from the closing years of the fourteenth century onwards, and attracted several different poets working with different poetic forms, although the authors almost always remained anonymous.

The same literary historians who fell into a philological trap nonetheless contributed a great deal of solid research that sheds light on the settings in which these poems were produced and consumed.[6] Francesco Novati points out that the observable variants in the first group of longer poems might well suggest they were actually meant for a variety of social groups.[7] He drew attention to the fact that this specific collection of texts adopted a particular poetic form, one that might suggest its use. The example published in the Appendix is composed of quatrains (with an AABB rhyme) and, more precisely, comprises two couplets with paired rhymes that form a kind of 'false quatrain'.[8] Novati pointed out that the couplet was often used to "comment" pictures or illustrations, which is why he suggested that this group of texts might actually have been associated with an image of *Pomona* that has since been lost. This hypothesis, although difficult to prove, does not lack plausibility, above all if one thinks of the *Tacuina sanitatis* (both illustrated and non-illustrated versions), which enjoyed extraordinary success at much the same time. Furthermore, the overtly didactic nature of these "poems" is reminiscent of the *Tacuina*.

For some of the texts in the second and less homogenous, group of poems, it has been possible to better document the setting in which they were produced and consumed. At least two of these poems were composed for the Florentine *Signoria*: the supreme governing body of the city.[9] Such an elite audience speaks for itself, but it is worth briefly recalling that, at the time these verses were written, this Florentine institution comprised nine Priors who were quite literally locked up in the Palazzo della Signoria for their two-month term of office in order to avoid all forms of external pressure. This forced seclusion was, undoubtedly, one of the reasons for which poets known as *canterini* were appointed to entertain them as of 1350. This practice was, of course, not limited to Florence, since "official" poets were also found in other Italian cities in the fourteenth and fifteenth centuries.[10]

The texts that can be attributed to the *canterini* of Florence only bear superficial resemblance to the first group of longer poems composed in "false" quatrains. Indeed, they are much more sophisticated from a literary point of view and use another poetic form: *terza rima*. These poets—usually known only by their first name—adopted a tripartite classification of fruit also found in the first group of poems, yet differ noticeably in that there is no description of the different characteristics of particular fruits, just lists of named varieties accompanied with very little commentary. These lists can be impressively long. In the poem by Pietro Canterino of Siena (Pietro Corsellini), for instance, appear the names of seven varieties of grapes, eleven kinds of pears, and as many as fifteen different types of figs.[11] That this was not simply a literary device is evident from the fact that the poems were performed in the same place and on the same occasions as the fruit in question was actually served. The coincidence of both menu and poetic conceit is borne out by account books relating to the dining table of the *Signoria* of Florence. While lists of expenditures on food tend to be quite laconic, they nonetheless reveal that the cornucopia of fruits mentioned in the poems corresponded with the many varieties consumed by the Priors. Thus, for example, "sanichole" and "rugine" pears, as well as "apiuole" and "chalamagnie" apples not only appear in Pietro Cantarino's poem but also in the surviving accounts of the high table.[12]

Throughout Europe, fruit was a luxury foodstuff that appeared on the tables of the rich and powerful. The Signoria of Florence was certainly no exception to this rule, and indeed large quantities of fresh and dried fruit were purchased for their meals. Elsewhere I have shown that the Signoria spent around 10% of its food budget on fruit,[13] a percentage that increased significantly for banquets. The interest shown in fruit by the *Mensa della Signoria* in late medieval/early Renaissance Florence was, however, hardly exceptional; similar purchases were made for the high table of the Burgundian court in the fifteenth century, as well as for banquets of Spanish confraternities in the same period.[14]

The price of fruit could soar, especially at the beginning and the end of the season for any one variety,[15] but over and above its high market price, it was a foodstuff that was perceived as being "noble." By growing far above the ground, fruit was considered to have been the object of a long "digestion" of the lowly, terrestrial traits absorbed by the roots, a "digestion" that vegetables could never achieve because of their proximity to the soil. This important sublimation of the terrestrial element—which is always mentioned in dietary, medical and agronomic treatises of the time[16]—helps explain why poets regarded fruits as a subject worthy of the Florentine elite.

On closer look, it is possible that the two groups of poetry identified earlier are not as distinct as they might first seem. Indeed, it is possible that the lists of the second group are simply notes, or a kind of *pro memoria*, known and used by poets who then composed the works that ended up in the first group. The reason for suspecting this is that the poetic compositions of the second, more rudimentary group are often found in manuscripts containing short texts on a variety of different topics.[17] It is well known that poets often kept notebooks to jot down material relevant to their work. For example, the notebook (or *zibaldone*) belonging to Antonio Pucci (1309?-1388?) contained historical and mythological names, stories from the Bible, chivalric romances, legends, notions concerning the "nature" of women, childrearing methods, and observations on doctors, priests, notaries, and so on.[18] A similar potpourri of topics can be found in the manuscripts containing poems on fruit.

Most of the poems on fruit start with the classification scheme according to which there were only three different kinds of fruit, yet the specific number of fruits taken into consideration varies from one poem to another. In some cases thirty-six fruits are mentioned (three times twelve), in other cases thirty (three times ten), or just twenty-one (three times seven). Whatever the number chosen, the classification is always tripartite. Moreover, the number of fruits belonging to each category is always the same, suggesting a sort of symmetry and order.

Once this classification has been announced at the beginning of the text, the poet moves on to deal with the fruits themselves and discusses them one by one. Thus, for example, the first fruits discussed are those edible inside (walnuts, hazelnuts, chestnuts), the next are those edible outside (peaches, apricots) and, finally, fruits that can be eaten whole (figs, pears, quinces, apples). The question that inevitably arises is whether the three groups or "classes" of fruits highlighted by the poets also reflected the views of doctors and dietitians. Several clues suggest this was the case. For example, doctors and dietitians saw fruits with an edible inner part (nuts of all kinds, but also oranges, lemons and pomegranates) as being "unlike any other fruit" and meriting separate treatment. Indeed, they were deemed the only healthy fruits, above all because they did not undergo the much feared process of "corruption" (rotting?) associated with succulent varieties.[19] This approach suggests at the very least a kind of covert grouping. Whatever the case, it is easy to imagine that, if poets and doctors held the same opinion of specific fruits, they also had a similar way of looking at the rest of this food category.

One example among many is offered by a quatrain dedicated to pine nuts that echoes what a doctor-dietitian had to say about them. According to the poet:

Caldo son fructo: e 'l mio nome è pigna	I am a hot fruit and my name is pine nut
Bona in confecto e quaxi in medicina	I am good when candied and almost a/ medicine
E mia confectione si è apellata	
Dagli spizieri per nome pignochata.	When I am candied I am called By apothecaries: *'pignochata'*.[20]

Over a century later, Baldassarre Pisanelli, a doctor from Bologna and author of the *Trattato della natura de' cibi et del bere...* (first published in 1583), declared that pine nuts were good to eat, but as a medicine they were barely short of miraculous since this fruit could cure at least a dozen different maladies.[21] The similarity of the opinions held by poets and doctors is even more striking in their assessment of dried dates. In the words of the poets:

Dattaro som e tutto il mio dilecto	Date am I and delicious I taste
Si è quando de mi se fa confecto.	When I am candied...[22]

Pisanelli fully agrees with this treatment of the fruit when he states that dates "are no good, at any time of the year, for any age group, and for any complexion, except when they are candied with sugar."[23]

The verses dedicated to each fruit are often packed with information and touch on different aspects of their consumption. They mention food practices, dietary recommendations and sometimes the medicinal properties of the fruit. The walnut, for example, speaks in the first person to announce that:

Noce son calda e de mi se rasona	Walnut, I am hot and it is said of me
Chi de poxe lo pesso sonto sana e bona	That after fish I am tasty and healthy,
De mi se fa bon olio e molto valio	I make good oil and I am well suited
A temperare la forteza de l'alio.	To temper the strength of garlic.[24]

This anonymous fourteenth-century poem reminds us, from the very first line, that the walnut was considered "hot" by humoral medicine[25] and that this virtue allowed it to correct the excess moisture of fish. Furthermore, the quatrain mentions that walnuts could be used to make oil, and that they were often associated with garlic in cooking. It should be added that the dietary advice offered by these verses regarding the consumption of walnuts after eating fish was not original. All dietary treatises and even cookbooks mentioned this custom, but intriguingly these didactic poets also felt obliged to recall it.

In another quatrain, it is the almond that discusses the culinary purposes for which it was used, in ways that have all but disappeared from Western cuisines.

Amigdola som, nemica de' rubaldi,	I am the almond, enemy of the ribald,
Dolci vivande e bianchissimo latte.	Sweet dishes and very white milk.
Caldo è 'l mio cibo e molto volentieri	I am hot food, and most willingly
Me tengono in stançone li spicieri.	Apothecaries store me in their shops.[26]

The allusion to almond milk, an ingredient used in large quantities in fourteenth- and fifteenth-century cookery, reminds us once again that the texts refer to commonplace practices.

Similarly, the verses dedicated to pomegranates underscore the reputation enjoyed by this particularly 'healthy' fruit, recommended as a remedy against many ailments by dietary treatises and agronomic texts.[27] They also mention a culinary use that has now vanished in Europe, which consisted in adding pomegranate juice to meat dishes.

Pomo granato sonto chiamato mostoxo	'Mostoxo' pomegranate I am called,
Che lo malato de sede fo stare zoioxo	The ill and the thirsty I make happy
E tute le ore son bon con lo rosto	At any time of day I am good with roasts
E per astrenzere de mi se fa mosto.	And for an astringent, they make juice/ of me.[28]

Both doctors and moralists advised the inclusion of acidic ingredients in meals since it was believed that they helped to dry up over-abundant humours. This is the explanation for which lemon, vinegar, verjus and even oranges were used to accompany meat dishes. The moral importance given to acidic ingredients in late medieval cooking is particularly evident, for example, in Boccaccio's *Corbaccio*. The plot of this tale recounts the many shortcomings of a widow, recounted by the ghost of her deceased husband to the man who has fallen in love with her; the ghost warns him of all her shortcomings, including gluttony and its direct consequence: lust. In describing the food she consumed, Boccaccio points out that she never wanted to include acidic ingredients in her meals and, furthermore, that she avoided "Aspics, salted meat and all other acid or bitter things [which] were mortal enemies because they were said to be drying."[29]

The authors of the poems on fruit also reminded their readers that they had to take various precautions when eating fruit. Peaches, for example, should be accompanied by wine, whereas figs required water. The reason for this advice was that the first were considered humorally cold and therefore had to be corrected with a hot substance such as wine. Figs, on the other hand, were considered humorally hot fruits and thus had to be tempered by a cold element. Traces of the idea that some fruits were hot and others cold survived until the nineteenth century, as is suggested by proverbs that still repeated the dictum: "Water for figs, and wine for pears or peaches."[30]

Sometimes poets writing on fruit did not limit themselves to commenting on the dietary or medicinal virtues of the same but went further, opening the door to other associations. This is particularly true of the hazelnut, which starts by describing itself much like all the other fruits, but ends on a completely different register.

E sonto per nome nizola chiamata,	My name is hazelnut,
Vechia e novella da ziaschuno amata:	Dry or fresh I am loved by everyone,
Caldo son fructo; mio drito camino	I am a hot fruit and lead straight
Si è il bordelo e onde si vende lo bon vino.	To the brothel or the place that sells/
	good wine.[31]

What was the logic behind an association like this? The somewhat indirect reasoning seems to be based on the current opinion that hazelnuts were able to "increase the size of the brain,"[32] the brain in turn was directly linked to the production of sperm, and wine, of course, "heated" the body and predisposed to lust. As scholarly work on sexuality and medical knowledge in the Middle Ages has shown, there were at least three distinct theories regarding the places where sperm was produced in the body.[33] Medical discourse put forth a theory of "pangenesis," which asserted that sperm was produced all over the body, and "hemogenesis," which argued for its production in the blood. But a third theory, which interests us most here, was the continuation of some deeply held beliefs, confirmed by as eminent an authority as Albert the Great. In accordance with this third theory, sperm was produced in the brain and, indeed, both appeared to be made of the same substance. Moreover, there was a direct link between that organ and seminal emission; most medical authorities believed that excess sexual activity reduced its dimensions. Given such convictions, it can be understood that hazelnuts were seen as a kind of remedy to protect the brain in preparation for visiting a brothel.

Such erotic associations crop up often in the poetic treatment of fruit. In the case of the fig, the texts play on a pun that, at least in Italian, is easier to understand.

Dolce son ficho maturo, dolce e secho	When ripe I am sweet fig, sweet when dried
E' multi oxelli me gustam con lo becho	Many birds taste me with their beak
In oni mane son bon alle persone	Every day I am good to people
Anche de mi se fa dirixione.	And I also serve to mock.[34]

In this last quatrain, innuendo is based on birds and figs as well-known sym-bols of sexuality in fourteenth- and fifteenth-century Italy.[35] Not only did birds "peck" figs, in a clear allusion to heterosexual intercourse, but the obscene gesture of the "fig" would have also been known by the readers (or listening audience) of these verses.[36]

Poems in Praise of Fruit and Learned Sources

As we have seen, the poetic texts examined here owe many of their ideas and much of their content to medical and dietary theories. Such "learned" knowl-edge was hardly restricted to the medical profession, but was also disseminat-ed by a vast number of texts: above all by the *tacuina sanitatis* (unfortunately studied almost exclusively in their elite illustrated form) and plague treatises. These two types of sources, literary genres in their own right, enjoyed a wide circulation, even though it is difficult to quantify the precise extent of this phenomenon.[37] Plague treatises, for example, are known to have multiplied exponentially in number after 1348, and systematically dedicated chapters to the question of food and diets to be observed before and during the outbreak of any wave of pestilence. As for the *tacuina sanitatis*, while they have cer-tainly been less well-studied than plague treatises, they were nonetheless in vogue in the same period and expanded the circulation of similar information. Evidently, both of these sources contributed to a commonplace, shared knowl-edge that also appears in poetic compositions on fruit.

There is yet another and relatively neglected source that can also help con-textualize the fruit culture of the poets. The source in question is a long trea-tise on cosmography composed by Ristoro d'Arezzo in 1282, a treatise whose influence and circulation have been underestimated, although it has recently regained visibility thanks to a belated critical edition.[38] While it might not have been known directly to the poets writing on fruit, it does seem to contain notions that were familiar at the time since they made (direct or indirect) use of ideas similar to those of Ristoro. The anonymous poet states that:

Fructi nati si son in questo mondo	Fruit born in this world is
Lungi, traversi, alchuni ch'é ritondo	Long, transversal, and some are round
Tall' è dolce dentro e talle quale di fuore	Some are sweet inside, and some outside
E alchuni d'ambi duy dona sapore.	Some other ones from both [parts]/
	give taste [39]

Ristoro d'Arezzo developed this idea in a more complex and articulate way, but the basic premise remains the same; he explains the different types of fruit with the (Aristotelian) theory of opposites:

> Everything ... must have its opposite ... and for this reason we find ... a variety of opposite plants, contrary to one another; thus we find thick and thin plants, one is long and another short, one armed, like those with sharp thorns, and another unarmed ... one whose peel runs lengthwise, another with its peel running across, one with a thin peel, another thick, one with leaves as large as its fruits and seeds, while another has small ones.[40]

And further on, Ristoro explicitly enunciates the familiar trope:

> ...in some fruits we find the sweet part on the outside and the bitter inside, like the peach ... and on the contrary, we find a fruit that is bitter on the outside and sweet inside, like the walnut...[41]

An even more specific example of the direct or indirect debt the poets had to the ideas set out by Ristoro d'Arezzo regards a fruit that seems to have held a particular fascination: the peach. Here, too, the similarities appear more in terms of content than in the exact wording. According to the verses of one poet:

I' son chiamata per mio nome pescha,	I am called by the name of peach,
buona non sono dove vin non si mescha	I do not taste good if wine is not poured,
e chi trarrà lo nocciol dal mio cientro,	Anyone pulling the stone from my center
ben calda troverà l'anima dentro.	Will find my hot soul inside.[42]

Here the poet is clearly alluding to a characteristic of the peach that seems to have astonished all authors at the time. Both poets and the learned cosmographer from Arezzo were clearly struck by the tripartite structure of this fruit, composed of meat, pit and edible kernel. While the poets expressed themselves in the concise terms dictated by their quatrains, Ristoro provides a more elaborate explanation for this natural phenomenon in cosmographic terms:

> The intellectual virtue of heaven ... always wonderfully chooses the mixed humours: such as hot humours and cold, wet and dry ones, which are conveyed [to the fruit] through the very thin stalk. Continuing the separation, it places the sweet part on one side of the fruit, the bitter part on the other side, and the 'earthy' part on yet another side, as is wonderfully achieved and chosen [sic] in the peach ... (where) we find the bitter part inside which has become the soul, the sweet part outside, which is the pulp, and the hard, 'earthy' part between the two, and that forms the stone ... almost as hard as iron, as if the peach were the result of much study to make us know...[43]

For Ristoro, the peach could therefore be seen almost as a prototype of all fruits, a sort of model for detailed study. With its three clearly differentiated and visible components, this fruit seemed to didactically explain that the sweet, the bitter and the "earthy" parts were basic components of all fruits and, depending on the mix, resulted in the variety of produce available to mankind.

★★★

The genre of fruit poetry, and the didactic declamation of it in front of the convivial assembly of the Florentine *Signoria*, suggests that fruit was invested with a particular importance and prestige. This special role was further confirmed and reinforced by the treatment of fruit in the realm of natural philosophy, where its superiority was self-evident. Yet, despite the importance accorded to fruit, it was not seen as a particularly healthy foodstuff. It is often reviled by doctors and dietitians, who abounded in warnings and detailed counsel as to when and how fruit should be consumed. Nevertheless, fruit remained, an important luxury item and a status symbol appearing on upper class tables and banquets. Considered more as a condiment than as a foodstuff that could actually nourish a person, fruit was credited with the capacity to modify humoral balances much in the same way as any of the six non-naturals were thought to influence the human body.[44] Fruit was thus comparable to spices, but unlike the latter was mostly humorally cold and wet, and in many cases was prone to rot (which caused it to be seen with dark suspicion).

The paradoxical attitude to fruit—on the one hand a recognized luxury item and status symbol, and on the other hand a foodstuff endowed with a dubious medical reputation—might provide an explanation for the markedly didactic nature of the poetry examined here. The verses convey an effort to simultaneously entertain and educate, but also (and maybe primarily) to advertise the cultural status of fruit in this period, a special status that is further confirmed by iconographic evidence, where fruit intended for both consumption and decoration is depicted on banquet tables and in *Last Suppers*.[45] These texts, and the public performance of the same, suggest the extent to which the consumption of fruit took place within a controlled and medicalized framework that made this status symbol safer to consume.

Annex I *De la condictione de li fructi*

Text reprinted from Francesco Novati, "Di due poesie del secolo XIV su 'La natura delle frutta': nuove comunicazioni," in *Giornale Storico della Letteratura Italiana*, vol. 18 (1891), 336–46.

Jehsus	Jesus
DE LA CONDICTIONE DE LI FRUCTI	ON THE CONDITION OF FRUITS
Fructi nati si son in questo mondo	Fruit born in this world is
Lungi, traversi, alchuni ch'è ritondo,	long, diagonal, and some are round,
Tal'è dolce dentro e talle quale di fuore	Some are sweet inside and some outside
E alchuni d'ambi duy dona sapore	Some other ones from both [parts] give taste
De tutti ve dirò alegramente:	Of all I will happily talk to you:
Parlo de dulci primamente.	I begin speaking about the sweet ones.
Plante sono sette che donan dolzore	Seven are the plants that give sweetness from
Lo fructo dentro, e quel lasciam de fuore:	the inside and where the outside is discarded.
Noze, nizole, mandole e la pigna	Walnut, hazelnut, almond and pine nut
Aranzo e lla castagna, se l'é fina*	Orange and chestnut, if it is a refined one*,
E poy lì poxe le pome granate	and then comes the pomegranate
Che sane sono per la zente amalate.	that is good for sick people.
Noce son calda e de mi se rasona	I am a walnut and am hot, of me they say
Chi de poxe lo pesso sonto sana e bona:	that after fish I am healthy and good:
De mi se fa bon olio e molto valio	From me good oil is made and I am good
A temperare la forteza de l'alio.	at tempering the strength of garlic.

E sonto per nome nizola chiamata,
Vechia e novella da ziaschuno amata:
Caldo son fructo: mio drito camino
Si è el bordelo e onde si vende lo bon vino.

I am called hazelnut
Dry or fresh, everybody loves me
I am a hot fruit that takes you straight to
the bordello and where good wine is sold.

Armandola sonto: de mi si sono fate
Dolce vivande e bianchissimo lacte:
Calda son secha, e multo voluntieri
Mi tengono in botega li spizieri.

I am the almond and with me they make
Sweet dishes and very white milk:
I am hot and dry and am kept,
Most willingly, in the shops of apothecaries.

Caldo son fructo: e 'l mio nome è pigna
Bona in confecto e quaxi in medicina:
E mia confectione si è appellata
Dagli spezieri per nome pignochata.

I am a hot fruit and my name is pine nut,
good when candied and almost like a/
                medicine:
my candied form is called,
by the apothecaries, "pignochata."

Aranzo sonto de ogni tempo verde,
E fiori e fructo in mi may no se perde:
De mi se fa ranciata; ogniun lo saza
Che yo son freda e bona con la vernaza.

I am an orange, at all times green,
In me flowers and fruit are never lost:
With me orange juice is made;/
                everybody is satiated
I am cold and good with vernaccia [wine].

E sonto per nome chiamata castagna,
Fructo nutrente a zente de montagna:
Bona son cotta e cruda in oni mane,
E assay n'è che me manducha in pane.

I am called a chestnut,
A nutritious fruit for mountain people:
Every day I am good, cooked and raw,
And many are those who eat me as bread.

Pomo granato sonto chiamato mostoxo,
Che lo malato de sede fo stare zoioxo,
E tute ore son bon con lo rosto,
E per astrezere de mi se fa mosto.

'Mostoxo' pomegranate I am called,
The ill and the thirsty I make happy,
At any time of day I am good with roasts,
And as an astringent, they make juice of me.

DE QUELLE CHE ÀNNO L'OSSO ZOÈ L'ARMA	OF THOSE THAT HAVE A BONE OR ARMOR

Plante siamo septe, che donamo sapore
Non quell'è de dentro, ma quell'è di/
                          fuore:
Nespolle e brugne, cirexe e maregne
Cornali e dattali che àno....
E anche v'è lo persicho sì chomo ve dico,
A chuy se monda no è vero amicho.

We are seven plants that provide taste
Not with the inside but rather with the/
                          outside:
Medlar and plum, cherries and sour cherries
Cornelian cherry and dates that have...
And there is also the peach which, I tell you,
Is not to be peeled for a real friend.

Nespola sonto che apayro l'inverno,
Quando lo richo gode e à sozorno:
E sonto fructo che sonto sazevole,
E a povera zente molto dispiacevole.

Medlar I am and appear in winter,
When the rich are enjoying their sojourn:
And am a fruit that satiates,
And am not much liked by the poor.

E sonto brugna, negra biancha e vermiglia
A chi me manza o con denti m'apilia,
Lo fazo astinzere in su la fede mia,
E vederme che de mi facia chacia.

I am the plum, black, white and vermilion
Those who eat me or seize me with their/
                          teeth,
Trust me to make you feel astringency,
And will see me who hunts for me.

E sonto per nome chiamata cirexa,
La quale payro de mazo lo bel mexe,
E non sonto fructo de grande valimento,
Ma ogni zente conforto in el mio/
                          comenzamento.

And my name is cherry,
I show up in May the beautiful month,
And am not a fruit of great value,
But everybody I comfort when I ripen.

Marena sonto che sonto gentilescha
E l'apetito de ziaschuno rifrescha;
E in la state per la gran calura
Sopra ogni fructo rendo fredura.

Sour cherry I am and am noble
Everybody's appetite I renew;
And in Summer when it is very hot
Above all other fruit I refresh.

Sonto cornaio con lo colore vermiglio
A chi me manza e a chi me dà del pilio
Lo fluxo del corpo senza infenzere
Tostamente eio lo fo astrenzere.

I am the vermilion colored cornelian cherry
Those who eat me and decidedly consume/
                                              me
The flux of their body without a doubt and
Immediately I constrict.

Persicho sonto asay fredo mondato,
E con la scorza son più temperato:
E chi non volle che ciò li faza venino,
Quanto po' beva del bon vino.

Peach, I am quite cold when peeled,
But more tempered with my skin:
Those who do not want me to be a poison,
Should drink good wine as much as/
                                              possible.

DE FRUCTI CHE SON BONI DENTRO E DI FUORI

FRUIT THAT IS GOOD INSIDE AND OUT

Plante sono septe, senza far più posso,
Di quali se manza lo mezo e lla scorza:
Ficho e pero e pomo e lo cologno,
E sorbo e cedro, a chi el fa bixogno.
Perchè de rimanenti no ne pare pigro
Apresso a questo pono la mora negra.

Seven are the plants, no more can I/
                                        [mention],
Of which we eat the center and the peel:
Fig and pear, persimmon and quince,
Sorb and citron, for those who need us.
So as not to appear lazy
Let me add to these the black mulberry.

Dolce son ficho maturo, dolce e secho,
E multi oxelli me gustam con lo becho;
In oni mane son bon alle persone;
Anche de mi se fa dirixione.

When ripe, I am sweet fig, sweet when dried,
Many birds taste me with their beak;
Every day I am good to people;
And I also serve to mock.

Eyo son pera, prexa per ragione	I am the pear, eaten in moderation
Chi dò conforto alla digestione;	I comfort your digestion;
E la persona chi è saza e dota	And the person who is sage and wise
Me manza cruda e melior son cotta.	Eats me cooked if he has judgement and / measure.

Citrono sonto: veruno corugno me dice;   I am the quince and some call me "corugno;"
E per astringere sono le mie pendice.   My *pendice* (?) are for constricting.
Li speciari perchè sia delicata   In order to be delicate, apothecaries
De mi con zucharo si fa cidronata.   From me with sugar make quince syrup.

Sorba sonto de chi pocho se prova;   Sorb I am of which little is tasted;
Chi no me crede pò vedere la prova;   He who does not believe me can see the / proof;
Savere sen pò veruna dignitate   Can there be any dignity
Di cui è stato inne le stranie contrade.   In one who comes from strange places.

E sonto per nome apelato el cedro,   And I am called by the name of citron,
Esi reluxo quaxi como el vedro;   I shine almost like glass;
E innel gustare quaxi e paro felle;   And tasting me I am almost like bile;
Però la zente me manza con melle.   Which is why people eat me with honey.

Io mora gelsa con dolce fructo;   I, mulberry from a tree, am a sweet fruit;
Innel gustare ò lo mio sapore tuto,   In savoring me I give all of my taste,
E chi me manza rinfrescho al matino,   And he who eats me in the morning I refresh,
E molta zente de mi se fa vino.   And many people make wine with me.

Finis   End

---

* This refers to the distinction between the wild chestnut (*Castanea sativa* or sweet chestnut) and the selected, cultivated varieties usually referred to as "marroni" in Italian, distinguished by both their bigger size and fewer interior partitions.

Notes

First published as "Savoir de poète ou savoir de botaniste? Les fruits dans la poèsie italienne du 15ᵉ siècle," *Médiévales*, n. 16 (1989), Festschrift in honor of Andrée Haudricourt, 131–146. Translated by Lucinda Byatt with revisions by the author.

1. It is worth remembering that there were very few studies on plants and their use as food-stuffs (before the mid-sixteenth century) when the present article was first published. Most of this research had been presented at the following colloquia: "L'Ambiente vegetale nell'alto medioevo" (Spoleto, 30 March–5 April 1989) (now published as *L'Ambiente vegetale nell'Alto Medioevo*, Spoleto, Presso la sede del centro, 1990), and "Il Mondo delle piante. Cultura, rappresentazioni e usi sociali dal XIII al XVII secolo" (Florence, 3–5 May 1989) now published as *Le Monde végétal (XIIᵉ-XVIIᵉ siècles): savoirs et usages sociaux*, edited by A. J. Grieco, O. Redon, and L. Tongiorgi Tomasi, (Paris: Presses Universitaires de Vincennes, 1993). Since these publications, the bibliography has grown exponentially.

2. See in particular Francesco Novati, "Di due poesie del sec. XIV su 'la natura dei frutti': nuove communicazioni," *Giornale storico della letteratura italiana* vol. 18, 1891, 336–354; ibid., "Le poesie sulla natura della frutta e i canterini del comune di Firenze nel Trecento," *Giornale storico della letteratura italiana*, vol. 19, 1892, 55–79; Flaminio Pellegrini, "Di due poesie del sec. XIV su 'la natura della frutta': comunicazione da manoscritti," *Giornale storico della letteratura italiana*, vol. 16, 1890, 341–352; Lodovico Frati, "La natura delle frutta secondo un nuovo testo," *Giornale storico della letteratura italiana*, vol. 21, 1894, 206–209; Antonio Medin, *Il Propugnatore*, N.S. vol. 4, part II, 1871, 213.

3. For a list, no doubt incomplete, of the poems in question, see the articles in the previous note. To the poems published by nineteenth-century scholars should be added another one found by Bruno Laurioux in an early sixteenth-century Italian manuscript from a private collection (the now regrettably disbanded collection of Oscar Bagnasco). See note 15 below.

4. Although these texts have not been the subject of a detailed linguistic study, there is no doubt that some of them contain typically Tuscan expressions, while others contain Venetian dialectal forms.

5. For a list, description and publication of some poems in this group of texts see Novati 1891; Pellegrini 1890; Antonio Medin 1871; and Lodovico Frati 1894.

6. For what follows I have relied on the work by Novati 1892 and on Francesco Flamini, *La lirica toscana del Rinascimento anteriore ai tempi del Magnifico*, (first edition Pisa 1891; anastatic reprint Florence: Le Lettere, 1977).

7. Novati 1891, 349–350, believes that the quatrains dedicated to medlars are written from two different, even opposite points of view.

"Nespola sonto che apayro l'inverno, quando lo richo gode e à sozorno;	"I am the medlar that appears in winter, when the rich enjoy and are in *villegiatura;*
e sonto fructo che sonto sazevole e a povera zente molto despiazevole."	I am fruit that fills and is not at all pleasing to poor folk."
"Nespola son, nemica de' ribaldi, che non maturo per li tempi caldi; allor maturo che 'l freddo mi tocca: molto son buona al ghusto e alla bocca."	"Medlar I am, enemy of ribalds, I do not ripen during the hot season; I ripen when the first frosts come: I am very good to taste and in the mouth."

8. Ibid., 343.

9. On this subject, see above all Novati 1892, 55–79. It is worth recalling that the *Signoria* was the supreme magistracy of the city of Florence from its creation in June 1282 to the rise to power of the Medici in 1434 and beyond.

10. Ibid., especially 63–64.

11. Ibid., 59–60. The text is untranslatable since it consists above all in named varieties:

"Fichi d'ogni maniera più sobrana:

bianchi e castagnuoli e botantani,

cigholi e fichi sechi a la toschana;

E picioluti, ucedegli e pissani,

perugin, badalon, grossi e menuti,

neri, corbini, sanghuegni, romani..."

12. In December 1398, for example, when apples and pears were in season, the accounts mention buying *apiole* apples which cost anywhere between 0,66 and 0,90 d. each, *malateste* apples between 1,20 d. to 1,32 d. each and *rugine* pears 2,40 and 2,88 d. each. That fruit was a rather expensive item can be appreciated by the fact that, the same month, pork cost the Mensa an average of 20 d./lb. For more on this see Allen J. Grieco, *Classes sociales, nourriture et imaginaire alimentaire en Italie (XIVe-XVe siècles)*, Doctorat de 3e cycle, Ecole des Hautes Etudes en Sciences Sociales, Paris 1987, unpublished dissertation, table 18, 149.

13. For this and what follows see ibid., table 3, 21.

14. Monique Sommé, "L'Alimentation quotidienne à la court de Bourgogne au milieu du XVe siècle," *Bulletin Philologique et Historique (1968)*, Paris: Bibliothèque Nationale, 1972, vol. 1, 103–117; Aline Rucquoi, "Alimentation des riches, alimentation des pauvres dans une ville castillane au XVe siècle," in *Manger et Boire au Moyen Âge*, edited by D. Menjot, (Nice: Faculté des Lettres et Sciences Humaines de Nice, 1984), 1, 297–311.

15. For a discussion of fruit prices, see ibid., 142–155.

16. Ibid., 176 passim.

17. See, for example, the description of the manuscript containing the text published by Pellegrini 1890, 342. Furthermore, see the "Classificazione dei frutti," in Ms 19 described in *Bibliothèque Internationale de Gastronomie, Catalogo del fondo italiano e latino delle opere di gastronomia del sec. XIV–XIX*, edited by O. Bagnasco, (Vaduz, Edizioni B.IN.G, 1994), vol. 2, 1820. This manuscript was brought to my attention by Bruno Laurioux.

18. Flamini 1977, 156–57.

19. On health-giving fruits, see Grieco 1987, 126–28.

20. See Novati 1891, 338 and 345 but also Pellegrini 1890, 348.

21. Concerning pine nuts see the anastatic reprint edition published by Forni, Bologna, 1980 of the Venice, 1611 edition, 26.

22. Pellegrini 1890, 346.

23. "Non sono buoni in nessun tempo per nessuna età, complessione, salvo che quando sono conditi con zuccaro," Pisanelli 1980, 28.

24. See Novati 1891, 337 and 344; Pellegrini 1890, 347; Frati 1894, 206.

25. Pisanelli 1980, 22, regards dried walnuts as "... hot in the third degree and dry in the beginning of the second degree." ("Le secche sono, calde nel 3. grado e secche nel principio del 2. Grado.")

26. Pellegrini 1890, 347.

27. See, for example, the late fourteenth-century agronomic treatise composed by Corniolo Della Cornia, *La Divina villa*, edited by Lucia Bonelli Conenna, (Siena: Accademia dei Fisiocritici, 1982).

28. Novati 1891, 338.

29. "Le gelatine, la carne salata e ogni altra cosa acetosa o agra, perché si dice asciugano, erano sue nimiche mortali," Giovanni Boccaccio, *Corbaccio*, edited by Pier Giorgio Ricci, (Turin: Einaudi, 1977; first edition, Milan/Naples, 1952), 49.

30. Giuseppe Giusti, "Water to fig, and wine to pear (or peach)." "Al fico l'acqua, e alla pera (o alla pèsca) il vino," *Raccolta di proverbi toscani*, (Florence: Edizioni Medicee, 1971; first edition 1853), 306.

31. Novati 1891, 337.

32. "...accrescono il cervello..." In this respect see Pisanelli 1980, 23, but also *Il Libro di casa Cerruti (ms. Series Nova 2644, Vienna, Osterreichische Nationalbibliothek)*, (Milan: Arnaldo Mondadori, 1983), 75 which makes the link between brain and sexuality because it states that hazelnuts "stimulate the brain and generate concupiscence" "Stimolano il cervello e inducono alla concupiscenza."

33. For what follows as well as the following example of Albert the Great, I have drawn on the work of Danielle Jacquart and Claude Thomasset, *Sexualité et savoir medical au Moyen Age* (Paris: P.U.F., 1985), above all 77–79.

34. Novati 1891, 340.

35. On the subject of birds and lust, see Grieco 1987, 99–110. This has now been explored in much greater detail in Allen J. Grieco, "From Roosters to Cocks: Renaissance Dietary Theory and Sexuality," in *Erotic Cultures of Renaissance Italy*, edited by S. F. Matthews-Grieco (Aldershot: Ashgate, 2010), 89–140.

36. This gesture recalls the "fica," a vulgar name for the female sexual organ.

37. On the subject of plague treatises, see the bibliographic review of Italian manuscripts by Karl Sudhoff, "Pestschriften aus den ersten 150 Jahren nach der Epidemie des 'Schwarzen Tod' 1348: IV, Italienisches des 14. Jahrhunderts," *Archiv für Geschichte der Medizin*, Bd. 5, H. 4–5 (December 1911), 332–396.; "Pestschriften aus den ersten 150 Jahren nach der Epidemie des 'Schwarzen Tod' 1348: V Aus Italien (Fortsetzung) und Wien," *Archiv für Geschichte der Medizin*, Bd. 6, H.5 (January 1913), 313–379.

38. Ristoro d'Arezzo, *La Composizione del mondo colle sue cascioni*, edited by A. Morino, (Florence: Accademia della Crusca, 1976).

39. Novati 1891, 336.

40. "E ogne cosa ... dea avere lo suo oposito ... e per questa cascione trovamo queste sue plante tutte opposite e variate e contrarie l'una de l'altra, e tale è grossa e tal è suttile, e tale è longa e tale è corta, e tale è armata, come so' quelle c'hano le spine acute, e tale so' sciarmate, ... e en tale va la corcia per lo lungo e en tale per traverso, e tale ha la corcia sutile e tale grossa, e tale ha le follia e le poma e li semi grandi, e tali li ha piccoli." Ristoro d'Arezzo 1976, 146.

41. "...e en tale trovamo lo dolce de fore e l'amaro dentro, come la perseca ... E per questo oposito tale trovamo amara de fore e dolce dentro, come la noce." Ibid., 147.

42. Novati 1891, 345.

43. "E la virtude intellettiva del cielo ... sceliendo sempre mirabilmente l'umore mesto aseme; como l'umore caldo e lo freddo, e l'umedo e lo secco, lo quale ella porta entro lo picio molto sutile. Divisando sempre, va ponendo la parte dolce da l'uno lato del pomo e l'amaro da l'altro, e la parte terestra da l'altro, secondo che noi trovamo scelto e lavorato mirabilmente e.lla persica ... ché trovamo posto la parte amara dentro e fattane l'anema, e la parte dolce posta de fore, fattane la polpa, e la parte dura terestra posta e.llo mezzo entra l'una e l'altra, fattone el nocciolo, la o' sta rachiusa l'anima, durissimo quasi come lo ferro, com'elli fosse fatto per grandissimo studio, per farese conósciare..." Ristoro d'Arezzo 1976, 148.

44. The six non-naturals are: air; exercise (motion and rest); sleeping and waking; food and drink; excretion; and passions (i.e. emotions). On fruit in the Medieval medical thinking see the excellent article by Marilyn Nicoud, "I medici medievali e la frutta: un prodotto ambiguo," in *Le parole della frutta: Storia, saperi, immagini tra medioevo ed età contemporanea*, edited by I. Naso, (Turin: Silvio Zamorani, 2012), 91–108.

45. On the decorative aspects of fruit see chapter 12, 217–219.

Chapter 9
The Social Order of Nature and the Natural Order of Society in Late Thirteenth and Early Fourteenth-Century Italy

The eleventh and twelfth centuries "rediscovered" nature.[1] This rediscovery came about at a time when Western Europe was witnessing the (re)birth of cities, and was beginning to embark upon a long process of urbanization. A new need to understand how nature functioned, how it was structured, and how it was related not only to God but also to man led to a great deal of speculation on the part of theologians and natural philosophers, and, somewhat later, authors writing on agricultural matters. In other words, the rediscovery of nature seems to have been linked, directly or indirectly, to the growth of a new urban culture that made scholars—both men and women[2]—more conscious of the larger environment in which they lived. The following pages are a very preliminary attempt to examine attitudes to nature, and man's relationship to nature, in one of the most highly urbanized regions of Europe—central and northern Italy—in the late thirteenth and fourteenth centuries.

The radical change of man's relationship to nature transformed what had been a symbiotic relationship into a subject-object relationship.[3] Such a fundamental transformation brought about an equally profound shift in worldview since, as Keith Thomas has observed, by the sixteenth century one can easily find what he calls a "breathtakingly anthropocentric spirit."[4] Thomas analyses this new outlook on nature through the work of English preachers. As he points out, theologians felt that "human ascendancy [over the rest of creation] was... central to the Divine plan,"[5] thus reconfirming what Lynn White Jr. affirmed some fifteen years earlier, when he stated that Christianity is "the most anthropocentric religion the world has seen."[6]

The process whereby man came to see nature as something quite separate from himself and created for his exclusive use was still evolving in medieval Italy, where the natural world and the social world continued to be seen as inextricably linked to each other. A variety of sources show not only the extent to which the natural world penetrated the social sphere, but also how the social order structured the perception of the natural world. This mirror image relationship between nature and society current in this period has seldom been pointed out and even less studied, despite the fact that the methodological tools have been available for some time to undertake such an inquiry.

A particularly fruitful way to study a subject as vast and as complicated as man' s relationship to nature was first broached by Emile Durkheim's and Marcel Mauss's long essay "De quelques formes primitives de classification" (1903).[7] The authors of this essay pointed out that in "primitive" societies (their terminology was, of course, germane to their time) it is quite impossible to separate the social structure of the human group studied from the way in which this group perceives and classifies nature. This essay is at the root of a line of inquiry which has greatly influenced the work of anthropologists, and especially the various branches of ethno science. A wealth of case studies conducted amongst many different peoples has repeatedly brought to light the fact that traditional societies project their social order onto nature by means of a similarly structured classificatory system.[8]

Historians seem to have overlooked the possibilities offered by such an approach which, while particularly well-adapted to the study of man's relationship to nature in non-western populations, is equally applicable to medieval history. In fact, ever since the late Middle Ages, and even more so since the Renaissance, the Western world has gradually abandoned traditional cognitive systems (usually considered part of popular culture), even though pockets of traditional knowledge, clearly derived from such ancient systems, have survived to this day in various parts of Europe.[9] It would, of course, be naive to think that such traditional knowledge is comparable to scientific and experimental methods. Using the criteria of modern experimental science in order to understand and explain the traditional systems of the past (and present) is a kind of anachronism, which tends to gloss over or even hide the way in which these systems worked. It is for this reason that historians must not make the mistake of dismissing the study of traditional cosmologies and classificatory systems as a quaint and purely antiquarian pursuit. These systems worked both as projections of the social order onto nature and, in turn, as a justification of the social order as being "natural." A better understanding of these neglected systems can elucidate the complex network of social representations that structured Italian society in this period.

In the following pages I would like to draw attention to the way in which medieval Italy projected its social order onto the natural world, as well as demonstrate the extent to which man's sense of being separate from nature was not yet a totally assimilated idea. The separation of the spheres of nature and of the social world of man, so readily accepted by us today, was, at this time, hardly complete. An example of this can be found in a little known cosmographical treatise by Ristoro d'Arezzo, *La Composizione del mondo colle sue cascioni* (1282),[10] where a number of parallelisms between man and nature are evoked. Ristoro, for whom little biographical data is available, reminded his readers of current analogies between the human body and nature (microcosm and macrocosm) whereby "the flesh of human beings" can be compared "to the earth, the soft stones to cartilage, the hard stones to bones, the blood flowing in our veins to the water flowing in the earth's body and the hairs of the human body to plants."[11] Such a close association between the human body and the natural world was not just a set of literary turns of phrase, since the "mirror effect" between the microcosm and the macrocosm actually determined a weakening of the conceptual boundaries that separated the human body and the environment. The result was an overlapping of the two that can be found in a variety of different sources, as will become apparent in the following pages.

Marie Christine Pouchelle's analysis of a surgical treatise by Henri de Mondeville († ca. 1320) reveals how a surgeon would regularly have recourse to similes taken from the animal world, the vegetable world and even the mineral world in order to describe the interior of the human body and the sicknesses that afflicted it.[12] Mondeville's comparisons with the inanimate world included such items as stones and earth, similar to Ristoro's treatise, but he also added many others, such as gypsum, plaster, sand, salt and glass. Like Ristoro, Mondeville saw the hairs of the human body as being akin to trees, but he also developed other analogies comparing veins to roots, the optic nerve to a reed, the human body to wood, and the small round bones found in joints to cherry seeds. Similes taken from the animal world were no less common; Mondeville compared nerves to worms, the retina to a spider's web, the elbow to a bird's beak, etc. Such associations worked because most medieval doctors believed, along with Albertus Magnus, that the most rudimentary forms of the soul (the animal and vegetative souls) presided over those functions of growth, nutrition and reproduction that were shared by plants, animals and human beings alike.[13] As a result, every human being was believed to incorporate elements belonging to both the plant and animal worlds.

In Mondeville's treatise there is a highly significant opposition between the inside and the outside of the body, wherein a human or domestic (*domesticus*) inside is opposed to a wild (*silvestris*) or natural outside. This neat separation was, however, not always maintained by this medieval surgeon, since certain bones or interior organs were commonly described by means of similes drawn from nature (as seen above). Furthermore, the cohabitation of man and nature in Mondeville's treatise is not always descriptive and neutral. For example, sickness in the human body is understood quite literally, as an invasion of nature, as he makes a very strong link between pathological states and the animal, vegetable and mineral worlds.[14] Mondeville considers a lack of separateness between man and nature to be a source of sickness: most of the illnesses that he identifies (with descriptors taken from nature), are skin problems and growths concerning the surface of the human body, i.e. the border area between the inside and the outside.[15]

Man was also believed to possess a "vegetative" soul that informed some functions in his body, which meant that the presence of the plant world perceived within the human body was strongly anthropomorphized. A *topos* of thirteenth and fourteenth-century literary, agricultural, and medical authors had it that trees were upside-down men and men were upside-down trees. According to this idea, the organs and functions of a human being were reversed compared to those in a plant. Many authors reminded their readers that human beings had their "roots" in the sky as opposed to sinking them into the earth like plants. In agronomical literature composed in the course of the Trecento, this reversal was used as an explanatory model in which human-vegetable comparisons were worked out in minute detail.

The examples I would like to look at here are mostly taken from a little-known central Italian agricultural treatise composed by Corniolo della Cornia.[16] In the second book of this treatise, where he analyses the "nature" of plants, he reminds his readers that "plants are said to be a reversed man" and then tries to show how this works, beginning with the way in which plants produce leafy branches, flowers and fruit. According to Corniolo, flowers were the "purest" part of the plant, since they "almost always recreate with their color, the human face; with their odor, the sense of smell in human beings; and with their softness, the sense of touch."[17] Such a surprising comparison might well be at the root of a tradition in botanical illustration which saw anthropomorphic and zoomorphic forms in plants[18] that survived in Western European manuscripts up to the end of the fifteenth century, but disappears in the work of sixteenth-century botanists who began depicting plants in a more realistic manner.[19]

The idea that a tree was a reversed human being was only one of a number of similarities that were believed to exist between plants and the human body. According to Pietro de' Crescenzi 's *Liber Commodorum Ruralium*, "the earth ... is a kind of stomach ... and this is the reason for which they [plants] push their roots into the earth a little like a mouth that sucks food."[20] Corniolo della Cornia also reminds his readers that, in Italian, the word "tronco" was used both to signify a tree trunk and the torso of a person, while the word "occhio" was used both to signify the buds of a plant and the eyes of a person.[21] According to Corniolo, it was possible to find "in the body of a tree, as in any animal, skin, flesh, nerves, veins, bones, marrow and fat."[22]

These shared characteristics went even farther. Not only did plants grow for the same reason that human beings grew—both were endowed with a "vegetative" soul—but like human beings, plants also possessed a "digestive" process. Plants were, however, assigned an ascending digestive system in order to respect the idea of the inverted man, as opposed to the descending digestion of human beings. Furthermore, plant digestion did not occur only when "food" was absorbed by the roots, nor did it happen via any particular "organ," but rather throughout the entire vertical development of the plant. The terrestrial food that they absorbed with their roots was slowly digested, turned into sap, and subsequently transformed into leaves, flowers, and fruit.

It was thought that the digestive process of plants could be demonstrated, as many authors asserted that incisions at different heights in tree trunks produced a sap of different quality: the higher the incision the better the sap. This was the reason for which Pietro de' Crescenzi could state that "...the food of plants is more insipid at the level of the roots of a plant and, the further we get from the roots, the better the taste of this food..."[23] For much the same reason Corniola della Cornia declared that the fruit from the top of a tree was "tastier," whereas the fruit from lower branches, close to the earth, was "insipid."[24] The taller the plant, the longer the digestion process, and the longer the digestion, the more the earthbound principles were transformed into a superior, more ethereal food. In human beings, on the other hand, the digestive process followed exactly the opposite course since it transformed the food into a substance that was returned to the earth.

Numerous other examples could be mentioned of how the plant world and the human sphere were conceptually interconnected and interpenetrating, but perhaps one of the most eloquent is again provided by trees, which were thought to exhibit a series of human-like characteristics when it came to problems of health. Corniolo della Cornia points out more than once that plants have pathological states that are similar to those of men. First of all, they react like men to either a lack of food or an excessive fertilization. Secondly, they have the same pains that develop in the arms of human beings, only that they feel them in their branches and limbs.[25] Even the pruning of trees is not seen as something specific to plants. According to Corniola della Cornia, pruning and gardening techniques such as cutting the roots of trees, inserting stones into a cut at the base of a plant, and the removal of bark, were all comparable to the principle of bloodletting and the effects the latter had on the human body.[26]

Over and above medical analogies linking the human body to nature and nature to the human body, there existed another set of analogies which were no longer between the individual body and nature but rather between the body social and nature. Just as rich in examples as the first, these demonstrate the various ways in which the social order was projected onto nature and, inversely, how the natural order was projected onto society.

In late medieval and Renaissance Italy, a tacit code determined the choices made with regard to food according to its supposed suitability for different social strata (at least for those social classes who could afford the luxury of choice).[27] The writings of doctors, dietitians, and the *tacuinum sanitatis* all pair social hierarchies with a vertical and equally hierarchical ordering of the animal and plant world. According to this vertical construct, the higher the food-stuff the "better" it was, and the "better" it was, the more suitable it became for the rich and powerful denizens of the world. Consequently, fruit that grew high off the ground was somehow inherently better and nobler than leafy vegetables that grew in the ground. The same reasoning was applied to the meat of birds,[28] as opposed to the meat of quadrupeds, which was considered much inferior. To explain this somewhat mechanical code, which can be empirically observed in a variety of sources (not only the "scientific" texts mentioned above but also in medieval encyclopedias and even in literary texts), it is necessary to identify the unifying theory underlying the hierarchies of nature and society.

The idea that the rich were meant to eat fruit from trees while the poor were meant to eat vegetables, a fruit of the earth, may seem rather contrived, but in the thirteenth and fourteenth centuries this dichotomy was rooted in shared convictions. According to the worldview current at the time, God had created both the natural world and human society according to the same vertical and hierarchical principle that ordered the entire universe. This order of things was described as a kind of ladder or chain along which all of creation was distributed in a divinely preordained sequence, usually referred to as the *"Great Chain of Being."*[29] According to Ristoro d'Arezzo, since both man and nature were informed by the same vertical ordering principle, the higher a man was situated in society and the higher a plant or animal was situated on the *Great Chain of Being*, the more noble and more perfect they were.[30] Like many other authors in his time (and long afterwards), Ristoro felt that nature and society were so closely linked to each other that society had a "natural" order and nature had a "social" order. One of the outcomes of the "mirror effect" which connected these two worlds was to suggest that there had to be a kind of parallelism whereby the upper strata of society were considered naturally destined to eat the foods belonging to the upper reaches of the world of nature. The idea that the produce of nature was not all the same—since it was hierarchically ordered—and that specific plants could be linked to specific sectors of society thus seemed perfectly plausible.[31]

Another, rather different example of how the natural world and the social body were organized according to a similar structuring principle can be found in comments made by Corniolo della Cornia regarding an epidemiological model shared by both plants and human societies. As he pointed out, the sicknesses that attacked trees behaved much like the plague which afflicted human beings. The selective singling out of species observed in the pathological states of plants could be compared to the way in which specific epidemics struck different human groups "sometimes the servants, sometimes the city people and sometimes the country people."[32]

Nature was also thought to govern some of the most basic social institutions, thus lending them what was felt to be an unchanging quality, typical of the natural world. A further example of parallels between these two spheres is provided by a "natural symbol" used to represent the relationships that structured the world of human affairs.[33] Once again, trees provide a particularly satisfactory analogy that could express, in a rich and articulated way, a set of social ties: the family tree. The origin of this metaphor has been examined by Christiane Klapisch Zuber,[34] who has demonstrated how this "natural" form took on a social valence.

The adoption of the tree as a symbol on which to hang the ancestry of a family did not come about all at once but rather was adopted in distinct and significant stages. Although, as Klapisch-Zuber's article points out, there is at least one example of a genealogical "tree" as early as the end of the twelfth century, the earliest representations did not take on the shape we are familiar with today. From the tenth to the fourteenth centuries, genealogies were often decorated with roots, branches, leaves, and flowers, but were constructed in such a way that the tree was seen as having its roots in the sky, a trunk growing down and the branches yet farther down, in order to respect the idea that a family descended from a common ancestor. Such representations worked perfectly well with the idea, mentioned above, of man as an upside-down plant, but presented some obvious problems in portraying family and kinship ties. The solution was to invert the direction in which the generations succeeded each other, so that the ancestor was placed at the trunk, while his "descendants" nestled in the branches above. It is doubtless not a coincidence that this reversal of genealogical representations came about towards the beginning of the sixteenth century, at a time when European botanical knowledge was rapidly evolving away from traditional classification systems and towards the first manifestations of a modern systematic order.[35]

The separation between man and nature on the one hand, and between the social body and nature on the other, was thus far from complete in Italian culture of the late Middle Ages. The overlap of these spheres seems to have been still very strong, even though some of the analogies of a surgeon like Mondeville might be considered premonitory signs of a progressive separation. Such a process, extremely slow in its unfolding, should ideally be documented on a much longer time scale than what has been attempted here, especially as the present study is an essentially synchronic approach to the question. Extending the inquiry towards the High Middle Ages and the Early Modern period would permit a more diachronic understanding of the convergence/divergence of the worlds of man and nature.

Notes

First published as "The Social Order of Nature and the Natural Order of Society in Late 13th–Early 14th Century Italy," in *Miscellanea Mediaevalia* 21/2 (Berlin/New York: W. de Gruyter, 1992), 898–907. This version has been somewhat edited for inclusion in this volume. Certain material reappears in other chapters, but has been retained as germane to the material discussed here.

1. Marie-Dominique Chenu, *La Théologie au douzième siècle*, Paris: Vrin, 1957, especially chapter one.
2. Any discussion of ideas on nature in the thirteenth century must include Hildegard of Bingen.
3. See above all Aaron Gourevitch, *Les Catégories de la culture medieval*, (Paris: Gallimard, 1983), translation of *Kategorii srednevekovoj kul'tury*, (Moscow, 1972), introduction and chapter one.
4. Keith Thomas, *Man and the Natural World: A History of the Modern Sensibility* (New York: Pantheon, 1983), 18.
5. Ibid.
6. Lynn White Jr., *The Historical Roots of our Ecologic Crisis*, in *Science* 155; reprinted as chapter 5 of *Machina ex Deo: Essays in the Dynamism of Western Culture*, (Cambridge: MIT Press, 1968).
7. Emile Durckheim and Marcel Mauss, *De quelques formes primitives de classification: contribution à l'étude des représentations collectives*, in *Année Sociologique* 6 (1901–1902).
8. For a bibliography of the work done in this domain see Giorgio R. Cardona, *La Foresta di piume: manuale di etnoscienza*, (Rome/Bari: Laterza, 1985).
9. An excellent example of such survivals can be found in the study done by Pierre Lieutaghi, *L'herbe qui renouvelle: un aspect de la médecine traditionelle en Haute-Provence*, (Paris: Maison des Sciences de l'Homme, 1986). The eating of bitter salads in spring as a kind of purifying cure very obviously harks back to the humoral theory and its correspondence with to the different seasons.
10. Ristoro d'Arezzo, *La Composizione del mondo colle sue cascioni*, edited by A. Morino, (Florence, Accademia della Crusca, 1976).
11. Ibid., 35.
12. Marie-Christine Pouchelle, *Corps et chirurgie à l'apogée du Moyen-Age* (Paris: Flammarion, 1983). This list of similes between the body and the animal, vegetable and mineral worlds is taken from the very useful appendix III, 354–59.
13. See Joan Cadden, "Albertus Magnus' Universal Physiology: the Example of Nutrition," in *Albertus Magnus and the Sciences: Commemorative Essays 1980*, edited by J. Weisheipl, (Toronto: Pontifical Institute, 1980), above all 324.
14. For a wealth of examples see Pouchelle 1983, 274–275 and 283–284.
15. Pouchelle 1983, 271 passim.
16. I have here chosen Corniolo della Cornia's treatise although, for chronological reasons, Pietro de' Crescenzi's treatise would have been a better example. Such a choice is dictated, above all, by the fact that there is no reliable edition of the *Liber Commodorum Ruralium* (Jean-Louis Gaulin's edition of this fundamental agricultural text was unfortunately never completed).
17. Corniolo della Cornia, *La Divina Villa*, edited by L. Bonelli Conenna, (Siena: Accademia dei Fisiocritici, 1982), 42.
18. Concerning the history of herbals, there is the useful (albeit antiquated) book by Agnes Arber, *Herbals, their Origin and Evolution: a Chapter in the History of Botany (1470–1670)*, (Cambridge, 1912; 2nd ed. rewritten and enl. Darien: Hafner, 1970). For a more recent approach, particularly useful for the relationship

between man and the plant world, see Pierre Lieutaghi's introduction to, Platearius, Matthaeus. *Le livre des simples médicines d'après le manuscrit français 12322 de la Bibliothèque nationale de Paris*, edited and presented by P. Lieutaghi, (Paris: Ozalid/Bibliothèque Nationale, 1986).

19. For an Italian example from the fifteenth century, where a tradition of anthropomorphic illustrations cohabits with increasing interest in realism, see Stefania Ragazzini, *Un Erbario del XV secolo. Il ms. 106 della Biblioteca di Botanica dell'Università di Firenze*, (Florence: Olschki, 1983).

20. Pietro de' Crescenzi, *Trattato dell' agricoltura di ... traslatato nella favella fiorentina, rivisto dallo 'nferigno accademico della crusca*, (Bologna, 1784), 43 and 48. For another example of this simile, see Corniolo della Cornia 1982, 38 and 41.

21. Corniolo della Cornia 1982, 183. It is worth pointing out that "trunk" and "eye" are still used in the description of plants today.

22. Ibid. 38. He also points out that wild trees (sic.) have no fat, just like wild animals!

23. Pietro de' Crescenzi 1784, 50.

24. Ibid. 47.

25. Ibid. 186.

26. Ibid. 180.

27. For a more detailed discussion of what follows see Allen J. Grieco, "Les utilisations sociales des fruits et légumes dans l'Italie médiévale," in *Le Grand Livre des Fruits et légumes: histoire, culture et usage*, edited by D. Meiller and P. Vannier, (Paris: La Manufacture, 1991 b), and, above all, "The Politics of pre-Linnean Plant Classification," in *I Tatti Studies* 4 (1991 a), (now chapter 10 in the present volume).

28. A medieval favorite and a choice confirmed by archeological evidence, for example, G. Clark, L. Constantini, A. Finetti, J. Giorgi et al., "The Food Refuse of an Affluent Urban Household in the Late Fourteenth Century: Faunal and Botanical Remains from the Palazzo Vitelleschi, Tarquinia (Viterbo)," in *Papers of the British School at Rome* 57 (1989), 233–239.

29. Curiously enough, the authors who have examined the *"Great Chain of Being"* have not (to my knowledge) noticed the parallelism between the order of nature and the order of society. See, for example, Arthur O. Lovejoy, *"The Great Chain of Being,"* Cambridge (Mass.), 1936; E. M. W. Tillyard, *The Elizabethan World Picture*, (Harmondsworth: Penguin, 1968; first ed. London, 1943). See also the more recent and more analytical study by Edward P. Mahoney, "Metaphysical Foundations of the Hierarchy of Being According to Some Late-Medieval and Renaissance Philosophers," in *Philosophies of Existence Ancient and Medieval* edited by P. Morewedge, New York, 1982.

30. Ristoro d'Arezzo 1976, 35–36, where he puts the two orders in parallel.

31. For an example of how the social order was projected onto the plant world see Grieco (1991b).

32. Corniolo della Cornia 1982, 185.

33. I am using the term somewhat differently from Mary Douglas, *Natural Symbols: Explorations in Cosmology*, London, 1970.

34. Christiane Klapisch-Zuber, "The Genesis of the Family Tree," *I Tatti Studies*, 4 (1991). The same author has since published a more complete study: *L'Ombre des ancêtres. Essai sur l'imaginaire médiéval de la parenté* (Paris: Fayard, 2000).

35. Much of the terminology used to describe grafting techniques in fourteenth- and fifteenth-century French, English and Italian is the same as the terminology used to refer to families. Thus, for example the English words "stock" and "scion" have a double meaning that seems to have been in existence well before the visual innovation of genealogical trees. For a somewhat more extended discussion of grafting techniques and terminology see Allen J. Grieco, "Reflections sur l'histoire des fruits aux Moyen Age," in *Cahiers du Léopard d'Or*, 2 (1992b).

Chapter 10
The Social Politics of Pre-Linnaean Botanical Classification

Vegetable gardens, often mentioned in the statutes of Italian cities, fulfilled a vitally important function in providing for the needs of a society where famine was a relatively constant phenomenon. Although little has been written concerning late medieval and early Renaissance vegetable gardens it is now known that they occupied large tracts of land both inside and outside the cities of the past.[1] The produce of these gardens was relatively cheap and abundant, and thus, for a primarily economic reason, vegetables had a prominent place in the poor man's diet in Western Europe from the fourteenth to the sixteenth century. Yet vegetable diets and poverty were felt to be intimately linked to each other beyond questions of economic necessity. From Boccaccio on, the authors of *novelle* identify both the urban poor and the peasantry by calling them onion eaters, fava bean eaters, garlic eaters, and other such epithets. This kind of attitude allows the *novelle* authors to make use of food as a satirical device where the mere mention of certain vegetables classifies the eater once and for all.[2]

One of Sabadino degli Arienti's *novelle* (contained in his collection of stories, *Le Porretane*, probably composed in 1492) shows us the "emblematic" use that could be made of a typical poor man's food: garlic. In this story a valet asks his prince to knight him. His master patiently explains that this is quite impossible due to the lowly social origins of valets, but, since the valet refuses to understand his reasoning, the prince decides to ridicule him by ordering a coat of arms suitable to the occasion. The result is as follows:

...on an azure background there was a hand sprinkling salt on a head of garlic ... above the shield there was a sun that made the azure background more solemn and, in the place of the crested helm, there was a very beautiful woman, representing Virtue, holding her nose and covering her mouth to show that she was disgusted by the smell of garlic.[3]

Beyond the obvious opposition between virtue and the lack of virtue (the young woman and the head of garlic), this coat of arms contains another coded message. Its iconography alludes to the cosmic and unchanging order of things. On the one hand there are the noble elements: air (the azure background) and fire (the sun) which, of course, fit perfectly in the world of the nobility and consequently in a coat of arms. Yet the valet's coat of arms also contains a less noble element: earth (symbolized by the garlic), which represents his intrusion into the harmony of the upper spheres. A few pages later Sabadino degli Arienti points out—for the benefit of all those who might not have caught this rather esoteric joke—that "garlic is always food for peasants, and this even when it is sometimes artificially civilized by inserting it into roasted geese."[4]

The link between vegetables and the lower social orders is always highly evident, to the extent that it sometimes constitutes a quasi-symbiotic relationship. Doctors, dietitians, and the authors of *novelle* are often guilty of a significant inversion when they affirm that the great quantities of vegetables eaten by the poor are the result of a physiological necessity rather than a diet imposed on them for economic reasons. A rather tardy and ironic example of such an inversion can be found in the tragicomic story of Bertoldo, a peasant from the mountains, who died at Court because he was not given the proper food to keep him in health. The author of this popular tale, Giulio Cesare Croce (1550–1609), explains the predicament of his hero in what amounts to a parody of a literary and medical tradition that was still very much alive. The problem was quite simply that:

The doctors, not knowing his complexion, gave him remedies that would have been suitable for the gentlemen and knights of the court. He [Bertoldo], who knew his own nature, asked that they bring him a pot of fava beans with some onions and some turnips cooked in the ashes of the fire. He knew that with such food he would be cured.[5]

Unfortunately the doctors did not understand this constitutional need and Bertoldo died. As a consequence, the epitaph on his tomb stone stresses, with great economy of means, the idea that diet and social class are closely linked and that this link has an ineluctable quality, the disregard of which entails its own punishment:

He died painfully because he was not given any turnips and fava beans,
He who is used to turnips must not eat meat pies,
He who is used to a hoe must not take a spear in his hand,
He who is used to the fields must not go and live at Court.[6]

Fruit, on the other hand, was eaten by and associated with a completely different social milieu. Doctors, dietitians, and agronomists never failed to speak of the deleterious effects fruit had on those who ate it. It was common knowledge that fruit was supposed to be unhealthy. During outbreaks of the plague, health authorities even forbade the importing of fruit since it was thought that it paved the way for sickness.[7] However, this negative aura did not seem to impress the wealthier segments of the population for whom fruit was a recently acquired luxury item and whose tastes for it probably explain the developing cultivation of fruit trees in central and northern Italy from the end of the thirteenth century. The exceptionally high prices attained by fruit, especially when it came from afar or when it was out of season, can leave no doubt as to its desirability both as a foodstuff and as a status symbol.[8]

As with vegetables, doctors and *novelle* authors tended to confuse fruit with the social classes that ate such fare. In fact, variations on a story illustrating the social and alimentary transgression perpetrated by a peasant who dares to eat fruit can be found in practically all the *novelle* collections of the fourteenth and fifteenth centuries. The example I would like to give is again taken from the *Porretane* of Sabadino degli Arienti (rather than another author) because it is particularly explicit and also because it introduces the idea behind the title to this chapter.[9] According to the story, a peasant repeatedly steals peaches from the garden of a rich land owner. When the land owner finally catches the thief, he does not speak of the monetary value of what has been stolen. The comment he makes is essentially based on reaffirming class differences. Thus he says to the peasant:

> Next time leave the fruit for people like me and eat the fruit of the people like you,
> in other words: turnips, garlic, leeks, onions, and shallots with sorghum bread.[10]

The idea that the rich were meant to eat fruit from trees while the poor were meant to eat vegetables, a fruit of the earth, may seem more or less senseless to us, but in the fourteenth and fifteenth centuries this idea did not seem at all arbitrary. In fact, this dichotomy was connected to a well-defined conception of the hierarchical order of things. According to the world view current at this time, there existed a series of analogies between the world of plants and the world of human beings. God had created the world of plants according to the same laws which governed human society, both being structured by a vertical and hierarchical principle that ordered the entire universe. This order of things was usually described as a kind of ladder or chain along which all of creation was distributed in a divinely preordained order.[11]

Ristoro d'Arezzo's cosmographical treatise, *La Composizione del mondo colle sue cascioni* (composed in 1282), compared and juxtaposed the order of nature to the order of society just as many authors had done before him. He reminded his readers of the well known analogies between the human body and nature (microcosm and macrocosm) whereby "the flesh" (of human beings) is compared "to the earth, the soft stones to cartilage, the hard stones to bones, the blood flowing in our veins to the water flowing in the earth's body, and the hairs (of the human body) to plants."[12] However, beyond these well-known analogies, Ristoro also drew another kind of parallel between nature and society. According to him, both were informed by the same vertical ordering principle according to which the higher a man or a plant was situated on the *Great Chain of Being*, the nobler and more perfect they were. And, like Ristoro, many authors—at least through the sixteenth century—felt that nature and society were so closely linked to each other that it could be said that society had a "natural" order and nature had a "social" order.

One of the outcomes of the mirror effect which united these two worlds was the development of a kind of parallelism whereby the upper strata of society were considered "naturally" destined to eat foods belonging to the upper reaches of the world of nature. It would take too long to trace here the development of this parallelism between nature and culture from the end of the thirteenth to the early seventeenth century.[13] Let it suffice, for the time being, to say that there seems to have been a steady development of this idea in the period under review. For Ristoro the comparison was still somewhat lopsided. On the one hand, he perceived nature as being highly stratified, whereas, on the other hand, he described a social body that could be subdivided into only two separate groups (those who *think* and those who *labour*).[14] By the sixteenth century, however, the terms of comparison seemed to be more balanced, since the perception of society had become far more complex and stratified.[15]

The idea that the produce of nature was not all the same (since it was hierarchically ordered) and that specific plants were associated with specific sectors of society thus became increasingly plausible. Furthermore, given the importance of a cosmological order in both society and the plant world, it is hardly surprising that sixteenth-century treatises on nobility always dedicate at least one chapter to the touchy problem of a correct diet for this social elite. In sixteenth-century France, Spain, and Italy,[16] for example, treatises on nobility echo contemporary medical literature and even go so far as to prescribe a specific diet for pregnant noblewomen. Since "food ends up modifying the body and the behavior of those who eat it,"[17] a mother's improper diet could even impair the *nobility* of a child before it was born.

The question which arises at this point is how did people choose "appropriate" foods? What were the rules and criteria for a "proper" diet? And what was the code that gave, simultaneously, a dietary and a social meaning to fruit and vegetables? These questions cannot be answered unless we examine the classification system that the fourteenth and fifteenth imposed on the world of plants.

Some Elements of Medieval Plant Classification

In the Middle Ages, and for a long time thereafter, it was thought that the plant world was part of the continuous chain connecting the world of inanimate objects—situated at the bottom of the *Great Chain of Being*—to the animal world, which was situated above the plant world. At the bottom of the plant world, where it came into contact with the world of inanimate things, Ristoro d'Arezzo and his contemporaries placed a kind of plant that he described as part stone and part plant. He called this plant "stone moss" (it was probably nothing more than lichen). At the other end of the plant world—after climbing up all of the various rungs of the *Chain of Being*—were to be found plants endowed with animal qualities. In this group of plants Ristoro placed what he called "erba viva" (actually sponge, as we find out later) which is characterized by the fact that, "when you touch it, it feels this and flees and shrinks into itself."[18] In other words, at the bottom of the ladder he placed a plant that had stone-like qualities whereas at the top he placed a sentient plant with animal-like qualities. All the plants of creation could be placed between these two extremes while respecting however, an ascending/descending order in which each plant was thought to be nobler than the preceding one but less noble than the following one. No two plants could have the same degree of nobility.

We must now turn, more specifically, to the classification of plants within the extremes just indicated. Before proceeding with this task it should be pointed out that plant categories and classification systems existed, of course, long before Linnaeus introduced the modern taxonomic order that is still in use. However, medieval (and to a certain extent even Renaissance) plant classification is best studied by historians in much the same way that ethnologists study non-western botanical classification. In fact, the pre-Linnaean classificatory system (like those systems studied by the ethnobotanists) can be distinguished from the "scientific" system constructed by the great Swedish botanist by the fact that it relies on implied categories. It is for this reason that ethnobotanists speak of "*covert* or *implicit* categories,*" which are responsible for the structuring of botanical knowledge.[19] Let us now try to isolate some of these implicit categories in the botanical system of late medieval and early Renaissance Europe.

Whoever decides to write a history of botany beginning with the Middle Ages (and this is a task that, to my knowledge, has not been undertaken) might begin their search for pre-Linnaean plant categories in the work of the most important of medieval botanists: Albert the Great. A careful analysis of his treatise *De vegetabilibus libri VII* shows that he breaks the plant world down into six distinct categories:[20]

1. tree *(arbor):* all woody plants with a single trunk from their roots.
2. arborescent shrub *(frutex magnus).*
3. shrub *(arbustum):* woody plants with numerous main stems from their roots.
4. bush *(frutex):* woody plants with many equal and relatively slender branches from the base.
5. ? vine *(rubus):* an only partially woody plant with long branches such as ivy and other types of vines and creepers.
6. herbaceous plants subdivided into:
a) *olus virens* or *olus* including all those with a leafy stem of considerable size (cabbage, for example), and
b) those with all or most of the leaves being radical (i.e. without a stem such as spinach, for example).

This classification was based, above all, on plant morphology. It will soon become evident, however, that these categories are also a classification in terms of the "nobility" or "perfection" of the plants in question.

Albertus Magnus' morphological ordering—principle, inherited from classical antiquity via the works of Aristotle he knew so well—was to underlie botanical classifications for a very long time. Even the great botanists of the sixteenth-century, who are usually considered the first botanists to work on a classification system, continued to organize the plant world according to the concept of the *Great Chain of Being.*

For example, Matthias de L'Obel (Matthias Lobelius, 1538–1616) and Gaspard Bauhin (Casparus Bauhinus, 1550–1624), both botanists who contributed decisively to the development of modern plant classification, were convinced that there was a general principle underlying the plant world and that one could recognize a "progression from the simplest forms to the more complex ones."[21] According to this idea, the simplest forms of plant life were the grasses, and the more complex forms were represented by trees.

If one turns to the work of doctors and dietitians, it soon becomes obvious that they adopted a similar and yet simplified version of the classification used by Albert the Great. According to them, the plant world could be subdivided into five distinct groups or categories. The first group, the one which contained the most noble plants, includes all of the trees, shrubs, and bushes that produce fruit. The second group includes all of the plants producing different types of grains (wheat, rye, millet, etc.). The third group includes all the different types of herbaceous plants whose upper foliage is eaten (parsley, mint, spinach, etc.). The fourth group includes all plants of which the roots are eaten (turnips, carrots, etc.). The fifth and last group is the one that includes what was called in contemporary Italian *agrumi* (not to be confused with its present day meaning). *Agrumi* were all those plants which in medieval and Renaissance taste theory were considered to have an "acrid" taste,[22] those we today group in the category of bulbous plants (onions, leek, garlic, shallots).[23] This simplified classification used by doctors and dietitians was, of course, no longer based exclusively on plant morphology. While doctors and dietitians let themselves be guided by this principle, they also added a pragmatic dimension by adopting the edible part as a classificatory criterion. Such a choice is not overly surprising. It might be pointed out that the distinguished sixteenth-century botanist Andrea Cesalpino (1519–1603), who was also the second director of the botanical garden at Pisa, tried, with some success, to classify plants according to their fruit and/or seeds in his *De Plantis libri XVI* (Florence, 1583).[24]

While each system of classification developed by botanists, doctors, and dietitians might seem to be different, all of them were constructed according to a *vertical ordering principle* applied in what seems to us today to be a surprisingly mechanical way. All express the idea that plants which grow to be tall are endowed with a particular nobility. For this reason, trees and the fruit that they produce are considered to be superior. Conversely, all fruits that do not grow high off the ground—such as melons and strawberries—do not enjoy such a superiority and are usually considered to be vulgar, unhealthy, or even dangerous.

Melons: a Lowly Fruit

Having examined some of the more general presuppositions governing the way in which the plant world was thought to be ordered, it is now necessary to examine in detail a specific plant or group of plants in order to understand the workings of this universal classificatory system. The specific example I have chosen is that of a "family" of plants that did not fit easily into the contemporary taxonomic system, namely the different types of melons as well as the entire family of the cucurbits *(cucurbitacea),* which includes all cucumbers, squashes, gourds, pumpkins, and melons. As we shall see, both the contradictions and the loop holes that appear where the classificatory system was most problematical can tell us a great deal about its fundamental ordering principles.

The family of the cucurbits posed a problem to the world order envisaged by the botanists of pre-Linnaean Europe. This was because it constituted an anomaly. In fact, all melons and cucurbits in general occupied an intermediary position between two well-defined groups of plants. According to Albert the Great's classification, they are a typical example of the *rubus,* in itself an intermediary category for which the best and yet unsatisfactory translation might be "vine" or "creeper," since the exact translation "brambles" is hardly helpful. In fact, the more one examines this category of Albert the Great, the more it becomes apparent that it is a hybrid category including all those plants for which the basic distinctions—"woody" and "herbaceous"—no longer hold true.[25] Melons and cucurbits are neither woody nor typically herbaceous plants. While they might be said to be rather more herbaceous, they do produce fruit (botanically speaking, succulent fruit), characteristic usually associated with woody plants.

The telltale signs of a classificatory problem with regard to these plants appears in the different and contradictory ways in which authors tried to classify them. For example, in a famous treatise on diet composed towards the end of the thirteenth century, Aldobrandino of Siena classifies pumpkins, melons, and cucumbers (all cucurbits) as different types of *fruit.*[26] On the other hand, Corniolo della Cornia—whose fourteenth-century agricultural treatise has been published in 1982 for the first time—considers these same plants to be *vegetables*.[27] Certain Piedmontese authors of juridical texts also choose to see melons and the rest of the cucurbits family as vegetables, which choice surprised the historian who worked on these sources.[28] If we now turn to five illustrated *tacuina sanitatis* from the end of the fourteenth century, which have been published by Luisa Cogliati Arano, the results are just as discordant. The Ms. Lat. Nouv. Acq. 1673 of the Bibliothèque Nationale of Paris, the Ms. 1041 of the Bibliothèque Universitaire of Liege and the Ms. 3054 of the Bibliothèque Municipale of Rouen classify melons and cucurbits as a kind of vegetable, while the Ms. Series Nova 2644 of the Vienna National Library and the Ms. 4182 of the Casanatense in Rome classify these same plants as a kind of link between the domain of fruit and that of vegetables.[29] (I might add, at this point, that the classificatory differences to be found in these *tacuina* seem to me to invalidate the hypothesis that they should all be attributed to the same Milanese *bottega* of Giovannino de' Grassi, as Luisa Cogliati Arano would have it).

Yet another solution to this classificatory puzzle is proposed by the sixteenth-century dietary dictionary of Baldassarre Pisanelli. This doctor separates melons from other cucurbits and considers them to be a kind of fruit. He then proceeds to classify the rest (cucumbers, pumpkins, squashes, gourds) as forming a link between fruit and vegetables.[30] This solution is very close to our present day sensibilities but is, of course, in contradiction to modern botanical classification.

These hesitations, and the search for an appropriate place for this group of plants, is symptomatic of what may be called a classificatory doubt. Ever since Mary Douglas' work on *Purity and Danger*, we know that animals falling between two categories tend to be seen as a potential source of impurity.[31] The rule seems to hold for the plant world as well. Our melons and cucurbits are in exactly the same position, and anyone who has worked on medieval and Renaissance food knows what a bad and even sinister reputation the fruits of these plants had. Dietitians never failed to point out that a series of precautions had to be observed in eating them. Known to be extremely cold and humid (second and often third degree, according to the humoral theory), they were to be eaten only during the hottest summer days.[32] From a dietetic point of view, the extreme coldness of all these plants also required a series of corrective measures to make them less harmful. Basically this was done by adding or mixing foodstuffs that were "hot." As Jean-Louis Flandrin has pointed out, some of these practices have survived (salting melon, eating raw ham or figs with melons, etc.).[33] A sixteenth-century flyleaf containing a facetious "lamentation of the melons" provides a good example of how at least one of these cucurbits was viewed. Despairing of their evil reputation, these melons speak to the reader and try to convince him that the fruit he thinks is best of all is actually the worst, and vice versa:

> We were not born in poisonous places
> such as strange and mountainous forests;
> we were born in pleasant places,
> green meadows, vegetable gardens, and other such places;
> we are the dignified and beautiful melons.
> To what extent we are the friends of
> human nature can hardly be told.
> All fruits cast a dark shadow;
> Melons are better than figs;
> We are good, beautiful, and so delicious
> That everyone wants to eat us.[34]

The fact that the melons insist that they are healthier than figs (which, according to all doctors and dietitians, were the healthiest fruit), makes their lamentation almost sinister: they are sirens playing on the gluttony and weakness of human beings who should know better.

The doubtful position of cucurbits in general, and melons in particular, within the classification system of late medieval and early Renaissance Europe caused these plants to acquire a curious mythology which surfaces in a variety of ways. To begin with, melons became the symbols of illusory achievements in sixteenth-century emblem books. According to the most common emblem concerning melons, these plants would grow up a fir tree and thus reach incredible heights without any effort only, as soon as their support was removed, to fall to the ground.[35] This emblem is very effective in portraying the imperfect vertical characteristics of these plants and creepers in general.

Yet more significant is the fact that melons were associated with (and contributed to) the widespread fame of a mythical being: the vegetable lamb or *agnus scythicus,* which Louis XI of France was so extremely curious about that he wrote Lorenzo de' Medici in an attempt to acquire one.[36] The earliest account of this mythical creature (at least in Western Europe) seems to be that of the Franciscan traveller, Odoric of Pordenone (ca. 1286–1331). In the course of his voyage to the Orient (begun in 1318) he saw:

> An animal the size of a little lamb which was white and whose wool was like cotton … I asked what this was and was told that there is a mountain called Caspeos on which grow large sized melons. When they are ripe they open up and out comes this animal…[37]

In its own way, the mythical story of the vegetable lamb confirms the doubtful position of melons in the classification system of the period. One might even add that phenomena like the vegetable lamb could materialize only where classificatory systems left the door open to what one might call "logical" marvels. In fact, in all such hinge locations of the taxonomic order (i.e. areas between two categories), appeared new "marvels" which caught the fantasy of the scientific and lay public of late medieval and Renaissance Europe.

Another such marvel, even better known at the time in Europe than the vegetable lamb, was the barnacle goose. The reproductive phase of this goose *(Branta leucopsis)* takes place in the arctic and thus might have constituted a kind of enigma which was explained in two different ways. According to the first theory, this bird began its life as a barnacle and when it reached maturity left the sea to become a bird. According to the other theory, it began life as a fruit that fell into the sea, in time became a barnacle and then, finally, in its last stage, became a bird.[38] The myth must have been widely believed, since the barnacle goose was eaten during Lent in various parts of Northern Europe where it was considered a kind of fish.

The High and the Low of the Plant World

The values attributed to the hierarchy of the plant world were, of course, based on the presupposition that plants at the top of the ladder were closer to God and those at the bottom were farther away. This principle, whereby *high = good* and *low = bad,* is at least partially responsible for the fact that herbaceous plants were considered less noble than fruit trees. Edible roots that actually grew into the ground were, in turn, considered more vulgar than herbaceous plants.

This code, which structured and gave meaning to the visible world, can be detected in many different sources. All dietitians went out of their way to remind their readers that the topmost parts of plants were always better to eat. Hence the fruit at the top of the tree was better than what grew close to the ground and the topmost leaves of a vegetable were always better than the lower ones. It was for this reason, no doubt, that treatises on diets tended to show a rather unusual and suspicious predilection for hops. This plant, which is capable of growing some fifteen to seventeen feet high in just a few months, seems to have struck the imagination of dietary experts. One of them, Baldassarre Pisanelli, extolls its qualities in these terms:

> ...it produces perfect humours, equalises them ... and in particular it makes blood clear and pure. When they [hops] are cooked they ... become a food whose virtue is without comparison and thus they produce positive effects in those who eat of them.[39]

Despite the fact that vegetables were usually condemned by dietitians, this panegyric on hops continues for another half a page. It finally ends with a question which highlights this theoretical preconception on the part of the author. The question he asks is particularly disarming: why do so few people eat such a superior food? What Pisanelli does not seem to understand is that cosmologically induced values do not necessarily coincide with taste.

On a less anecdotal level, it is the general theory of plant growth and plant digestion, current in the fourteenth to sixteenth centuries, which can best explain how the conception of high and low became so deeply rooted in the supposedly natural order of diet and society. Medieval authors agreed with each other in saying that plants were able to grow because of "attraction forces" existing between two different principles. Most authors speak of a celestial force (sometimes the sun) which attracted a terrestrial principle. Ristoro d'Arezzo, for example, described this attraction in the following manner:

> ...the sky ... a little like a seal impresses its image into wax, attracts the humours of the earth to it and turns them into trunks, branches, flowers and leaves.[40]

Writing at the end of the fourteenth century, Corniolo della Cornia used a similar image when he reminded his readers that:

> The nourishing principle for plants comes from the earth. The generating principle of fruit is the sun, and this is why the earth is referred to as the mother of plants and the sun is referred to as the father.[41]

In both of these cases, plant growth was considered to be a kind of ascending movement due to the attraction exerted by the sky. At first, this explanation does not seem to carry with it any particular value judgment, although a closer look at the problem of plant growth soon reveals the hierarchy of values which structures botanical theory. In fact, the growth of plants and the "digestive" process that permits their growth were seen as similar to that of human beings, even though the process was somehow reversed insofar as the digestive process of plants ascended while that of human beings descended. This seemed all the more logical since plants were often thought of as human beings in reverse.

Plants thus "digested" the terrestrial food that they absorbed with their roots and turned it into sap, which was then transformed into leaves, flowers, and fruit. It was thought that this digestive process of plants could be observed empirically by making a series of incisions at different heights in tree trunks and, as Pietro de' Crescenzi pointed out, the higher the incision the "better" the sap: "...the food of plants is more insipid at the level of the roots of a plant and, the further we get from the roots, the better the taste of this food..."[42] For much the same reason another author asserted that the fruit from the top of a tree is "tastier" whereas the fruit from the branches closest to the earth is "insipid."[43] The taller the plant, the longer the digestion process, and the longer the digestion, the more the inferior earthbound sources were transformed into some kind of superior, more ethereal, food.

The importance ascribed to a "good" (which meant, above all, a "long" and thus thorough) digestion was due to the fact that the earthbound elements absorbed by the roots of plants had to be transformed into something more or less fit for human consumption. According to the agronomists, the least digested sap produced leaves, a food that is often referred to as fit for animals or for the poorest urban and rural populations. The better digested sap produced flowers which, as we well know, were eaten in many different ways all over medieval Europe. Best of all, the most perfectly digested sap produced fruit.

Everything, from the classification of the plant world according to a system of more or less "noble" plants to ideas about the growth of plants and their ability to reach upwards, reveals the extent to which late medieval and early Renaissance botanists, agronomists and dietitians did not conceive of a strict separation between the natural world and the social world of man. The *Great Chain of Being*, which is the inherent structuring principle behind the botanical and dietetic theories examined, was also the means by which social hierarchies were projected onto the natural world. In fact, the *Great Chain of Being* had a double function insofar as it classified the natural world as well as provided a social value for all of the plants it classified. This double function of classifying and evaluating contributed to making vegetables into a lowly food fit for the poor while helping fruit to become an attribute of the powerful, who made sure that it was always served on their tables as both reminder and confirmation of their social superiority.

Notes

First published as "The Social Politics of pre-Linnean Botanical Classification," *I Tatti Studies* 4, 1991, 131–149.

1. Henri Bresc, "Les jardins de Palerme (1290–1460)," in *Mélanges de l'Ecole Francaise de Rome – Temps Modernes* 84, no. 1, 1972, 55–127; Alfio Cortonesi, *Il Lavoro del contadino: uomini, tecniche, colture nella Tuscia tardomedievale* (Bologna: Clueb, 1988), 3–48.

2. Concerning the use of literary texts as a source for historians, see Peter Salwa, "Fiction e realtà: novella come fonte storica," *I Tatti Studies* 1, (1985): 189–205.

3. "Il principe adunque, factose secretamente pignere, in uno bello scudo, in campo de finissimo azuro, una mano che salava uno capo d'aglio in uno saliero e, desopra il scudo, uno sole che solenizava tutto il campo azuro, e per cimiero una bellisima damisella, in luoco de la virtute, che si chiudeva il naso e strengeva la boca, dimostrando essere forte offesa da l'odore de l'aglio." Giovanni Sabadino Degli Arienti, *Le Porretane*, edited by B. Basile. (Rome: Salerno, 1981), 241.

4. Ibid., 243: "...l'aglio che sempre e cibo rusticano, quantunque a le volte artificiosamente civile se faza ponendose nel corpo de li arostiti pavari..."

5. "I medici non conoscendo la sua complessione gli facevano i rimedi che si fanno alli gentiluomini e cavalieri di corte; ma esso, che conosceva la sua natura teneva domandato a quelli ch'gli portassero una pentola di fagiuoli con la cipolla dentro e delle rape cotte sotto la cenere, perché sapeva lui che con tali cibi saria guarito..." Giulio Cesare Croce, *Le Sottilissime astuzie di Bertoldo; Le Piacevoli e ridicolose simplicità di Bertoldino*, edited by P. Camporesi (Turin: Einaudi, 1978), 74.

6. Ibid., 75: "Morì con aspri duoli..." and then
"Per non poter mangiar rape e fagiuoli.
Chi è uso alle rape non vada ai pasticci.
Chi è uso alla zappa non pigli la lancia.
Chi è uso al campo non vada alla corte."

7. "Tutte le frutta nocive vietarono a entrare nella città come susine acerbe, mandorle in erba, fave fresche, fichi, e ogni frutta non utile e non sana," Marchionne Di Coppo Stefani, *Cronica Fiorentina*, edited by N. Rodolico, (Città di Castello, 1903), RR.II.SS., 30,1, T. XXX, fasc. 4, P. 1, rub. 634, 231.

8. With respect to the little known history of fruit and its prices in the late Middle Ages, see Allen J. Grieco, "Classes sociales, nourriture et imaginaire alimentaire en Italie (XIVe-XVe siècle)," Doctorat 3e cycle, Ecole des Hautes Etudes en Sciences Sociales, 1987, ch. 4. See also the more accessible Allen J. Grieco, "Savoir de poete ou savoir de botaniste? Les fruits dans la poèsie italienne du XVe siècle," *Médiévales* 16–17, 1989, 131–146 (chapter 8 in the present volume); and Allen J. Grieco, "Les utilisations sociales des fruits et légumes dans l'Italie médiévale," in *Le Grand livre des fruits et des légumes: histoire, culture et usage*, edited by Daniel Meiller and Paul Vannier (Paris: La Manufacture, 1991 b), 150–54.

9. Other examples of this *topos* may be found in Giovanni Sercambi, *Novelle*, edited by G. Sinicropi, (Florence: Le Lettere, 1995) novella CXXXVIIII, 1130; and Franco Sacchetti, *Il Trecentonovelle*, edited by A. Lanza (Florence: Sansoni, 1984), novella LXXXIX and XCI, 185–86 and 188–91.

10. "Un'altra volta lassa stare le fructe de li mei pari e mangia delle tue che sono le rape, gli agli, porri, cepolle e le scalogne col pan di sorgo." Sabadino degli Arienti 1981, 332.

11. Curiously enough, the authors who examined the Great Chain of Being did not, to my

knowledge, notice the parallelism between the order of nature and the order of society, even though Emil Durckheim and Marcel Mauss, *De quelques formes primitives de classification: contribution à l'étude des représentations collectives*, in *Année Sociologique* 6 (1901–1902) had already drawn attention to this phenomenon. The classical study is, of course, Arthur O. Lovejoy, *The Great Chain of Being*, Cambridge (Mass.), 1936. See also the somewhat more descriptive book by E. M. W. Tillyard, *The Elizabethan World Picture*, (Harmondsworth: Penguin, 1968; first ed. London, 1943), and the more analytical and complete article by Edward P. Mahoney, "Metaphysical Foundations of the Hierarchy of Being According to Some Late-Medieval and Renaissance Philosophers," in *Philosophies of Existence Ancient and Medieval*, edited by P. Morewedge, New York, 1982, (I am grateful to James Hankins for this last reference).

12. Ristoro d'Arezzo, *La Composizione del mondo colle sue cascioni*, edited by A. Morino, (Florence: Accademia della Crusca, 1976), 35.

13. For a somewhat more detailed analysis see Allen J. Grieco, "The Social Order of Nature and the Natural Order of Society in late 13th–early 14th Century Italy," in *Miscellanea Mediaevalia* 21, no. 2. Berlin/New York, 1992a, 898–907 (chapter 9 in the present volume).

14. Ristoro d'Arezzo 1976, 36. According to George G. Jones, "The Function of Food in German Literature," *Speculum* 35, no. 1 (1960), 78–86, a very similar bipartite image of society seems to underlie German literature of the thirteenth-century even though the categories he names, *nobility* and *peasantry*, are different.

15. An excellent example of how sixteenth-century writers perceived the complexity of social stratification may be seen in Tommaso Garzoni da Bagnacavallo, *La Piazza universale di tutte le professioni del mondo e nobili ed ignobili...* Venice, 1586.

16. Concerning sixteenth-century treatises on nobility, see José A. Maravall, *Potere, onore,*

élites nella Spagna del secolo d'oro, translated by M. L. Nasali-Rocca di Corneliano (Bologna: Il Mulino, 1986) and Arlette Jouanna, *Mythes et hiérarchies dans la France du XVIᵉ siècle*, (Paris: Hachette, 1977).

17. Jouanna 1977, 24.

18. Ristoro d'Arezzo 1976, 35.

19. The ethnobotanical literature produced in the last thirty-forty years in the wake of André G. Haudricourt, and Louis Hédin, *L'Homme et les plantes cultivées*, (Paris: Métailé, 1987; first ed., 1943) is truly staggering. The earliest formulation of this concept is to be found in Harold C. Conklin, "The Relation of Hanunòo Culture to the Plant Word," Ph.D. dissertation, Yale University, 1954. For a well informed and useful guide to the concepts and a bibliography of available studies see Giorgio R. Cardona, *La Foresta di piume: manuale di etnoscienza*, (Rome/Bari: Laterza, 1985), above all ch. 7. See also Brent Berlin, Dennis E. Breedlove and Peter H. Raven, "Covert Categories and Folk Taxonomies," *American Anthropologist* 70, (1968): 290–99.

20. For the following analysis of plant morphology in Albert the Great, I owe much to T. A. Sprague, "Plant morphology in Albertus Magnus," *Kew Gardens Bulletin of Miscellaneous Information 9*, (1933): 430–440.

21. Agnes Arber, *Herbals, their Origin and Evolution: a Chapter in the History of Botany (1470–1670)*, (2nd ed. rewritten and enl., Cambridge, 1953; first ed. Cambridge, 1912), 181. The only serious study of pre-Linnaean botanical knowledge that is readily available, this otherwise commendable book is tainted by a certain amount of positivist thinking. It is worth pointing out that the progression from "simple" forms of plant life to more "complex" ones" in Renaissance botanical theory elicited a revealing comment by Agnes Arber when she reminded her readers that this antiquated theory had nothing to do with Darwin's ideas about the evolution of species!

22. Concerning late medieval and Renaissance taste theory, see the regrettably unpublished thesis of Rashmi Patni, "L'Assaisonnement dans la cuisine française entre le XIVe et le XVIe siècle," Doctorat 3e cycle, Ecole des Hautes Etudes en Sciences Sociales, 1989, above all 135–64. See also Allen J. Grieco, "Medieval and Renaissance Wines: Taste, Dietary Theory, and How to 'Choose' the Right Wine (14th–16th Centuries)," in *Mediaevalia*, vol. 30, (2009), 15–42 (chapter 6 in the present volume).

23. This classification may be found in many of the treatises on diet from Aldobrandino of Siena up to the end of the sixteenth century. See, for example, Aldobrandino da Siena, *Le Régime du corps*, edited by L. Landouzy and R. Pepin, (Geneva: Slatkine, 1978; first edition Paris, 1911); Gieronimo De' Manfredi, *Libro intitolato il perché*, Bologna, 1474; Baldassarre Pisanelli, *Trattato della natura de' cibi et del bere*, (Bologna: Forni, 1980; anastatic reprint of the Venice, 1611, edition).

24. Arber 1953, 164. Even John Ray (1627–1705) proposed a classificatory scheme based on the fruit and leaves of plants (*Historia plantarum, species hactenus editas aliasque insuper multas noviter inventas et descriptas complectens...*, London, 1686–1704, 3 vols.

25. To a certain extent this "classificatory unease" can be explained by the fact that creepers are relatively rare in the temperate areas of the world and thus constitute an apparent anomaly. The populations living in tropical areas of the world where creepers are well represented have developed classificatory systems where these plants are fully integrated. Cardona 1985, 123.

26. Aldobrandino da Siena 1911, table of contents, 260.

27. Corniolo della Cornia, *La Divina Villa*, edited by Lucia Bonelli Conenna, (Siena: Accademia dei Fisiocritici, 1982), book 6, esp. 308–10, 317–18, etc.

28. Anna Maria Nada-Patrone, *Il Cibo del ricco e il cibo del povero* (Turin: Centro Studi Piemontesi, 1981), 141.

29. I have reconstructed the order in which cucurbits appear in these manuscripts from the useful index in Luisa Cogliati Arano, *Tacuinum sanitatis*, (Milan: Electa, 1979), 141–145.

30. Baldassarre Pisanelli, *Trattato della natura de' cibi et del bere*, Venice, 1611, (reprint edition Bologna: Forni, 1980), 4, 62 and 68.

31. Mary Douglas, *Purity and Danger. An Analysis of Concepts of Pollution and Taboo*, (Harmondsworth, Penguin, 1970), above all ch. 3.

32. Out of the many possible examples, see Pisanelli 1611, 4, 62 and 68; Tommaso del Garbo, *Consiglio contro a pistolenza*, edited by P. Ferrato (Bologna, 1866), 29.

33. Jean-Louis Flandrin, "Medicine et habitude alimentaires anciennes," in *Pratiques et discours alimentaires à la Renaissance*, edited by J.-C. Margolin and R. Sauzet, (Paris: Maisonneuve et Larose, 1982), above all 89–90.

34. *Lamento di meloni in barcelletta. Et un capitolo in lode de l'uva*, n.p. (but probably northern Italy), n.d. [16th century], Biblioteca Nazionale, Florence, E.6. 6.154.II, n. 24.

35. Arthur Henckel and Albrecht Schöne, *Emblemata. Handbuch zur Sinnbildkunst des XVI und XVII Jahrhunderts*, (Stuttgart, 1967), cols. 331–32.

36. Johan Huizinga, *The Waning of the Middle Ages*, Harmondsworth, 1968, 181.

37. "...una bestiola grande como un agnelecto, la quale era bianca e la lana era proprio como un bambago ... Io adomandai che cosa era questa: me fu resposto ... affermandome e giurandome ch'el e uno monte che se chiama Caspeos nel quale nasce peponi grandi, e quando sonno maturi se aprono et esscene fora questa bestiola." For lack of better editions I have used Odorichus, *De rebus incognitis: Odorico da Pordenone nella prima*

edizione a stampa del 1513, edited by L. Monaco and G. C. Testa, (Pordenone: Camera di Commercio, 1986), 88.

38. Concerning the barnacle goose see Grieco 1987, 112–14.

39. "Generano humore perfetto, agguagliano gli humori … e particolarmente fanno il sangue chiaro & puro … Perdendo nella cottura ogni ventosità, e si fanno cibi di virtù incomparabile, con grand beneficio di chi l'usa," Pisanelli 1611, 46–47.

40. "…l'cielo … la quale elli significa e ha in sé, come lo sugello significa e ha en sé e 'ntende de fare e de pònare e lla cera la figura ch'elli ha en sé; e trarà enverso se l'umore de la terra, e faranne el pedone e 1i rami e 1i fiori e le follie" Ristoro d'Arezzo 1976, 147–48.

41. "El principio del cibo de le piante è da la terra. El principio de la generatione de fructi è dal sole et però la terra è dicta madre de le piante, el sole padre." Corniolo della Cornia 1982, 52.

42. Pietro Crescenzi, *Trattato della agricoltura: traslatato nella favella fiorentina, rivisto dallo 'nferigno accademico della Crusca,* (Bologna: Istituto delle Scienze, 1784), 50. Unfortunately we do not yet have an edition of this important agricultural treatise of the Middle Ages. As is usual, I am quoting from the eighteenth-century translation mentioned above.

43. Corniolo della Cornia 1982, 47.

III. Food in Literary and Visual Discourse

Chapter 11
What's in a Detail:
More Chickens in Renaissance
Birth Scenes

In some cases a detail embedded in an image will resonate with the rest of the painting and add meaning to it. This can happen when the viewer is able to read and contextualize it within the representation as a whole, or more appropriately for an historian, within the context of the social and cultural period in which the image was produced. Much has been written about details in paintings since the days when Kenneth Clark published *One Hundred Details from Pictures in the National Gallery*, a book that took advantage of developments in photography that had made it possible to reproduce high-quality details.[1] His brief introduction pointed out, "It may be true that a work of art can be recognized in the first second, but this does not exhaust its potentialities." The details he was submitting to the readers, accompanied by brief comments, "show us some of the rewards of patient scrutiny."[2] On quite another conceptual level is Daniel Arasse's attempt to discuss the multiple ways in which details can develop the significance of a painting, reach out to the viewer, and open additional windows of meaning.[3] The examples he discusses demonstrate his debt to semiotics and range from details that are "invisible" to elements that furnish supplementary allegorical commentary. There are also details that resist analysis, and others where the artist enters the picture by representing himself in the reflection of a mirror. Such examples, as Arasse points out, are, however, not meant to constitute a catalogue of the types of details that might be isolated in paintings of a given period. In fact, he concludes that "une 'histoire du détail' est impossible."[4] What I would like to do in these few pages is to reverse the proposition and show that at least sometimes "l'histoire est dans le détail."

The following contribution is based on an apparently minor detail in the *Birth of the Virgin* depicted in the *predella* of an altarpiece of the *Annunciation* from circa 1450, attributed to the Master of Signa, located in the Berenson Collection at Villa I Tatti. The detail I would like to contextualize is the depiction, in the left-hand part of the scene, of a woman carrying on her head a wicker basket containing two black hens (Plate 3). The figure is about to enter a door that leads to the room in which St. Anne is lying on a bed, having just given birth to the Virgin Mary. Two other women are engaged in a conversation with St. Anne and yet two others bathe the infant girl. A rapid look at the woman carrying the basket might suggest to the viewer that this figure was added for no particular reason other than to provide some sort of local color. Those who have in mind other depictions of the Birth of the Virgin or, for that matter, the Birth of St. John the Baptist might look at this scene and wonder why a different sort of detail—another, standard trademark of such depictions—is conspicuously absent: where is the cooked chicken that is often shown being served to the newly delivered mother, be she St. Anne or St. Elizabeth?[5] This important Italian (but not exclusively Italian) birth ritual of the late Middle Ages and the Renaissance was based on widespread dietary theories that ascribed to capons and to chickens in general 'warming' and restorative characteristics. Such qualities made fowl a natural fare for sick people, including newly delivered women, who were considered to be in need of such foods after giving birth.[6] The question that logically arises in the viewer's mind is: why did the Master of Signa choose to paint the scene at a somewhat earlier moment in time, when the food for the confined mother was being brought to the house?

Even a rapid search amongst birth scenes from the fourteenth to sixteenth centuries shows that different artists choose different time frames, resulting in a certain number of variants in the representation of this particular food ritual. In these depictions it becomes increasingly clear that above and beyond what amount to minor variations in the staging of birth scenes there must have also been some variability in parts of the dietary ritual itself. This is particularly noticeable in childbirth scenes that give anecdotal importance to contemporary customs. In fact, a serial examination of birth scenes provides a list of actions and details that ultimately permit us to understand the chicken ritual more fully.

While the Master of Signa chooses to show us the delivery of live chickens, a much more frequent choice turns out to be the one of portraying the delivery of chickens that have already been killed in preparation for cooking. In many fourteenth-century images we see them as they are being brought to the house, wrapped up in a cloth, but with a tell tale humped bulge, as can be seen in Giotto's *Birth of the Virgin* in the Scrovegni Chapel in Padua, in Pietro Lorenzetti 's *Birth of the Virgin* (Museo dell 'Opera del Duomo, Siena), or in Giovanni da Milano's *Birth of the Virgin* (Rinuccini Chapel, Santa Croce, Florence) (Plate 4). Sometimes the plucked and prepared chicken is in full view, as is the case in both the *Birth of the Virgin* by the Master of the Ashmolean Predella (Ashmolean Museum, Oxford), and the *Birth of St. John the Baptist* by Giusto de' Menabuoi (Baptistery, Padua). Ultimately, however, these are all examples of how this detail appears in a time frame, or narrative moment that precedes the actual presentation or consumption of the food. An interesting variant in which such birds are portrayed simultaneously in different phases of preparation is Vittore Carpaccio's *Birth of the Virgin* (Accademia Carrara, Bergamo) (Plate 8) of the first decade of the sixteenth century. Here the artist depicts a woman plucking a chicken in the background and another woman cooking a chicken in the kitchen in the middle ground, while in the foreground St. Anne is being served a bowl of what we can presume is chicken broth that is being cooled by being dripped from a spoon. Yet other representations concentrate on the preparation of food in a nearby kitchen, as is the case with the early fifteenth-century *Birth of the Virgin* on the triptych attributed to Master of the Osservanza (National Gallery, London), (Plate 5) where on the right-hand panel two women are at work in a kitchen. One of them squats in front of the pots boiling over the fire and holds a tray with a bowl of broth.

Finally, there are many depictions that focus exclusively on the actual serving of the ritual food to the newly delivered mother during her confinement. This moment constitutes the most important phase of the bedroom activities around which all of these images are predicated. Here again variants emerge, above all in the preparation of the food that is served (even though the possibilities are not limitless): there is roasted or boiled chicken, chicken broth and, more rarely, eggs or a combination of any of these three. In Italian depictions both broth and chicken are common[7] and sometimes even presented together, as in the case of

Sano di Pietro's *Birth of the Virgin* in Asciano (Plate 6 and 7). Much less frequent is the presence of eggs, for which Italian sources are not particularly prolific. So far my search has turned up only a few examples, such as the *Birth of the Virgin* of ca. 1470–80 by a Veronese painter[8] and another *Birth of the Virgin* by a Dalmatian artist working around 1375–1400 (National Gallery, London), where a man is seen delivering a large chest full of eggs.[9] In Italian paintings the three elements do not seem ever to have come together in one image, whereas this 'trilogy' of foods was often portrayed by Spanish artists of the same period, who used them as a metaphor for the Alpha and Omega of the life cycle.[10]

All these ingenious variants in the depiction of the food served to a newly delivered woman can be understood in terms of artists being forced by the very nature of their medium to portray a synchronic moment of the ritual or, to use a more cinematic metaphor, forced to adopt a "still frame" in a sequence of events. Since the ritual was so well known to all their viewers it was possible to represent any one of the many moments constituting the entire sequence beginning with the delivery of the chickens and ending with the final act consisting in the cooling and consumption of the broth. The familiarity of the viewers with this ritual made it possible to rely on a complicity whereby they could be counted on to reconstruct the sequence of events on the basis of one detail. Choosing a new and unusual moment in the sequence must have constituted a kind of inventive game that artists and viewers could engage in. The number of representations that have survived and their countless variants suggest that such visual clues fed on (and perhaps also reinforced) contemporary cultural practice.

This examination of the chicken as a recurrent detail in birth scenes can be concluded with the words of Daniel Arasse:

> Once a detail has been deciphered by an historian, once the resistance to its interpretation has been overcome, then the current reading, the detail, becomes normal, almost banal. Its singularity disappears and is integrated harmoniously into the explanation developed by the historian. The enigma is resolved, the 'surprise' wiped out...[11]

And, I will add, that such a detail once again becomes "just a detail."

Notes

First published as "What's in a Detail: More Chickens in Renaissance Birth Scenes," in *Renaissance Studies in Honor of Joseph Connors,* (Florence: Villa I Tatti, 2013), vol. 2, 150–154.

1. Published in a limited edition for the Trustees of the Museum in 1938, it was followed up by Kenneth Clark, *More Details from Pictures in the National Gallery,* London, 1941.
2. Kenneth Clark, *One Hundred Details from the National Gallery,* London, 1938, vi.
3. I am, of course, referring to Daniel Arasse, *Le détail. Pour une histoire rapprochée de la peinture,* (Paris: Flammarion, 1992).
4. Arasse 1992, 12.
5. Jacqueline Musacchio has written on this practice associated with childbirth on a variety of occasions. See her article "Pregnancy and Poultry in Renaissance Italy," *Source,* XVI, 1997, 3–9; her volume *The Art and Ritual of Childbirth in Renaissance Italy,* (New Haven/London: Yale University Press, 1999), 40–41; and *Art, Marriage, and Family in the Florentine Renaissance Palace,* (New Haven/London: Yale University Press, 2008), 40 for a fifteenth-century and a sixteenth-century childbirth scodella used to serve chicken broth. For an excellent recent overview, see Massimo Moretti, "Confini domestici. Ruoli e immagini femminili nella pittura della Controriforma," Florence, 2007, last consulted at http://www.fupress.net/index.php/sdd/article/view/2178/2099 on August 5, 2018.
6. The dietary discourses developed by medieval doctors to substantiate this idea are hard to summarize in just a few words. For a discussion of this belief, see among others my article on "From Roosters to Cocks: Renaissance Dietary Theory and Sexuality," in *Erotic Cultures of Renaissance Italy,* edited by Sara Matthews-Grieco, (Aldershot: Ashgate, 2010). See also Giovanni Marinello and

Girolamo Mercurio, *Medicina per le donne nel Cinquecento,* edited by M. L. Altieri, C. Mazzotta, A. Chiantera, and P. Antheri, (Turin: UTET, 1992).
7. Some examples, other than the ones already mentioned, are Sano di Pietro, *Birth of the Virgin,* University of Michigan Museum of Art, Ann Arbor; Benozzo Gozzoli, *Birth of the Virgin,* tabernacle of the Visitation, Museo Benozzo Gozzoli, Castelfiorentino; Giulio Campagnola, *Birth of the Virgin,* Scuola del Carmine, Padua; and a mid-fifteenth-century desco da parto with the *Birth of a Saint,* Galleria Giorgio Franchetti, Ca' d' Oro, Venice.
8. I would like to thank Mattia Vinco, who identified this image as one of three predella panels sold by Salamon in Milan in 1988 (lot 102, as by a Paduan-Veronese master of around 1470–80) and suggested an attribution to Francesco dai Libri.
9. See https://www.nationalgallery.org.uk/paintings/dalmatianvenetian-saint-joachim-and-the-angel-the-birth-of-the-virgin (last accessed 25/8/2018).
10. This information is derived from a paper given by Maria del Carmen Garcia Herrero on "Hens and Eggs at the Beginning of Life in the Hispanic Middle Ages," at the Conference on *Food and Beliefs/Alimentation et Croyances,* 10–11 December 2004, Tours now published as "Huevos y gallinas en los inicios de la vida," in María del Carmen Garcia Herrero, *Artesans de vida. Mujeres de la Edad Media,* (Zaragoza: Institución Fernando el Católico, 2009), 109–125.
11. "Une fois le détail déchiffré par l'historien, une fois vaincu la résistance qu'il offrait à une lecture courante, le détail devient comme normal, banal presque. Sa singularité s'évanouit et s'intègre harmonieusement au système d'explication mis au point par l'historien. L'énigme est résolue, la 'surprise' effacée." Arasse 1992, 10.

Chapter 12
Food and Good Manners
in Florentine Last Suppers

Last Suppers (also known as *Cenacoli*), and food-related subjects represented in convent refectories, have long remained the almost exclusive domain of art historians.[1] Yet religious representations of eating and dining tables also offer historians of food a particularly rich "source," despite the difficulties that images present in terms of their contextualization and interpretation. Although the history of the material culture of convents and convent dining is still somewhat in its infancy,[2] the following pages will attempt to throw light on aspects of food history that influenced the pictorial content of Florentine *Cenacoli* in the late Middle Ages and Renaissance.

Frescoes, paintings and other iconographic media have documented—often with greater precision than archival sources—changes that occurred in the way people interacted with the food they consumed as well as the evolution of eating practices in this period. Of course, an iconographic source does not necessarily reflect "reality" in a direct or literal manner, and most historians are well aware of the allusive and symbolic value of images, especially in the case of the foods represented in religious subjects. However, in order not to err through anachronism, we need to place foodstuffs in their contemporary cultural context,[3] so that they can be "decoded" and their material or allegorical meaning correctly interpreted.

One of the objects usually represented in *Last Suppers* provides potentially misleading information that can lead to a "mis-reading" of the items in front of the diners. As of the early fourteenth century, there is an almost obsessive use of glass vessels in *Cenacoli*, usually filled with red wine. The quasi-constant presence of such glasses responds, in all probability, to the striking pictorial effect of transparent glass and ruby red wine more than to the use of glass drinking vessels in contemporary dining practices, which took much longer to become generalized. The presence of red wine has often been interpreted as a reference to the Passion, but the visual fascination with transparency also extends (albeit more rarely) to white wine or transparent water. An example of this can be found in the glasses and carafes depicted in the (large) *Last Supper* by Domenico Ghirlandaio in the refectory at Ognissanti, where the rich yellow color of the wine contrasts with the red cherries on the table (Plate 9). Other *Last Suppers* by Stefano di Antonio di Vanni—at Sant'Andrea a Cercina (Plate 10) and in the former *Spedale di San Matteo,* now the Accademia di Belle Arti (Plate 12)—feature water carafes on the table, probably meant to dilute the wine according to current dining practice. Another explicit reference to the practice of diluting wine with water, appears in the (small) *Last Supper* painted by Domenico Ghirlandaio in the refectory at San Marco, where eight carafes are positioned in four pairs on the table, each pair containing red wine and water.

It is here worth remembering that wine was never drunk pure but was always diluted with water in proportions that depended on the type of wine consumed as well as on the taste or specific requirements of individual drinkers.[4] Indeed, drinking undiluted wine was regarded as unusual behavior (denoting a lack of temperance) until the late eighteenth century, when this custom became more common. The adding of water to wine often constituted an important ritual: it was performed at banquets by the *bottigliere* (butler) or the *coppiere* (cupbearer), two officials who are described in some detail by sixteenth-century treatises dealing with such events. However, the assistants who served at table generally do not appear in *Last Suppers,* or are almost hidden, as can be seen in the *terra verde* frescoes at the former *Spedale di San Matteo,* where a small group of servants are barely visible on the far left of the pictorial space (Plate 11).

On the whole, *Last Suppers* were portrayed as intimate meals, where the confusion of the banquet, with its accompanying retinue of pages, grooms, cupbearers, carvers and stewards, was eliminated in order to further emphasize the sacred nature of the setting. Other dining scenes were not as hindered by such a devotional purpose. The *Wedding at Cana* for example—a subject that is much less frequent in the convent refectories, and appears later than the *Last Supper*—introduces us to a setting where a miraculous event takes place in a more animated social context, with a significantly expanded range of descriptive details. Thus a *Wedding at Cana* fresco by Bernardino Poccetti, completed in 1604 for the Vallombrosan monastery of *San Bartolomeo a Ripoli*, features a number of servants or stewards (in the right foreground), handling the amphorae where the water is about to be miraculously turned into wine (Plate 13). These stewards are the equivalent of the court butlers of the sixteenth and seventeenth centuries who were responsible for handling the wine and water for the table. However, the butlers never served the guests directly; this was the task of the much more important cupbearer, who can be seen in the Poccetti fresco, about to present a glass of wine to the Lord. The care with which he holds the glass in his right hand, and the small salver in his left hand, are consistent with Domenico Romoli's description of this ritual in his treatise on the "art of the table," published a few decades earlier (*La Singolare dottrina*, 1560). When describing the cupbearer's duties, Romoli writes, among other things, that "he must wear a priest's beret … and when he goes to collect the cup or the glass he shall adjust the hat." But above all he states that "he will carry with his arm raised and steady" the glass he will give to the diner. Romoli provides detailed instructions regarding this ritual: when the cupbearer has "appeared before his lord, … [he] will uncover the glass with his right hand" by removing the salver "…and having performed the *credenza*, [i.e. having tasted some of the wine poured from the glass into the salver, to show that it was not poisoned] and added water, he will then place the salver below the glass."[5] In his fresco, Poccetti depicts the cupbearer in the precise act of placing the salver he has just used to taste the wine under the glass (Plate 13).

Visual representations often testify, almost unconsciously, to the slow development of etiquette, to changes in ways of eating and various other aspects of the history of food and its consumption. Between the fourteenth and the sixteenth centuries, a striking example of the evolution of dining customs can be found in *Last Suppers*. In the early part of this period, representations of

the *Last Supper* in monastic refectories show how guests shared a trencher between two commensals, as well as other tableware (glasses and knives), but
by the sixteenth century each guest begins to have his personal table setting
with individual tableware. A good example of this transition is provided in a
Last Supper by Stefano d'Antonio di Vanni in the presbytery at Sant'Andrea,
Cercina (ca. 1440–1460?), painted in a style that Luisa Vertova rightly identifies
as belonging to a "current of outmoded painters" (Plate 10).[6] Yet it is clear that
the table setting was hardly outmoded, but more in keeping with the times.
The painter has positioned a shared trencher in front of each pair of apostles,
but the "privatization" of eating utensils and the eating space (as described by
Jean-Louis Flandrin for the early modern period)[7] is surprisingly advanced.
Although the Stefano d'Antonio di Vanni fresco still shows pairs of apostles
sharing trenchers, each person at the table has their own knife and glass. This
is a significant change from fourteenth-century depictions, such as the well
known *Last Supper* by Duccio di Buoninsegna on the back of his *Maestà* (Siena,
Museo dell'Opera Metropolitana, 1308–1311), where commensals share tableware (Plate 14).

Despite the small dimensions of the panel, Duccio includes a wealth of
detail; it is even possible to see the embroidery on the tablecloth, an attractive glazed ceramic jug, as well as the bread and wafers allotted to the apostles. However, there are only three bowls, four glasses and four knives to be
shared among the company, which objects eloquently document what was
still a widespread, collective use of tableware. The descriptive value of such
images has often been undervalued, owing to a lack of interest in the foods
and objects present on the table, or to an exaggerated tendency to enhance
their symbolic significance to the detriment of their documentary value. The
bread and *cialdoni* (a kind of rolled up wafer) in Duccio's small panel—a detail that appears in many other contemporary and later depictions[8]—suggest
a symbolic meaning, but it is also true that such little breads were actually
served at wealthy tables in the fourteenth century (see, for example, the accounts for the table of the Florentine *Signoria*, dating from 1344).[9]

Even the fruit on the tables of dining scenes commissioned for refectories
in Florence (as well as other locations in central-northern Italy) calls for an

interpretation that cannot be restricted to the exclusively symbolic.[10] It has often been suggested that the characteristic red cherries appearing on the tables are reminiscent of Christ's blood and therefore the Passion, but the presence of many other types of fruit (other than red) suggests the need for other readings. *Last Suppers*, above all those from the fifteenth century, often feature a profusion of fruit that is prominently displayed against a white tablecloth. In addition to the usual cherries there are also oranges, like those in the Ognissanti refectory, or lemons and pears, like those in the *Convento della Croce* (San Casciano Val di Pesa). It is also worth recalling the beautiful trays of figs alongside the table painted in the *Cenacolo di Fuligno* (formerly the church of Sant'Onofrio), and the melons in the *Convento della Calza*. To these examples of various fruits should be added the magnificent citrus trees visible in the background of almost identical *Last Suppers* by Ghirlandaio: the larger version in the Church of Ognissanti (1480) (Plate 9) and the smaller one in San Marco (1483/4?). Even the *Last Supper* at the *Spedale di San Matteo* features fruit, though in this case it is still not on the table but rather on a tray carried by a servant at the extreme left of the scene (Plate 12).

Nearly all these fruits would have been out of season for the time of year (early Spring) in which the scene purportedly took place, and so it is not possible to speak of realism in any strict sense of the word. The presence of fruit can perhaps best be explained by the particular importance accorded to this kind of foodstuff by the most affluent classes of the time. Not only did fruit command a high price, especially when out of season, but it was quite simply, a luxury item. Not considered a staple, although beautiful and decorative, fruit was thought to lack any nutritional value and was seen more as a "condiment" appropriate for social (and religious) elites.[11]

The conviction that fruit was not suitable fare for the lower classes can also be found in literary sources of the late Middle Ages and Renaissance. A well-known plot (occurring in several novelle and analyzed at greater length in chapter 10) featured a peasant who stole his master's fruit; the story ends with the thief being reminded that fruit was for gentlemen, whereas vegetables were for peasants. The distinction between "high" fruits that grew on trees (suitable for the rich and powerful), as opposed to "low" tubers that grew underground (appropriate for the poor), was a commonplace at this time, and was justified on both medical and cosmological grounds: the products of nature furthest from the earth were considered the best, and thus "naturally" due to the higher social orders.[12]

Less well known, but equally significant, is the existence of a minor literary genre dedicated exclusively to fruit, in vogue between the fourteenth and fifteenth centuries. Initially limited to Tuscany, it spread to other areas in Italy, as is apparent in surviving versions composed in different Italian dialects.[13] Some of these early fifteenth-century texts were the work of the Florentine popular poets known as *canterini,* performers who, in some cases, were paid by the Florentine *Signoria* to entertain the Priors sitting at the most important table in the city. The texts composed for this civic institution, were considerably more sophisticated than their fourteenth-century counterparts, and often voiced an opinion as to what were the best varieties of each kind of fruit. In one of these poetic texts, composed by Pietro Corsellini of Siena (also known as Pietro Canterino), we find him praising seven different grape varieties, eleven kinds of pears and no fewer than fifteen different varieties of figs.

Not only was the Florentine *Signoria* entertained with poetic descriptions of fruit, but considerable quantities of real fruit were served at the table of the Priors. To give an idea of the importance of this luxury food, thought to be superfluous in terms of nutritional value, and thus a kind of "extra," it might be pointed out that, in 1344, some 10% of the money spent by the *Mensa della Signoria* was devoted to fruit. The accounts mention many varieties served at table; there was seasonal produce such as pears and cherries, but every day throughout the year they were given expensive oranges (either imported or an exotic, locally grown fruit). The oranges served a specific purpose since the Priors used them above all to squeeze juice onto their roast meat, thus "tempering" their viands.

The genuine passion for fruit shown by the elites can also be gauged by their interest in its cultivation, the history of which still needs to be written. Leon Battista Alberti dedicated the most flowery descriptions in his *Libri della Famiglia* to the various kinds of pine nuts imported from Sicily and Puglia and later grown by Niccolaio Alberti, before concluding that "It would be a long tale to recount all the exotic and diverse fruits which that most gentlemanly of people planted in his garden, all arranged in rows by his own hand, so that one could see and admire them with ease."[14] Yet this passion for fruit, which is so evident among the social elites of Florence and other parts of the peninsula, ran counter to the advice of doctors and dietary treatises of the period, which almost always singled out the consumption of fresh fruit as dangerous and unhealthy. Both the medieval *Tacuinum sanitatis* and the popular dietary handbooks of the sixteenth century assert the dangers of such foodstuffs.

Despite medical diffidence, consumption remained high amongst the wealthy, almost certainly because this particular foodstuff continued to be a status symbol on socially important tables for a long time. A particularly striking example of the *longue durée* of this custom is furnished by a royal banquet hosted by Louis IX of France (Saint Louis) at the Franciscan monastery of Sens in 1248. Salimbene de Adam (a Franciscan friar and a chronicler born in Parma) provides an eye-witness account of that event in his *Cronica*, in which he not only stresses the importance of fruit at the feast but also casts light on the strategic presence of fruit seen in *Last Suppers*. Salimbene recalls the royal banquet saying:

> So we received on that day first cherries, then the whitest bread. Plenty of excellent wine, truly worthy of the [King's] magnificence ... Afterwards we had fresh broad beans cooked in milk, fish, crabs, rolls of eel, rice with almond milk and powdered cinnamon, boiled eel in a delicious sauce, pies and fresh cheese. The fruit that was served was abundant and beautiful.[15]

Other details in the *Last Suppers* of Florentine refectories—details that are usually overlooked by the literature on the subject—can also provide relevant information for the food historian. As mentioned earlier on, it was normal, at least until the late Quattrocento, to share a meal with a companion who ate from the same trencher, a practice that required a particular etiquette in sharing food and drink (Plate 15).[16] This special relationship is dealt with in treatises on good manners, such as the *De Quinquaginta Curialitatibus ad Mensam*,[17] composed by Bonvesin da la Riva, a *magister* who was also a member of the

Umiliati (a Franciscan tertiary order). Composed in the late thirteenth century, this treatise on manners to be observed at table listed some fifty rules, of which a considerable number are dedicated to sharing a trencher and glass. The fourth rule mentions that neither diner should start to eat unless one of the two has blessed the food. Other rules are more down to earth, such as the tenth, which advises wiping one's mouth before drinking out of the shared cup to avoid disgusting the other. Similarly, rule eleven reminds diners not to proffer the cup to their companion so as not to inconvenience him, and leave him free to do what he wishes, provided the cup is within reach. Yet another rule, the twenty-first, advises against picking through the pieces of meat or egg on the trencher so as not to disgust, once again, one's dining partner, while rule twenty three states that bread should not be dipped in the wine and then fished out again (since it would bother Bonvesin, the author, himself!). However, maybe the most striking rules were the two that suggested that diners behave respectfully towards their companion (whether man or woman) and, furthermore, to both prepare and offer them the tastiest mouthfuls (rules twenty-five and twenty-six).

Apart from the anecdotal value of these rules, they highlight what might be described as the social dynamics of the trencher, a situation in which a dining partner was paired with another person, with whom they would interact more intimately than with the rest of the commensals, and be obliged to adjust their manners accordingly. Thus, in many *Last Suppers*, particularly the earliest ones, the apostles are depicted turning towards one another. A good example of this is a *Last Supper* by an anonymous thirteenth-century mosaic artist preserved in St Mark's, Venice (Plate 16), where almost all the apostles are paired, except for St John, St Peter and Christ, who are separated from the others (in order to highlight the specific roles assigned to them by the Byzantine canonical tradition).[18] So too Giotto, who innovated on many visual conventions, nonetheless continued to portray the dining dynamic imposed by shared trenchers in the Arena (Scrovegni) Chapel depiction of the *Last Supper* (Plate 17). The apostles seen from the back (two pairs) and those facing the viewer (again two pairs) clearly turn to their dining companions, and in the case of the pair on the bottom right, a trencher is distinctly visible between them. The key players at the table are, here again, set apart on the far left of the table: Jesus and St. Thomas, St. Peter, St. John and the yellow-robed Judas.

Even later depictions, including those in Florentine refectories up to the late fifteenth century, continued to portray this way of pairing the apostles at table. This is apparent in the mid fifteenth-century *Last Supper* at Sant'Andrea a Cercina (Plate 10), and even more clearly (although in a very different pictorial style) in a *Cenacolo* painted by Cosimo Rosselli in 1481–1482 in the Sistine Chapel in Rome.[19] With the passage of time, the dramatic depiction of this New Testament episode changes and Christ is placed increasingly at the centre of the composition. In some versions, this centrality mobilizes the figures closer to Christ, leaving pairs of apostles on the right and on the left, set slightly apart from the action and apparently intent on conversing and dining—as in the *Last Supper* by Sogliani in the refectory of Santa Maria di Candeli (ca. 1510).[20] Here the somewhat abrupt division of the scene, divided between three lunettes, highlights this same kind of separation. Similar groupings of diners can be seen in the work of Franciabigio in the Convento della Calza (1514), and that of Domenico Ghirlandaio in the Church of Ognissanti (1480). Gradually, a central Christ came to dominate the entire composition. Perhaps the most influential example of this is Leonardo's *Last Supper* (1494/98) in Santa Maria delle Grazie in Milan, where all the apostles were now seated (or standing) before their individual plates, and most are turned towards the center of the composition and focused on Jesus.

In conclusion, it might be useful to recall the more general context in which these representations of the *Last Supper* should be placed. Refectories were spaces where meals were consumed, and therefore the choice of table-related iconography was certainly not coincidental. In her work on the Florentine *Cenacolo*, Luisa Vertova suggested that

> The idea of decorating the room where a religious community ate its meals with meal-related subjects taken from the Old and New Testament, or from the community's favourite Lives of the Saints, is an obvious one … But this vaguely edifying and meditative function only appears in the decoration of Florentine refectories at the time of Poccetti and Giovanni da San Giovanni, namely when the monumental painting of refectories was in its death throes.[21]

As she convincingly argues, the *Last Suppers* of the earlier period were not intended to be a narrative or merely decorative subject, but rather a profession of Christian faith that would serve as a prologue to the Crucifixion, another religious subject that was often represented in the same room as a *Last Supper*.

Sometimes the dining tables depicted in *Last Suppers* do not have much food on them, like the one portrayed in the fourteenth-century refectory at Santa Croce (completed ca. 1350). But whereas a *Cenacolo* may not feature much more than bread and wine, other food-related subjects can contribute to the iconographic program of a room dedicated to taking meals. In the Florentine refectory frescoed by Taddeo Gaddi, the act of eating is depicted three more times, over and above the *Last Supper*: Saint Louis of Toulouse is shown feeding the poor in Florence, there is the story of a priest who interrupted his Easter dinner to share it with Saint Benedict and, lastly, Christ is represented eating in the house of Simon the Pharisee while St Mary Magdalen anoints his feet.

In other settings, representing yet other dining scenes, the tables depicted can be abundantly supplied, as in the *Marriage at Cana* painted by an unknown Florentine artist in the church of San Giorgio alla Costa (late sixteenth century/early seventeenth century). From the sixteenth century onwards, the visual arts develop a variety of subjects evoking the act of eating and portray tables that can vary greatly in terms of how richly they are laid. A particularly frugal table is that of *The Providence of the Dominicans,* by Giovanni Antonio Sogliani in the large refectory at San Marco (1536), where the only "edible" thing on the table is salt. An example of a rich table is the *Miracle of Manna* by Alessandro Allori in the church of Santa Maria Novella (completed in 1597), where platters are laden with white Manna and roast fowl.[22] Finally, a more mysterious and mystical meal is conveyed by the curiously tilted (and therefore almost entirely hidden) table surface in the *Dinner at Bethany*, painted by Giovanni da San Giovanni in the refectory of Santa Trinità (ca. 1630).

In what way might these images have served as *exempla* to the monks and lay brethren who ate their meals beneath them? As in all complex cultural phenomena, one explanation does not rule out others, but here it makes sense to approach this question from the perspective of the food historian. The emergence of a visual interest in the subject of a table surrounded by diners can certainly be correlated with the fact that the first texts to discuss good manners (and good manners when dining) first emerged from the monastic environment.[23] The most influential of these texts were translated into Italian (and other vernaculars) as of the thirteenth century, and appear to have been modeled on both the *De istitutione novitiorum* of Hugh of Saint Victor, who died in 1141, and Petrus Alphonsi's *Disciplina clericalis*, composed at around the same time. Yet another important text from the clerical world were two short but resonant chapters (*De curialitatibus in mensa conservandis* and the *De ministratione decenti*) of the *Morale scholarium* composed by John of Garland (ca. 1192–ca. 1272). These echo much of the same general advice given by predecessors, and were to be expanded upon in the following centuries by authors who further developed the guidelines of civility.

An increasing interest in rules aimed at fostering polite table manners appears in texts written by monastic authors such as Bonvesin da la Riva (ca. 1240–ca. 1313) and, somewhat later, Francesc Eiximenis (1330–1409), a Franciscan monk who began a vast encyclopedia in Catalan known as *Lo Crestià* that remained incomplete. The third book of this latter undertaking (often referred to as *Terç del Crestià*, and composed most probably in 1382) contained some 47 chapters dedicated to the table but also, more generally, to the "Christian" way of eating and drinking, with far more details than the treatise authored by Bonvesin a century earlier. The attention that the monastic world paid to good manners, over and above the diet religious orders were meant to follow, was evident in the images chosen for their refectories. The tables and diners depicted on the walls of dining halls, facing the religious community, presented a model to imitate. Indeed, the extent to which these images were meant to function as a kind of mirror at times becomes quite explicit, as in the case of the *Last Supper* in the former Spedale di San Matteo, thanks to the inclusion of a lector on the far right. This figure stands at the end of the high table (Plate 11) to read aloud to Christ and the apostles, reflecting the current practice of reading the Holy Scriptures during (otherwise silent) refectory meals, a custom common to all religious orders. The insertion of a contemporary monk in a biblical dining scene commissioned for a monastic dining hall was, however, not entirely unusual. A later, but even more ingenious example of the "mirror effect" of such a tableau is the monumental painting of the *Banquet of Esther and Ahasuerus* by Giorgio Vasari (1549), originally located in the refectory of the Benedictine Badia at Arezzo. On the shiny metal surface of a vessel placed in the foreground, at the feet of the guests seated at the table, can be seen the reflected figure of a standing monk, captured in the act of contemplating the painting and thereby becoming both audience and subject of this Old Testament dining scene.

Notes

First published as "Cibi e buone maniere nei sacri conviti," in *La tradizione fiorentina dei cenacoli*, edited by Cristina Acidini Luchinat and Rosanna C. Proto Pisani, (Florence: Scala, 1997), 69–79. Translation by Lucinda Byatt with revisions by the author. Some changes have been made in the present version (notably adding the names of painters, location of frescos, their date of execution and when possible a link to find a good reproduction). This seemed advisable since the original article appeared in a volume where that information was provided.

1. In Italian usage the term cenacolo refers to both the room where the conventual meal was served and the depiction of the *Last Supper* suggesting their close association. For an early approach that, somewhat exceptionally, refers to social history, see Dominique Rigaux, *A la*

Table du Seigneur: L'Eucharistie chez les Primitifs Italiens 1250–1497, (Paris: Cerf, 1989), and by the same author, "La Cène aux Ecrevisses. Table et Spiritualité dans les Alpes Italiennes au Quattrocento," in *La Sociabilité à table*, edited by M. Aurell, O. Dumoulin and F. Thelamon, (Rouen: University of Rouen, 1992), 217–228. In the intervening years more work has been done in this direction. See, for example, Stefanie Felicitas Ohlig, *Florentiner Refektorien. Form, Funktion und die Progamme ihrer Fresken*, (Engelsbach/Frankfurt/Munich/New York: Hänsell-Hohenhausen, 2000) and Diana Hiller, *Gendered Perceptions in Florentine Last Supper frescoes c. 1350–1490*, (Farnham: Ashgate, 2014).

2. When this essay was written, the bibliography on this topic was limited to: Barbara Harvey, "Monastic Diet, XIIIth–XVIth Centuries: Problems and Perspectives," in Simonetta Cavaciocchi (ed.), *Alimentazione e nutrizione nei*

secoli XIII–XVIII, (Florence: Le Monnier, 1997), 611–41; Marek Derwich, *La vie quotidienne des moines et chanoines réguliers au Moyen Age et Temps modernes* (Wroclaw: Institut d'Histoire de l'Université, 1995). Since then, more research has appeared; an overview of the recent literature can be found in Sylvio Hermann De Franceschi, "Discipline alimentaire et morale monastique à l'âge classique. Approches casuistiques de l'observance du jeûne et de l'abstinence en milieu régulier (XVIIᵉ-XVIIIᵉ siècles)," *Food & History*, vol. 16.1 (2018).

3. The importance of the setting is particularly evident for images that were specifically conceived for refectories, as Luisa Vertova stresses from the outset in her book on *I Cenacoli fiorentini*, (Turin: ERI, 1965), 7.

4. For more on the proper choice of wine see chapter 6.

5. "...doveria portare berrette da preti ... et quando anderà a pigliar la coppa o il bicchiere accomodi la sua berretta..." and regarding the glass "...lo porterà rilevato e fermo di braccio..." Once he actually serves the wine "...comparso inanzi al suo signore con la mano destra scuopra il bicchiere ... et fatta la credenza, et inacquato il vino, ponga sotto il bicchiere la tazza," Domenico Romoli, *La Singolar Dottrina*, (Venice, 1560), 14v.

6. "...corrente di pittori ritardatari," Vertova 1965, 40.

7. See the chapter, "La distinction par le goût," in *Histoire de la vie privée*, edited by Philippe Aries and Georges Duby, (Paris: Seuil, 1985), vol. 3, 267–309.

8. For example, Stefano di Antonio di Vanni's previously mentioned *Last Supper* in the Spedale di San Matteo.

9. On the *Signoria* see Giovanna Frosini, *Il cibo e i signori. La mensa dei priori di Firenze nel quinto decennio del sec. XIV*, (Florence: Accademia della Crusca, 1993), especially 54–56.

10. See the numerous examples of *Last Suppers* with fruit reproduced in Isidoro

Marcionetti, *I Cenacoli della Svizzera Italiana*, (Lugano: Marcionetti, 1981). I would like to thank Massimo Danzi (University of Geneva) for drawing my attention to this publication.

11. For more on the importance of fruit in this period see chapters 8 and 10. See also the excellent article by Marilyn Nicoud, "I medici medievali e la frutta: un prodotto ambiguo," in *Le parole della frutta: Storia, saperi, immagini tra medioevo ed età contemporanea*, edited by Irma Naso, (Turin: Silvio Zamorani, 2012), 91–108.

12. For the reasons underlying this way of seeing fruit, and for what follows on the poems dedicated to fruit, also see my three articles: "The Social Politics of pre-Linnean Botanical Classification," *I Tatti Studies*, 4, 1991 (chapter 10 in the present volume); "Les utilisations sociales des fruits et légumes dans l'Italie médiévale," *Le Grand livre des fruits et légumes: histoire, culture et usage*, edited by D. Meier and P. Vannier, (Paris: La Manufacture, 1991); and "Savoir de poète ou savoir de botaniste? Les fruits dans la poésie italienne du 15ᵉ siècle," in *Médiévales*, 16 (1989), (now translated as chapter 8 in the present volume).

13. Some of the following points are also discussed, albeit in greater detail, in chapter 8, but could not be removed here without weakening the present argument.

14. "Sarebbe lunga storia racontare quanta strana e diversa quantità di frutti quello uomo gentilissimo piantasse negli orti suoi, tutti di sua mano posti a ordine, a filo, da guardalli e lodalli volentieri" Leon Battista Alberti, *I Libri della famiglia*, edited by R. Romano and A. Tenenti, (Turin: Einaudi, 1969), 241.

15. "Habuimus igitur illa die primo cerasa, postea panem albidissimum; vinum quoque, ut magnificentia regia dignum erat, abundans et precipuum ponebatur ... Postea habuimus fabas recentes cum lacte de coctas, pisces et cancros, pastilles anguillarum, risum cum

lacte amigdalarum et pulvere cynamomi, anguillas assata cum optimo salsamento, turtas et iunctas et fructus necessarios habuimus abundanter atque decenter." Salimbene de Adam, *Cronica*, edited by F. Bernini, (Bari: Laterza, 1942), vol. 1, 321.

16. For a fresco illustrating this point (geographically closer to where Bonvesin de la Riva's treatise was composed), see the little-known Cristoforo da Seregno e bottega, *Last Supper* in the church of San Bernardo a Monte Carasso, Ticino, second half of the 15th century (Plate 15).

17. The standard edition of this treatise is by Gianfranco Contini, *Cinque volgari di Bonvesin de la Riva*, Modena 1937, but there is now a more recent version: Bonvesin de la Riva, *I volgari di Bonvesin de la Riva*, edited by A. M. Gökçen, (New York: Peter Lang, 1996).

18. On the canonical gestures assigned to Christ, John the Evangelist and Saint Peter, see Vertova 1965, 18 passim. Much of this had already been pointed out by Frederick Adama van Scheltema, *Über die Entwiklung der Abendmahlsdarstellung von der byzantinischen Mosaikkunst bis zur niederländischen Malerei des 17. Jahrhunderts*, (Leipzig, 1912).

19. For a reproduction see https://it.wikipedia.org/wiki/Cosimo_Rosselli#/media/File:Cosimo_Rosselli_Ultima_cena.jpg (last accessed 22/08/2018).

20. For reproductions of this *Last Supper* and the following two see:
—Cenacolo di Candeli (Giovanni Antonio Sogliani):   https://it.wikipedia.org/wiki/Cenacolo_di_Candeli#/media/File:Giovanni_antonio_sogliani,_ultima_cena,_1511-14_ca._01.JPG. (last accessed 22/08/2018).;

—Cenacolo della Calza (Franciabigio): https://it.wikipedia.org/wiki/Cenacolo_della_Calza#/media/File:Cenacolo_della_calza,_Franciabigio1.jpg (last accessed 22/08/2018).

—Cenacolo di Ognissanti (Ghirlandaio) https://it.wikipedia.org/wiki/Cenacoli_di_Firenze#/media/File:Domenico_ghirlandaio,_cenacolo_di_ognissanti_01.jpg   (last accessed 22/08/2018).

21. "L'idea di decorare l'ambiente ove una comunità religiosa consuma i pasti con soggetti attinenti al pasteggiare dall'Antico e dal Nuovo Testamento o dalle Vite dei Santi più cari alla comunità, è abbastanza ovvia … Ma questa funzione vagamente edificante e meditativa è riconoscibile nella decorazione dei refettori fiorentini soltanto al tempo del Poccetti e di Giovanni da San Giovanni, cioè quando la pittura monumentale dei refettori entra in agonia" Vertova 1965, 14.

22. For illustrations of these frescos see:— Sogliani, San Marco: https://upload.wikimedia.org/wikipedia/commons/b/be/Giovanni_antonio_sogliani%2C_san_domenico_e_i_frati_serviti_dagli_angeli.jpg;—Allori, S. Maria Novella: https://upload.wikimedia.org/wikipedia/commons/7/7e/Alessandro_allori%2C_caduta_della_manna%2C_05.JPG (last accessed 22/08/2018).

23. For more information on clerical authors of treatises on dining etiquette and a bibliography on this topic, see Allen Grieco and Andrea Manciulli, "La codificazione del modo di stare a tavola," in *Et coquatur ponendo. Cultura della cucina e della tavola in Europa tra medioevo ed età moderna*, (Exhibition catalogue), (Prato: Istituto Datini, 1996), 109–123.

Chapter 13
The Eaten Heart: Social Order, Sexuality and the Wilderness

The somewhat macabre but fascinating legend of the eaten heart is well-known to philologists. It has been enormously successful in literature: not only has it circulated for more than six centuries, but it has also given rise to countless variations in practically every European country. Its dissemination has been such that a complete account would require much more space than is available here. Therefore, renouncing any attempt at an overview, the following pages will focus specifically on a hitherto unnoticed aspect of this literary *topos*[1] that will throw new light on both literary and iconographic versions of this story.

The earliest reference to this story appears in a version of the *Tristan* legend attributed to an Anglo-Norman troubadour, known as Thomas of Britain. It is generally acknowledged that this version was composed possibly sometime between 1165 and 1170, and may have been the source for the German translation by Gottfried von Strassburg, dating from the end of the twelfth or very early thirteenth century. Only a few isolated fragments have survived from the Thomas of Britain version: as she waits for Tristan to return, Iseult passes the time playing the harp and singing the *Lay of Guiron*. The eight verses of this *Lay* tell the story of the Count of Guiron, who was killed by his mistress's husband and whose heart was fed to her through trickery. This short, unfinished story was expanded and embellished upon in numerous variations. As it slowly spread throughout medieval Europe, it became a major literary theme.[2]

Although this is not the place to explore all the instances in which this story appears, it is important to outline the main steps of its growing fortune. Between the twelfth and fifteenth centuries, the story of the eaten heart moved in all geographical directions. Its earliest appearance in Germany can be found in *Die Herzemäre* by Konrad von Würzburg (d.1287), a poem written in Middle High German. In the early thirteenth century, the same basic story reappeared in the *Lay of Ignauré* also known as the *Lay of the Prisoner*, written in *Langue d'Oïl* by an anonymous poet.[3] In this version, the story of the eaten heart is unchanged, except that the adulterous lover is killed by the husbands of twelve women. At about the same time, two Provençal biographies, written in *Langue d'Oc*, associated this legend with the lives of two different troubadours from the south of France: Lignauré or Linhaure (the *senhal* for Raimbaut d'Aurenga), active in the second half of the twelfth century, and Guillem de Cabestany (in Occitan Guilhem de Cabestanh), active in the early thirteenth century.[4] The tale also appears in the well-known *Roman du châtelain de Coucy et de la dame de Fayel*, dating from the late thirteenth century.

A sixteenth-century version of *Von des Brembergers End und Tod* attributes the theme of the eaten heart to the German *Minnesinger*, Reinmann von Brennenberg, who lived in the mid thirteenth century. In England, the tale does not seem to have been known before the *Knight of Courtesy*, a fifteenth-century poem of five hundred verses written in Middle English. However, the relatively late arrival of this literary theme was compensated by its success in the sixteenth century, when it appeared in numerous English plays and in poems translated from Italian.[5] Furthermore, versions of the story can be found in Spain,[6] Sweden[7] and in popular ballads throughout Europe, from the sixteenth through the eighteenth century.

While the dissemination of the legend of the eaten heart was Europe-wide, it became most successful in Italy, where it was circulated and even adopted by celebrated authors. Its first known use is in a collection of one hundred stories, often referred to as *Il Novellino*, composed in the late thirteenth century.[8] Tale number sixty-two is an interesting variation, reminiscent of the *Lay of Ignauré*, since it tells of several women tricked into eating the heart of their lover. This rudimentary and concise version falls short of the much more sophisticated renditions of this theme that were soon to appear. In Dante's *Vita Nuova* (chapter III), a personification of Love appears to the poet, holding Beatrice in its arms. Love proffers her the heart of the poet, trying all kinds of ruses to make the woman eat the heart, which she ends up doing unwillingly and expressing disgust. Dante's version of the story seems, at first, quite different to the stories of adultery mentioned so far, but even if the absence of a jealous husband leaves the love triangle incomplete, it does not change the basic act of eating the lover's heart.[9]

Perhaps the richest and most interesting uses of this story appear in Boccaccio, since he uses the motif at least three different times, in each case introducing subtle alterations. The first is in a long poem written during the Neapolitan period of his life. *Filostrato* (VI, 24) presents an unexpected role reversal. In this poem, Troilus, son of Priam, is in love with Cressida. Grieved by the long absence of his beloved and doubting her fidelity, Troilus falls asleep and dreams that she is being attacked and knocked down by a boar that is actually the Achaean hero Diomedes. The boar then gouges out her heart. Cressida neither struggles nor cries, indeed she seems to take pleasure in her fate.

> Troilus ... in a dream he saw the perilous sin of her who made him languish. He seemed to hear a great and unpleasant trampling in a shady wood. Upon raising his head thereat he seemed to behold a great charging boar. And then afterwards it seemed to him that he saw beneath its feet Cressida, whose heart it tore forth with its snout. And as it seemed, little cared Cressida for so great a hurt, but almost did she take pleasure in what the beast was doing.[10]

Boccaccio was more respectful of previous literary traditions regarding the theme of the eaten heart when he composed *The Decameron* some ten years after *Il Filostrato*. The best example of his fidelity to the theme is to be found in the novella IV, 9, a tale that has been the object of a vast amount of scholarly work.[11] The narrative structure preserves the typical love triangle in which the husband takes revenge on his wife by killing her lover and duping her into eating his heart. Moreover, it also quite closely reflects the group of tales in which a poet becomes the victim. The *Decameron* story of Guiglielmo Rossiglione, his wife and her lover echoes rather uncannily one of the Provençal troubadour biographies mentioned earlier on. Boccaccio sets his novella in Provence, describes the lover as a knight instead of a poet, and calls him Guiglielmo Guardastagno (thus using the same first name as the jealous husband). The adulterous victim's Italian name is perhaps also a deliberate reference to the thirteenth-century troubadour associated with the story of the eaten heart: Guillem de Cabestany.[12]

The third time that Boccaccio used this motif, again in *The Decameron*, was in a more figurative sense since the story does not end with the actual consumption of a heart. In this version, Tancred, Prince of Salerno and father of Ghismunda, discovers that his daughter has a lover whom she meets at night. In his wrath, he kills the transgressor and sends his heart in a golden cup to Ghismunda. Her despair prompts her to pour poison over the heart and then to commit suicide by drinking the contents. Here, there is no jealous husband, because Ghismunda is a young widow, and the husband is replaced by an angry father who, in neglecting his daughter's need to remarry, is ultimately guilty of her death.

The theme of the eaten heart continued to have success in the Italian peninsula. Giovanni Sercambi (1348–1424) adapted it twice in his collection of *novelle*, written in Lucca in the early fifteenth century. In both cases, the author respected the basic narrative plot while altering some of the details: in one story the heart is replaced in a sinister manner by the lover's face (novella 135), and in the other by his sexual organs (novella 150).[13]

Let me conclude this brief introduction to this literary motif by mentioning two important scholarly interpretations by Odile Redon and Milad Doueihi.[14] In each analysis, emphasis is put (to a greater or to a lesser degree) on the idea that this story represents the fantasy of 'devouring' the lover, symbolized by his heart or other essential body parts. Although this "psychological" reading might seem quite plausible, at an implicit level, it does overlook the possibility of an explicit model that could help to put the story into a cultural context, and in the process help explain the presence of some curious details. Readers today struggle to understand this oft-repeated and strange tale because we are no longer familiar with contextual references that would have been much more obvious to a late Medieval and Early Modern audience. The missing clue to understanding the primary symbolism and implications of the story of the eaten heart can be found among the rituals and mythology of boar hunting studied by Claudine Fabre-Vassas.[15]

Boar Hunting Rituals

Many of the customs surrounding boar hunting have a long history, as confirmed by medieval hunting treatises describing practices that are still carried out today.[16] These treatises offer a fascinating example of the historical "longue durée," what Jacques Le Goff defined as "a Middle Ages to which we are still bound by the uncut thread of oral culture."[17] The boar hunt traditionally involves a relatively large group of hunters, but the hunter who kills a male animal is responsible for carrying out an essential ritual: castrating the boar immediately, and bleeding it out by cutting its throat with a long knife. This mutilation and bleeding is, according to hunters and medieval treatises, essential to prevent the "wild taste" of the animal (believed to be particularly concentrated in the genitals) from spreading to the rest of its body, as it would make the flesh rank and inedible. Indeed, most sources insist on the fact that the carcass of a boar that is not treated in this manner must be thrown away because its smell will become unbearable. This "wild taste," translated as *ferum* or *salvajum* in the Midi and as *selvatico* in Italy, applies particularly to males because of their sexuality, which was seen as being particularly wild and uncontrolled.

This hunting ritual, and the beliefs it is based on, are especially associated with boars but also with some other wild animals, like wolves and squirrels. It has a long pedigree as it makes an early appearance in Aristotle's *Historia animalium*, in the works of Latin agronomists, as well as in medieval hunting treatises.[18] According to early zoological theory, male boars were believed to have an excessive sexuality: young boars without sows were driven to rubbing their sexual organs so violently against a tree that they castrated themselves, and boar meat, even if carefully preserved, would become rank and bloated during the rutting season.[19]

The wild taste of the boar was not only due to the sexual organs of the animal, for the hunter also had to bleed the animal out as soon as possible to prevent the bad taste of "wildness" from spreading and contaminating the flesh. In addition, even when the precautions of castration and bleeding were scrupulously observed, the *ferum* within the animal could not be completely eliminated. Indeed, it was thought that all its viscera contained elements of the "wild" environment in which it lived. As a result, when the moment came to share the carcass among the hunters, a clear distinction was made (and is still made) between the offal and other body parts. The hunter who killed the boar took (and today still takes)[20] the testicles, the head and the beast's entrails— heart, liver, spleen, tongue, kidneys, lungs—as a special reward and as a mark of distinction. In the Middle Ages, the rest of the carcass was divided between the hunters of the party according to complex rules, and in the present day, according to a somewhat more egalitarian mode.

Today, any questions concerning the final use of the entrails are usually met with an embarrassed wall of silence. Hunting treatises from the medieval period are also unclear on this point, and only mention the fact that these parts of the boar are fought over by the hunters and their dogs.[21] This curious silence hides what might be termed a "deep symbolic investment," as explained by the ethnologist Fabre-Vassas. Even though—in the present and in the past— hunters do not explicitly appear to give any particular importance to these organs, more probing questions reveal that this is far from being the case, as the organs are tacitly understood to be prized trophies. Surprisingly, considering the implicit importance accorded to offal, it is only said to be consumed by the dogs participating in the hunt, since by eating this fare they are thought to absorb the *ferum* or *salvajum* circulating in the beast. As is also suggested by medieval hunting treatises, these parts of the boar are believed to imbue the dogs with the wild nature of the animal and makes them better hunters. Nevertheless, it has become clear in present day field work (and this potentially casts light on some of the ambiguities of medieval hunting accounts) that some hunters—frequently the best ones whose exceptional skills are legendary—might eat these animal parts themselves. The act of eating them, which usually takes place in private, is perceived in contradictory terms. Even if denigrated or openly condemned, it is nevertheless secretly admired: what is shameful for ordinary humans becomes a worthy act for outstanding hunters. This ambiguity resides in the fact that eating the boar's interior organs certainly helps to improve the skills of a good hunter, but also endows him with the animal's excessive sexuality.[22]

The Eaten Heart

The rituals of medieval and present-day boar hunting, and the means by which the animal's "wild nature" is overcome, can help cast new light on some of the narrative details in the history of the eaten heart. Starting with one of the earliest versions of this story, the *Lai d'Ignauré*, the similarities appear to be particularly evident. Ignauré is the owner of a small castle where live twelve married knights who partake their meals with him. One day, the wife of one of the knights suggests playing a game in which all of the twelve wives will participate. One of them is chosen to act as the confessor, while the eleven others whisper into her ear the name of their lover: they discover to their amazement that, in each case, it is Ignauré. They then decide to retaliate and ambush him in an orchard where they will stab him to death. When captured by the women, Ignauré persuades them to spare his life by promising to choose just one of them to whom he will remain faithful. This choice, which is described as being contrary to nature, proves fatal because, as the anonymous poet puts it, he becomes like a mouse that has only one bolt-hole. Being limited to just one lover, his frequent nocturnal visits soon become known to everybody. His past and present adultery is found out by the deceived husbands, who finally trap him. In their fury, the revenge consists in first bleeding him to death and then castrating him. His sexual organs and his heart are then served to the unfaithful wives, who are unaware of what they are consuming but, when they realize it, they decide to never eat anything less noble and thus starve themselves to death.[23]

If the later versions of the eaten heart motif are not quite as explicit, it is probably because the allusion to boar hunting was generally understood, and readers were likely to show more appreciation for variations around the central theme than for mere repetition. Normally, it was only the lover's heart that was given to the unfaithful woman, but as we have seen, there are also examples where the face or genitals accompany or replace the heart.[24] While these variations may appear confusing, in the context of hunting rituals they become more comprehensible: both the genitals and the head were trophies kept by the hunter who killed the boar.

Even the most obscure versions of this story reveal telltale clues regarding the lore and symbolism of boar hunting. For example, in Boccaccio's *Filostrato,* Troilus dreams that Diomedes, in the form of a (sexually excessive) boar, encounters Cressida in a wooded area where he knocks her down. It is clear that the ease with which Cressida gives in to the boar and lets him take her heart is synonymous with her infidelity to Troilus. What might appear a somewhat abstruse metaphor must have been much more transparent to readers familiar with the zoological theories that attributed a mythical sexuality to this animal. Boccaccio thus plays with the elements of the eaten heart motif in a surprising, perhaps entertaining way, by inverting the roles: here it is the woman that undergoes the lover's fate and the boar/Diomedes who removes her heart. This version of the tale could be appreciated by a reader with a knowledge of the code and the allusions Boccaccio was playing with. From this perspective, the imagined tryst between Diomedes and Cressida was characterized by a wild and unrestrained sexuality, further underscored by setting the scene in a "shady wood"—the same setting in which boar hunts took place.

Of equal interest are the subtle but nonetheless telling details that emerge in the tale of Guiglielmo Rossiglione in *Decameron* (IV, 9). From the outset, the content of the story is foreshadowed as it is recounted by the character Filostrato, whose name means literally: "he who is overcome by love." In this tale, two Provençal knights are the best of friends and share a series of traits. Both have the same first name, both own a castle with a following of vassals, both enjoy taking part in tournaments, and above all both wear the same livery in these jousts. Nevertheless, their deep friendship turns to implacable hatred when the knight Guiglielmo Rossiglione discovers that his friend Guiglielmo Guardastagno has betrayed him by seducing his wife, the one thing they cannot share. Boccaccio chooses to locate the dramatic assassination of the lover in an ambush. Staged, once again, in a nearby forest, the assassination is reminiscent of a boar hunting battue, in which the animal is awaited by the hunters ready to ambush him. Furthermore, although Guiglielmo Rossiglione kills his rival like a boar, with a lance, he does so in a very particular manner. Boccaccio clearly states that the lover is killed *"con una lancia sopra mano,"*[25] which means that the spear is held above shoulder height, pointing down.

This was not a usual hold, above all for a jousting champion like Guiglielmo Rossiglione. Instead of being carried like a lance, it is here used as a spear, a weapon more suited to a hunter than a jouster. And in case the allusion to the hunt was not sufficiently clear, Guiglielmo Rossiglione's heart is later on identified as a "boar's heart" when it is consigned for the cook to be prepared and served as an "exquisite dish."[26]

Boccaccio was doubtless more than familiar with boar hunting rituals, as is suggested by his repeated use of them in a figurative way. This familiarity—and doubtless that of his audience—is further confirmed by the story of Nastagio degli Onesti (*Decameron*, V, 8). This well-known and much commented novella was also illustrated by Botticelli in a series of panels depicting various phases of the story, with details that stayed very close to the literary model it was illustrating (Plate 18, 19 and 20). Boccaccio's novella re-proposes the familiar hunting metaphors, even though this time they are not used to evoke passionate love but, on the contrary, punishment for unrequited love. In this case the rejection of love might seem quite the opposite of a passionate (sexualized) love, even symmetrically opposed to it. Yet an unreasonable rejection could also be seen as an antisocial act, and equally likely to upset the accepted order of social relations. In other words, a radical and fervent refusal of love could be equated to a kind of untamed, wild behavior.

The story recounts that a young man from Ravenna, Nastagio degli Onesti, tries in vain to court a young girl from the Traversari family, spending much of his family fortune in the process. Despite his assiduous courtship, the young woman remains "cruda e dura e salvatica" (literally: raw, harsh and wild).[27] Saddened by his failure, he takes refuge in a forest near Ravenna where he can brood on his disappointment. One day he suddenly hears terrible shrieks and sees a naked woman running towards him, pursued by two mastiffs and a hunter on horseback. The dogs snap at her savagely and Nastagio's first reaction is to defend the damsel using the branch of a tree (Plate 18). However, the hunter convinces him not to intervene by telling his tragic story. The woman he is chasing had once spurned his amorous advances, plunging him into such despair that he had committed suicide. It was for this reason that he was now condemned to eternally hunt the woman he had loved and to kill her every time he caught up with her. He explains to a horrified Nastagio the procedure used to hunt his prey (Plate 19).

> Every time I catch up with her, I kill her with this same rapier[28] by which I took my life; then I slit her back open, and (as you will now observe for yourself) I tear from her body that hard, cold heart to which neither love nor pity could ever gain access, and together with the rest of her entrails I cast it to the dogs to feed upon.

In case this was not sufficiently eloquent, Boccaccio then describes in even more detail the scene that occurred before Nastagio's eyes, now that the woman was at the hunter's mercy, to the point of repeating the detail about feeding the heart and entrails to the dogs (Plate 20):

> Applying all his strength, the knight plunged his rapier into the middle of her breast and out again at the other side, whereupon the girl fell on her face, still sobbing and screaming, whilst the knight, having laid hold of a dagger, slashed open her back, extracted her heart and everything else around it, and hurled it to the two mastiffs, who devoured it greedily...[29]

The novella then goes on to recount how Nastagio realizes that the hunting scene endlessly repeats every Friday in the same place at the same time. This gives him the idea to invite a large group of people, with the pretext of offering a meal in the place where they too will be able witness the killing, and seats the recalcitrant young Traversari woman with the best possible view of the spectacle. The didactic event is not lost on her; she changes her mind and marries the hitherto thwarted suitor. The concluding remarks of the novella suggest that what she has witnessed has made her identify with the victim since she

> realized that these matters had more to do with herself than with any of the other guests ... consequently, she already had the sensation of fleeing before her enraged suitor, with the mastiffs tearing away at her haunches.

It all ends with her finally accepting her suitor, announcing to her father and mother—"to their enormous satisfaction"[30]—that she would marry Nastagio.

Boar, Sexuality and Lust

The literary use of boar hunting customs and the lore attached to it as a metaphor of excessive sexuality and unbridled lust (or its opposite, unrelenting refusal) was not confined to literature. It also surfaces in a number of iconographic sources other than Botticelli's panels representing the story of Nastagio degli Onesti. A frequent example that comes to mind are allegories of Lust, one of the seven deadly sins. At times this sin is personified by a woman gazing into a mirror while reclining on a boar (Plate 21), or even carrying a banner on which the animal is painted.[31] Yet more explicit is the monstrous human/boar figure in Giovanni da Modena's rendition of Hell and the sinners guilty of Lust in the Cappella Bolognini (San Petronio, Bologna) painted ca. 1415 (Plate 22 and 23). Here a boar-headed devil is assigned only to this particular sin, and is not found in any of the other parts of Hell, where the rest of the deadly sins are located.

Although it has often been affirmed that lust was associated with pigs rather than boars,[32] this assertion should be nuanced because of the difficulty of distinguishing these two animals in Medieval and Renaissance art. As is well known, medieval pigs often resembled boars. Furthermore, the two species often mated, thus further confusing things. Both were usually depicted as having a black and hairy coat as well as bristly hairs down their backs, making it practically impossible to distinguish one from the other in painting. Even the presence of tusks does not necessarily confirm that a boar is being represented. Pigs had (and still have) tusks, although prominent tusks were generally used by artists as a signifier for the wild beast.[33] A telltale characteristic of the boar is its straight snout, as opposed to the curved, upturned nose of the pig, yet this detail might have been more difficult for the viewer to identify.[34] Correct identification of boar versus pig thus relied more on context, such as a hunting scene. The taxonomic confusion that still prevails today is increased by the fact that more than one European language refers to the boar as a "wild pig," which may explain why the sin of lust also came to be associated with pigs.[35]

The literary examples mentioned so far highlight the frequency with which ritual customs linked to boar hunting emerge in many variations on the eaten heart story, where the evocation of these rituals in a text is sometimes *implicit* and sometimes *explicit*. Yet, no matter how relevant this interpretative key might be for these stories, it cannot be automatically extended to all symbolic uses of the heart (or other human organs) that frequently appear in medieval culture. An example of the latter is a tale recounted by the troubadours as well as by many Italian poets of the thirteenth and fourteenth centuries. This tale uses a vivid and gory literary trope to convey the sense of being a "victim" of love: a woman "steals" the affections of the man she loves by (metaphorically) plunging her hands into his chest in order to tear out his beating heart.[36] Another example of the symbolic importance of the heart and other body parts in the Middle Ages is provided by the funeral rites of the kings of France. Although these rites were condemned in the late thirteenth century, they were still in use during the reign of François I (1494–1547). The dead king's body was divided into three parts—heart, entrails and the rest—and prepared for separate burials in separate places, according to the sovereign's wishes.[37]

As for the eaten heart motif, it usually appears in the context of a love triangle. The majority of these stories follow a basic structure in which the forbidden love between a man and a woman destroys the established ties between the woman and her legitimate husband or father. The lovers' "wild" and unruly passion is associated with the unbridled sexual appetite of boars, and is responsible for destabilizing the civic and domestic "order" represented by marriage and the family. If the male lover's lustfulness is a destructive force comparable to a boar's wild and excessive sexuality, even the woman is held responsible for her socially dangerous transgression. Her role is to keep in check such untamed and disorderly behavior on the part of men, not encourage it. A telling visual example of this feminine role is provided by Lorenzo Leonbruno's *Boar hunt* (1522–23), where two women in floating robes spear a gigantic boar. (Plate 24). Similar to other visual evocations of "virtuous" women who overcome symbols of lust (the Virgin Mary trampling a snake, or Botticelli's *Pallas and the Centaur*), this lunette fresco in the Palazzo Ducale in Mantua transforms delicate women into boar hunters, thus reinforcing the current conceit according to which the role of virtuous court women was to "civilize" brutish, uncouth men.[38]

In the eaten heart paradigm, the adulterous woman is responsible for her lascivious lover's death. She is fed his heart, in the same way that a hunter is rewarded with the heart of the boar he kills.[39] Her undisciplined violation of social rules—be she complicit in Lust or unavailable in courtship—is punished in a variety of ways, amongst which an involuntary and taboo culinary transgression: eating human flesh. In contemporary hunting practice, literature and art, the many variants on the tale of the eaten heart expose the intimate connections between food, ritual behavior and social order.

Notes

First published as "Le thème du coeur mangé: l'ordre, le sauvage et la sauvagerie," in *La sociabilité à table: commensalité et convivialité à travers les âges* edited by Martin Aurell, Olivier Dumoulin and Françoise Thélamon, (Rouen: Publications de l'Université de Rouen, 1992), 21–28. The present version contains more illustrations than the original, as well as a somewhat modified text to account for them. Translated by Lucinda Byatt with revisions by the author.

1. See Gaston Paris, *Histoire littéraire de la France*, Paris 1887, vol. 28, 375 *passim* now also available at https://archive.org/details/histoirelittra28riveuoft. (last accessed 21/08/2018).

2. Among the works that are useful for the study of the circulation of this theme, see: Antti Aarne, *The Types of the Folktale: A Classification and bibliography*, translated and expanded by Stith Thompson, (Helsinki: Academia

scientiarium fennica, 1961), 2nd edition; Stith Thompson, *Motif-index of Folk Literature*, (Bloomington: University Press, 1955–58); Dominic P. Rotunda, *Motif-Index of the Italian Novella in Prose*, (New York, Haskell House, 1973; first ed. Bloomington (Ind.), University Press, 1942).

3. For a recent edition, translation and commentary see Glyn S. Burgess and Leslie C. Brook, *The Old French Lays of Ignaure*, Oiselet and Amours, (Cambridge: D.S. Brewer, 2010).

4. While the Lignauré biography is a very short one, see Alfred Pillet and Henry Carstens, *Bibliographie der Troubadours*, (Halle: Nieymeyer, 1933), the biography of Guilhem de Cabestanh is richer in detail and survived in no less than four versions that have been published by Guido Favati, *Biografie trovadoriche. Testi provenzali dei sec. XIII e XIV*, (Bologna: Palmaverde, 1961). Little is known about the life of this second troubadour and, at present, nothing explains his being associated with the story of the eaten heart. See Arthur Långfors, "The Troubadour Guilhem de Cabestanh," *Annales du Midi*, 26, 1934, 353.

5. With regard to the English *fortuna* of this legend, see Laura A. Hibbard Loomis, *Medieval Romance in England. A Study of the Sources and Analogues of the non-Cyclic Metrical Romances*, (New York: Burt Franklin, 1960; first ed. Oxford: University Press, 1924), especially 253–60.

6. On this motif in Spanish literature, see John D. Williams, "Notes on the Legend of the Eaten Heart in Spain," *Hispanic Review*, vol. 26, 1958, 91–98.

7. An eighteenth-century Swedish version is mentioned by Hibbard Loomis, 1960, 256–57.

8. This collection of tales, written in an Italian that linguists have identified as Florentine, can be dated between 1281 and 1300 thanks to the historical events it mentions. For a reliable edition see *Il "Novellino,"* in *Prosa del Duecento*, edited by Cesare Segre and Mario Marti, (Milan/Naples: Ricciardi, 1959), vol. 3, 793–881.

9. For a discussion of this somewhat obscure allegory and its links to other variants of the eaten heart, see Henri Hauvette, "La 39e nouvelle du *Decameron* et la légende du coeur mangé," *Romania*, 41, 1912, 196.

10. Troilo, e'n sogno vide il periglioso
fallo di quella che'l facea languire;
ché gli parea, per entro un bosco ombroso,
un gran fracasso e spiacevol sentire;
per che, levato il capo, gli sembiava
un gran cinghiar veder valicava.
E poi appresso gli parve vedere
sotto a' suoi piè Criseida, alla quale
col grifo il cor traeva, ed al parere
di lui Criseida di così gran male
non si curava, ma quasi piacere
prendia di cio che facea l'animale...

Giovanni Boccaccio, *Il Filostrato*, in *Tutte le Opere di Giovanni Boccaccio*, edited by Vittore Branca, (Milan: Mondadori, 1964), VII, 23–24. English translation is from Giovanni Boccacio, *Filostrato*, translated by Nathaniel Griffin and Arthur Myrik, (Cambridge, Ontario: In Parentheses Publications, 1999), 106, accessed at https://www.yorku.ca/inpar/filostrato_griffin.pdf (last accessed 19/06/2018)

11. An ample bibliography of the work dedicated to this story is found in Giovanni Boccaccio, *Decameron*, edited by Vittore Branca, (Turin: Einaudi, 1980), XCIV–XCV, XCVII–XCVIII, 471, note 1, and 563–64, note 1. Since this article appeared the topic has continued to interest scholars and has produced additional bibliography. Somewhat more recent books on this subject are by Mariella di Maio, *Il cuore mangiato: Storia di un tema letterario dal Medioevo all'Ottocento*, (Milan: Guerrini, 1996) and Milad Doueihi, *A Perverse History of the Human Heart*, (Cambridge: Harvard University Press, 1997).

12. A troubadour whose Occitan name, Guillem Cabestaing, is even closer to Boccaccio's "Guardastagno."

13. Giovanni Sercambi, *Novelle*, edited by Giovanni Sinicropi, (Florence: Le Lettere, 1995).

14. Odile Redon, "Themes alimentaires dans les nouvelles toscanes des XIVe et XVe siècles," in *Quaderni medievali*, 11, 1981, reprinted in *"De finibus Tuscie." Il medioevo in Toscana*, edited by Franco Cardini, (Florence: Arnaud, 1989), 208–10; Milad Doueihi, "The Lure of the Heart," in *Stanford French Review*, 14, 1990, 66–68.

15. The following description of boar hunting, its rituals and its mythology owes much to an article by Claudine Fabre-Vassas, "Le partage du ferum. Un rite de chasse au sanglier," in *Etudes rurales*, 87–88 (1982), 377–400. The geographic area studied by this ethnologist covers the south of France, from the Rhone valley to the Spanish border. The practice of these customs in other areas has not been studied, even though they seem to be very similar in many parts of continental Europe, as suggested by Fabre-Vassas herself in a brief mention of Portuguese variants. The ritual she describes is, in any case, still practiced in central Italy, as I was able to establish by talking to hunters who belonged to well-organized boar-hunting associations from the upper Valdarno valley in Tuscany and the region around Siena. I would like to thank Alfredo (Palle) Fantoni for his patience and help in understanding boar hunting rituals in present day Tuscany, a subject hunters do not readily talk about.

16. The medieval treatises cited by C. Fabre-Vassas (both of which written in the second half of the fourteenth century) are Gaston III Phoebus, Count of Foix, *Livre de chasse*, edited by Gunnar Tilander, *Cynegetica*, 18, 1971, and Henri de Ferrières, *Le Livre de chasse du Roy Modus*, edited by Gunnar Tilander, (Limoges: Ardant 1973).

17. "Un Moyen Age auquel nous relie encore le fil non coupé de l'oralité." Citation from Jacques LeGoff, "Pour un long Moyen Age," in *L'imaginaire médiéval*, (Paris: Gallimard, 1985), 13. My translation.

18. See C. Fabre-Vassas 1982, 379.

19. Ibid., 380.

20. The designation of the boar's organs as a trophy reserved to the hunter who killed it has been documented in Italy, Southern France and Portugal, the three places where field work has been done.

21. Ibid., 384.

22. Ibid., 393.

23. In these stories, the fact of regarding such macabre meals as "noble" food has become a commonplace; for example, see *Decameron*, IV, 9.

24. See for example Giovanni Sercambi 1995, novella 135, 1089–1093 and novella 150, 1265–1270.

25. Boccaccio, *Decameron*, 1980, 566. In English "...brandishing a lance above his head..." Giovanni Boccaccio, *The Decameron*, translated by G. H. McWilliam, (Harmondsworth: Penguin, 1982; first ed. 1972), 350.

26. Boccaccio, *The Decameron*, 1982, 351. "Prenderai quell cuor di cinghiare e fa che tu ne facci una vivandetta migliore e la più dilettevole a mangiar che tu sai..." Boccaccio 1980, 567.

27. Boccaccio, *Decameron*, 1980, 672. Translated by McWilliam, *The Decameron*, 1982, 419 as "cruel, harsh and unfriendly" which is etymologically far from the original.

28. More correctly the Italian word "stocco" should have been translated as "estoc" or "tuck sword." This was a weapon developed in the 14th century as an improved longsword. The very long, strong blade did not have cutting edges and was used to penetrate chain mail as well as for hunting boar and other large animals. The rapier is a weapon developed in the 17th century.

29. I am citing the McWilliam translation mentioned in note 24. In the original, Boccaccio, *Decameron*, 1982, 676–77 the passages are: "... quante volte io la giungo, tante con questo stocco, con quale io uccisi me, uccido lei e aprola per ischiena, e quel cuor duro e freddo, nel qual mai né amor né pietà poterono entrare, con l'altre interiora insieme, sì come tu vedrai incontanente, le caccio di corpo e dolle mangiare a questi cani" and "...con lo stocco in mano ... a quella

dette con tutta sua forza per mezzo del petto e passolla dall'altra parte. Il qual colpo come la giovane ebbe ricevuto, cosí cadde boccone sempre piagnendo e gridando: e il cavaliere, messo mano a un coltello, quella aprí nelle reni, e fuori trattone il cuore e ogni altra cosa da torno, a' due mastini il gittò, li quali affamatissimi incontanente il mangiarono."

30. Boccaccio, *The Decameron*, 1982, 425. "…al padre e alla madre disse che era contenta d'essere sposa di Nastagio, di che essi furon contenti molto." Boccaccio, *Decameron*, 1980, 680.

31. See, for example, *Reallexikon zur Deutschen Kunst-Geschichte*, edited by Otto Schmitt, Ernst Gall and Ludwig H. Heydenreich, Stuttgart, Alfred Druckenmüller, 1956, instalment 42, cols. 671 and 673, and the *Lexikon der Christlichen Ikonographie*, edited by Engelbert Kirschbaum, Rome, Freiburg, Basel, Vienna: Herder, 1971, vol. 3, col. 22. I thank Julian Kliemann for this useful reference.

32. See Mireille Vincent-Cassy, "Les animaux et les Péchés capitaux: de la symbolique a l'emblématique," *Le monde animal et ses représentations au moyen-âge (XIᵉ-XVᵉ siècles)*, Actes du congrès de la Société des historiens médiévistes de l'enseignement supérieur public, vol. 15 (1984), 121–32.

33. A useful illustration of using tusks as signifiers can be found in representations of St. Anthony's companion pig. From the fourteenth to the sixteenth century, this domestic animal was shown without tusks, or then with a relatively small set.

34. On the difficulty of distinguishing boars (*Sus scrofa*) from domestic pigs (*Sus scrofa domesticus*) see: *Pigs and Humans: 10.000 years of interaction*, edited by Umberto Albarella, Keith Dobney et al., (Oxford: University Press, 2007), especially Leif Anderson, "The molecular basis for phenotypic changes during pig domestication," chapter 3, 42–54; Umberto Albarella, Filippo Manconi, Jean-Denis Vigne and Peter Rowley-Conway, "Ethnoarchaelogy of pig husbandry in Sardinia and Corsica," chapter 16, 285–307.

35. Three examples of this interpretation—probably incorrectly identified as pigs (see previous note)—can be found in images nos. 51, 82 and 84 of Rosemond Tuve, *Allegorical Imagery. Some Medieval Books and their Posterity*, (Princeton: University Press, 1966), 182 and 210. In all three images, the prominent, curved tusks are emphasized, suggesting that the animal is meant to be a boar.

36. The tale of the metaphorical extraction of the lover's heart enjoyed a similar success to the eaten heart motif, and is used by many different poets: Bernart de Ventadour, Guiraut de Salinhac, Paulet de Marseilha, Raimbaut de Vaqueiras, Sordello di Goito, Guido Cavalcanti, Cino da Pistoia, Francesco da Barberino and Petrarch himself. For the list and the developments around these themes, see Michele Scherillo, *Alcuni capitoli della biografia di Dante*, (Turin: Loescher, 1896), 229–31.

37. Concerning the distribution of royal organs see, among other studies: Ralph Giesey, *The Royal Funeral Ceremony in Renaissance France*, (Geneva: Droz, 1960; reprint edition 1983), 19–22; *Handwörterbuch des Deutschen Aberglaubens*, edited by Hans Bächtold-Stäubli and Eduard Hoffmann-Krayer, (Berlin and Leipzig: W. De Gruyter, 1930–31), vol. 3, col. 1799.

38. The medieval allegory of the *Psychomachia* with a female protagonist had a certain amount of success in Renaissance courts, where it reinforced aristocratic mores. See the concise overview relative to prints and engravings by: Sara F. Matthews-Grieco, *Ange ou diablesse. La représentation de la femme au XVIᵉ siècle*, (Paris: Flammarion, 1991), "'Virtus' ou l'honneur au féminin," 106–64.

39. The contrast between illicit love and passionate love was, of course, one of the more salient themes in the literature of the troubadours. On this point see Moshe Lazar, *Amour courtois et fin'amors dans la littérature du XIIᵉ siècle*, (Paris: Kliencksieck, 1964).

Chapter 14
Vegetable Diets, Hermits and Melancholy in Late Medieval and Renaissance Italy[1]

Attempts to understand the food intake of the past using modern scientific criteria (calories, vitamins, subdivision into elements etc.) will inevitably over-look the social, cultural and historical dimensions that had a powerful impact on the formation of dietary habits. In the past people had a very different un-derstanding of food and its effects on the body, which understanding must be taken into account by any historical approach to food and diets. Contemporary representations and mental constructs open a window onto the history of taste and the properties ascribed to different foods, permitting historians to better document—and explain—changing patterns of consumption.

The beliefs and attitudes affecting food behavior in the late Middle Ages and the Renaissance are invariably based on humoral theory and on the *Great Chain of Being*, two essential epistemological tools inherited from Classical Antiquity (but also constantly enriched and adapted over time). These provid-ed the mental scaffolding that defined the way in which people perceived and understood food and foodstuffs. However, the intention here is not to broach such vast topics as the *Chain of Being*[2] and how it developed historically, nor, for that matter, to explore the equally complex world of the four elements and humoral theory.[3] More simply, what will be examined here are a couple of the key aspects of this pre-modern cosmological system, highlighting the way in which it determined how certain foods were thought of (and experienced) in the period under examination.

According to the *Great Chain of Being*, the universe had a vertical structure, starting with God and Heaven at the top, and ending, at the bottom, with the Satan and Hell. Between these two extremes was located all of creation, including all of the animals and plants in the natural world. Like nature itself, the *Chain of Being* was divided into four separate levels, corresponding to the four elements and ranked in descending order: on the top was fire, then air, water and at the very bottom, earth (Fig. 3). Each of these elements contained the living organisms particular to it. Mythological creatures like the phoenix and salamander lived in the element fire, whereas all bird species were associated with air. Water contained fish, shells, crabs, etc., and, finally, all plants grew in (or on) the earth. Quadrupeds, since they walked on the earth, although clearly not rooted in it like plants, were also associated with that element.[4]

As a cosmological classification system, the *Great Chain of Being* not only described and ordered the natural world but also provided a framework for supporting social and cultural meanings, amongst which values ascribed to food.[5] The premise was that God had created the natural world and human society according to the same principles, and that consequently both were organized with the same rigid vertical hierarchy in mind. For example, the higher up an animal or a plant was located in the *Great Chain of Being*, and the higher up an individual was placed in society, the more noble and perfect they evidently had to be. One of the results of this mirror effect between these two hierarchical systems was to suggest a sort of parallelism, whereby the higher tiers of society were meant to eat the foods produced by the higher spheres of the natural world, and the inferior ranks were expected to consume products from the lower levels.

Thus: birds, which belonged to the higher echelons of the *Chain*, were regarded by doctors, dietitians, agronomists and theologians as a food that could not be eaten by all and sundry on any occasion.[6] Indeed, according to humoral theory, all birds were "hot," and this made them suitable for only two specific groups. The first, comprised of the powerful and those who ruled, almost had a duty to consume poultry and fowl, not only because it was deemed the dietetically correct fare for social elites, but also because it confirmed their "natural" vocation to exercise power. The second group was that of the sick. In this case it was thought that a weakened state, or "loss of heat" could be effectively

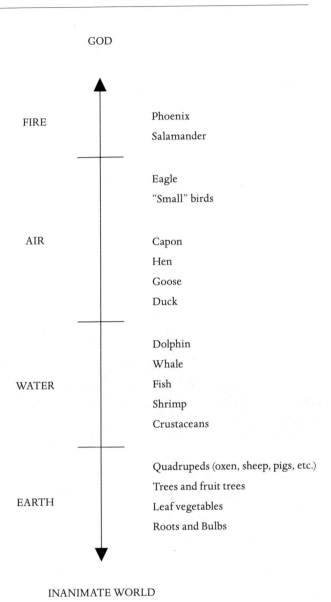

Fig. 3 The *Great Chain of Being*

countered by humorally "hot" foodstuffs. As for those who belonged to neither group, they were expected to prudently avoid eating fowl, since they would otherwise risk encountering a number of serious problems, not the least of which an excessive heating of the body, with a consequent onset of lust. This risk was taken quite seriously, to the extent that a moralist like Bernardino of Siena advised widows not to eat birds because they might become unchaste.[7] Bernardino was not the only one who thought this possible: the Florentine notary Ser Lapo Mazzei also espouses this widespread belief in some of his letters. Every time he wanted to remind his friend. Francesco di Marco Datini, a wealthy merchant from Prato, of the "past sins" Francesco had committed (notably resulting in his illegitimate children), Mazzei would allude to the fact that his friend had been very fond of partridge.[8]

Moving down the social hierarchy, and placed below those who were permitted by birth or rank to eat fowl, came a middle group (shopkeepers, artisans, etc.) who did not number among the powerful or the poor but who, because of their station in life and more restricted means, were supposed to eat the meat of quadrupeds (veal, mutton, pork, etc.). Lastly, came the group that is of particular interest for this chapter: the poor, who were relegated to the bottom of the social ladder. The foods they were meant to eat also came from the lower reaches of the *Great Chain* and thus, for the most part, from the plant world.

Even in the lowly domain of plants, closely associated with the element earth, there was a hierarchical ranking at work (Fig. 4).[9] Indeed, tall plants (such as fruit trees) were reserved for the wealthy, while low ones that grew on or in the ground (leaf vegetables, pulses, root vegetables, etc.) were essentially thought of as food fit for the poor.[10] The most humble of these plants—such as annuals (beans, lettuce, cabbage, etc.), and to an even greater extent roots or bulbs that grow underground (carrots, onions, etc.)—were often considered only fit for animals, even though they were staple foods for the humble folk who ate them. Given their particularly low status, vegetables also had what might appear to be a paradoxical use: they were deliberately chosen as an exceedingly simple foodstuff (demonstrating humility) by religious orders, and were believed to provide the principle diet of hermits (Plate 25 and 29).

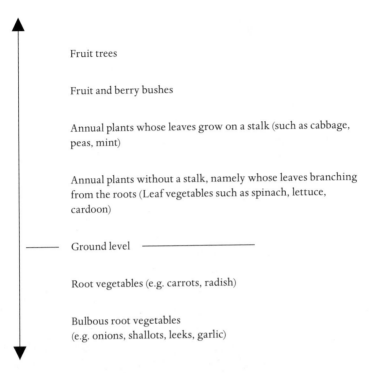

Fruit trees

Fruit and berry bushes

Annual plants whose leaves grow on a stalk (such as cabbage, peas, mint)

Annual plants without a stalk, namely whose leaves branching from the roots (Leaf vegetables such as spinach, lettuce, cardoon)

Ground level

Root vegetables (e.g. carrots, radish)

Bulbous root vegetables
(e.g. onions, shallots, leeks, garlic)

Fig. 4 Hierarchy of the Plant World

Vegetable Diets

The diverse social and religious connotations of vegetables raises two questions that need to be examined in some detail. First of all, what might be the similarities and differences between diets that followed an essentially vegetable-based regimen? Second, once the characteristics of different vegetable diets have been identified, how do these foods, located in the lower rungs of the *Chain of Being*, convey the cultural presuppositions behind these regimens?

A diet of leaf vegetables, bulbs (onions, garlic) and roots (carrots, turnips), accompanied by bread and water, was closely identified with specific social groups and/or with certain periods of the year, such as Lent. The largest group comprised the poor, who, for evident economic reasons, found it hard to buy anything else than vegetables, and for whom meat remained a rarely-consumed commodity.[11] In fact, these foodstuffs were so strongly equated with poverty and humility that a frugal diet of this nature (supplemented by a little fish when it could be afforded), was associated with the forty days of Lent as well as other days or times of the year when penance had to be observed. It will thus hardly come as a surprise that vegetable diets generally represented the rule (if not the norm) for most monastic orders. Monks and nuns were meant to follow such regimes in a spirit of permanent penance, and regarded them as a way of fighting off the temptations of the flesh (i.e. gluttony and lust).[12] But if vegetable-based diets were normally regarded as being reserved to the poor and those belonging to monastic orders, they were also seen as characteristic of another small but symbolically important group: hermits (religious recluses) and people who had become lost in remote areas, forests or deserts, all of whom lived on what they could gather in the wild. The difference, of course, was that individuals lost in nature had no choice but to eat humble and wild foods, while hermits adopted this regimen as a particularly radical form of abstinence.

To our modern eyes, the different vegetable diets adopted by the three social groups mentioned—the poor, members of religious orders, and hermits—may appear broadly similar, but this sort of generalization would be misleading because it does not take into account distinctions that were considered fundamental at the time. Late medieval and Renaissance doctors, authors of agricultural treatises and even theologians, carefully distinguished between different kinds of vegetable-based diets, and linked each with quite different types of people. Different vegetable diets, practiced by one group or the other, were more or less strict, and therefore more or less ascetic.

The least strict regimen was associated with the poorer classes, followed by the diet recommended for monastic and conventual orders, and culminating with the strictest and most penitential of them all: the food eaten by hermits and those who had to survive gathering wild plants. Whereas the poor ate large amounts of cooked vegetables, they did consume meat when they could afford it. A more austere regime was followed by religious orders, who were supposed to voluntarily follow a diet that consisted above all in vegetables, meat being served on particular feast days, and then only in moderation.[13] But even more drastically impoverished was the nourishment of religious recluses living in the wild and those lost in the wilderness, insofar as they were said to gather and eat the leaves and roots of wild plants (Plate 27). This was regarded as a deprivation diet, whether followed voluntarily or by necessity, and was seen as a radical departure from the more usual vegetable fare, since there was a fundamental difference between eating cultivated vegetables and wild plants. Medical doctors, agronomists and theologians all agreed that wild plants had a negative effect on the human body because, among other things, they produced an excess of black bile,[14] a humor that could leave visible "signs" on the individual, and even cause deviant behavior, as we will see.

As a form of dietary penance, vegetable diets were imposed periodically on society as a whole since the Church *required* all the faithful (at least those in good health) to restrict their diets to vegetables and fish during Lent as well as on other specified fast days.[15] The few religious orders that adopted this diet throughout the calendar year not only embraced a life-style of perpetual penance, but also performed an act of humility, signifying closeness to the poor via the food that this section of the population consumed. Such a regime was, however, still far from the mortifying diet practiced by hermits, which derived from a different frame of reference. Considering the medical and dietary theories current in this period, a closer look at the way hermits ate, and some of the lore surrounding the food they consumed, will shed light on the unspoken rules governing eremitic fare and the meanings associated with such a diet in late medieval and Renaissance Europe.

Literary and iconographic sources provide abundant material on hermits and their diet, but before examining this material, it is necessary to introduce three key oppositions within the *Great Chain of Being* that bear heavily upon the eremitic regimen. The oppositions in question are nature/culture, hot/cold and cooked/raw. These oppositions are meant to be seen as a continuum between two extremes—varying in degree, along the axis from one end to the other—and can be seen as working in parallel to the hierarchical structure of the *Great Chain of Being* (Fig. 5). To take one of these parallels as an example—the hot/cold axis—it functions as follows: the higher an item moves up

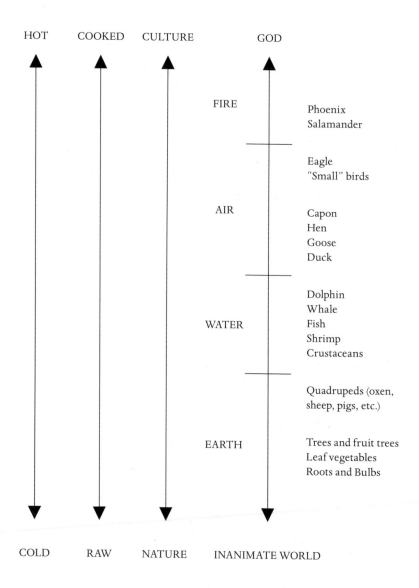

Fig. 5 The *Great Chain of Being* compared to some other oppositions.

the *Chain* (from the cold to the hot end), the more the plants and animals distributed along this vertical cosmological system will be endowed with a hot humoral composition. Thus birds, which belonged to the element air (hot and wet), were quite logically considered hotter than fish, which belonged to the element water (cold and wet), while lower down the hot/cold axis, the *Chain of Being* descends into the even colder realm of plants and the element earth (cold and dry). The cooked/raw and culture/nature oppositions worked in much the same way. In other words, the top end of the *Chain* was not only the "hot" end of things, but was also associated with "cooked" foods and the sphere of "culture;" the lower reaches of the *Chain of Being* were the "cold" strata, occupied by the "raw" foods from the world of plants/"nature."[16]

As has already been mentioned, it was a commonly held opinion that society had a natural order, and that the most appropriate diet for any specific individual connected their social rank with the equivalent rank of foodstuffs on the *Chain of Being*.[17] Foodstuffs (and in this instance, plants) that belonged to the lower end of the *Chain*—i.e. at the "nature" end of things—were thus "naturally" appropriate for specific social groups (the poor, religious orders, hermits). Yet, as pointed out before, all plant-based diets were not considered equal. Cooking vegetables was a way of improving upon their cold and raw nature, and the "better" vegetables were the cultivated ones grown in kitchen gardens.[18] The domestication of plants thus introduced a corrective principle that attenuated the unhealthy qualities of wild varieties. Medical and scientific knowledge of the time considered both of these corrective factors—cooking and cultivation—to markedly lessen the harmful effects inherent in a vegetable diet where "nature" was all too present.[19] Together these correctives could transform meals based on vegetables into more "civilized" fare.

The severe diet of hermits was, however, not corrected by either one of these two conditions. Not only did they feed from the lowest end of the *Chain of Being*, but most hermits intensified the "natural" character of their diet by consuming the wild plants they gathered without even cooking them. Their diet was therefore regarded as an extreme one, so close to being "wild" that it actually resembled that of animals. The only thing that kept them from eating like beasts was their use of bread, a product that symbolically linked them to human society (Plate 28).

Like the places they chose to live (forests and deserts), their diet was a further confirmation of the secluded position they occupied on the margins of the civilized world, on its outermost confines where nature merged into chaos.

The Knight and the Hermit

The idea that the hermit/eater of raw foods occupies a liminal space between nature and culture is a theme frequently encountered in literary sources. One of the most vivid illustrations of this topos is to be found in Chrétien de Troyes (fl. 1160–ca. 1181), *Yvain, or the knight with the Lion* (composed between 1177 and 1181).[20] A passage in *Yvain* bears on the notion of the liminal area between nature and culture, setting the stage for the significant episode of Yvain's "insanity" (provoked by his being rejected by his wife Laudine). The passage begins at the point where, out of grief, he goes mad and leaves, by degrees, the civilized world. He first abandons the knights of his company and goes as far as possible from their tents and pavilions. Yvain's self-distancing from human company is followed by a "storm breaking loose in his brain" that has him tearing at his flesh and stripping off his clothes. He flees through "fallow" and "plowed" fields, which belong to a strictly agricultural, domesticated landscape ("Lors se li monte un torbeillons/El Chief, si grant que il forsane;/Si se dessire et se depane/fuit par chans et par arees," vs 2805–07).[21] The knights who go to search for him do so in the wrong places, since they are looking in hedgerows (*haies*) and "orchards" (*vergiers*), which are also cultivated, agricultural spaces. In his mad flight, Yvain reaches what Chrétien de Troyes calls a *parc*. What is meant by this term is an enclosed tract of land used for grazing animals, usually near forests, and therefore a transitional terrain that bridges the civilized world that Yvain is fleeing and the wilderness, where hunting and gathering take place.[22]

In the border area of the *parc* he encounters a last human being, whom the poet calls a *garçon*. This is a term that had distinctly negative connotations in the twelfth century as it referred to a member of the lowest social class.[23] Yvain steals a bow and arrow from this young man, thus obtaining a simple hunting weapon that will allow him to survive, even though it was hardly an appropriate weapon for a knight. Finally, he leaves even the *parc* and begins to live in the forest. There, the naked Yvain is also said to be overcome by oblivion (*Porqant mes ne li sovenoit/De rien que onques eüst feite*, vs 2822–23). Abandoning the faculty of memory (an eminently human trait), he begins to live exclusively by hunting. With his bow and arrow he kills wild animals, which he eats raw in the same way as a predatory beast (*Les bestes par le bois agueite,/Si les ocit; et se manjue/La venison trestote crue.* vs 2824–26). At this point he can be said to have truly abandoned the world of culture and fully embraced a "crazed" and "wild" existence (*hom forsenez et salvage*, vs 2828) comparable to that of a savage beast.

After living like this for several months, Yvain slowly recovers from his madness and returns to civilization in equally progressive and symbolic stages. Particularly significant is that the first part of his reintegration takes place thanks to a hermit, who was "slash-and-burning" (*Et li hermites essartoit.* vs 2831), a form of farming that is more nomadic than static and, in the Middle Ages, mostly practiced in forests in order to clear land for cultivation.[24] The lone hermit, who is a kind of mirror image of the *garçon*, is terrorized by the naked man who suddenly appears at his doorstep. He nevertheless takes pity on the crazed man, leaving him some bread and a pitcher of fresh water on a window ledge. This most basic of cooked and "civilized" foodstuffs is thus placed in a kind of framed passageway (the window) between the wilderness of the forest and the interior of the hermit's simple hut. Significantly, the hermit's bread is of the worst quality, stronger and more bitter than any the former Knight had ever tasted (*Ne cuit que onques de si fort/Ne de si aspre eüst gosté*, vs 2844–45), i.e. just barely civilized bread, far from good quality, white bread made from wheat flour. All the same, and even though distracted by his madness, Yvain ravenously eats this offering, and it is precisely this bread and the jar of water that sets in motion a slow but steady progression back towards human society.

In response to the hermit's basic offering of food and drink, Yvain deposits hunted game for the hermit on the same ledge. This, in turn, allows the hermit to "transform" such wild food into more civilized fare by skinning the wild beasts and cooking them. The hermit then leaves the cooked meat on the same ledge, along with the usual bread and water. This very simple transaction is, to all effects, an extended metaphor for a basic economic exchange. Although the hermit does not partake of the cooked game, he "sells" (*vandre*) the skins of these animals in order to "buy" (*acheter*) the most basic kind of bread for his visitor: unleavened and made with "barley and oats" (*D'orge et de soigle sanz levain*, vs 2878). It is equally significant that the hermit cooks the meat for Yvain but does so without salt or pepper (*Venison sanz sel et sanz poivre*, vs 2874). Both the humble kind of bread and the wholly unseasoned game represent the lowest rung of culture and, at the same time, what might be called the lowest common denominator in terms of cooked and civilized food. It is precisely this "threshold" food (on the cusp of the civilized and the uncivilized, of culture and nature), that creates a transition that will allow Yvain to regain the human world.

It is useful to dwell on the details of this story, not only because they highlight clear-cut differences between period concepts of nature and culture—as illustrated by the foods eaten by Yvain and the way some of them are prepared—but also because they draw attention to the way how all three axes of oppositions (nature/culture, cooked/raw, hot/cold) function in parallel to the *Chain of Being* (see Fig. 5). The tale of Yvain's madness not only demonstrates how all of these concepts are related to each other, but also how they belong to a structure which permits us to understand eremitical diets as the lowest, but still "human," end of the *Great Chain of Being*. Yvain's decision to return to the world of culture is made possible and facilitated by the mediation of a person who nourishes himself at the lowest level of the *Chain*: a hermit. Considered inferior even to the poor, hermits and eaters of raw foods constitute the very last outpost of human civilization before entering the wilderness.

Melancholic bodies

Such a liminal status was seen as potentially dangerous, for the radical regimen of hermits could be responsible for a series of harmful effects.[25] The "wild," gathered plants that made up the hermits' diet (and were eaten raw), as well as their choice of water over wine,[26] were thought to possibly cause serious physical and mental disorders. While eating habits of this type might manifest the spiritual greatness of some individuals, they could also accentuate existing weaknesses in those who did not measure up to such exacting standards. Indeed, according to humoral theory, the severe diet of the holy men who lived in the forests and deserts was liable to provoke an excessive humoral cooling of the body. This condition could produce, as a result, a pathological form of melancholy that, in some hermits, could even induce them to break society's most basic rules and laws (those of the "civilized" world). In some cases they could break their vow of chastity, or worse still, become guilty of theft or even murder. In Boccaccio's *Decameron* (III, 10), there is a satirical treatment of this idea that plays on its fundamental premise. In this tale, a young and naive daughter of a wealthy man leaves her house and wanders into Thebes, a legendary gathering place for hermits. There she is fed, by an old and wise member of this community, the same kind of food he himself consumes, a typical hermit diet of "roots of plants, wild fruit, dates and water." She then visits other hermits residing in Thebes until she finally encounters a young one, who seduces her with an unlikely ruse, thereby confirming the negative stereotype of the lascivious hermit.[27] His name, Rustico, plays on a double meaning since it can refer to both a hermit saint of that name,[28] but also (and more likely in Boccaccio's case) a rustic/lower class character reminiscent of the clever peasant. In fact, not only does the hermit Rustico opportunistically have his way with the young woman, but he also ends up marrying her, abandoning his ascetic life and obtaining her father's vast fortune.

A similar but more serious example of the dangers inherent in a hermit's lifestyle appears in legends featuring Saint Alban (and apocryphally, in the Middle Ages, John Chrysostom). According to a Tuscan version from the fourteenth century, Saint Alban had been living for many years in a "dark and wild forest," living on the usual "roots of plants, wild fruit and the water of fountains in this dark valley."[29] One day a king's daughter, who had become lost in the forest during a hunt, burst into the hermit's lonely presence and begged for help. The appearance of such a young and beautiful woman made him lose his head (although he had long wondered why men did not prefer to die rather than commit the sin of lust). Forgetting his saintly life and concomitant vow of chastity, he rapes the young woman. Then, realizing the enormity of his sin, he compounds it by killing his visitor, burying her body and denying to search parties any knowledge of her whereabouts.

Aggravated by an extreme diet and its deleterious effect on the human body, the already transgressively antisocial behavior of hermits was fraught with dangers. Dietetic theory held that eating raw wild plants, and especially an excessive consumption of such fare, could result in humoral imbalances in the body, causing cold and melancholic humors to take over and even resulting in a form of madness. An excess of melancholy was, however, not solely attributed to diet (although the type of food consumed played an important role), it could also be the result of a predisposition, stage of life, or a series of other factors.[30] Evidence of commonly held theories about *melancholia* surfaces, yet again, in the latter part of the legend of St Alban. Alban realizes the gravity of his crimes (rape, murder and perjury) and decides that his penance will take on a much harsher form: he will not only observe an even stricter diet, but also will never again stand upright. Eating food appropriate for animals, the hermit also crawls like a brute beast, head down, in order to never see the sky.[31] When hunters come by his burrow, their dogs do not recognize that the creature they have flushed out is actually a human being (Saint Alban/John Chrysostom) because he moves on all fours, in a posture that is often referred to as the essential difference between beasts and human beings (Plate 29). However, as Klibansky, Panofsky and Saxl have stressed in their work on melancholy, this posture, which obliges the person to constantly look down, is nothing more than a misinterpretation of the Greek word (κατηφής) which means "depressed" (literally, "looking at the ground").[32]

There were yet other reasons for thinking that the disorders observed in hermits (and others who followed their diets) were symptoms of melancholia. Since the first formulation of this pathological state in Aristotle's *Problemata Physica* (XXX.1), it was held that a disposition towards melancholy could lead to lascivious behavior.[33] On the positive side of this complex and at times contradictory state, Aristotle held that melancholics were also prone to trances and ecstasies, like the Sibyls and soothsayers.[34] These characteristics appear again in the portrayals of medieval hermits, afflicted by both of the symptoms described by Aristotle.

The comparison between the Classical model and the medieval version of melancholy can be carried even further. The idea that an immoderate consumption of plants and vegetables risked turning a person into melancholic also entailed a telltale sign that was thought intrinsic to such people: their skin color changed. A dark, tanned tint—referred to as a "black" skin color—was yet another sign of a melancholic disposition, as black bile would become the dominant humor in the body. Unsurprisingly, many hermits are described (and even portrayed in paintings) as having markedly dark-colored skin. A good example of the transformations brought about by an eremitical lifestyle is provided by Mary of Egypt. After living for many years in the desert and eating wild plants and roots to expiate her sins, she lost the beauty for which she had been renowned as a courtesan in Alexandria and became a "black and withered body."[35]

The poor who ate a similar diet—albeit less extreme—were believed to undergo similar alterations in the color of their skin, to the point that peasants were recognized first and foremost by their dark skin tone. This tanned appearance was not simply attributed to their exposure to the sun, but to their eating largely from the lower end of the plant world. This characteristic of the lower social orders is humorously exploited in a tale from Franco Sacchetti's *Trecentonovelle*. In the novella in question, a town dweller married to a woman from the countryside asked her, one night, to end her prayers and finally undress for bed. Misled by his wife's "brown" (*monachino*) colored skin, the husband had not realized she was already naked. Worried by the incident, the wife decides to prepare a special abrasive cream made with herbs with which she hopes "to remove this surface layer of *wild* skin which appeared as a result of my life in the country." Her husband finds out and dissuades her by arguing that, "the more you remove your skin, the blacker you'll become."[36] The moral of the story is that the inherent color of a farmer's daughter cannot be disguised, and the more she tries to remedy the defect, the more her true nature will show through.

By the twelfth century, with the recovery and first translations of Aristotelian texts, the cause and effect relationship between certain diets, melancholic temperament and dark skin became a much discussed topic, animating a debate that lasted well beyond the sixteenth century.[37] But we should not surmise that ideas about the effects of specific diets were restricted to philosophical and medical circles, since the same associations circulated in a variety of cultural products, including visual media and literary texts. In the *Decameron*, the novella that best illustrates the dark skin attributed to melancholics is the tale of Beritola (II,

6),[38] wife of a Neapolitan nobleman, who finds herself a fugitive on the island of Ponza with her two children. Every day, Beritola would leave her children on the beach with her attendants while she withdrew to a grotto and cried over her sad fate. One day, while she is not with her children, they and her retinue are kidnapped by passing pirates. The distraught mother does not eat all day, but soon, driven by hunger, she begins to gather wild plants that she feeds on. This becomes her daily diet and, as the author clearly states (repeating it at least twice), she survives solely on wild plants and water. Significantly, Boccaccio uses the verb *pascere* (to graze) instead of *mangiare* (eat), which would have been the correct verb to use for human beings. Beritola's descent into a wild state, caused by her diet and provoked by her grief, is completed by her adopting two roebucks that she discovers in a cave and that she breastfeeds with the milk her children can no longer be given. After several months the noblewoman is found by the dogs of a couple who come to the island. Although there could be some confusion regarding whether the dogs are hunting the roebuck or Beritola herself, Boccaccio does make a point of describing her as nothing less than "a wild animal."[39] Above all, her physical appearance has changed since she is now described as being "brown, thin and hairy,"[40] all typical characteristics attributed to melancholics and brought about by the diet of hermits.[41]

Although this is certainly not the place to retrace the complex reception of Aristotelian ideas on melancholy in the Middle Ages, which have received much scholarly attention, it is clear that melancholy and its allied phenomena of dark skin, hairiness, and a raw and "wild" diet, were all well known. The work of Isidore of Seville, Bede, Albert the Great and William of Auvergne, along with that of many other minor authors, indirectly relayed Aristotelian theory to the Middle Ages, even before more reliable texts were made available in Europe. These authoritative figures also argued, as did Aristotle, that melancholic persons were naturally gifted with a temperament that inclined them to more spiritual predispositions. William of Auvergne, who wrote in the first half of the thirteenth century, reminded his readers that a melancholic temperament distanced men from worldly matters, and induced enlightenment and revelation, but that too great a preoccupation with the supernatural could degenerate into an extreme form of melancholy easily confused with madness.[42]

To return to the eating habits of hermits, the diet they adopted may well have been a kind of body technique used in the hope of modifying, at least in part, their natural constitution in order to be more receptive to the supernatural powers with which they wished to commune. To do so, they would have deliberately generated melancholic humors in their bodies by following a diet that combined raw, cold and wild foodstuffs that had an occult, quasi-mysterious significance. While a diet based on wild plants, herbs and roots could constitute a choice, a way of living to facilitate the supernatural powers to which hermits aspired, it nonetheless had to be carefully controlled by those who practiced it, to avoid falling into the many pitfalls of excessive melancholy. Ordinary mortals dared not engage in such a diet and even hermits had to practice it with extreme caution, since the price for ascetic hubris could be deviant behavior and even insanity.

* * *

This exploration of some of the concepts and convictions that accompanied an apparently marginal aspect of food discourse on plant-based diets has provided a vantage point from which to survey the *Great Chain of Being*. As a widely-shared cosmological construct, it heavily conditioned the social and symbolic meaning invested in food, and in turn influenced consumption patterns in late medieval and Renaissance Italy. While medical doctors and dietitians might have advised special foods for special illnesses or states of mind, the basic cultural construction remained that of the *Chain of Being*, reinforced by the basic oppositions: culture/nature, cooked/raw, hot/cold, high/low. While these pairs of oppositions are present in many other cultural contexts, here they take on meanings specific to this historical period.

The effect that vegetable based diets were believed to have on the body commanded a consensus of opinion that surfaces in literary sources, in visual media, and in medical and dietetic texts, revealing how firmly rooted and widespread these notions actually were. Such convictions contributed to a structured and convergent discourse regarding the effects that eating cooked or raw vegetables, or consuming greens gathered in the wild, might have on human health. Defined and described by the *Great Chain of Being*, these beliefs and cultural constructs provide important insights into the organization of a complex food system that held sway in the later Middle Ages and Renaissance.

Notes

First published as «Les plantes, les régimes végétariens et la mélancolie à la fin du Moyen Age et au début de la Renaissance italienne», in *Le monde végétal (XIIe-XVIIe siècles): savoirs et usages sociaux*, edited by Allen J. Grieco, Odile Redon, Lucia Tongiorgi Tomasi, (Paris: Presses Universitaires de Vincennes, 1993), 11–29. The present version is the result of a translation by Lucinda Byatt with revisions by the author.

1. I would like to thank Jan Ziolkowski for reading and offering useful comments on an earlier version of this article. Any shortcomings remain, of course, entirely mine.
2. The standard work on the *Chain of Being* remains Arthur O. Lovejoy, *The Great Chain of Being* (Cambridge: Harvard University Press, 1936). For a more recent study, see Edward P. Mahoney, "Metaphysical Foundations of the Hierarchy of Being according to some Late Medieval Philosophers," in *Philosophers of Existence Ancient and Medieval* edited by P. Morewedge (New York: Fordham University Press, 1982), 165–257, and by the same author, "Lovejoy and the Hierarchy of Being," *Journal of the History of Ideas*, vol. 48, 2 (1987), 211–30. The *Great Chain of Being* is further examined, with particular attention to food history, in chapter 5, 6, 10 and in the conclusion.
3. On the four elements and humoral theory in this period, see *Les Quatre éléments et la culture*

médiévale, edited by D. Buschinger and A. Crépin (Actes du Colloque d'Amiens, 25–27 March 1982), (Göppingen: Kümmerle Verlag, 1983).
4. This location of quadrupeds in the *Great Chain of Being* is somewhat different from the one proposed in the original version of this article and reflects my present understanding of where they were situated.
5. For a more detailed discussion see Allen J. Grieco, "The Social Order of Nature and the Natural Order of Society in Late thirteenth- to early fourteenth-century Italy," in *Miscellanea Mediaevalia* 21, no. 2, (Berlin/New York: W. De Gruyter, 1992), 898–907 (chapter 9 in the present volume).
6. The following paragraph on birds and their alleged effects on the human body according to late fourteenth-century Italian medical and theological knowledge draws on Grieco 1987. (This theme has now been explored in much greater detail in my article "From Roosters to Cocks: Renaissance Dietary Theory and Sexuality," in *Erotic Cultures of Renaissance Italy*, edited by S. F. Matthews-Grieco (Aldershot: Ashgate, 2010), 89–140.
7. Bernardino da Siena, *Prediche volgari sul campo di Siena 1427*, edited by C. Delcorno (Milan: Rusconi, 1989), vol. 1, no. 22, 633.
8. Ser Lapo Mazzei, *Lettere a Francesco Datini*, edited by C. Guasti (Florence: Le Monnier, 1880), Letter CCCLVI (undated but 1407?), vol. 2, 104.

9. This hierarchy is more closely examined and presented in chapter 10.

10. For a more detailed analysis of the relations between social classes and vegetable-based diets, see Allen J. Grieco, "Les utilisations sociales des fruits et légumes dans l'Italie médiévale," in *Le Grand livre des fruits et légumes: histoire, culture et usage*, edited by D. Meiller and P. Vannier (Paris: La Manufacture, 1991), 151–54, and idem., "The Social Politics of Pre-Linnaean Botanical Classification," *I Tatti Studies*, 4 (1991), 131–49 (chapter 10 in the present volume).

11. Almost all the available data concerning meat consumption in Mediterranean Europe confirms the largely vegetable diet of the poor. For an example see Giampiero Nigro, *Gli Uomini dell'Irco. Indagini sui consumi di carne nel basso Medioevo, Prato alla fine del '300*, (Florence: Le Monnier, 1983), above all ch. 4. For a more nuanced opinion see Ramón A. Banegas López, *Europa carnivora. Comprar y comer carne en el mundo urbano bajomedieval*, (Gijón: Trea, 2012).

12. This is what the Monastic rules affirm, though the diets that were actually followed would seem to have been much less strict. See, for example, the Benedictine abbey of Westminster in the late 15th century – early 16th century London, examined by Barbara Harvey, *Living and Dying in England 1100–1540: the monastic experience*, (Oxford: University Press, 1996; first edition 1993), chapter 2, "Diet," above all 59–61 and Fig. II.1, 57.

13. Chapter 39 of the Benedictine rule (adopted by many others) actually forbids the meat of quadrupeds to all monks except for those who are sick.

14. Concerning this humor and its effect on the body see Grieco 1987, especially chapter 3.

15. Fridays, Saturdays (in some places), Ember days, etc.

16. These opposites and their relationship with the *Great Chain of Being* are a speculative hypothesis, here submitted as a heuristic scheme relating to the *Chain of Being* as a cosmological system. The opposition between the raw and the cooked in medieval medicine and dietetics has not, to my knowledge, been dealt with in any systematic way, despite its obvious importance.

17. This mechanism is discussed in greater detail in both chapters 9 and 10.

18. Consuming raw vegetables by choice, other than when forced to by exterior circumstances or for penance, is a distinctly modern practice that still awaits to be studied.

19. This discourse was reversed in the case of medicinal plants, which were considered to be more powerful and efficacious when gathered in the wild.

20. This poem is beautifully analyzed in an article by Jacques le Goff and Pierre Vidal-Naquet, whose Lévi-Straussian approach reveals the dynamic between nature and culture, although the implications of food remain unexplored. The following discussion owes much to: Jacques Le Goff and Pierre Vidal-Naquet, "Lévi-Strauss en Brocéliande. Esquisse pour une analyse d'un roman courtois," in *Claude Lévi-Strauss*, "Idée," (1979), republished in Jacques Le Goff, *L'imaginaire médiéval* (Paris: Gallimard, 1985), 151–187.

21. For a brief discussion of the term see Le Goff, Vidal-Naquet 1979, republished in Le Goff 1985, 156.

22. This and the following citations are from the online version of *Yvain ou le Chevalier au Lion* last consulted 26 June 2018 at http://atilf.atilf.fr/gsouvay/dect/download/Yvain.xml (last accessed 20/8/2018) provided by the exemplary *Dictionnaire Électronique de Chrétien de Troyes* and its wealth of linguistic resources.

23. On this see Le Goff and Vidal-Naquet 1979, in Le Goff 1985, 156 and note 5. See also the *Dictionnaire Électronique de Chrétien de Troyes* which confirms these negative connotations.

24. For a useful article on this topic see Anita Guerreau-Jalabert, "Aliments symboliques et symbolique de la table dans les romans arthuriens (XIIe–XIIIe siècles)," *Annales ESC* 47, 1992, especially 565–66.

25. On this agricultural technique see the classical study by Emilio Sereni, "Terra nuova e buoi rossi: Le tecniche del debbio e la storia dei disboscamenti e dissodamenti in Italia," reprinted in *Terra nuova e buoi rossi e altri saggi per una storia dell'agricoltura europea*, (Turin: Einaudi, 1982), 2–100.

26. A good example of this diet can be found in "Il Guglielmo dell'epopea e il Guglielmo Toscano," in *Leggende Cristiane del Trecento*, edited by G. De Luca (Turin: Einaudi, 1977; first edition, 1954), 79: "E continuamente osservava e digiuni eziandio e dì delle feste; e tre dì della settimana beveva vino, tanto poco che non aveva altro che un poco di colore, e mangiava molto poco di cotto e sottilmente viveva; e gli altri dì digiunava in pane e acqua … e mangiava erbe crude sanza alcuno condimento." (And he constantly observed and fasted, even on feast days; and on three days a week he drank wine, so little that he only had a little color, and ate very little cooked food, and he lived frugally; and on the other days he fasted on bread and water … and ate raw herbage without any dressing.).

27. "…e dandole alquanto da mangiare radici d'erbe e pomi salvatici e datteri e bere acqua…" Giovanni Boccaccio, *Decameron*, edited by V. Branca (Turin: Einaudi 1987), 445. On the topos of the lascivious hermit, as well as earlier and later versions of the same, see 443, note 1. For a slightly later version of this story see Franco Sacchetti, *Il Trecentonovelle*, edited by A. Lanza (Florence: Sansoni, 1984), Novella CI, 203.

28. Regarding this see the *Decameron*, edited by V. Branca, 1987, 445, note 4.

29. "…in salvatico e scurissimo luogo" and "…quivi viveva di radici d'erbe e di pomi salvatichi e d'acque di fontane, ch'èrono in quello scuro vallone," "La Leggenda di Sant' Albano," in *Leggende cristiane del Trecento*, 1977, 41 and 43.

30. The following discussion on melancholy owes much to the pioneering work done by Raymond Klibansky, Erwin Panofsky and Fritz Saxl, *Saturn and Melancholy. Studies in the History of Natural Philosophy, Religion and Art* (Nendeln/Liechtenstein: Kraus Reprints, 1979) (first edition 1964).

31. "… si puose in cuore di … mai mangiare se non erbe, e di non andar mai se non carpone, e di mai non guardare verso 'l cielo," in "La Leggenda di Sant' Albano," in *Leggende cristiane del Trecento*, 1977, 44.

32. Klibansky, Panofsky and Saxl 1979, 50.

33. For an explanation of this association, see ibid., 21–22, 30, 34.

34. Ibid., 32.

35. "Leggenda di Santa Maria Egiziaca," in *Leggende Cristiane del Trecento*, edited by G. De Luca (Turin: Einaudi, 1977; first ed. 1954), 17–18.

36. "È che io mi voglio levare questa carne salvatica di sopra, che per stare in contado è arrozzita" to which he answers "… e quanto più cavi, più mi pare che truovi il nero." The word "wild" is, of course, underlined by me. Sacchetti 1984, Novella XCIX, 200–201.

37. Klibansky, Panofsky and Saxl 1979, 81, 82, 85, note 47, 112, 115–16. On how diets can modify humoral constitutions (including melancholy) see the fifteenth-century treatise by Michele Savonarola, *Libreto de tutte le cosse che se magnano*, edited by J. Nystedt (Stockholm: Almqvist-Wiksell International, 1988), 193.

38. I would like to thank Elissa Weaver for having drawn my attention to the relevance of this novella.

39. "Et così dimorando la gentil donna divenuta fiera…" Boccaccio 1987, 205.

40. "…vedendo costei che bruna, magra et pelosa divenuta era…" ibid., 206.

41. See, for example, Klibansky, Panofsky and Saxl 1979, 59 and 71.

42. Ibid., 73–74.

Afterword

The articles collected in this volume have repeatedly suggested the importance of two distinct but closely interrelated epistemological constructs: the
doctrine of the four elements and the concept of the *Great Chain of Being*. Both
provided cosmological systems that were rooted in theological beliefs, and
provided a framework within which to "read" and "explain" the functioning
of the material world. Originally inherited from Antiquity, these cosmological
systems were modified and reformulated as of the end of the twelfth century
by authors of medieval encyclopedias, in an attempt to reconcile biblical explanations of the universe with Aristotelian theories.

Between the mid-twelfth and mid-thirteenth century, much of the
Aristotelian corpus had became available in Latin, thanks mostly to translations from the Arabic. It was these translations that were enthusiastically exploited by medieval philosophers and natural historians. Without a doubt, the
medieval encyclopedia was one of the most important vehicles for the re-in-
tegration of this knowledge into the Western world-view. Alexander Neckam
(*De naturis rerum*, ca. 1190), Bartholomaeus Anglicus (*De proprietatibus rerum*,
1240), Thomas de Cantimpré (*Liber de natura rerum*, 1228–1244), Vincent
of Beauvais (*Speculum maius*, ca. 1254)—not to speak of Albertus Magnus
(ca. 1193–1280)—were among the more influential early natural philosophers
in this field. The impact of these authors and their texts is measurable in
at least two different ways. To begin with, there are a considerable number
of surviving manuscripts and translations, further diffused by the many
print editions that appeared as of the second half of the fifteenth century.

Bartolomeus Anglicus, for example, was translated into Italian, Provençal, French, English, Spanish, Flemish and Anglo-Norman, and was published in no less than 12 Latin and 9 French editions before 1500. Even Vincent of Beauvais' unwieldy *Speculum naturale* (one of the three parts comprising his *Speculum maius*, with its 32 books, 3708 chapters and circa 1,260,000 words), continued to have an "immense success up until the 17th century."[1] Secondly, the wide-reaching impact of these encyclopedias can be measured by the fact that they were compiled by clerics, primarily for other clerics, in order to provide them with an understanding of the workings of the universe and material for their sermons. As a result, these texts became not only the source material of preachers throughout Christendom but also the backbone of the fundamental teachings passed on in universities, where the medieval encyclopedia flourished well into the Early Modern period.

These highly influential compendiums of learning, that reigned more or less unchallenged until the scientific revolution, systematically presented what, at the time, was considered a comprehensive state of current knowledge. A consistent amount of attention was thus dedicated to cosmological theory, derived from the natural philosophy of Aristotle and reconciled with Christian theology.[2] The cosmological framework adopted by late medieval encyclopedists privileged a vertical and hierarchical approach that superseded an earlier representation of a cosmos ordered from the center out, in a series of concentric circles. This vertical and hierarchical ordering of nature had an enormous success, even after the medieval encyclopedists were replaced by a new wave of sixteenth-century humanist natural philosophers,[3] and would continue to hold sway, not the least because many of the encyclopedias were still being published throughout the early modern period.

The center-out (or outside-in), concentric world view, as well as the later, vertically ordered hierarchical model, nonetheless shared some basic cosmological concepts. On the outside of the concentric cosmological diagrams representing the universe—or at the very top of the vertical model—were the "incorruptible" celestial spheres, which included everything from the moon to the farthest reaches of the firmament. On the inner (or lower) part of such diagrams was an area that went from the moon down to the center of the earth, a space characterized by the fact that it was "corruptible." This "sub-lunar" region was subsequently subdivided into four concentric spheres or tiers, formed by the four elements. These were represented as circles progressively farther out from the center (in the concentric diagrams) or as successively higher levels (in the vertical model), but always respected the following order: earth, water, air and fire.

Visual representations of the concentric circles version of the cosmos were in circulation as of the thirteenth century,[4] even though written accounts began significantly earlier (such as Honorious of Autun's influential *Ymago mundi,* ca. 1120). This cosmological model retained its popularity for centuries, as can be seen in a great number of manuscripts but also in prominent public spaces, where they could be seen and explained to a less educated public. An early "public" example is Giusto de' Menabuoi's *Creation of the world,* (ca. 1375) in the baptistery of Padova, but this visually engaging motif was to enjoy success well into the 15th century, as seen in Giovanni di Paolo's *Creation and expulsion from paradise* (ca. 1445) (Plate 30).[5]

The four concentric circles of the elements implied a hierarchical order in relation to the center that became explicit in the vertical model: the elements were always "above" or "below" one another with respect to the element earth, which occupied the center and thus the "lowest" position. Within each one of these elements the medieval encyclopedists placed all known plants and animals (including mythological creatures) in hierarchical order, progressively occupying the successive strata that constitute the *Great Chain of Being.* Each one of the four elements thus contained its own specific creatures, including those that were suitable for human consumption: earth was the domain of plants and four legged animals, water the realm of fish and all aquatic creatures, air garnered all of the birds and, finally, fire was the home of mythological animals such as the phoenix and the salamander.[6] This vertical ordering of the sub-lunar sphere was pursued not only in thirteenth-century encyclopedias, but was to continue to provide a basic structure in fifteenth- and sixteenth- century medical and scientific literature, including the work of humanist natural philosophers such as Gessner and Aldrovandi.[7]

The doctrine of the four elements and the *Great Chain of Being* was deeply ingrained in medieval and Renaissance culture, permeating the thinking of philosophers, doctors, dietitians, botanists and zoologists (such knowledge had long been an integral part of the university curriculum), but also spilling over into a much vaster sector of the population that had no such learning. The extent to which cosmological knowledge had become part of commonplace culture was already evident in the fourteenth century (in both poetry and the novella, for example) and continued to grow and permeate both Italian and European culture in all media. By the sixteenth century, basic cosmological references to the four elements and the hierarchy of the natural world could be used by artists in paintings, secure in the knowledge that they would be readily understood by their public. A grandiose example of this is the mythological rendering of the four elements in the *Sala degli Elementi* frescoes in Palazzo Vecchio by Vasari and Cristofano Gherardi, executed between 1555 and 1557. More humble versions frequently appeared in the international market for painted pictures as of the second half of the century. An example of the theme of the four elements with their respective plants or animals, executed for somewhat less exalted circles, is the set of four paintings presently at the Brera Gallery in Milan (Plates 31, 32, 33 and 34).[8] Found in Vincenzo Campi's workshop at his death, they first appear in a 1611 inventory drawn up by his widow. At some unspecified date after 1621 (when the widow Campi had drawn up a second will), the paintings passed to the Hieronymite Convent of Saint Sigismund in Cremona, only to end up in the Brera when the convent was closed during the Napoleonic period. Their original location in Campi's workshop suggests that they might have been models the artist could show to prospective buyers, a hypothesis that is born out by the almost identical versions he sold around 1580 to Hans Fugger (1531–1598), destined to decorate the wealthy German businessman's dining room in Kirchheim (Bavaria).

The four Campi paintings in the Brera and those in Kirchheim, as well as numerous other versions and imitations of this set held in museums and private collections, are usually referred to as *The Fruit Seller*, *The Poultry Vendors*, *The Fishmongers* and *The Kitchen*. Despite their individual subject matter, as a whole they refer to the four elements, where the kitchen scene (with fire) provides the necessary conceit to complete the cosmological reference.[9] Such food-themed, four-elements sets of paintings—illustrating the plentiful produce of Earth,

Water, Air and the essential transformative power of Fire[10]—have a number of shared characteristics. First of all, the individual paintings do not combine products derived from the different elements, whereas genre paintings or still-lifes in this period often mix them. Secondly, the paintings in question (and other series of this type) were clearly intended as companion pieces, meant to be displayed together. All four paintings in the Brera are almost exactly the same size,[11] while the ones bought by Hans Fugger have identical dimensions (142 × 215 cm). Finally, the theme underlying the serial production of Campi's paintings were derived from Northern models. Campi's pictures owed much to two Flemish painters who had explored the same subject at least one decade earlier: Pieter Aertsen (ca. 1508–1575) and his pupil Joachim Beuckelaer (ca. 1535–1575). Beuckelaer's paintings in particular—known as the *Four Elements* (1569–70), now at the National Gallery in London—are thought to have been painted for a dining room in Ghent,[12] while another group of paintings by Beuckelaer on this same theme once hung in the banquet hall of the Palazzo del Giardino in Parma. As these three examples suggest, by the second half of the 16th century, the motif of the abundance of nature, subdivided in an orderly manner according to the four elements, had become an appropriate decorative subject for the dining rooms of the wealthy throughout Europe.

Artists could therefore work tacitly within the cosmographic scheme of the four elements and the universal ordering system of the *Great Chain of Being*, at the same time as medical practitioners could tacitly refer to this world view in dietary treatises that presumed a common—albeit less learned—store of knowledge on the part of their patients. This presumption of a commonly-held knowledge is apparent, for example, in the mid-fifteenth century treatise on foodstuffs and dietary advice composed by the Ferrarese doctor, Michele Savonarola (often cited in this volume), for his patron Borso d'Este. In his advice book, Savonarola draws heavily upon the familiar ordering principles involving both the elements and the *Chain of Being*. In the dedication to the treatise, he makes a point of telling Borso that the subject matter has been presented "So as to make you remember these things more easily..." and that, to this effect, "...I will present them in their order, since the Philosopher [the allusion is to Aristotle] says order helps memory."[13] This "order" allowed

Savonarola to categorize the entire range of foodstuffs served at the Ducal table, including items that were considered to be on the cusp between two elements (earth and water), such as snails, frogs and beaver. It is noteworthy that he not only speaks of the "order" with which he has organized his subject matter, but also presupposes that this order would be recognized, understood and remembered by his reader, almost as a mnemonic trigger or a dietetic memory palace. Significantly, while the approach Savonarola adopted must have been relatively well consolidated by the mid-Quattrocento, it became quasi-universal in the following century, when dietary advice had literally morphed into nothing less than a popular genre. Baldassare Pisanelli's highly successful *Trattato della natura de' cibi et del bere,* first published in 1583 was one of the most popular of many sixteenth-century texts in this vein (twenty-five editions before 1650). Pisanelli's treatise followed much the same order and categories as those observed in Savonarola's work, more than a century earlier, as did the plethora of less successful texts of the same ilk.

All foodstuffs consumed by human beings were thus considered part of an ordered, natural system, and were classified and understood within this framework. The rigidly hierarchical taxonomy introduced by the *Great Chain of Being,* (and the four elements that reinforced it), gave every plant, animal, fish and bird a unique position in the same way that every link in a chain has a unique place. Each plant or animal was therefore either above or below another, and the hierarchy of the *Chain of Being* had a mirror effect with regard to the equally hierarchical social system: a social order that paralleled the natural order. Ultimately, this cosmographic hierarchy served a double function. On the one hand, it assigned a specific place to every foodstuff within a classificatory system. On the other hand, it introduced a hierarchical order that ruled over the resulting system, in parallel with the social world. The result was—to use a linguistic metaphor—that while foodstuffs might be considered "words," the classification system provided the "grammar" for a "language of food." According to this language, elements of which have been examined in this collection of articles, social distinctions could be communicated in a clear and intelligible way via specific foodstuffs and prepared dishes much in the same way that social status could be transmitted by clothing, possessions, or other systems of signs.

* * *

The pervasive cosmological system that was so deeply rooted in medieval and Renaissance thinking (most easily referred to as the *Great Chain of Being*) also made its way to the New World in the mental baggage of European explorers, travelers and settlers. It left its distinctive imprint on the way an uncharted nature was perceived by these travelers, but also influenced their efforts to classify previously unknown plants and animals. The accounts of learned chroniclers and observers amply testify to this phenomenon, beginning with the influential writings of Pietro Martire d'Anghiera (1457–1526), who never actually set foot in the New World but wrote about it on the basis of reports he received from those who had experienced it directly. Much the same can be said regarding the work of a more direct observer, Gonzalo Fernández de Oviedo (1478–1557), whose complete *Historia general y natural de las Indias* was not published until the middle of the nineteenth century, but still constitutes a monument to the classificatory bias that a curious mind applied to describing and understanding nature in the New World.

Such classificatory baggage was not only the purview of humanists, whose training shows through their writings, but can also be found among merchants, doctors, explorers and conquistadors. The disparate narratives of these other authors provide a collective (albeit less learned and often quite mundane) confirmation of how the hierarchical and cosmological order continued to provide a way of understanding and interpreting nature and, above all, guided travelers in the choices they had to make on a daily basis.[14] In a world where most of the foodstuffs were foreign—at least until more familiar foods could be produced *in loco*—the danger of eating *like* a native (and thus *becoming* a native) or, worse still, doing irremediable harm by consuming unknown fare, was a very real concern.[15] Such dangers were a persuasive incentive to adhere to deeply ingrained explanatory schemes regarding the properties of foods. Preconceptions and classificatory schemes remained a powerful influence for a long time, being both rooted in natural philosophy (as it had trickled down to these authors) and confirmed by the absolute authority of divine (Christian) cosmology.

Generations of preachers had been raised on the cosmological lessons taught by Medieval encyclopedias, and the missionaries who found themselves in the New World contributed to spreading this world view well beyond the European continent: through sermons, the printed word and images. An extraordinary image of the *Great Chain of Being* that illustrates how this cosmology made its way to the Americas (and back again), is a print conceived by Diego Valadés (Plate 35). Valadés was a Franciscan, born in Mexico in the 1530s. Trained in his country of birth, he became active as a missionary for approximately thirty years before moving to Europe in 1571. Although little is known about him, he seems to have risen rapidly in the ranks of his order, publishing a book entitled *Rhetorica Christiana* in Perugia in 1579. Some of the detailed engravings in this volume were signed with "Valadés *fecit*" (in one case "Valadés *inventor*"), which implies that he was the author of these particular compositions. In a beautifully detailed representation of the *Great Chain of Being* (signed *fecit*), complete with a selection of animals belonging to each tier, Valadés includes the figure of God and the celestial hierarchy that medieval angelology placed above human beings. He also includes Hell and its denizens, placed below the element earth. By including the heavenly and infernal tiers, Valadés reminded the viewer that this cosmological order and the doctrine of the four elements was ultimately also a theological dogma, giving meaning to a natural world that provided humanity with food, on both sides of the Atlantic.

Notes

1. Benoît Beyer de Ryke, "Le miroir du monde: un parcours dans l'encyclopédisme médiéval," *Revue Belge de philosophie et d'histoire*, vol. 81, number 4 (2003), 1264.

2. For a useful overview from Isidore of Seville through the fifteenth century see the survey article by Beyer de Ryke, 2003, as well as a more recent study regarding the scholastic period by Mary Franklin-Brown, *Reading the World: Encyclopedic Writing in the Scholastic Age*, (Chicago: University Press, 2012).

3. This new wave of natural philosophers were responsible not only for producing a more systematic body of work but also for

rethinking the nascent fields of botany, zoology, ichthyology and ornithology as of the third decade of the sixteenth century.

4. An early example of this is to be found in the thirteenth-century copy of Hildegard of Bingen's, *Liber Divinorum Operum*, Biblioteca Statale (Lucca), *Codex Latinum 1942*, c. 9 available at http://expositions.bnf.fr/ciel/grand/4-099.htm. The concentric cosmos is also common in late thirteenth/early fourteenth century illustrations of Gossuin de Metz, *Ymage du Monde* manuscripts such as the Bibliothèque Nationale de France, Ms. *Fr. 2174*, fol. 69 v. or Ms. *Fr. 574*, fol. 136 v. (both of which can be viewed on Gallica).

5. On Giovanni di Paolo and the origin of his iconography, see above all Laurinda S. Dixon, "Giovanni di Paolo's Cosmology," *The Art Bulletin*, Vol. 67, No. 4 (1985): 606, 610. See also Ingeborg Bähr, "Zum ursprünglichen Standort und zur Ikonographie des Dominikaner-Retabels von Giovanni di Paolo in den Uffizien," *Mitteilungen des Kunsthistorischen Institutes in Florenz*, XLVI (2002), Heft 1, 74–120.

6. For a graphic rendition of this see Figure 14.1, 245.

7. A relatively rare variant to this ordering principle uses an alphabetical approach which, however, does not contradict the hierarchy established by the *Great Chain of Being*.

8. For the following I have relied on the work of Valérie Boudier, *La cuisine du Peintre. Scène de genre et nourriture au Cinquecento*, (Tours/Rennes: Presses Universitaires François Rabelais/Presses Universitaires de Rennes,

2010), especially 51–54 and 167–187 and Claudia Goldstein, *Pieter Bruegel and the Culture of the Early Modern Dinner Party*, (Farnham/Burlington: Ashgate, 2013), notably chapter 5.

9. Such series are not always exclusively about the four elements, since they often contain details referring to religious motifs regarding the refusal of earthly bounty in favor of a more spiritual one. Thus Beuckelaer's "Fire" at the National Gallery in London is also an illustration of the story of Christ in the house of Martha and Mary.

10. On the negative/dangerous value represented by raw foods in the Middle Ages and the Renaissance see chapter 14, 256 *passim*.

11. The measures of the Brera versions are: "Kitchen" 145 × 220 cm, "Fruit vendor" 143 × 213 cm, "Poulterers" 147 × 215 cm and "Fishmonger" 144.5 × 217 cm.

12. Goldstein, 2013, 11 (note 35) and 125–146.

13. "Et azò che di tale cosse te faza più memorioso, le ponerò cum suo ordine ché, come dice il Phylosopho, l'ordine fa ala memoria" and "Seguitando adunque diremo cum questo ordine tale" Michele Savonarola, *Libreto di tutte le cosse che se magnano: un'opera di dietetica del sec. XV*, edited by Jane Nystedt (Stockholm: Almquist & Wiksell International, 1988), 57.

14. This is a topic that I plan to broach in a book to be co-authored with Davide Domenici (University of Bologna) and Gregorio Saldarriaga (University of Antioquia, Medellin).

15. On this see the landmark work of Rebecca Earle, *The Body of the Conquistador. Food, Race and the Colonial Experience in Spanish America, 1492–1700*, (Cambridge: University Press, 2013).

Plates

1. Ugolino di Nerio, *Last Supper*, ca. 1325–30, tempera and gold on wood. New York, The Metropolitan Museum of Art, Robert Lehman Collection.
2. Unknown Piedmontese or Lombard artist, *Last Supper*, ca. 1503–1522, fresco. Bessans (Savoie), Chapelle Sainte Antoine.

3. Master of Signa, *Birth of the Virgin*, ca. 1450, predella panel of the altarpiece of the *Annunciation*, tempera and gold on wood. Florence, Villa I Tatti, Berenson Collection.
4. Giovanni da Milano, *Birth of the Virgin*, 1365, fresco. Florence, Santa Croce, Cappella Rinuccini.

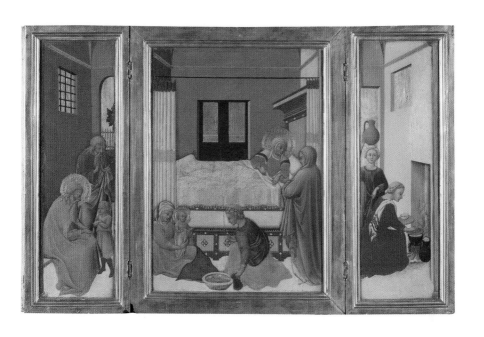

5. Master of the Osservanza, *Birth of the Virgin*, ca. 1440, tempera on wood. London, The National Gallery.

6. Sano di Pietro, *Birth of the Virgin*, 1437–39, tempera and gold on wood. Asciano, Museo di Palazzo Corboli.

7. Sano di Pietro, *Birth of the Virgin*, 1437–39, detail, tempera and gold on wood. Asciano, Museo di Palazzo Corboli.

8. Vittore Carpaccio, *Birth of the Virgin*, 1504–1508, tempera on canvas. Bergamo, Accademia Carrara.

9. Domenico Ghirlandaio, *Last Supper*, 1480, detail, fresco.
Florence, Cenacolo di Ognissanti.

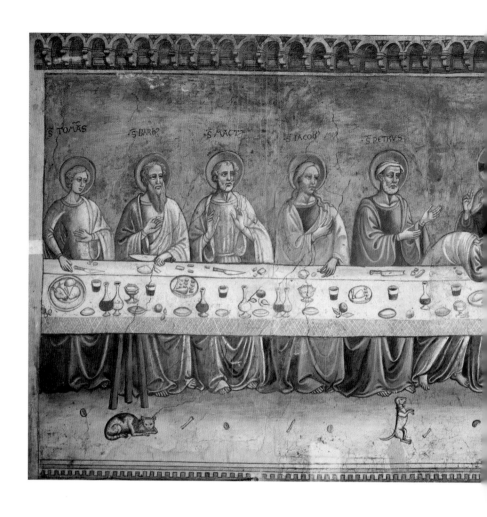

10. Stefano d'Antonio di Vanni, *Last Supper*, 1440–50, fresco.
Sesto Fiorentino, Sant'Andrea a Cercina.

S ANDŘ · S IACOB·MAŘ · S FILIPP · S SIMONI · S TADE·

11. Stefano d'Antonio di Vanni, *Last Supper*, 1465–67, detail (left hand side), fresco. Florence, Spedale di San Matteo (now Accademia di Belle Arti).

12. Stefano d'Antonio di Vanni, *Last Supper*, 1465–67, detail (right hand side), fresco. Florence, Spedale di San Matteo (now Accademia di Belle Arti).

13. Bernardino Poccetti, *Wedding at Cana*, 1604, detail, fresco.
Badia a Ripoli, Florence.

14. Duccio di Buoninsegna, *Last Supper*, between 1308 and 1311, tempera on wood. Siena, Museo dell'Opera Metropolitana.

15. Cristoforo da Seregno e bottega, *Last Supper*, ca. 1450, fresco.
Monte Carasso (Ticino, Switzerland), Church of San Bernardo.
16. Anonymous artist, *Last Supper*, 13th-century, mosaic. Venice, St Mark's Basilica.

17. Giotto, *Last Supper*, ca. 1304–1306, fresco. Padua, Scrovegni Chapel.

18. Sandro Botticelli, *Scenes from the Story of Nastagio degli Onesti*, *Encounter in the Forest*, 1483, mixed method on panel. Madrid, Prado.

19. Sandro Botticelli, *Scenes from the Story of Nastagio degli Onesti, Killing in the Forest*, 1483, mixed method on panel. Madrid, Prado.

20. Sandro Botticelli, *Scenes from the Story of Nastagio degli Onesti. Killing in the Forest*, 1483, detail of dogs eating heart and entrails. Madrid, Prado.

21. Stefano di Giovanni Sassetta, *Saint Francis in ecstasy*, 1437–1444, detail of "Vanity reclining on a boar," tempera on panel. Berenson Collection, Villa I Tatti, Florence.

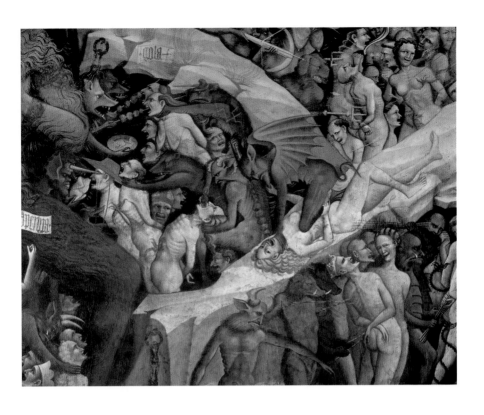

22. Giovanni da Modena, *Hell*, 1410–15, detail with punishment of the Lustful, fresco. Bologna, Basilica di San Petronio, Cappella Bolognini.

23. Giovanni da Modena, *Hell*, 1410–15, detail with punishment of the Lustful with a boar's head, fresco. Bologna, Basilica di San Petronio, Cappella Bolognini.

24. Lorenzo Leonbruno, *Women hunting a boar*, 1522–23, fresco. Mantova, Palazzo Ducale, Sala Grande (Scalcheria).

Clarus Hybernorum regione FIACRIVS horti
Exiqui cultor, prodigiosa facit. 18

Dum signat fossam in fossa multa insilit arbos
Dum sedet in saxo, saxum abit in Cathedram.

25. Raphael Sadeler (after Maarten de Vos), *Saint Fiacre*, 1595–1600, engraving.
From the series *Oraculum Anachoreticum*, Venice, 1595–1600.

26. Jan Brueghel the Elder or 'Velvet Brueghel,' *Six Villages: Hermit Praying before an Icon*, 1597, oil on copper. Milan, Veneranda Biblioteca Ambrosiana.

Patria QVIRIACO cunctis eft nota Corinthus   Cui leo feruat olus, dum differit atq̃ precator,
Sed magis ignoti culta Natupha soli.   24   Sollicitat nubes atq̃ Acherunta fugat.   9

27. Raphael Sadeler (after Maarten de Vos), *Saint Quiriacus*, 1594, engraving.
From the series *Sylvae sacrae monumenta… anachoretarum*, Venice, 1593–94.

Exuit ARNVLPHVS mitram, clerumq Metensem
Deserit, et missis omnibus antra subit   12.

Iungitur hic Christo: cunctis dat verba salutis:
Inq crucis signo plurima mira facit.

28. Raphael Sadeler (after Maarten de Vos), *Saint Arnulphus of Metz,* 1598, engraving. From the series *Trophaeum vitae solitariae,* Venice, 1598.

Dœmone quam soluit casti vox ante puellam,
Hanc violans mačta mox IOANNIS amor. 15.

In spæubus tandem soluens pro crimine pœnas,
Est venatori serpere visus humo.

29. Raphael Sadeler (after Maarten de Vos), *Sancti Joannis* (Saint John Chrysostom), 1598, engraving. From the series *Trophæum Vitæ Solitariæ*, Venice, 1598.

30. Giovanni di Paolo (Giovanni di Paolo di Grazia), *The Creation of the World and the Expulsion from Paradise*, 1445, tempera and gold on wood. New York, The Metropolitan Museum of Art, Robert Lehman Collection.

31. Vincenzo Campi, *The Fruit Seller (Earth)*, ca. 1578–1581, oil on canvas.
Milan, Pinacoteca di Brera.

32. Vincenzo Campi, *Fishmongers (Water)*, ca. 1576–1580, oil on canvas.
Milano, Pinacoteca di Brera.

33. Vincenzo Campi, *Fowl sellers (Air)*, ca. 1590–91, oil on canvas. Milan, Pinacoteca di Brera.

34. Vincenzo Campi, *Kitchen (Fire)*, ca. 1590–91, oil on canvas. Milan, Pinacoteca di Brera.

35. *Great Chain of Being*, from Didacus (Diego) Valadés, *Rhetorica Christiana*. Perugia, 1579.

Bibliography

MANUSCRIPT SOURCES

Archivio di Stato, Firenze (ASF):

Acquisti e Doni, 302, 1.

Camera del comune, Mensa dei Signori above all no. 13, 15, 17, 26 and 68.

Archivio dell' Ospedale degli Innocenti Firenze (AOIF):

s. XII, no. 2

Spese minute et straordinarie dello Spedale delli Innocenti B (1451–1463), 5342.

Biblioteca Medicea Laurenziana, Firenze: *Ashburnham*, 1216.

Biblioteca Nazionale, Firenze:

E.6. 6.154.II, n. 24. *Lamento di meloni in barcelletta. Et un capitolo in lode de l'uva*, n.p. (but probably northern Italy), n.d. [16th century].

PRIMARY PRINTED SOURCES

Adami, Antonio. *Il Novitiato del Maestro di casa*, Rome: 1657.

Alberti, Leon Battista. *Libri della famiglia*, edited by Ruggiero Romano and Alberto Tenenti, Turin: Einaudi, 1969.

——. *De Iciarchia*, in *Opere Volgari*, edited by Cecil Grayson, Bari: Laterza, 1966, vol. II.

Aldobrandino, da Siena. *Le Régime du corps*, edited by Louis Landouzy and Roger Pépin, (Paris: Champion, 1911; reprint edition Geneva: Slatkine, 1978

——. Rossella Baldini, "Zucchero Benciveni, 'La Santà del Corpo'. Volgarizzamento del'Régime du corps' di Aldobrandino da Siena (a. 1310) nella copia coeva di Lapo di Neri Corsini (Laur. Pl. LXXIII 47)," in *Studi di Lessicografia Italiana* (1998), vol. 15, 21–300.

Belon, Pierre. *Histoire naturelle des estranges poissons marins*, Paris: Regnaud Chaudiere, 1551.

——. *De Aquatilibus libri duo*, Paris: Charles Estienne, 1553.

Benzi, Ugo. *Tractato utilissimo circa la Conservazione della Sanitade*, Milan: Petri de Corneno, 1481.

Bernardino, da Siena. *Le prediche volgari detti nella Piazza del Campo l'anno 1427*, 3 vols., edited by Luciano Banchi, Siena: 1880–1888.

——. *Prediche volgari sul campo di Siena 1427*, 2 vols., edited by Carlo Delcorno, Milan: Rusconi, 1989.

Boccaccio, Giovanni. *Decameron*, edited by Vittore Branca, Turin: Einaudi, 1980.

——. *Il Corbaccio*, edited by Pier Giorgio Ricci Milan/Naples: Ricciardi/ Einaudi, 1977.

——. *Il Filostrato*, in *Tutte le Opere di Giovanni Boccaccio*, edited by Vittore Branca, Milan: Mondadori, 1964.

——. *Filostrato*, translated by Nathaniel Griffin and Arthur Myrik, (Cambridge, Ontario: In Parentheses Publications, 1999), 106. This is now also available at: http://www.yorku.ca/inpar/filostrato_griffin.pdf

Bonvesin da la Riva, *De quinquaginta curialitatibus ad mensam*, in *Poeti del Duecento*, edited by Gianfranco Contini, Milan/ Naples: Ricciardi, 1960, vol. 2, tome 1.

——. *I volgari di Bonvesin de la Riva*, edited by Adnan M. Gökçen, New York: Peter Lang, 1996.

Buon vino, favola lunga: vite e vino nei proverbi delle regioni italiane, edited by Maria Luciana Buseghin, Perugia: Electa Editori Umbri, 1992.

Campano, Bishop Giannantonio. *Trasimeno felice. Trasimeni descriptio seu de felicitate Trasimeni*, edited and translated by Cipriano Conti, introduction and notes by Ebe Pianta, Foligno: Edizioni dell'Arquata, 1992.

Castellani, Francesco di Matteo. *Ricordanze I. Ricordanze A (1436–1459)*, edited by Giovanni Ciappelli, Florence: Olschki, 1992.

———. *Ricordanze II. Ricordanze e Giornale B (1459–1485)*, edited by Giovanni Ciappelli, Florence: Olschki, 1995.

Castiglione, Baldassarre. *Il libro del Cortegiano*, edited by Giulio Preti, Turin: Einaudi, 1965.

Celebrino, Eustachio. *Refettorio, Opera Nova che insegna apparechiar una mensa*, Venice, 1526 (reprint edition, Campoformido, Udine: Ribis, 1993).

Cogliati Arano, Luisa. *Tacuinum sanitatis*, Milan: Electa, 1979.

Cornaro, Alvise. *La vita sobria*, edited by A. Di Benedetto, Milan: Tea, 1993.

Cotrugli, Benedetto Raguseo. *Il libro dell'arte di mercatura*, edited by Ugo Tucci, Venice: Arsenale, 1990.

Crescenzi, Pietro de'. *Trattato dell' agricoltura di ... traslatato nella favella fiorentina, rivisto dallo'nferigno accademico della crusca*, Bologna, 1784.

Crivellati, Cesare. *Trattato dell'uso et modo di dare il vino nelle malattie acute*, Rome, 1550, reprint edition Bologna: Forni, 1989.

Giovanni Battista Croce, *Della eccellenza e diversità de i vini che nella Montagna di Torino si fanno e del modo di farli*, Turin, 1606; reprint edition Bologna: Forni, 1980.

Croce, Giulio Cesare. *Le Sottilissime astuzie di Bertoldo; Le Piacevoli e ridicolose simplicità di Bertoldino*, edited by Piero Camporesi, Turin: Einaudi, 1978.

Cronache Senesi in *Rerum Italicarum Scriptores*, Bologna: 1934, vol. 15, part 6.

Dallington, Sir Robert. *A Survey of the Great Dukes State of Tuscany, in the Year of Our Lord 1596*, London: Edward Blount, 1605 (facsimile reprint, Amsterdam: Walter J. Johnson/Theatrum Orbis Terrarum, 1974).

Datini, Francesco. *Le Lettere di Franceso Datini alla moglie Margherita (1385–1410)*, edited by Elena Cecchi, Prato: Società Pratese di Storia Patria, 1990.

Dei, Benedetto. *La Cronica*, edited by Roberto Barducci, Florence: Papafava, 1984.

Della Cornia, Corniolo. *La Divina Villa*, edited by Lucia Bonelli Conenna, Siena: Accademia dei Fisiocritici, 1982.

"Dottrina del vivere o Lettera a Raimondo". *Scrittori di religione del Trecento*, edited by Don G. De Luca, Turin: Einaudi, 1977, vol. 3, 461–466.

Felici, Costanzo. *Dell'insalata e piante che in qualunque modo vengono per cibo del'homo*, edited by Guido Arbizzoni, Urbino: Quattroventi, 1986.

Ferrières, Henri de. *Le Livre de chasse du Roy Modus*, edited by Gunnar Tilander, Limoges: Ardant 1973.

Fiera, Giovanni Battista. *Coena. Delle virtù delle erbe e quella parte dell'Arte medica che consistenella regola del vitto*, translation by Maria Grazia Fiorini Galassi, Mantua: Provincia di Mantova/Casa del Mantegna, 1992.

Ficino, Marsilio. *Consilio contro la pestilenzia (1481)*, edited by Enrico Musacchio, Bologna: Cappelli, 1983.

Florio, John. *A World of words or the most copious, and exact Dictionarie in Italian and English*, London, 1598.

Garbo, Tommaso del. *Consiglio contro a pistolenza*, edited by Pietro Ferrato, Bologna: G. Romagnoli, 1866.

Garzoni, Tommaso. *La Piazza universale di tutte le professioni del mondo e nobili ed ignobili...*, Venice: Giovanni Battista Somasco, 1585.

———. *La Piazza universale di tutte le professioni del mondo*, edited by Paolo Cherchi and Beatrice Collina, Turin: Einaudi, 1996.

Gaston III Phoebus, Count of Foix. *Livre de chasse*, edited by Gunnar Tilander, *Cynegetica*, 18, 1971.

Gessner, Conrad. *Historiae animalium liber IIII qui est de piscium & aquatilium animantium natura*, Zürich: Froschauer, 1558.

Gherardi, Giovanni. *Il Paradiso degli Alberti*, edited by Antonio Lanza, Rome: Salerno, 1975.

Giovio, Paolo. *De Romanis piscibus libellus*, Rome: Francesco Minunzio Calvo, 1524.

——. *Lettere*, edited by Giuseppe Guido Ferrero, Rome: Poligrafo dello Stato, Libreria dello Stato, 1956–58, vol. 2

Guazzo, Stefano. *La Civil conversazione*, edited by Amedeo Quondam, Modena: Panini, 1993.

"Guglielmo dell'epopea e il Guglielmo Toscano, Il". *Leggende Cristiane del Trecento*, edited byDon Giuseppe De Luca, Turin: Einaudi, 1977 (first edition, 1954), 47–92.

"Leggenda di Sant' Albano, La". *Leggende Cristiane del Trecento*, edited by Don Giuseppe De Luca, Turin: Einaudi, 1977 (first edition, 1954), 41–46.

"Leggenda di Santa Maria Egiziaca, Dalla". *Leggende Cristiane del Trecento*, edited by Don Giuseppe De Luca, Turin: Einaudi, 1977 (first edition, 1954), 15–24.

Lancerio, Sante. "Della qualità dei vini," in Emilio Faccioli, *L'Arte della cucina in Italia. Libri di ricette e trattati sulla civiltà della tavola dal XIV al XIX secolo*, Turin: Einaudi, 1987, 329–355.

Leggende Cristiane del Trecento, edited by Giuseppe De Luca, Turin: Einaudi, 1977 (first edition, 1954).

Libro di cucina del secolo XIV, edited by Ludovico Frati, Leghorn: 1899; anastatic reprint, Bologna: Forni, 1979.

Malatesta, Fiordiano. *Operetta non meno utile che dilettevole della natura et qualità di tutti pesci sino al giorno d'hoggi conosciuti dal mondo: composta in ottava rima da Malatesta Fiordiano da Rimino*, Rimini: Bernardino Pasini, 1576.

Manfredi, Girolamo. *Libro intitolato il perché*, Bologna: 1629 (first Italian edition Bologna, 1474).

Mazzei, Ser Lapo. *Lettere di un notaro a un mercante del sec. XIV*, edited by Cesare Guasti, Florence: Successori Le Monnier, 1880.

Messisbugo, Christoforo di. *Libro novo nel qual s'insegna a far d'ogni sorte di vivanda*, Venice: 1557; reprint edition, Bologna: Forni, 1982.

Morelli, Giovanni di Pagolo. *Ricordi*, edited by Vittore Branca, Florence: Le Monnier, 1957.

Novelle inedite intorno a Bernabò Visconti, published by Piero Ginori Conti, Florence: Fondazione Ginori Conti, 1940.

Il "Novellino", in *La Prosa del Duecento*, edited by Cesare Segre and Mario Marti, Milan/Naples: Ricciardi, 1959, vol. 3, 793–881

Odorico da Pordenone, *De rebus incognitis: Odorico da Pordenone nella prima edizione a stampa del 1513*, edited by Lucio Monaco and Giulio C. Testa, Pordenone: Camera di Commercio, 1986.

Ordine et Officij de Casa de lo Illustrissimo Signor Duca de Urbino, edited by Sabine Eiche, Urbino: Accademia Raffaello, 1999.

Passerini, Luigi. *Genealogia e storia della famiglia Panciatichi*, Florence: 1858.

Piccolomini, Enea Silvio. *I Commentarii*, 2 vols., edited by Luigi Totaro, Milan: Adelphi, 2004

Pisanelli, Baldassare. *Trattato della natura de' cibi et del bere*, (Bologna: Forni, 1980; anastatic edition of the Venice 1611 ed.)

Platina (Bartolomeo Sacchi), *Il piacere onesto e la buona salute*, edited by Emilio Faccioli, Turin: Einaudi, 1985.

——. *On Right Pleasure and Good Health: a critical edition and translation of "De Honesta voluptate et valetudine"*, Mary Ella Milham,

Tempe: Medieval & Renaissance Texts and Studies, 1998.

Platearius, Matthaeus. *Le livre des simples médicines d'après le manuscrit français 12322 de la Bibliothèque nationale de Paris*, edited and presented by Pierre Lieutaghi, Paris: Ozalid/ Bibliothèque Nationale, 1986.

Pontano, Giovanni. *I Trattati delle virtù sociali*, edited by F. Tateo, Rome: Edizioni dell'Ateneo 1965.

Pontormo, Jacopo. *Il libro mio*, edited by Salvatore Nigro, Genoa: Costa e Nolan, 1984.

Priscianese, Francesco. *Del Governo della corte d'un Signore in Roma*, edited by Lorenzo Bartolucci, Città di Castello, 1883 (1st ed., Rome, 1543).

Raccolta di proverbi toscani nuovamente ampliata da quella di Giuseppe Giusti, edited by Giovanni Capponi, Florence: 1911 (reprint edition Florence: Edizioni Medicee, 1971).

Ray, John. *Historia plantarum, species hactenus editas aliasque insuper multas noviter inventas et descriptas complectens...*, London: 1686–1704, 3 vols.

Reguardati, Benedetto. *Libellus de conservatione sanitatis*, Rome: Joannes Philippus de Lignamine, 1475.

Ristoro d'Arezzo, *La Composizione del mondo colle sue cascioni*, edited by Alberto Morino, Florence: Accademia della Crusca, 1976.

Romoli, Domenico. *La singolare dottrina*, Venice: 1560.

Rondelet, Guillaume. *De piscibus marinis libri XVIII*, Lyons, 1554.

———. *Universae aquatilium historiae pars altera*, Lyons, 1555.

Rucellai, Giovanni di Pagolo. *Zibaldone*, edited by Gabriella Battista, Florence: Sismel, 2013.

Sacchetti, Franco. *Il Trecentonovelle*, edited by Antonio Lanza, Florence: Sansoni, 1984.

Sabadino Degli Arienti, Giovanni. *Le Porretane*, edited by Bruno Basile, Rome: Salerno, 1981.

Salimbene da Parma. *Cronica*, 2 vols., edited by Ferdinando Bernini, Bari: Laterza, 1942.

Salviani, Ippolito, *Aquatilium animalium historiae*, Rome: Hippolytum Saluianum, 1557–58.

Savonarola, Michele. *Libreto de tutte le cosse che se magnano*, critical edition by Jane Nystedt, Stockholm: Alquist & Wiksell, 1988.

Scappi, Bartolomeo. *Opera*, Venice: 1570 (reprint edition, Bologna: Forni, 1981).

Scrittori di Religione del Trecento. Volgarizzamenti, edited by Don G. De Luca, 3 vols. Turin: Einaudi, 1977 (first ed., Milan/Naples: Ricciardi, 1954).

Sermini, Gentile (Pseudo), *Novelle*, critical edition and comment by Monica Marchi, Pisa: ETS, 2012.

Sercambi, Giovanni. *Novelle*, edited by Giovanni Sinicropi, 2 vols., Bari: Laterza, 1972.

Sercambi, Giovanni. *Novelle*, edited by Giovanni Sinicropi, 2 vols., Florence: Le lettere, 1995.

Stefani, Marchionne Di Coppo. *Cronica Fiorentina*, edited by Niccolò Rodolico, Città di Castello: 1903, RR.II.SS., 30,1, T. XXX, fasc. 4, P. 1.

Thierriat, Florentin de. *Trois Traictez Scavoir, 1. De la Noblesse de Race, 2. De la Noblesse Civille 3. Des Immunitez des Ignobles*, Paris: Lucas Bruneau, 1606.

Ugolino da Montecatini. "Consiglio medico ad Averardo de' Medici," edited by Francesco Baldasseroni and Giustiniano Degli Azzi, *Archivio Storico Italiano*, serie quinta, no. 38, 1906, 140–152.

SECONDARY SOURCES CITED

Adama van Scheltema, Frederick. *Über die Entwiklung der Abendmahlsdarstellung von der byzantinischen Mosaikkunst bis zur niederländischen Malerei des 17. Jahrhunderts*, Leipzig, 1912.

Albala, Ken. *Eating Right in the Renaissance*, Berkeley: University of California Press, 2002.

Albini, Giuliana. *Città e ospedali nella Lombardia Medievale*, Bologna: CLUEB, 1993.

———. "Ospedali e cibo in età medievale" in *Carità e governo delle povertà (secoli XII–XV)*, Milan: Unicopli, 2002, 211–225.

Arasse, Daniel. *Le détail. Pour une histoire rapprochée de la peinture*, Paris: Flammarion, 1992.

Arber, Agnes. *Herbals, their Origin and Evolution: a Chapter in the History of Botany (1470–1670)*, 2nd rewritten and enl. ed., Cambridge, 1953 (first ed. 1912).

Aarne, Antti. *The Types of the Folktale: A Classification and bibliography*, translated and expanded by Stith Thompson, Helsinki: Academia scientarium fennica, 1961, 2nd edition

Balletto, Laura. "I lavoratori dei cantieri navali (Liguria secc. XII–XIV)," in *Artigiani e salariati. Il mondo del lavoro nell'Italia dei secoli XI–XV*, Pistoia: 1984, 103–153.

Banegas López, Ramón A. *Europa carnivora. Comprar y comer carne en el mundo urbano bajomedieval*, Gijón: Trea, 2012.

Barthes, Roland. *Mythologies*, Paris: Les Lettres Nouvelles, 1957

———. "Pour une psycho-sociologie de l'alimentation contemporaine", in *Annales. Économies, Sociétés, Civilisations*, vol. 16, n. 5, (1961), 977–986.

Bascapè, Giacomo C. "L'assistenza e la beneficenza a Milano dall'alto medioevo alla fine della dinastia Sforzesca", in *Storia di Milano:*

(1500–1535). Tra Francia e Spagna, vol. VIII, Milan: Fondazione Treccani degli Alfieri, 1957, 387–419.

Belli, Maddalena et al., *La Cucina di un ospedale del Trecento. Gli spazi, gli oggetti, il cibo nel Santa Maria della Scala di Siena*, Ospedaletto (Pisa): Pacini, 2004.

Bettoni, Anna. "Cibo e rimedio. I meloni di Montaigne," in *Codici del Gusto*, edited by Maria Grazia Profeti, Milan: Franco Angeli, 1992, 265–274.

Bibliothèque Internationale de Gastronomie, Catalogo del fondo italiano e latino delle opere di gastronomia del sec. XIV–XIX, 3 vols., edited by Orazio Bagnasco, Vaduz: Edizioni B.IN.G, 1994).

Bonardi, Antonio. *Il Lusso di altri tempi in Padova: studio storico con documenti inediti*, Venice: Libreria Emiliana, 1909.

Berlin, Brent; Dennis E. Breedlove and Peter H. Raven, "Covert Categories and Folk Taxonomies," *American Anthropologist* 70, (1968), 290–299.

Bresc, Henri. "Les jardins de Palerme (1290–1460)", in *Mélanges de l'Ecole Francaise de Rome –Temps Modernes* 84, no. 1, 1972, 55–127.

Burgess, Glyn S. and Leslie C. Brook, *The Old French Lays of Ignaure, Oiselet and Amours*, Cambridge: D.S. Brewer, 2010.

Cadden, Joan. "Albertus Magnus' Universal Physiology: the Example of Nutrition," in *Albertus Magnus and the Sciences: Commemorative Essays 1980*, edited by James Weisheipl, Toronto: Pontifical Institute, 1980, 321–340.

Cardona, Giorgio R. *La Foresta di piume: manuale di etnoscienza*, (Rome/Bari: Laterza, 1985).

Carnevale Schianca, Enrico. *La Cucina medievale: lessico, storia, preparazione*, Florence, Leo Olschki, 2011.

Ceppari, Maria A. and Turrini, Patrizia. *Il Mulino delle vanità. Lusso e cerimonie nella Siena medievale*, Siena: Il Leccio, 1993.

Chambers, David S. "Bartolomeo Marasca, master of cardinal Gonzaga's household (1462–1469)," in *Renaissance Cardinals and their Worldly Problems*, Aldershot/Brookfield: Variorum, 1997, 265–283.

Chenu, Marie-Dominique. *La Théologie au douzieme siècle*, Paris: Vrin, 1957.

Cherici, Ugo. *L'Assistenza all'infanzia ed il R. Spedale degli Innocenti di Firenze*, Florence: Vallechi, 1932.

Clark, Gillian and L. Constantini, A. Finetti, J. Giorgi et al., "The Food Refuse of an Affluent Urban Household in the Late Fourteenth Century: Faunal and Botanical Remains from the Palazzo Vitelleschi, Tarquinia (Viterbo)," in *Papers of the British School at Rome* 57 (1989), 201– 302.

Clark, Kenneth. *One Hundred Details from the National Gallery*, London, 1938.

———. *More Details from Pictures in the National Gallery*, London, 1941.

Cogliati Arano, Luisa. *Tacuinum sanitatis*, Milan: Electa, 1979.

Conklin, Harold C. "The Relation of Hanunòo Culture to the Plant Word," Ph.D. dissertation, Yale University, 1954.

Cortonesi, Alfio. *Il Lavoro del contadino: uomini, tecniche, colture nella Tuscia tardomedievale*, Bologna: Clueb, 1988.

Conti, Elio. *La Formazione della Struttura Agraria Moderna nel Contado Fiorentino*, Rome: Istituto Storico Italiano per il Medioevo, 1966, vol. 3, part 1.

Cortonesi, Alfio. "Le spese 'In victualibus' della Domus Helemonsine Sancti Petri di Roma", in *Archeologia Medievale*, vol. 8 (1981), 193–225.

Cosenza, Mario Emilio. *Biographical and Bibliographical Dictionary of the Italian Humanists and the World of Classical Scholarship in Italy 1300–1800*, 6 vols., 2d ed. rev. and enl. (Boston: G.K. Hall, 1962).

Di Maio, Mariella. *Il cuore mangiato: Storia dei un tema letterario dal Medioevo all'Ottocento*, Milan: Guerrini, 1996.

"Dossier Histoire de l'alimentation", in *Annales ESC*, vol. 30, n. 2–3 (1975).

Doueihi, Milad. "The Lure of the Heart," in *Stanford French Review*, 14, 1990, 66–68.

———. *A Perverse History of the Human Heart*, Cambridge: Harvard University Press, 1997.

Douglas, Mary. *Natural Symbols: Explorations in Cosmology*, London, 1970.

———. *Purity and Danger. An Analysis of Concepts of Pollution and Taboo*, (Harmondsworth: Penguin, 1970).

Durckheim, Emile and Marcel Mauss, *De quelques formes primitives de classification: contributionà l'étude des representations collectives*, Année Sociologique 6 (1901–1902).

Dyer, Christopher. *Standards of living in the later Middle Ages: social change in England, ca. 1200–1520*, Cambridge/New York: Cambridge University Press, 1989.

Emiliani-Giudici, Paolo. *Storia politica dei municipi italiani*, Florence, 1851.

Et coquatur ponendo: Cultura della cucina e della tavola in Europa tra medioevo ed età moderna, catalogue of the Prato exhibition (Spring 1996), Prato: Istituto Internazionale di Storia Economica "Francesco Datini", 1996.

Fabre-Vassas, Claudine. "Le partage du ferum. Un rite de chasse au sanglier," in *Etudes rurales*, 87–88 (1982), 377–400.

Faccioli, Emilio. *L'Arte della cucina in Italia. Libri di ricette e trattati sulla civiltà della tavola dal XIV al XIX secolo*, Turin: Einaudi, 1987.

Fantoni, Marcello. "Feticci di prestigio: il dono alla corte medicea", in *Rituale, Cerimoniale, Etichetta*, edited by Sergio Bertelli and Giuliano Crifò, Milan: Bompiani, 1985, 141–161.

Favati, Guido. *Biografie trovadoriche. Testi provenzali dei sec. XIII e XIV*, Bologna: Palmaverde, 1961.

Fery-Hue, Françoise. "Le Régime du Corps de Aldebrandin de Sienne: tradition manuscrite et diffusion," in *Actes du Congrès National des Sociétés Savante, Section Histoire Médiévale*, Montpellier, 1985, vol. 1, 113–134.

Flamini, Francesco. *La lirica toscana del Rinascimento anteriore ai tempi del Magnifico*, first edition Pisa, 1891; anastatic reprint Florence: Le Lettere, 1977.

Flandrin, Jean-Louis. "Médecine et habitudes alimentaires anciennes," in *Pratiques et discours alimentaires à la Renaissance*, edited by Jean-Claude Margolin and Robert Sauzet, Paris: Maisonneuve et Larose, 1982, 85–95.

——. "Internationalisme, nationalisme et régionalisme dans la cuisine des XIVᵉ et XVᵉ siècles: le témoignage des livres de cuisine", in *Manger et boire au Moyen Âge*, Paris: Belles Lettres, 1984, vol. 2, 75–91.

——. "La distinction par le goût", in *Histoire de la vie privée*, edited by Philippe Aries and Georges Duby, Paris: Seuil, 1985, vol. 3, 267–309.

——. "Structure des menus français et anglais aux XIVᵉ et XVᵉ siècles", in *Du manuscrit à la table. Essai sur la cuisine au Moyen Age*, Paris/Montréal: Champion/Slatkine and Les Presses de l'Université de Montréal, 1992, 173–192.

——. "Les légumes dans les livres de cuisine français du XIVᵉ au XVIIIᵉ siècle,"in *Le Monde végétal (XIIᵉ–XVIIᵉ siècles): savoirs et usages sociaux*, edited by Allen J. Grieco, Odile Redon and Lucia Tongiorgi Tomasi, Saint-Denis: Presses Universitaires de Vincennes, 1993, 71–85.

——. *L'ordre des mets*, (Paris: Odile Jacob, 2002).

——. Jean-Louis Flandrin and Odile Redon, "Les livres de cuisine italiens des 14ᵉ et 15ᵉ siècles," in *Archeologia Medievale* 8, 1981, 393–408.

Folena, Gianfranco. "Per la storia della ittionomia volgare. Tra cucina e scienza naturale," in *Bollettino dell'Atlante Linguistico Mediterraneo*, 5–6 (1963–1964), now in *Il linguaggio del caos. Studi sul bilinguismo rinascimentale* (Turin: Bollati Boringhieri 1991), 169–199.

Food: A Culinary History, edited by Jean-Louis Flandrin and Massimo Montanari, New York: Columbia University Press, 1999.

Fragnito, Gigliola. "La trattatistica cinque e seicentesca sulla corte cardinalizia," in *Annali dell'Istituto Italo-germanico di Trento*, 1991, 135–185.

Frati, Lodovico. "La natura delle frutta secondo un nuovo testo," *Giornale storico della letteratura italiana* vol. 21, 1894, 206–209.

Frosini, Giovanna. *Il Cibo e i signori. La mensa dei Priori di Firenze nel quinto decennio del sec. XIV*, Florence: Accademia della Crusca, 1993.

Gaulin, Jean-Louis and Allen J. Grieco, *Dalla vite al vino. Fonti e problemi della vitivinicoltura italiana medievale*, Bologna: Clueb, 1994.

Gavitt, Philip. *Charity and Children in Renaissance Florence: The Ospedale degli Innocenti*, Ann Arbor: University of Michigan Press, 1990.

Gelli, Simona and Giuliano Pinto, "La presenza dell'Ospedale nel contado (sec. XV)", in *Gli Innocenti e Firenze nei secoli: un ospedale, un archivio, una città*, edited by Lucia Sandri, (Florence: Spes, 1996), 95–108.

Giesey, Ralph. *The Royal Funeral Ceremony in Renaissance France*, Geneva: Droz, 1960; reprint edition 1983.

Goldthwaite, Richard. "The Economic and Social World of Italian Renaissance Maiolica", *Renaissance Quarterly* 42, 1, 1989, 1–32.

Gourevitch, Aaron. *Les Catégories de la culture medieval*, Paris: Gallimard, 1983 (translation of *Kategorii srednevekovoj kul'tury*, Moscow, 1972).

Grieco, Allen J. *Classes sociales, nourriture et imaginaire alimentaire en Italie (XIVe–XVe siècles)*, unpublished PhD thesis, École des Hautes Études en Sciences Sociales, (Paris, 1987).

——. "Savoir de poète ou savoir de botaniste? Les fruits dans la poèsie italienne du 15e siècle", *Médiévales*, n. 16 (1989), Festschrift in honor of Andrée Haudricourt, 131–146.

——. "Le gout du vin entre doux et amer: essai sur la classification des vins au Moyen Age," in *Le vin des historiens*, edited by Gilbert Garrier, Suze-la-Rousse: Université du vin, 1990, 89–97.

——. "The Social Politics of Pre-Linnaean Botanical Classification," *I Tatti Studies* 4 (1991a), 131–149.

——. "Les utilisations sociales des fruits et légumes dans l'Italie médiévale," in *Le Grand Livre des Fruits et légumes: histoire, culture et usage*, edited by Daniel Meiller and Paul Vannier, Paris: La Manufacture, 1991b, 151–154.

——. "The Social Order of Nature and the Natural Order of Society in Late 13th-Early 14th Century Italy", in *Miscellanea Mediaevalia* 21/2, Berlin/New York: W. de Gruyter, 1992a, 898–907.

——. "Reflections sur l'histoire des fruits aux Moyen Age," in *Çahiers du Léopard d'Or*, 2, 1992b, 145–153.

——. "Il vitto di un ospedale: pratica, distinzioni sociali e teorie mediche alla metà del Quattrocento" in *Gli Innocenti e Firenze nei secoli: un ospedale, un archivio, una città*, edited by Lucia Sandri, Florence, Spes, 1996a, 85–92.

——. "La Gastronomia del XVI secolo: tra scienza e cultura," in *Et coquatur ponendo: Cultura della cucina e della tavola in Europa tra medioevo ed età moderna*, catalogue of the Prato exhibition (Spring 1996), Prato: Istituto Internazionale di Storia Economica "Francesco Datini", 1996b, 143–153.

——. and Andrea Manciulli, "La codificazione del modo di stare a tavola", in *Et coquatur ponendo. Cultura della cucina e della tavola in Europa tra medioevo ed età moderna*, catalogue of the Prato exhibition (Spring 1996), Prato: Istituto Internazionale di Storia Economica "Francesco Datini", 1996c, 109–123.

——. "Cibi e buone maniere nei sacri conviti", in *La tradizione fiorentina dei cenacoli*, edited by Cristina Acidini Luchinat and Rosanna C. Proto Pisani, Florence: Scala, 1997, 69–79.

——. and Sandri, Lucia, eds., *Ospedali e città: Italia del Centro-Nord, XIII–XVI secolo*, Florence: Le Lettere, 1997.

——. "Conviviality in a Renaissance Court: the *Ordine et Officij* and the Court of Urbino", in *Ordine et Officij de Casa de lo Illustrissimo Signor Duca de Urbino*, edited by Sabine Eiche, Urbino: Accademia Raffaello, 1999, 37–44.

——. "Food and Social Classes in Late Medieval and Renaissance Italy" in *Food: a culinary history*, New York: Columbia University Press, 1999, 302–312. (First English language version)

——. "Le repas en Italie à la fin du Moyen-Age et à la Renaissance," in *Tables d'Europe, tables d'ailleurs*, edited by Jean-Louis Flandrin and Jane Cobbi, Paris: Odile Jacob, 1999, 117–149.

——. "Fiordiano Malatesta da Rimini e i trattati di ittiologia della metà del Cinquecento", in *Scrivere il medioevo: lo spazio, la santità, il cibo,* edited by B. Laurioux and L. Moulinier-Brogi, (Rome: Viella, 2001), 305–317.

———. "Medieval and Renaissance Wines: Taste, Dietary Theory, and How to 'Choose' the Right Wine (14th–16th Centuries)", in *Mediaevalia,* vol. 30, (2009), 15–42.

———. "From Roosters to Cocks: Renaissance Dietary Theory and Sexuality", in *Erotic Culturesof Renaissance Italy,* edited by Sara F. Matthews-Grieco, Aldershot: Ashgate, 2010, 89–140.

Guerreau-Jalabert, Anita "Aliments symboliques et symbolique de la table dans les romans arthuriens (XIIᵉ–XIIIᵉ siècles)", *Annales ESC* 47, 3, 1992, 561–594.

Guida ai vitigni d'Italia, edited by Fabio Giavedoni and Maurizio Gily, Bra: Slow Food, 2005.

Handwörterbuch des Deutschen Aberglaubens, edited by Hans Bächtold-Stäubli and Eduard Hoffmann-Krayer, Berlin and Leipzig: W. De Gruyter, 1930–31.

Harvey, Barbara. *Living and Dying in England 1100–1540: the monastic experience,* Oxford: University Press, 1996 (first edition 1993).

———. "Monastic Diet, XIIIth–XVIth Centuries: Problems and Perspectives", in *Alimentazione e nutrizione nei secoli XIII–XVIII,* edited by Simonetta Cavaciocchi, Florence: Le Monnier, 1997, 611–641.

Haudricourt, André G. and Louis Hédin, *L'Homme et les plantes cultivées,* Paris: Métailé, 1987 (first ed., 1943).

Hauvette, Henri. "La 39ᵉ nouvelle du *Decameron* et la légende du coeur mangé", *Romania,* 41, 1912, 184–205.

Henckel, Arthur and Albrecht Schöne, *Emblemata. Handbuch zur Sinnbildkunst des XVI und XVII Jahrhunderts,* Stuttgart: Metzler, 1967.

Henderson, John. *The Renaissance Hospital. Healing the Body and Healing the Soul,* New Haven and London: Yale University Press, 2006.

Hibbard Loomis, Laura A. *Medieval Romance in England. A Study of the Sources and Analogues of the non-Cyclic Metrical Romances,* New York: Burt Franklin, 1960 (first ed. Oxford: University Press, 1924).

Hiller, Diana. *Gendered Perceptions in Florentine Last Supper frescoes c. 1350–1490,* Farnham: Ashgate, 2014.

Huizinga, Johan. *The Waning of the Middle Ages,* Harmondsworth: Penguin, 1968.

Hurtubise, Pierre. "La table d'un cardinal de la Renaissance. Aspects de la cuisine et de l'hospitalité à Rome au milieu du XVIᵉ siècle," *Mélanges d'archéologie et d'histoire de l'École française de Rome,* 92,1 (1982), 249–282.

Jacquart, Danielle and Claude Thomasset, *Sexualité et savoir medical au Moyen Age,* Paris: P.U.F., 1985.

Jéhanno, Christine. "L'alimentation hospitalière à la fin du Moyen Âge. L'exemple de l'hôtel Dieu de Paris", in *Hospitäler in Mittelalter und Früher Neuzeit. Frankreich, Deutschland und Italien. Eine vergleichende Geschichte, Hôpitaux en France, Allemagne et Italie: une étude comparée (Moyen Âge et Temps modernes),* Munich: Oldenbour, 2007, 107–162.

Jones, George G. "The Function of Food in German Literature", *Speculum* 35, 1 (1960), 78–86.

Jouanna, Arlette. *Ordre social: mythes et hiérarchies dans la France du XVIᵉ siècle.* Paris: Hachette, 1977.

Klapisch-Zuber, Christiane. *L'Ombre des ancêtres. Essai sur l'imaginaire médiéval de la parenté,* Paris: Fayard, 2000.

———. " The genesis of the family tree", *I Tatti Studies,* 4 (1991), 105–129.

———. "Les noces florentines et leurs cuisiniers," in *La sociabilité à table. Commensalité et convivialité à travers les âges* (Actes du colloque de Rouen, 14–17 novembre 1990), edited by Martin Aurell, Olivier Dumoulin and Françoise Thelamon, Rouen: University of Rouen, 1992, 193–199.

Klibansky, Raymond; Erwin Panofsky and Fritz Saxl, *Saturn and Melancholy. Studies in the History of Natural Philosophy, Religion and Art*, Nendeln/Liechtenstein: Kraus Reprints, 1979 (first edition 1964).

Krug-Richter, Barbara. *Zwischen Fasten und Festmahl. Hospitalverpflegung in Münster 1540 bis 1650*, Stuttgart: Steiner, 1994.

Lambert, Carole. "Survivance d'usages culinaires anciens dans la cuisine québécoise." In *Actes du colloque "Manger: de France à la Nouvelle-France," Textes colligés et présentés par Yves Bergeron et Gérald Parisé, Ethnologie XII*, no. 3 (1990): 61–64.

Långfors, Arthur. "Le Troubadour Guilhem de Cabestanh", *Annales du Midi*, vol. 26, n. 101, 102, 103, (1914) 5–51, 189–225, 349–356.

La Roncière, Charles de. *Prix et salaires à Florence au XIVe siècle, 1280–1380*, Rome: École française de Rome, 1982.

Laurioux, Bruno. "I libri di cucina italiani alla fine del Medioevo: un nuovo bilancio", *Archivio Storico Italiano*, vol. 154, n. 1 (1996), 33–58.

———. *Les Livres de cuisine médiévaux*, Turnhout: Brepols, 1997.

———. *Le Règne de Taillevent. Livres et pratiques culinaires à la fin du Moyen Âge*, Paris: Publications de la Sorbonne, 1997.

Law, John E. "The *Ordini et officij*: aspects of context and content," in *Ordine et officij de casa de lo illustrissimo Signor Duca de Urbino*, edited by Sabine Eiche, Urbino: Accademia Raffaello, 1999, 13–35.

Lazar, Moshe. *Amour courtois et fin'amors dans la littérature du XIIe siècle*, Paris: Klienchsieck, 1964.

Le Goff, Jacques. "Au moyen âge. Temps de l'église et temps du marchand," in *Pour un autre Moyen âge*, Paris: Gallimard, 1977, 19–45.

———. and Pierre Vidal-Naquet, "Lévi-Strauss en Brocéliande. Esquisse pour une analyse d'un roman courtois," in *Claude Lévi-Strauss*, "Idée," (1979), republished in Jacques Le Goff, *L'imaginaire médiéval*, Paris: Gallimard, 1985, 151–187.

———. "Pour un long Moyen Age", in *L'imaginaire medieval*, Paris: Gallimard, 1985, 7–13.

Lehmann, Gilly. "The Late Medieval menu in England. A Reappraisal", *Food & History*, vol. 1, n.1 (2003), 49–83.

Lexikon der Christlichen Ikonographie, edited by E. Kirschbaum, Rome, Freiburg, Basel, Vienna: Herder, 1971.

Lieutaghi, Pierre. *L'herbe qui renouvelle: un aspect de la médecine traditionelle en Haute-Provence*, Paris: Maison des Sciences de l'Homme, 1986.

Loux, Françoise and Richard, Pierre. *Sagesses du corps: la santé et la maladie dans les proverbes français*, Paris: Maisonneuve et Larose, 1978.

Lovejoy, Arthur O. *The Great Chain of Being*, Cambridge (Mass.), 1936.

Mahoney, Edward P. "Metaphysical Foundations of the Hierarchy of Being According to Some Late-Medieval and Renaissance Philosophers," in *Philosophies of Existence Ancient and Medieval* edited by Parviz Morewedge, New York, 1982, 165–257.

———. "Lovejoy and the Hierarchy of Being," *Journal of the History of Ideas*, vol. 48, 2 (1987), 211–230.

Malacarne, Giancarlo. *Sulla Mensa del Principe. Alimentazione e banchetti alla corte dei Gonzaga*, (Modena: Il Bulino, 2000).

Manger et boire au Moyen âge, 2 vols., edited by Denis Menjot, Paris : Belles lettres, 1984.

Maravall, José A. *Potere, onore, élites nella Spagna del secolo d'oro*, translated by Maria L. Nasali-Rocca di Corneliano, Bologna: Il Mulino, 1986.

Marcionetti, Isidoro. *I Cenacoli della Svizzera Italiana*, Lugano: Marcionetti, 1981.

Matthews-Grieco, Sara F. *Ange ou diablesse. La représentation de la femme au XVIe siècle*, (Paris: Flammarion, 1991).

Mazzi, Curzio. "La mensa dei Priori di Firenze nel secolo XIV," *Archivio Storico Italiano* 5, 20, 1897, 336–368.

Melis, Federigo. *I Vini Italiani nel Medioevo*, edited by Anna Affortunati Parrini, Florence: Le Monnier, 1984.

——. "Il Consumo del vino a Firenze nei decenni attorno al 1400", in Federigo Melis, *I Vini Italiani nel Medioevo*, edited by Anna Affortunati Parrini, Florence: Le Monnier, 1984, 31– 96.

Milham, Mary Ellen. "La nascita del discorso gastronomico: Platina", in *Et coquatur ponendo: Cultura della cucina e della tavola in Europa tra medioevo ed età moderna*, catalogue of the Prato exhibition (Spring 1996), Prato: Istituto Internazionale di Storia Economica"Francesco Datini", 1996, 125–129.

——. *On Right Pleasure and Good Health: a critical edition and translation of "De Honesta voluptate et valetudine"*, Mary Ella Milham, Tempe: Medieval & Renaissance Texts and Studies, 1998.

Minonzio, Franco. "Appunti sul 'De Romanis Piscibus' di Paolo Giovio", in *Periodico della Società Storica Comense*, n. 53 (1988–1989), 87–128.

Monde végétal (XIIe–XVIIe siècles): savoirs et usages sociaux (Le), edited by Allen J. Grieco, Odile Redon, and Lucia Tongiorgi Tomasi, Paris: Presses Universitaires de Vincennes, 1993.

Montanari, Massimo. *Il formaggio con le pere: la storia in un proverbio*, Bari: Laterza, 2008.

Massimo Moretti, "Confini domestici. Ruoli e immagini femminili nella pittura della Controriforma," Florence: University press, 2007, http://www.fupress.net/index.php/sdd/article/view/2178/2099

Musacchio, Jacqueline, "Pregnancy and Poultry in Renaissance Italy", *Source*, XVI, 1997, 3–9.

——. *The Art and Ritual of Childbirth in Renaissance Italy*, New Haven/London: Yale University Press, 1999.

——. *Art, Marriage, and Family in the Florentine Renaissance Palace*, New Haven/London: Yale University Press, 2008.

Nada-Patrone, Anna Maria. *Il Cibo del ricco e il cibo del povero*, Turin: Centro Studi Piemontesi, 1981.

Nicoud, Marilyn. *Les régimes de santé au Moyen Âge: naissance et diffusion d'une écriture médicale, XIIIe–XVe siècle*, 2 vols., Rome: École Française de Rome, 2007.

——. Marilyn Nicoud, "I medici medievali e la frutta: un prodotto ambiguo", in *Le parole della frutta: Storia, saperi, immagini tra medioevo ed età contemporanea*, edited by Irma Naso, Turin: Silvio Zamorani, 2012, 91–108.

Nigro, Giampiero. *Gli Uomini dell'Irco. Indagini sui consumi di carne nel basso Medioevo*, Prato alla fine del '300, Florence: Le Monnier, 1983.

Notaker, Henry. *A History of Cookbooks. From Kitchen to Page over Seven Centuries*, Oakland, California: University of California Press, 2017.

Novati, Francesco. "Di due poesie del sec. XIV su 'la natura dei frutti': nuove communicazioni,"*Giornale storico della letteratura italiana* vol. 18, 1891, 336–354.

——. "Le poesie sulla natura della frutta e i canterini del comune di Firenze nel Trecento", *Giornale storico della letteratura italiana* vol. 19, 1892, 55–79.

Ohlig, Stefanie. *Florentiner Refektorien. Form, Funktion und die Programme ihrer Fresken*, Engelsbach/Frankfurt/Munich/New York: Hänsel - Hohenhausen, 2000.

Origo, Iris. *The Merchant of Prato*, Harmondsworth: Penguin, 1979 (first English edition, 1963).

Paris, Gaston. *Histoire littéraire de la France*, vol. 28, Paris, 1887.

Patni, Rashmi. *L'Assaisonnement dans la cuisine française entre le XIVe et le XVIe siècle*, unpublished Ph. D. thesis, Ecole des Hautes Etudes en Sciences Sociales, 1989.

Pellegrini, Flaminio. "Di due poesie del sec. XIV su 'la natura della frutta': comunicazione da manoscritti," *Giornale storico della letteratura italiana* vol. 16, 1890, 341–352

Peruzzi, Piergiorgio. "Lavorare a Corte: *'ordine et officij.'* Domestici, familiari, cortigiani e funzionari al servizio del Duca d'Urbino," in *Federico di Montefeltro: lo Stato*, edited by Giorgio Chittolini, *et al.*, Rome: Bulzoni, 1986, 225–296.

Pigs and Humans: 10.000 years of interaction, edited by Umberto Albarella, Keith Dobney et al., Oxford: University Press, 2007.

Pillet, Alfred and Henry Carstens, *Bibliographie der Troubadours*, Halle: Nieymeyer, 1933.

Pinto, Olga. *Nuptialia. Saggio di bibliografia di scritti italiani pubblicati per nozze dal 1484 al 1799*, Florence: Olschki, 1971.

Polica, Sante. "Il tempo del lavoro in due realtà cittadine italiane: Venezia e Firenze (secc. XIII– XIV)," in *Lavorare nel Medio Evo. Rappresentazioni ed esempi dall'Italia dei secc. X–XVI*, Atti del Convegno del Centro di Studi della Spiritualità medievale (12–15 ottobre 1980), Todi: 1983, 35–64.

Pouchelle, Marie-Christine. *Corps et chirurgie à l'apogée du Moyen-Age*, Paris: Flammarion, 1983.

Pratiques et discours alimentaires à la Renaissance, edited by Jean-Claude Margolin and Robert Sauzet, Paris: Maisonneuve et Larose, 1982.

Price Zimmermann, T. C. "Renaissance Symposia," in *Essays presented to Myron P. Gilmore*, edited by Sergio Bertelli, Gloria Ramakus, Florence: La Nuova Italia, 1978, vol. I, 363–374.

——. *Paolo Giovio: the historian and the crisis of sixteenth-century Italy*, Princeton: Princeton University Press, 1995.

Quatre éléments dans la culture médiévale (Les), (Actes du Colloque d'Amiens, 25–27 March 1982), edited by Danielle Buschinger and André Crépin (Göppingen: Kümmerle, 1983).

Ragazzini, Stefania. *Un Erbario del XV secolo. Il ms. 106 della Biblioteca di Botanica dell'Università di Firenze*, Florence: Olschki, 1983.

Rainey, Ronald E., *Sumptuary Legislation in Renaissance Florence*, PhD thesis, Columbia, 1985 University Microfilms International, 1987.

Reallexikon zur Deutschen Kunst-Geschichte, edited by O. Schmitt, E. Gall and L.H. Heydenreich, Stuttgart, Alfred Druckenmüller, 1956.

Redon, Odile. "Thèmes alimentaires dans les nouvelles toscanes des XIVe et XVe siècles," in *Ricerche Storiche*, 26, 1, 1981, 3–16.

——. "La réglementation des banquets par les lois somptuaires dans les villes d'Italie (XIIIe–XVe siècles)," in *Du manuscrit à la table*, edited by C. Lambert, Montréal/Paris: Champion-Slatkine/Les Presses de l'Université de Montréal, 1992, 109–119.

Riccetti, Lucio. "Il cantiere edile negli anni della Peste Nera," in *Il Duomo di Orvieto*, edited by Lucio Riccetti, Bari: Laterza, 1988, 139–216.

Rigaux, Dominique. *A la Table du Seigneur: L'Eucharistie chez les Primitifs Italiens 1250–1497*, Paris: Cerf, 1989.

———. "La Cène aux Écrevisses. Table et Spiritualité dans les Alpes Italiennes au Quattrocento", in *La sociabilité à table. Commensalité et convivialité à travers les âges* (Actes du colloquede Rouen, 14–17 novembre 1990), edited by Martin Aurell, Olivier Dumoulin and Françoise Thelamon, Rouen: University of Rouen, 1992, 217–228.

Rivière, Daniele. "Le thème alimentaire dans le discours proverbial de la Renaissance française," in *Pratiques et discours alimentaires à la Renaissance*, edited by Jean-Claude Margolin and Robert Sauzet, Paris: Maisonneuve et Larose, 1982, 201–217.

Rotunda, Dominic P. *Motif-Index of the Italian Novella in Prose*, Bloomington (Ind.), University Press, 1942, (reprint ed. New York, Haskell House, 1973).

Rucquoi, Aline. "Alimentation des riches, alimentation des pauvres dans une ville castillane au XVe siècle", in *Manger et Boire au Moyen Âge*, edited by Denis Menjot, Nice: Faculté des Lettres et Sciences Humaines de Nice, 1984, vol. 1, 297–311.

Salwa, Peter. "*Fiction* e realtà: novella come fonte storica," *I Tatti Studies* 1, (1985): 189–205.

Sandri, Lucia. *L'Ospedale di S. Maria della Scala di S. Gimignano nel Quattrocento*, Castelfiorentino: Biblioteca della Miscellanea Storica della Valdelsa, 1982.

———. "I regimi alimentari negli ospedali fiorentini alla fine del Medio Evo e in Età Moderna" in *Aspetti di vita e di cultura fiorentina*, Florence: Accademia della Fiorentina, 1995, 3–15.

———. "Alimentazione e salute negli ospedali fiorentini tra Medioevo e Età Moderna", in *I Gusti della salute. Alimentazione, salute e sanità ieri e oggi*, Silea, Centro Italiano Storia Sanitaria Ospitaliera, 2000), 199–211.

Scherillo, Michele. *Alcuni capitoli della biografia di Dante*, Turin: Loescher, 1896.

Scholliers, Peter. "Twenty-five years of studying *un phénomène social total*. Food history writing on Europe in the 19th and 20th centuries", *Food, Culture and Society*, vol. 10, n. 3 (2007), 450–471.

———. "The Many Rooms in the House: Research on Past Foodways in Modern Europe", in *Writing Food History. A Global Perspective*, edited by Kyri Claflin and Peter Scholliers, (London/New York: Berg, 2012), 59–71.

Sereni, Emilio. "Terra nuova e buoi rossi: Le tecniche del debbio e la storia dei disboscamenti e dissodamenti in Italia", reprinted in *Terra nuova e buoi rossi e altri saggi per una storia dell'agricoltura europea*, (Turin: Einaudi, 1982), 2–100.

Siraisi, Nancy. *Taddeo Alderotti and his Pupils* (Princeton: University Press, 1981).

Sommé, Monique. "L'Alimentation quotidienne à la court de Bourgogne au milieu du XVe siècle," *Bulletin Philologique et Historique (1968)*, Paris: Bibliothèque Nationale, 1972, 1, 103–117

Sprague, T.A. "Plant morphology in Albertus Magnus," *Kew Gardens Bulletin of Miscellaneous Information* 9, (1933): 430–440.

Stouff, Louis. *Ravitaillement et alimentation en Provence aux XIVe et XVe siècles*, Paris/The Hague: Mouton, 1970.

Sudhoff, Karl. "Pestschriften aus den ersten 150 Jahren nach der Epidemie des 'schwarzen Todes' 1348. IV, Italienische des 14. Jahrhunderts," *Archiv für Geschichte der Medizin*, Bd.5, H. 4–5 (December 1911), 332–396.

———. "Pestschriften aus den ersten 150 Jahren nach der Epidemie des 'schwarzen Todes' 1348. V, Aus Italien (Fortsetzung) und Wien" in *Archiv für Geschichte der Medizin*, Bd. 6, H.5 (January 1913), 313–379.

Tillyard, E. M. W. *The Elizabethan World Picture*, Harmondsworth: Penguin, 1968; first ed. London, 1943.

Thomas, Keith. *Man and the Natural World: A History of the Modern Sensibility*, New York: Pantheon, 1983.

Thompson, Stith *Motif-index of Folk Literature*, (Bloomington: University Press, 1955–58).

Tonini, Carlo. "Malatesta Fiordiano. Alcuni ignoti particolari della sua vita. Poemetto dei Pesci, e altre Operette del medesimo," in *La Coltura letteraria e scientifica in Rimini dal secolo XIV ai primordi del XIX*, Rimini: Luisè, 1988 (first ed. Rimini, 1884), vol. 1, 293–314.

Tucci, Ugo. "L'alimentazione a bordo delle navi veneziane", *Studi Veneziani*, n.s. XIII (1987), 103–146.

Tuve, Rosemond. *Allegorical Imagery. Some Medieval Books and their Posterity*, Princeton: University Press, 1966

Vertova, Luisa. *I Cenacoli fiorentini*, Turin: ERI, 1965.

La vie quotidienne des moines et chanoines réguliers au Moyen Age et Temps modernes, edited by Marek Derwich, 2 vols., Wroclaw: Institut d'Histoire de l'Université, 1995.

Vincent-Cassy, Mireille. "Les animaux et les péchés capitaux: de la symbolique a l'emblématique", in *Le monde animal et ses représentations au moyen-âge (XIᵉ–XVᵉ siècles)*, Actes du congrès de la Société des historiens médiévistes de l'enseignement supérieur public, vol. 15 (1984), 121–132.

White, Lynn Jr. *The Historical Roots of our Ecologic Crisis*, in *Science* 155; reprinted as chapter 5 of *Machina ex Deo: Essays in the Dynamism of Western Culture*, Cambridge: MIT Press, 1968.

Williams, John D. "Notes on the Legend of the Eaten Heart in Spain," *Hispanic Review*, vol. 26, 1958, 91–98.

Index

Photo Credits

Bagno a Ripoli, Scala Archives, 1, 4, 9–12, 14,
16–17, 22-23, 30

Bergamo, Accademia Carrara, 8

Bologna, Fondazione Zeri, 24

Bucine (Arezzo), Allen Grieco, 13

Chicago, The Newberry Library, 25, 27–29, 35

Florence, Fratelli Alinari, 26

Florence, Villa I Tatti, Berenson Collection,
3, 21

London, The National Gallery, 5

Madrid, Museo nacional del Prado, 18–20

Milan, Pinacoteca di Brera, 31–34

Siena, Fabio Lensini, 6–7

Varese, Renzo Dionigi, 2, 15

Printed in the month of October 2019
on the presses of Monotipia Cremonese, Cremona

Ex Officina Libraria Jellinek et Gallerani